Yours truly,
W. H. Crogman.

PROGRESS OF A RACE

..OR..

THE REMARKABLE ADVANCEMENT OF THE AFRO-AMERICAN

From the Bondage of Slavery, Ignorance and Poverty
to the Freedom of Citizenship, Intelligence,
Affluence, Honor and Trust

BY

H. F. KLETZING, A. M. 1850-

AND

W. H. CROGMAN, A .M.

WITH AN INTRODUCTION

BY

BOOKER T. WASHINGTON,

Principal of Tuskegee Normal and Industrial Institute, Tuskegee, Alabama.

NEGRO UNIVERSITIES PRESS
NEW YORK

Originally published in 1897
by J. L. Nichols & Co., Atlanta, Ga.

Reprinted 1969 by
Negro Universities Press
A DIVISION OF GREENWOOD PUBLISHING CORP.
NEW YORK

SBN 8371-1382-2

PREFACE.

Our apology for presenting to the public a new book is not that there are not sufficient books already written on the Negro, but that to our knowledge there has been no attempt made to put into permanent form a record of his remarkable progress under freedom—a progress not equaled in the annals of history.

Although the "Progress of a Generation" might, as to time, more accurately bound the limits of our theme, we have preferred to record as well the struggles and triumphs of the Race in the dark days of bondage, for slavery, with all its appalling horrors, was nevertheless in a sense educative to the Race.

We are not ignorant of the fact that the eye of the critic will discern imperfections, but after much and labored research we have followed the plan that, in our judgment, would make the volume an incentive to greater progress in the future.

In the chapter on Noted Men and Women we may be charged with gross omissions, but the modesty of many men and women worthy of mention has prevented a record of noble lives. In other cases the manuscript did not reach us in time.

We have quoted largely from different authors, and wherever possible have given credit, but in some cases even this was not possible, as the author was not always known. We are especially indebted to Dr. Hubbard, of Meharry Medical College, and Prof. Spence, of Fisk University, for valuable information.

Our motive throughout has been that of an increasing desire to aid in the work of elevating the Race for which many noble lives have been given.

We shall feel well repaid for our labors, if, through the perusal of these pages, there shall be an incentive to even greater efforts, during the second generation of freedom. With the sincere hope that our efforts may aid in inducing the multitudes to catch the same spirit of progress that imbues their leaders, we send this volume forth.

THE AUTHORS.

BOOKER T. WASHINGTON.

INTRODUCTION.

The Progress of a Generation in the history of the Negro is the most fascinating study modern times possesses. Springing from the darkest depths of slavery and sorrowful ignorance to the heights of manhood and power almost at one bound, the Negro furnishes an unparalleled example of possibility. In the pages following, the authors have performed a duty at once difficult and needful—that of following the rise of the Negro through the different stages of his career. It is a task that merits respect, commands attention, and is, unhappily, too seldom attempted.

The task of a biographer of a people is too frequently a thankless one. In sifting out the conflicting elements which present themselves for his consideration he is apt to injure tradition. In using material which he thinks best he is likely to upset preconceived ideas of theorists. His work must be the result of careful thinking and an astonishing amount of *finesse* and diplomacy.

The historian of the Negro race has all this and more too. He must, in addition to the other duties which devolve upon him in his work, be able to prophecy and foresee the days to come. For the progress of the Negro is far from completed—it is yet in its incipient stage—and the eyes of the prophet must discern whither the road leads, upward or downward.

The unprecedented leap the Negro made when freed from the oppressing withes of bondage is more than deserving of a high place in history. It can never be chronicled. The world needs to know of what mettle these people are built. It needs to understand the vast possibility of a race, so much despised and so thoroughly able to prove without blare and flourish of trumpet its ability to hold its own and compete, after only thirty years of life, with those of centuries of lineage.

The dawn of new life is again gleaming behind the

horizon.   After the words were spoken which pronounced the Negro free, he hesitated a minute, then sprang towards the highest place at once.   It was not many days before he was heard from in all positions, in all walks of life; he was in high government positions, his name was on the most exclusive professional roles, yet the common horde lingered in surprised helplessness, wondering what next.   Such a state of affairs, though brilliant, was without foundation and could not last.   In building the structure of his race-life the Negro had begun at the top.   The cupola could not last without a foundation; the work was shaking without a firm support.   Of late years this is being realized, and we are turning our attention to the foundation work. It may be that some are blind to the crying needs of an absolute and unwrenchable foundation in the soil of the state, but those whose eyes are opened must realize that we can advance no further, or do no better work, until we have paused and implanted ourselves firmly.   The progress made thus far has been magnificent, but like the house built upon sands.   Ere we add another gable or tower to its structure we must insure it against the lash of the storm's fury by placing a solid rock beneath its surface.

This is where the progress of the Negro leads us today—to pause in the brilliant meteoric advance and stride forward henceforth as a solid phalanx of earnest, industrious toilers, for a merited place in the world's array of nations.   By the work-shop, the well-tilled farm, the scientifically conducted dairy, the mechanic's well-done work, our advance is now being noted. From gaining the wondering curiosity of the world for a chosen, brilliant few, we are compelling its respect and admiration for ourselves as a whole, as a people upon whom the stigma of idle dreaming can no longer be laid.

Thus, while the authors record in these pages the progress of the Negro within the past generation, let us hope that when another quarter century has passed away the race's biographer may have a still more promising story to tell.   Let us hope that it will be a story of a people taking part in the affairs of a nation—not in isolated cases, but as an integral part of a magnificent whole. Let us hope that there will be manufacturers, as well as senators; good and successful business men, as well as politicians; reputable artisans, as well as literateurs; millionaires, as well as laborers. Let us hope that the wave of industrial feeling now extending over the country may find its culmination in the unmistakable and solid foundation of a magnificent people, and crystallize a race into conformation with the highest standard reached by man in the present age.

BOOKER T. WASHINGTON,
Tuskegee Normal and Industrial Institute.
TUSKEGEE, ALA., August 8, 1897.

WE ARE RISING.

BY REV. GEORGE C. ROWE.

Among the sayings of our race,
    Suggestive and surprising,
That fill a most exalted place,
    Is, "Tell them we are rising!"

The question asked for right and truth,
    What to the North your greeting?
The answer from a Negro youth—
    "Tell them we are rising!"

Within Atlanta's classic halls,
    This youth, self-sacrificing,
Wrote high his name upon her walls,
    His motto: "We are rising!"

Out in the world he makes his mark,
    Danger and fear despising,
E'er soaring upward like the lark,
    My brethren: "We are rising!"

He meets the foe with voice and pen,
    With eloquence surprising!
Give us a chance, for we are men!
    Most surely we are rising!

Rising to take our place beside
    The noble, the aspiring;
With energy and conscious pride,
    To the best things, we're rising!

Within the class-room is his place,
    Greek, Latin, criticising,
To raise the youthful of his race,
    And show the world we're rising!

Go forth, my friend, upon your way,
    Each obstacle despising,
Prove by your efforts every day
    To all that we are arising!

In farming, trade and literature,
    A people enterprising!
Our churches, schools, and home life pure,
    Tell to the world we're rising!

NOTE.—About a score of years since, Gen. O. O. Howard, then connected with the Freedman's Bureau, on visiting one of the colored schools in Georgia, asked the children: "What message shall I take from you to the people of the North?" An intelligent boy answered promptly: "Tell them we are rising!" The boy was Richard Wright, of Augusta, Ga., who has since graduated from Atlanta University, ably filled the editorial chair, and is now President of the State Normal School, of College, Georgia.

TABLE OF CONTENTS.

CHAPTER I.

HISTORY OF THE RACE.

Unity of the race—Of one blood—No inferior race—The curse theory—Base of arguments—The proper interpretation — Josephus — Herodotus —The case stated—The color theory—Plants and animals—Gradations of color—Caucasians—Dr. Livingston—Equator to polar circles—From inland to coast—Black, a mark of reproach—Ideals of Negroes—God knows best—Antiquity—J. P. Jefferis—Further evidence—The word Negro—The term Negro—Africa for the Negroes—Deportation—Not well considered—Separation would not relieve—Not possible—Points of superiority—Physical characteristics — Distinguishing traits — Drink traffic — Ingenuity—In other continents—Unknown to Hebrews—Liberia—Sierra Leone—Purpose and preparation—Africa's future.

CHAPTER II.

SLAVERY.

Knowledge worth knowing—In Africa — Sources of slavery—Right of a free adult to sell himself—Insolvent debtors—Sale of criminals—Kidnapping—Capture in war—Slaves of slaves—Early history of slavery—Livingston's tomb—For what purpose—European plantation slavery—In Asia—Slavery in Portugal—Columbus—Slavery in the New World—First slaves—First liberty—Slavery in the United States—Slavery contended for—The slave trade—The slave dealer—Kidnapping—The middle passage—The slave dealer and President Lincoln—Profit—Slavery a curse—Fusion—Slavery not justifiable—Slavery degrading—A curious advertise-

CHAPTER III.

The Negro in the Revolution.

CHAPTER IV.

Anti-Slavery Agitation.

CHAPTER V.

CHAPTER VI.

THE NEGRO IN THE CIVIL WAR.

CHAPTER VII.

MORAL AND SOCIAL ADVANCEMENT.

CHAPTER VIII.

THE COLORED WOMAN OF TODAY.

CHAPTER IX.

PROGRESS IN INDUSTRIES.

CHAPTER X.

Financial Growth.

CHAPTER XI.

Mortality.

CHAPTER XII.

EDUCATIONAL IMPROVEMENT.

EDUCATIONAL INSTITUTIONS—INDUSTRIAL SCHOOLS—
THE PRESS.

CHAPTER XV.

CHAPTER XVI.

CHAPTER XVII.

ALPHABETICAL INDEX.

CHAPTER I.

HISTORY OF THE RACE.

Unity of the Race.—Attempts have been made in the past to prove that the Negro is not a human being. In this age of the world such a preposterous idea does not receive countenance. The remarkable progress of the Negro and the rapid disappearing of race malice and prejudice, have made this theory so absurd that to-day no one can be found to advocate it. It is, however, to be noted that as late as 1868 a minister of the South advocated this theory. Arguing from this standpoint he says, "Half an eye tells us the fate of the Negro on this continent is fixed, his doom is irrevocably sealed, he is out of his natural condition to which he aspires. If he is separated from *man* he sinks speedily to savage cannibalism. Men cannot refute the fixed decree of Omnipotence; nothing but the power of God can save the Negro from extinction. Four millions of blacks are doomed to extinction. The history of the Negro proves that he does not, never did possess, a self-directing, independent mind. The white man regards him as a natural, lawful slave, the Negro admits the fact and instinctively seeks the condition of slavery to man."

Of One Blood.—Why should we here refer to this theory so absurd and contradictory to all history? Not that we place any confidence in any of the arguments, nor that we will refute the arguments, they need no refutation; but that the young man of to-day, who is an American citizen, may know something of the tendency of the times when slavery existed.

To-day the universal belief is that God "Created of one blood all nations of man to dwell on the face of the earth." The unity of the race is demonstrated with emphasis in the possible and actual assimilation of all the races in the one man, and is distinctly shown in the personalities and careers of men like Benjamin Banneker, Frederick Douglass, and Alexander Dumas.

No Inferior Races.—God did not create an inferior race; there are races with inferior conditions, and these may be black or white, but, says Dr. Blyden, "There is no absolute or essential superiority on the one side, nor absolute or essential inferiority on the other. Man is a unity in the plan of salvation. No man is too inferior to be saved. In all the wondrous work of creation the making of man is God's crowning act, and whoever has His image has infallible credentials of his high origin and sonship. Man is our universal representative head and from him all peoples sprung. God never made a superior race nor an inferior one; and there is nothing in the heavens above, nor in the earth beneath, that can substantiate any such doctrine, "For God hath made of one blood all nations of men to dwell upon the face of the earth."

The Curse Theory.—Failing to establish the theory that the Negro is not a human being, we find an attempt on the part of those who would have held the Negro in perpetual slavery to show that he belongs to an inferior race. That against him an irrevocable curse has been pronounced. But the remarkable advancement of the race in all lines of activity has dispelled even the doubts of those who "hoped against hope" that this might be the case, and has scattered the mists of unbelief that rose above the horizon of a few of the Anglo-Saxon race.

Base of Arguments.—Such arguments are based upon passages of the scripture in which Noah cursed Canaan in these words: "Cursed be Canaan, a servant of servants shall he be unto his brethren. Blessed be the Lord God of Shem, and Canaan shall be his servant. God shall enlarge Japheth, and he shall dwell in the tents of Shem and Canaan shall be his servant." If this were a prophecy then the argument might have some weight, but it is considered a prophecy only by a very few writers, and these are those who would substantiate preconceived opinions thereby. The best evidence of a prophecy is its fulfillment. This statement was never fulfilled either in the case of Canaan, whose descendants have often conquered and been among the powerful nations of olden times, nor of Shem and Japheth, whose descendants were frequently enslaved. The Hebrews were in bondage in Egypt for centuries, they were the descendants of Shem; Egypt was peopled by the Children of Ham.

The Proper Interpretation.—We have neither inclination nor time to spend on extended argument against this theory so contradictory to all facts revealed by the light of true history and now no longer a question of debate, and yet a statement is necessary for the information of the youth who knows nothing of slavery, and the arguments and the attempts to hold in perpetual bondage a race destined to play an important part in the civilization and Christianization of the world. Noah was once a preacher of righteousness, but he afterward became drunk on the wine that he made. The exposure to which he was subjected by his drunken condition caused him in his irritable and self-defensive mood to utter these words, which cannot in any sense be prophetic. The best argument against

this theory is the remarkable progress of the race and
the moral and intellectual condition of the best of the
race in these closing years of the nineteenth century.

Josephus says: "The children of Ham possessed
the land from Syria to Amanus, and the mountains of
Libanus, seizing upon all the maritime ports and keeping them as their own. Of the four sons of Ham, time
has not at all hurt the name of Cush, for the Ethiopians
over whom he reigned are even at this day, both by
themselves and by all men in Asia, called Cushites."

Herodotus.—Herodotus states that Cambyses attempted to conquer Ethiopia but failed. He succeeded
in conquering Egypt, but he found the Ethiopian equal
to the Egyptian in refinement and intelligence and
superior in military skill. Cambyses attempted, by
means of spies and by means of various designs, to
entrap and enslave the Ethiopian, but was forced to
return to Egypt with but a remnant of his army.

The Case Stated.—Rev. Norman Wood puts it thus:
"Whereas, Noah got drunk and cursed Canaan, an
innocent party; and whereas, this curse was never
fulfilled; therefore, all to whom these presents may
come, greeting: Pagan, infidel, or pirate, are hereby
empowered to kidnap and to enslave all the sable
Africans who are descendants from Cush. We are here
reminded of the statement of Liliuokalani, the recent
dethroned queen of Hawaii, that the best blood of the
English flowed in her veins, because her grandfather
devoured Captain Cook."

The Color Theory.—Another argument in support
of the curse of Noah is the color of the African. This
argument also fails utterly when we take into account
the climatic influence. Climate, and climate alone, is
the sole cause. The predominant color of the inhabit-

ants of the tropical regions of Asia and Africa is black, while the whites are found in the temperate and cold regions. We see and admit the change which a few years produce in the complexion of a Caucasian going from our northern latitude into the tropics. If a few years make such great changes why shall we hesitate to recognize the changes of centuries and ages?

Plants and Animals.—There is perhaps no better evidence of the influence of climate upon man than to witness its effects upon plants and animals. The flowers of the north are almost invariably white, while the arctic rabbit is spotless white, and the fox and polar bear are either white or pale yellow. The lack of color in the northern regions of animals which possess color in more temperate regions can be attributed only to change of climate. The common bear is differently colored in different regions. The dog loses its coat in Africa, and has a smooth skin.

Gradations of Color.—Let us survey the gradations of color on the continent of Africa itself. The inhabitants of the north are whitest; and, as we advance southwards towards the line, we find in those countries in which the sun's rays fall more perpendicularly, the complexion gradually assumes a darker shade. And the same men whose color has been rendered black by the powerful influence of the sun, if they remove to the north, gradually become white (I mean their posterity), and eventually lose their dark color.

Caucasians.—The Portuguese, who planted themselves on the coast of Africa a few centuries ago, have been succeeded by descendants blacker than many Africans. On the coast of Malabar there are two colonies of Jews, the old colony and the new, separated

by color and known as the "black Jews" and the
"white Jews."

The old colony are the black Jews, and have been
longer subjected to the influence of the climate. The
hair of the black Jews is curly, showing a resemblance
to the Negro. The white Jews are as dark as the
Gypsies, and each generation is growing darker.

Dr. Livingstone says: "I was struck with the
appearance of the people in Londa and the neighborhood; they seemed more slender in form and their
color a lighter olive than any we had hitherto met."

Lower down the Zambesi, the same writer says:
"Most of the men are muscular, and have large,
ploughman hands. Their color is the same admixture,
from very dark to light olive, that we saw in Londa."

Equator to Polar Circles.—Under the equator we
have the deep black of the Negro, then the copper or
olive of the Moors of northern Africa; then the Spaniards and Italian, swarthy compared with other Europeans; the French, still darker than the English, while
the fair and florid complexion of England and Germany
passes more northerly into the bleached Scandinavian
white.

From Inland to Coast.—As we go westward we observe the light color predominating over the dark; and
then, again, when we come within the influence of the
dampness from the sea air, we find the shade deepened
into the general blackness of the coast population."

If these opinions, given by the best authorities, mean
anything, and if we shall credit them as having any
value, then the color line can be drawn only where
there is deep-seated prejudice.

Black, a Mark of Reproach.—Prof. Johnson, in his
school history, justly says: "Black is no mark of re-

proach to people who do not worship white.   The West Indians in the interior represent the devil as white. The American Indians make fun of the 'pale face' and so does the native African.   People in this country have been educated to believe in white because all that is good has been ascribed to the white race, both in pictures and words.   God, the angels and all the prophets are pictured white, and the devil is represented as black.''

Ideals of Negro.—The ideals of the Negro are the ideals of the white man.   The two races are both educated to one standard, that is, the white man's standard.   While the white man would have the Negro adopt his standard, at the same time there are those who would repel him; somewhat like putting on steam and throttling the valve.   True manhood knows no color.   While the ideals are the same, the standards the same, let all, black and white, aim to attain to a virtuous manhood that would impress itself upon mankind and make men more and more to see the ideals shine out in the lives of all true leaders.

God Knows Best.—George Williams says: "It is safe to say that when God dispersed the sons of Noah he fixed the 'bounds of their habitation,' and that from the earth and sky the various races have secured their civilization.   He sent the different nations into separate parts of the earth.   He gave to each its racial peculiarities and adaptability for the climate into which it went.   He gave color, language, and civilization; and, when by wisdom we fail to interpret his inscrutable ways, it is pleasant to know that 'he worketh all things after the counsel of his own mind.' "

Antiquity.—It is difficult to find a writer on ethnology or Egyptology who doubts the antiquity of the

Negroes as a distinct people from the dawn of history down to the present time. They are known as distinctly as any of the other families of men. Negroes are represented in Egyptian paintings. They formed the strength of the army of the King of Egypt. They came against the King of Rehoboam as well as the armies of Sesostris and Xerxes.

John P. Jefferis, who is not friendly to the Negro, in his criticism nevertheless makes this statement: "Every rational mind must readily conclude that the African race has been in existence as a distinct people over four thousand two hundred years, and how long before that period is a matter of conjecture only there being no reliable data on which to predict a reliable opinion."

Further Evidence.—Further evidence in favor of the antiquity of the Negro is found in Japan and Eastern Asia. In these large, magnificent temples, hoary with age, are found idols that are exact representations of woolly-headed Negroes; other inhabitants of the country have straight hair. But why accumulate evidence, when monuments, temples and pyramids rise up to declare the antiquity of the Negro race?

The Word Negro.—The word Negro is a name given to a considerable branch of the human family possessing certain physical characteristics which distinguish it in a very marked degree from the other branches or varieties of mankind. "It is not wise," says George Williams, "for intelligent Negroes in America to seek to drop the word 'Negro.' It is a good, strong and healthy word, and ought to live. It should be covered with glory; let Negroes do it."

The Term Negro.—The term, Negro, is properly applied to the races inhabiting that part of Africa lying

BRICKMAKING AT THE TUSKEGEE BRICKYARD.

between latitude 10 degrees north and 20 degrees south and to their descendants in the old and new world. It does not include the Egyptians, Berbers, Abyssinians, Hottentots, Nubians, etc., although in some writings it comprises these and other dark-skinned nations. One characteristic, however, the crisp hair, belongs only to the true Negro.

Africa for the Negroes.—Centuries of effort and centuries of corresponding failure have fully demonstrated that the white man cannot colonize the largest part of the great continent of Africa. It seems that, in the providence of God, this great and glorious continent is chiefly for the colored races, and especially for the Negro. Is it not possible that this great continent with its millions of Negroes occupying the most fertile portions, and in all more than one-half of the continent, is to be enlightened, civilized and Christianized by the American Negro?

Deportation.—Let it not be understood that the preceding paragraph argues in favor of deportation of the American Negro to Africa. This is impossible, but that the American Negro has a part in the elevation of the black brother of the dark continent is as true as that the Caucasian of America has a part in the Christianization of the white race in other parts of the world. The Negro is better adapted to the climate and can endure the hardships of mission work in Africa much better than the Caucasian.

Not Well Considered.—Booker T. Washington says: "I recall that a few months ago, when, on the occasion of six hundred deluded colored people sailing from Savannah for Liberia, some of the newspapers and not a few of the magazines gravely announced to an expectant people that the race problem was in process of solving itself. These newspapers and magazine writers did not take into consideration the important fact that perhaps before breakfast that same morning six hundred colored babies were born. I have a friend down in Georgia whose unfailing solution of the race problem is, that the Negro should be cooped up in some place, surrounded by a high fence, and kept separate from the whites. That would not even reach the dignity of touching the question, since it would be utterly impossible to keep the blacks inside the fence to say nothing of the impossible task of keeping the whites outside of it. If the Negroes were fenced in Africa the white men would break in at the first cry that gold existed in the inhabited territory. Besides, the Negro has never yet been able to exile himself to any place the white man would not follow him and break in."

Separation would Not Relieve.—"Talks for the Times" says: "If such a separation were even possible, are we simple enough to believe that that would relieve us of the presence of the white man? He who is scouring the seas, dredging the oceans, tunneling the mountains, boring his way into the frozen regions of the North, parceling out the continent of Africa, and giving civilization and laws to its tribes—it is not likely, I say, that this restless, energetic white brother will respect the boundary line of a state or territory at home; he has not done so in reference to the Indian; he would never do so in reference to us. Were it possible for us to go off to-morrow to some territory by ourselves, within a week the Connecticut Yankee would be there peddling his wooden nutmegs. The patent medicine man would be there selling his nostrums. The Georgia Cracker and the Kentucky horse-trader would be there with their horses and mules. The Southern white man would especially be there, for he has been so accustomed to us from his childhood that he does not feel at home without us, although sometimes, in the heat of political excitement, he wishes we were in Africa or a warmer place."

Not Possible.—Judge Gunby says: "The favorite remedy for the race problem with some has come to be the deportation of the Negroes. I am prepared to say with the utmost confidence that this remedy does not meet with general approval, although it is fair to concede that it has many able advocates. The Negroes do not desire to leave and the great majority of the whites do not want them to go. The enforced removal of the Negroes would be unnatural and unjust; cruel, bitter cruel, would be the task of tearing Negroes from their genial Southern homes, their Southern friends, their churches, their graveyards, and the haunts they love so well. Sadder than the melancholy processions that moved to the shore from Goldsmith's 'Deserted Village,' sadder than the doomed band of Acadian farmers that looked for the last time on their burning homes in Grand Pré, would be the final movement of the Negroes from the South. It would be worse than slavery; for the Negroes in a colony of their own would degenerate and speedily lose the civilization they have derived from contact with the whites. Such a crime would never be forgiven. It would raise a protest from whites and blacks alike and from an indignant world. The very stones would rise up and cry against it. Deportation is not conceivable; because, although a few might be transported to Africa or scattered elsewhere, yet reproduction will increase their number in spite of such trifling methods, and our only way to get rid of their presence in the country is to kill them—which would be difficult, for many of them already have guns."

Points of Superiority.—A certain writer says that the Negro has less nervous sensibility than the white, and is not subject to nervous afflictions. He is comparatively insensible to pain, bearing severe surgical operations well; he seldom has a fetid breath, but transpires much excrementious matter by means of glands of the skin, whose odorous secretion is well known. His skin is soft, and his silky hair, though called wool, does not present the characteristics of wool, and differs but little from that of other races except in color and in its curly and twisted form. He flourishes under the fiercest heat and unhealthy dampness of the tropics where the white man soon dies.

Physical Characteristics.—The physical characteristics of the black, or Negro, race are: A large and strong skeleton, long and thick skull, projecting jaws, skin from dark brown to black, woolly hair, thick lips, flat nose and wide nostrils. The typical color of the race is not coal black but the dark brown of a horse-chestnut. Observation shows that the darkest specimens are found on the borders where Negroes have been in contact with lighter races, while in the population of the Congo basin, which has been almost completely free from mixture, the dark-brown type prevails. It should, however, be understood, that there is as great a difference among Negroes as among Caucasians.

Distinguishing Traits.—The Africans, as a race, are passionately fond of music and have many ingeniously contrived musical instruments. While some of their inventions may have been borrowed from other people, it is a well established fact that they are the inventors of an ingenious musical instrument. They have a keen sense of the ridiculous and are of a cheerful disposition. They are naturally kind hearted and hospitable to strangers and are generally ready to receive instruction and to profit by it. They are quick to perceive the beauty of goodness and hence they generally appreciate the services of missionaries in their behalf, and, but for the curse of intoxicating drinks brought upon them by unscrupulous white traders, the dark continent would shine more brightly with the light of Him who is the light of the world.

Fidelity of the Negro.—During the Civil war the fidelity of the negro was tested to a most remarkable degree; and he stood the test. Nearly all able-bodied men of the South were in the Confederate army. Only helpless women and children, and old or disabled men were left with the slaves to care for the plantation houses. While the white-faced "Copperhead" of the North was aiding the South, the black-faced slave was caring for the helpless ones in Southern houses. Strange as it may seem, these same colored men knew that victory for the Union meant freedom for themselves. General Sherman, in describing his first day's experience on his famous "March to the Sea," says: "The negroes were simply frantic with joy. Whenever they heard my name, they clustered about my horse, shouting and praying in their peculiar style, which had a natural eloquence that would move a stone. I have witnessed hundreds, if not thousands, of such scenes.   *   *   *

"We made our bivouac, and I walked up to a plantation house close by, where were assembled many negroes, among them an old, gray-haired man, of as fine a head as I ever saw. I asked him if he understood about the war and its progress. He said he did; that he had been looking for the 'angel of the Lord' ever since he was knee-high, and, though we profess to be fighting for the Union, he supposed that slavery was the cause, and that our success was to be his freedom. I asked him if all the negro slaves comprehended this fact, and he said they surely did."

Every Union soldier escaping from Confederate prison-pen, knew that it was safe to make himself known to a colored man. No Union soldier ever asked in vain for help from his dusky brother.

Drink Traffic.—The drink traffic carried on by civilized nations in Africa is the curse of millions. The same ship that carries missionaries to its shores carries thousands of gallons of rum that does more to degrade the helpless and ignorant Negro than many missionaries through a lifetime can succeed in winning to a better life. Let it be known that the Christian (?) nations, Great Britain and the United States, are leaders in this degrading and soul destroying business. This can be permitted only where dollars and the greed of gain surpass in estimation the worth of true manhood and of immortal souls.

Ingenuity.—The African Negroes display considerable ingenuity in the manufacture of weapons, in the working of iron, in the weaving of mats, cloth and baskets from dyed grasses, in the dressing of the skins of animals, in the structure of their huts and household utensils and in the various implements and objects of use in a barbarous state of society.

In Other Continents.—In addition to Africa, Negroes are found in the United States, Brazil, West Indies, Peru, Arabia and the Cape Verd Islands. They are rare in Europe and the islands of the Pacific. Africa is, however, the native home of the Negro. Whenever he is found outside of this great continent it is because he has been carried away and subjected to slavery.

Unknown to Hebrews.—Negroes were almost unknown to Hebrews. They were unknown to the Greeks until the seventh century B. C. About twenty-three hundred years B. C. the Egyptians became acquainted with the Negroes, who helped them on their monuments as early as 1,600 years B. C.

Liberia.—Liberia is a Negro republic of western Africa, on the upper coast of Upper Guinea. It was founded by the American Colonization Company. The first expedition of eighty-six emigrants was sent out in February, 1820. It was organized as a home for the Negro of the United States. The suffering that slavery brought upon the Negro aroused his friends, and, following the plan of Wilberforce and other Englishmen, Liberia was founded as a refuge for the colored men who would avail themselves of its blessings.

The constitution of Liberia, like that of the United States, establishes an entire separation of the church from the state, but all citizens of the republic must belong to the Negro race. The constitution has recently been changed and this point has been modified. Its present constitution was adopted in 1847 and is similar to that of the Constitution of the United States. The article on slavery reads thus: "There shall be no slavery within the republic, nor shall any citizen of this republic, or any person residing therein, deal in slaves either within or without the republic."

The first years witnessed the struggle of a noble band of colored people who were seeking a new home on the edge of a continent given over to idolatry. Immigration went forward slowly, but the republic continued establishing and extending itself until it now numbers more than one million inhabitants. Already in 1853 Bishop Scott, of the M. E. Church, stated that the government of Liberia was extremely well administered. In his visit of several months he saw no intoxicated colonists and did not hear a profane word, the Sabbath was kept in a singularly strict manner and the church crowded with worshipers.

Agriculture is carried on with increasing success. Sugar was formerly the principal article of produce and of manufacture, but through the efforts of Mr. Morris, coffee has become the principal article. Rice, arrowroot and cocoa are also cultivated; trade is rapidly extending. Although the circumstances that led to the founding of this republic passed away when the shackles were torn from the Negroes of the South, yet it had done a vast amount of good before the days of the great rebellion, and to-day stands as a beacon light penetrating the darkness and gloom of Africa. May we not hope that through the ages to come the light of this Christian republic will reach the dark, trackless regions of African Paganism and bring millions to the brightness of its shining?

Sierra Leone.—Sierre Leone is under the protecting hand of England, it has a population of half a million. Freetown, the capital, is a well built city, with a population of about seventy thousand, not more than 150 whites. There is no friction among the races. A man is a man for what he is, what he knows and what he has. The west coast of Africa is often said to be a death trap on account of the malarial regions along the coast. This, however, is not substantiated by the reports from Freetown. While it has little or none of

the modern hygienic and sanitary improvements and
only six physicians, four colored and two white, the
death rate in 1896 was lower than that of Atlanta
with all her advantages of altitude, hospitals, water,
sewers and other modern sanitary improvements,
together with her several hundred physicians and three
medical colleges. The reason given for this is that in
Freetown the majority of the colored people are in a
position to take care of themselves; while in Atlanta
the death rate is greatly increased by poverty and
ignorance.

The Mayor of Freetown is a rich colored man. The
streets of the city are lighted with oil lamps, there are
no street cars, and only one railroad entering the city.
The people are industrious and intelligent and hate
ignorance. A man going there, if he wishes the respect
of the people, must be a good mechanic, lawyer, doctor
or preacher. An American common laborer finds no
open door for the African can be secured much cheaper.
Africa, like other parts of the civilized world, is calling
for brains, morals and money; without at least one of
these Africa does not want you.

Purpose and Preparation.—"Unless the Negro out
of Africa goes to Africa seeking a home because he has
none; goes on his own volition, with as correct a knowledge of Africa as may be obtained from the writings of
trustworthy African travelers and explorers and missionaries, reinforced by race loyalty, and with greater
confidence in himself and his race than in any alien
self and alien race; goes from a sense of duty imposed
by his Christian enlightenment, and not unprovided
with ability and previous experiences to organize and
control labor, with as ample means as he would go
from the Atlantic coast of the United States to the

Pacific slope for the purpose of engaging in business, he is wholly and entirely unsuited for Africa, and would impede by his presence not only the progress of Liberia (if he went thither) but any part of Africa by his unprofitable presence, and ought·to be denied the right to expatriate himself."

Africa's Future.—"If my opinion about the future were asked," says Heli Chatelain, "I should not hesitate to declare my conviction that within one hundred years all Bantu-land will contain more than 500,000,000 inhabitants, will equal Europe in civilization, will be united in a great United States of Central Africa under a new and improved edition of our American constitution, will both speak and write a common language, the mother-tongue of all Bantu dialects, as revived by scholars and enriched with the best developments of its daughters, and will produce masterpieces of literature, science, and art, vying with all the best that Europe and America will then be able to bring forth.

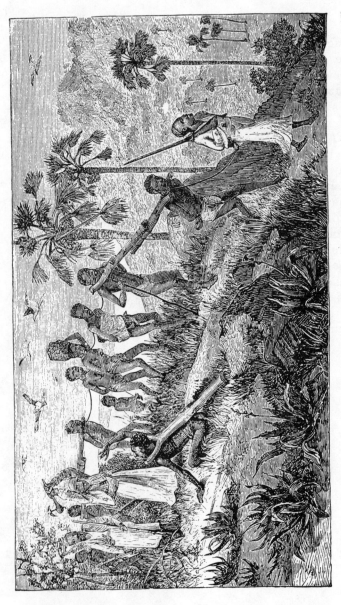

SLAVE TRADERS MARCHING THEIR CAPTIVES TO THE COAST, BUTCHERING DISABLED ONES ALONG THE WAY.

CHAPTER II.

Knowledge Worth Knowing.—Dr. Hamilton says: "The popular notions which have prevailed concerning African slavery have shaped imaginations and controlled opinions concerning the origin and destiny of the African race. Men have asserted boldly and arrogantly that the African people were designed in the very first cosmogony to be hewers of wood and drawers of water. Slavery was their natural relation. As the slaves in America within the recollection of the present generation have been Negroes, most persons have thought that all slaves have been Negroes. As Negroes have come from Africa, it has been commonly believed that all Africans were Negroes. As the sons of Ham in the dispersion went into Africa to live, it has been supposed that all Negroes were the sons of Ham. And as Ham is said in the book of Genesis to have looked on the nakedness of his drunken father and so incurred his anger that he visited the sin of the father on the son of Ham, and in his anger cried out, 'Cursed be Canaan; a servant of servants shall be unto his brethren,' it has been claimed scriptural warrant is found for the enslavement of all Negroes. Of such knowledge and such argument it is pertinent to affirm, in the language of Mr. Josh Billings, 'that it would be better not to know so many things than to know so many things that are not so.'"

In Africa.—From time immemorial slavery has existed in Africa. The oldest records of the human race, the inscriptions of the Nile valley, show us that

Negro slaves from the Soudan were then, as to-day, one of the principal articles of Egyptian trade.

Neither the institution of slavery nor the slave trade were introduced into Africa or forced upon the natives by Arabic, Moslems, or European Christians. At all times, so far as human knowledge goes, slavery has been a constituent element in the social order of Negro Africa. It is said of two or three African Negro tribes that they object to selling their own tribesmen, and oppose slave dealing in a general way. But these exceptions only confirm the rule that slavery is the universal practice of native Africa. There the trade in human beings is considered just as honest as trade in any other merchandise.

All those who want to work for the extinction of slavery in Africa should know from the start, that for one Arab or European slave-holder, slave-raider, or slave-dealer, there are hundreds of African slave-holders, slave-dealers and slave-raiders. Therefore, in their effort to conquer that monster they will have to face thousands of interested native opponents. This will be made clearer by a consideration of—

Sources of Slavery.—Chief among these is (1) the right of parents to sell their children. Every child born is the property of its maternal uncle; in a few tribes of its father. The uncle or the father has the right to dispose of his property as he pleases. He may even kill this human property and no one can prosecute him, claim damages, or demand his punishment. If he sells his children, separating child from mother, nobody seems to think he is doing wrong. The victim itself is expected not to protest against it more than a young girl of our land would protest against being sent to a boarding school for the first time.

(2.) **The Right of a Free Adult to Sell Himself.**—
Runaway slaves, or liberated slaves, rather than be kidnaped, prefer to sell themselves to masters of their
own choice. In times of famine hundreds are compelled to change their liberty for the food that will
keep body and soul together. In war, cowards would
rather live as slaves than die as freemen.

(3.) **Insolvent Debtors.**—Those who have lost all
resources of material, animal and human property,
sometimes give themselves for debt.

(4.) **Sale of Criminals by Legal Action.**—In Africa
there are no prisons, hence punishment is always paid
by death or the pay-
ment of a fine. If
the fine c a n n o t be
paid the individual is
sold to pay for it.

(5.) **Kidnaping.**
—This is much more
frequent than is gen-
erally supposed. The
kidnaped generally
resent the injustice
committed, and fre-
quently, with tears
in their eyes, enter-
tain a secret, though
forlorn, hope of re-
gaining their liberty
and r e t u r n i n g to
their homes.

AN EX-SLAVE.

(6.) **Capture in War.**—Captives are often committed
to slavery, many wars are often even made that captives may be taken and carried into slavery.

Slaves of Slaves.—It is not an unusual thing for slaves to own slaves, and in old Calabor plantation, slave-holding by slaves is so common that you often hear of slaves belonging to slaves of slaves. Any slave may by industry and thrift redeem himself, take his seat among the tribal headman, and aspire to the kingship.

Early History of Slavery.—The history of Negro slavery carried on by Europeans, beginning in Portugal over a period of 400 years, and involving the exportation by violence from their African homes of forty million of men, women and children, is one of exceeding and unimaginable bitterness. It is too late to criminate those who were responsible for beginning the slave trade and for perpetuating the system of bondage that grew out of it. Many of them were conscientious, Christian men, who worked without a thought of the wrong they were doing. Some of them really believed they were benefiting the Negro by buying him out of a condition of barbarism into the enlightening and purifying influences of Christianity.

AN EX-SLAVE.

Livingstone's Tomb.—On Livingstone's tomb-slab

ın Westminster Abbey are engraved these, among the last words which he wrote: "All I can add, in my solitude is: May Heaven's rich blessing come down on everyone, Americans, English and Turk, who will help to heal this open sore of the world, the slave trade."

For What Purpose.—Slaves are hunted by Moslems, Arabs, half-breeds, or Mohammedan Negroes, for the three following purposes: 1, To supply labor for their fields and plantations in the Soudan, in Zanzibar and the adjoining coast belt; 2, to supply Negresses for the harems of Turkey, especially Arabia, Egypt, Tripoli, and Morocco; 3, to obtain carriers for the trading caravans taking European goods to the interior and bringing down in exchange the tusks of ivory and the balls of rubber so much coveted by Europeans and Americans.

European Plantation Slavery.—Under the pretense of redeeming slaves from patriarchal native slavery these poor creatures are taken into European plantation slavery, which means that the slave has no more free time, no accumulation of property, no hope of redeeming one's self by thrift, no home life, no possibility of flight, but unremitting toil from morning until night in the broiling sun, under the lash of the driver, without pay, and often with insufficient food. His only prospect is that he is being worked slowly to death.

In Asia.—Slavery existed in Persia, China and India. Parents sold their children to be slaves. There was slavery among the Hebrews. All Africans are not Negroes, many of them are entirely distinct from the Negro—the idea that a slave is always black is erroneous. It is not Noah, nor Ham, nor Canaan, nor Africa, but sin and slavery that has cursed the Negro.

Portugal inaugurated the slave trade. Antonio Gonsalve brought home some gold dust and ten slaves in 1443. These were probably the first slaves taken from western Africa by Europeans. They were presented to Pope Martin V., and he conferred on Portugal the right of possession of all countries discovered between Cape Bojado and the Indies. Portugal also had the first of many chartered companies to trade in African gold and slaves.

AN EX-SLAVE.

Columbus began his intercourse with the natives of Africa by kidnapping and he gave the word for the opening of the slave trade.

Slavery in the New World. — African slavery was introduced into the New World by the Spaniards. Their cruelty to the inoffensive Indians in the islands of the West Indies had greatly reduced their numbers. The poor Indian had been reduced to slavery, and in order to prevent extermination the Spaniards resorted to importing slaves from Africa. The first cargo of Negro slaves was landed at San Domingo on the Island of Hayti in the year 1565. These were at once put to cultivating the plantations, and it was soon found that, as Rev. Wood says, "These hearty sons of Africa

not only survived the oppressive cruelty of their heart-
less taskmasters, but in time they rebelled against
them, and under their invincible 'Black Prince,' Toussaint, killed them in battle and drove them from the
island.''

First Slaves, First Liberty.—Bancroft aptly says:
"Hayti, the first spot in America that received African
slaves, was the first spot to set the example of African
liberty.''

Slavery in the United States.—Slaves were brought
by the Spaniards to Florida soon after the founding of
St. Augustine, in 1565, but the first slaves brought to
the colonies were landed at Jamestown, Va., in 1619,
by a Dutch trading vessel. Twenty Negroes were
exchanged for food and supplies. These had no personal rights, were doomed to service and ignorance by
law, and could not leave the plantation to which they
belonged without a written pass from their master.
They received no religious instruction, and were sometimes given to white ministers as pay for their services. It was, however, nearly a half century from
this time before the system of Negro slavery became
well established in the English colonies.

Slavery Contended for.—The slave trade was the
great industry contended for and carried on. In 1748
there were 97,000 slaves carried to America by all
nations, and up to that time the total number was
probably a million. During the eighteenth century six
millions were carried to America, besides the horrible
traffic which was kept up to the coasts of the Mediter-
ranean, to Egypt and Asia, which has been carried on
from time immemorial. It is estimated that the profits
of the slave trade in the seventeenth and eighteenth

centuries from the Dark Continent were equal to that on gold and all other products.

The Slave Trade.—We cannot in a few paragraphs, relate all the horrors and suffering entailed on the African race by means of the slave trade. While it is true that the revenue of the kings of the country sometimes depended on the sale of slaves, yet it remains as a blot on Christian England and America's record that they were the means of carrying out this cruel work. Some Americans, at least, went one step further, and, not content with selling slaves, sold their own sons and daughters.

The Slave Dealer.—Many chapters might be written upon the cruelties and inhuman treatment of the slave dealers, but as all who have engaged in this nefarious business have rendered their accounts to God, who is just, and have been justly dealt with, we will pen but a few items to show what the race has endured.

Kidnapping.—Probably the largest number of slaves were obtained by a system of kidnapping. In this case a village was often surrounded in the night and torches applied to the combustible huts; the able-bodied men and women were seized, bound, while children, the aged and infirm were cruelly murdered in the light of their burning homes. In journeying to the seashore, over rugged mountain sides and through fields of cacti, whose sharp thorns would lacerate and tear their flesh, they endured more than can be expressed. On reaching the coast the best of them were selected and placed on board ships, while those who had not endured the march, or were maimed, were often murdered in cold blood.

It is said that King Loango, "rather than incur the expense of feeding slaves for whom he found no mar-

ket, sent them to a side of a hill and cruelly butchered
them there.

Middle Passage.—The slave ships were frequently
crowded to such an extent that men were barely allowed
room enough to lie down.

Lord Palmerston says: "A Negro has not as much

CAPTURING SLAVES.

room in a sea ship as a corpse in a coffin." Bancroft
says: "The horrors of the middle passage correspond
to the infamy of the trade." Small vessels, of little
more than two hundred tons burden, were prepared
for the traffic, for these could most easily penetrate the
bays and rivers of the coast; and quickly obtaining

lading, could soonest hurry away from the deadly air of Western Africa. In such a bark, five hundred Negroes and more were stored, exciting wonder that men could have lived, within the tropics, cribbed in so few inches of room. The inequality•in force between the crew and the cargo, led to the use of manacles; the hands of stronger men were made fast together, and the right leg of one was chained to the left of another. The avarice of the trader was a partial guarantee of the security of life, as far as it depended upon him; the Negroes, as they came from the higher level to the seaside, poorly fed on the sad pilgrimage, sleeping at night on the damp earth, without covering, and often reaching the coast at unfavorable seasons, imbibed the seeds of disease, which confinement on board ship quickened into feverish activity. There have been examples where one-half of them—it has been said, even two-thirds of them—perished on the passage."

President Lincoln, who was always easily moved by appeals for mercy, when appealed to by a slave trader, promptly and sternly refused, although the appeal was very pathetic, and the man had served a long time in prison. The President said: "I could forgive the foulest murder for such an appeal, but the man who could go to Africa and rob her of her children and sell them into endless bondage, with no other motive than that of getting dollars and cents, is so much worse than the most depraved murderer that he can never receive a pardon at my hands. No! he may rot in jail before he shall have liberty by any act of mine."

Profit.—Dr. Roy says: "Before the annual meeting of the American Missionary Association, in 1859, Rev. Dr. George B. Cheever, from Harper's Encyclopedia of Commerce, made the following statements as to the

slave trade: For it every year twelve vessels were
fitted out by three cities each, Boston and Baltimore
being of the number, and from other places enough to
make forty slave ships, owned mostly by northern men.
Each made two trips a year, at a total cost of three
million dollars. The receipts being twenty million dollars, left for profit seventeen million dollars. One
voyage of the fleet would bring in twenty-four thousand
slaves, of whom four thousand were lost by death.
The two trips a year would make the total importation
forty thousand. These were mainly taken to Cuba,
but fifteen thousand were for the United States the
preceding year. A slave ship was landed after the war
broke out, in a distant part of the South, and there the
slaves were held till after the war. It has been estimated by Hon. John M. Langston and Col. Keating,
of the Memphis Appeal, that up to 1825, forty million
slaves had been imported to the West Indies and to the
American continent.

Slavery a Curse.—Some writers will insist that
American slavery has been a blessing to the race.
Slavery is dead, and there is no one that would revive
it. Ancient slavery may have been a step forward in
evolution, because it ended in emancipation, and ultimately in the fusion of the races. But American slavery was a long step backward.

It was carried on by a desire of Europeans in a lan-
guid climate to have the work done for them instead
of doing it themselves.

Fusion in the case of Negro slavery was fatally pre-
cluded by color; there could be no intermingling
except that which arose from the abuse of the Negro
woman by her white master. While household slavery
may frequently have been mild, the plantation slave

was overworked and tortured, and, with impunity, sometimes murdered. If certain writers are correct in attempting to show that the slave was contented in his bonds, why those fetters, those cruel slave laws, those bloodhounds? If he was fully content to live in slavery, why the laws that forbade the holding of meetings, the restraint from moving about freely, the liability to arrest when found alone, and the subjection to flogging when found away from the plantation Think of the revolting sights when, at public auction, husband and wife, parent and child, were sold apart, ·a sight of human cattle on the way to the auction and the advertisements of human flesh, especially of girls nearly white. Negro quarters on the plantation were hovels, his clothes rags, his food coarse, his life foul; it has been asserted that his life was happier than his African home, but it remains to be proven that this is the case.

Slavery Cannot Be Justified.—"Slavery cannot be justified," says Gov. Atkinson, "but may not God have intended that you, who are the descendants of those whom slavery has brought into the country, should pray and work for the redemption of your fatherland?"

Slavery Degrading.—Judge Stroud, in his "Sketch of the Laws Relating to Slavery," declares: "This maxim of civil law, the genuine and degrading principle of slavery, inasmuch as it places the slave on a level with brute animals, prevails universally in the slave-holding states." "It is plain that the dominion of the master is as unlimited as that which is tolerated by the laws of any civilized country in relation to brute animals to quadrupeds, to use the words of the civil law." To the unprincipled observer, at thirty-five years' distance, the whole system, as a system, was "the sum of all villianies," one universal harem, that, at the emancipation of the slave, had swept to the vortex of tyranny, degradation, fornication and diabolism of the most vicous character.

"In the case of Harris vs. Clarissa and others, in the March term, 1834, the chief justice, in delivering his opinion to the court, said: 'In Maryland, the issue (i. e., of female slaves) is considered not an accessory, but as a part of the use, like that of other female animals. Suppose a brood mare be hired for five years, the foals belong to him who has a part use of the dam. The slave in Maryland in this respect is placed on no higher or different ground.' "

The Slave Trade in the United States.—In 1774, the Articles of the Continental Association agreed that no more slaves should be imported and that the African slave trade should be wholly discontinued. These agreements were signed by the representatives of the colonies, but it was left to the next generation to carry out the agreement fully.

Abolishing African Slave Trade.—In his message to Congress at the commencement of the session in 1806, President Jefferson asked of that body the wisdom of abolishing African slave trade. The message was referred to a select committee, which reported a bill to prohibit the importation of slaves into the United States. This bill, of course, was fought by the Southern representatives. A long and fiery debate ensued and the act was finally passed, after several amendments, imposing a fine on persons engaged in the slave trade were added.

A Baltimore journal of this period says: "Dealing in slaves has become a large business. Establishments have been made in several places in Maryland and Virginia at which they are sold like cattle. These places of deposit are strongly bolted and are supplied with iron thumb- screws and gags ornamented with cows' skins, ofttimes bloody."

A Curious Advertisement in a religious paper of Richmond, in March, 1850, is found the following: "Who wants thirty-five thousand dollars in property. I am desirous to spend the balance of my life as a *minister, if the Lord permits*, and therefore offer for sale my farm, the Vineyard, adjoining to Williamsburg * * * and also about 40 servants, mostly young and likely, and rapidly increasing in number and value."

Effect on Slave Owners.—While the slave owner may have been hospitable, courteous, grave, the character of a true gentleman cannot be found where reigns domestic despotism, amidst whips, manacles and bloodhounds. The minds of young men were tainted by familiarity with slaves. With slavery always goes lust. If, as the advocates of slavery contended, the Negro was not a man, what were all these half-breeds to be called. The tendency of slavery in that which is not elevating in man is clearly seen in the inferiority of Southern to Northern life. Culture, invention, literature, scientific research, were not found South as long as slavery existed. It is only since slavery has been abolished that the South is beginning to rise in all these lines.

Not Content in Slavery.—The argument against the Negro is that he has never rebelled or resisted slavery, that his docility and contentment in slavery suggested that this was this normal condition. But we need understand the true condition of the Negro, his helplessness and lack of leadership, to see the falsity of such arguments. Negro insurrections, wherever the opportunity presented itself, were not wanting in the south land. We need but refer to what is called the Nat Turner insurrection to show that the Negro was struggling for freedom, and was not as docile as the white slaver would make him.

The influence of this bloody insurrection in which the lives of so many whites were taken spread throughout Virginia and the South. For years afterwards they lived in a state of dread for fear another Nat Turner might arise.

Serious Apprehensions.—"Talks from the Times" says: "During the days of slavery there were continuous and serious apprehensions on the part of masters. The whole South was under patrol every night, and the Negro, though regarded then, as many seem to regard him now, as a harmless, spiritless being, a 'scrub race,' a 'race of timid rabbits,' was an object of suspicion and distrust, and not infrequently was consternation thrown into whole states by apprehensions of servile uprisings."

Uncle Tom's Cabin.—Dr. Edwards says: "The key to 'Uncle Tom's Cabin' is one of the most abhorrent and appalling commentaries ever written on African slavery. It has made the cheek of many a slave-holder tingle. But the legislation at that time in Virginia was deemed a life and death question Nothing short of it, for the time being, could allay the painful and distressing excitement that prevailed everywhere throughout the country. It almost makes one's blood run cold, even at this remote period of time, to recall the trepidation and alarm that pervaded the whole community. The stoutest hearts were made to quail.

Negro Insurrection.—Rumors of Negro insurrection filled the air. Sleep ceased to be refreshing, haunted as it was by hideous dreams of murder, blood and arson. Mothers and maidens, and even little children, for months, not to say years, following the 'Nat Turner Insurrection,' looked pale and ghastly as the shadows of evening gathered around them, from the horrifying apprehension that with bludgeon they might be brained, or with torch might be burned to a crisp before morning. I speak from experience. Nor would I go through the agony of those years again for all the gold that ever passed hands in the Negro traffic from Colonial times till President Lincoln emancipated them with a stroke of his pen. Pharaoh and his people, under the visit of the destroying angel, when the first-born was convulsively quivering in the death struggle in every household, did not more earnestly desire the quick departure of the Hebrews out of the land of Egypt than did the great majority of the slave holders in the Carolinas and Virginias desire the removal of the Negroes from among them immediately after the Southampton Insurrection.''

Restriction of Slavery.—The African trade having been abolished, the next question that agitated the mind of the American abolitionist was that of restricting slavery; while the North would restrict it to its present limits, the South insisted that slavery should be permitted to be carried into the new territory and states as they entered the Union. The Congressional discussion of the slavery question aroused the anti-slavery sentiment of the North, and thereby hastened the day when it was possible to liberate the last slave.

Slavery in the Colonies.—Slavery was early introduced into all of the thirteen original colonies. But climate and other considerations proved that it was not so profitable to the Northern colonies as to those in

the South. After some years the Northern colonies
liberated their slaves and adopted laws against slavery.
While in the South, the large rice and cotton fields,
where labor was in demand, the slave was held in cruel
bondage, for no other reason than that of the profit
that it might bring the owner.

The Southern Colonists.—The Southern colonists
differed widely from the Northern in habits and style
of living. In place of thickly settled towns and villages, they had large plantations, and were surrounded
by a numerous household of servants. The Negro
quarters formed a hamlet apart, with its gardens and
poultry yards. An estate in those days was a little
empire. The planter had among his slaves men of
every trade, and they made most of the articles needed
for common use upon the plantation. There were
large sheds for cutting tobacco, and mills for grinding
corn and wheat. The tobacco was put up and con-
signed directly to England. The flour of the Mount
Vernon estate was packed under the eye of Washington
himself, and we are told that barrels of flour bearing
his brand passed in the West Indies market without
inspection.

Maryland and Delaware.—While the North liberated the slave, the Quakers of Maryland and Delaware
were rapidly emancipating theirs. Men felt that the
best interests of white society demanded that the curse
of slavery should be abolished. "The whole commerce
between master and slave," says Mr. Jefferson, "is a
perpetual exercising of the most boisterous passions,
our children see this and learn to imitate it. If a
parent could find no other motive for restraining the
temper of passion against his slave it should always be
a sufficient one that his child is present. The man

must be a prodigy that can retain his morals and manners undepraved by such circumstances, and what exe-
cration should come upon the statesman who permits
half the citizens thus to trample on the rights of others,
transform them into despots, and these into enemies,
destroy the morals of one, and the love of country of
the other."

It was often difficult to tell whether the slave or the
master was injured the more, the ignorance of the
slave hid from him the great evils of his condition,
while the intelligence of the owner revealed the baneful effects of slavery upon all who came within its area.
It made men sectional, licentious, profligate, cruel,
and selfishness paled the holy fire of patriotism.

Profitable in Maryland.—In Maryland the slave
trade became a profitable enterprise on account of its
rich soil and cultivation of tobacco. Labor was scarce,
and the Negro slave labor could be made as cheap as
his master's conscience and heart were small. Slavery
gained a foothold and at once became the bone and
sinew of the working force of the colony. While many
attempted to persuade themselves that slavery was an
institution indispensable to the success of the colony
here, as elsewhere, it was impossible to escape the bad
results of the trade which made men cruel and
avaricious.

Virginia.—There is no doubt that the colony of
Virginia purchased the first Negroes, and thus opened
the nefarious traffic in human flesh.

It may, however, be stated, that the first twenty
were forced upon the colony by the Dutch sailors who
were famishing and insisted upon the exchange of
Negroes for food.

It is to be noted that even after the institution of

slavery was founded, its growth was very slow in Virginia; according to the census of 1624, there were but twenty-two in the entire colony. The African slave trader was some time in learning that this colony was a ready market for his helpless victims. Whatever compunction of conscience the colonists had in reference to the sub-dealing in slaves, this was destroyed at the golden hopes of immense gains.

Slavery existed in this colony from 1619 until 1662, without any sanction of law, but in a later year slavery received the direct sanction of statutory law, and it was also made hereditary; with each returning year, this cruel inhuman institution flourished and magnified.

While in some colonies efforts were made to put down slavery from 1619 to 1775, there is nothing in history to show that Virginia ever sought to prohibit in any manner the importation of slaves. That she enriched herself by the slave trade cannot be doubted.

The slave had no personal rank; if he dared lift up a hand against any white man he was punished with lashes, or if he resisted his master he could be killed.

Virginia, the mother of Presidents, was also the mother of American slavery. In the absence of the slave trade which Great Britain had suffered, the demand for more Negroes in the cotton fields of the South was met by the conversion of Virginia, the old Dominion state, into a breeding state, a shameful, degrading end for the mother of Presidents.

New York.—An urgent and extraordinary demand for labor, rather than the cruel desire to traffic in human beings, led the Dutch to engage in Negro slave trade. The majority of them were employd on farms, and led quiet and sober lives. At first the Negro slave

was regarded as a cheap laborer, but after a time he
became a coveted chattel. It is stated that Queen
Elizabeth discouraged slavery and at one time
attempted to rebuke a slave dealer, but soon after was
found encouraging the slave trade. The condition of
the slaves in the Christian colony of New York was no
better than in many other colonies, they had no family
relations, for a long time lived together by common
consent, had no schools, neglected in life, and were
abandoned to burial in a common ditch after death.

The Negro Plot.—In 1741, through a combination of
circumstances, the Negroes of New York were accused
of plotting against the whites, and in less than three
months more than 150 Negroes were put into prison,
some of them burned at the stake, others hanged, some
transported, and the remainder pardoned. The hatred
and mistrust of the Negro was the occasion of much of
this supposed riot. Without evidence, and with the
mere form of a trial, many Negroes were convicted
and sentenced to death. The result of the supposed
Negro plot in New York is a stain upon the fair name
of that province. It is stated that the desperate valor
of the Negro in the war with Great Britain gave her
an opportunity to dispell injustice and wipe out with
his blood the dark stains of 1841.

Rhode Island.—The institution of slavery was never
established by statute in this colony, but in a few years
after the establishment of the government it became
so fully rooted that it was not possible to destroy it
without explicit and positive prohibition of law.

Demand for Ignorance.—The education of the Negro
in all colonies was considered to be a step against the
best interests of their masters. The flourishing of the

slave trade demanded that the slave be kept in ignorance.

New Jersey.—It is not known when slavery was introduced into New Jersey, but early in its history the Dutch, Quakers and the English held slaves, but were more humane in their treatment of them than in the other colonies. Legislation on the subject was not undertaken until about the middle of the eighteenth century, and at no time did it reach the severity that exhibited itself in the other parts of the country. In this colony alone, of all the colonies north or south, was the American Negro given the right of trial by jury. In Virginia, Maryland, Massachusetts and in all other colonies, the Negro went into the court convicted, and went out convicted, he was executed on the flimsiest evidence imaginable, but be it said to the praise of New Jersey that justice was shown towards the Negro in this colony as in no other. The Negro slave was given the privilege of being tried by jury and permitted to be sworn in the courts.

South Carolina.—In South Carolina the inhumanities of the slave trade reached its height. The entire slave population of this province was regarded as a chattel. Rice fields of this state demanded labor and the increase of the slave was almost phenomenal. The laws were not surpassed in stringency by any other colony, and it was unlawful for any free person to inhabit or trade with Negroes. The cruelties of the code are without parallel.

Goldwin Smith says: "In the upshot she became the typical slave state, the heart of slavery and the focus of all the ideas and all the ambitions connected with the system; while Charleston, her social capital and seaport, became the paradise of planter society with its luxury and pride. Her slave code transcended even that of Virginia in cruelty and expressed still more vividly the terrors of a dominant race. Every one who found a slave abroad without a pass was to flog him on the spot. All Negro houses were to be searched once a fortnight for arms and for stolen goods. For the fourth larceny a slave was to suffer death, and the kind of death was left to the discretion of the judge. For running away a fourth time a slave was to undergo mutilation. For punishing a slave so that he died no one was to suffer any penalty. For the wilful murder of a slave the penalty was a fine of forty pounds. It need not be supposed that the most revolting articles of the code were often put in force, or that they represent the general relations between master and slave.''

North Carolina.—In this colony there was but little improvement on the condition of the slave in South Carolina. If any Negro showed the least independence with white men he could be murdered in cold blood. The free Negro population was small and were not allowed any communion with the slaves; here, as elsewhere, the slave was left in a state of ignorance in order to further the interests of his master.

New Hampshire.—Early in the history of New Hampshire slavery was considered by the authorities as a wicked, hateful institution. The colony never passed any laws establishing slavery, but as early as 1714 passed several laws regarding the conduct and service of the slaves. In New Hampshire there were slaves up to the beginning of the war of the Revolution, but they were slaves in name only.

Massachusetts.—In Massachusetts, as well as in some other colonies, slavery was first introduced into individual families and afterwards into communities where, without the sanction of the law, usage and custom made it legal. Finally, men desiring to enjoy the field of unrequiting labor gave it the sanction of statutory law.

Pennsylvania.—Since the habit of enslaving the Negro spread through the colonies north and south, Pennsylvania, even, tolerated slaves within her borders. It is said that William Penn himself once owned slaves. Efforts were made in early years to pass laws emancipating slaves, but the mother country would not permit such laws at that time.

Slave-Breeding States.—After the establishing of our republic, Maryland, Virginia, Kentucky and Missouri were the border states of slavery. North of these the slave was free, and even in these states slavery was found to be an unprofitable business as far as labor was concerned. We may well then ask, "Why was not slavery abolished in these states?" For the simple reason that it was found that since the African slave trade was abolished the South needed an increasing number of slaves for the great plantations. Here was found a profitable business, and these states became breeding states for the propagation of the race, increasing the number so as to flood the markets of the South. One of the largest exports of these states was slaves. It was estimated that in 1836 the number sold from the single state of Virginia was 40,000, yielding a return of twenty-four million dollars. This business, horrible as it seems in our day, was licensed and protected by law, advertised in papers, and recognized as one of the branches of legitimate production of trade.

Not Universally Countenanced.—It must not be supposed that this trade was countenanced by all in the South, even there, there were men who denounced in

GRANDCHILDREN OF SLAVES.

strong and vehement language the barbarous custom of separating man and wife, mother and child, scattering families never to meet again until at the great day they meet their inhuman masters as common accusers. The pathetic scenes that presented themselves to the better element in the South brought words of condemnation against the remorseless traffic that presented scenes along the streets and highways where crowds of suffering victims whose "Miserable condition was second only to the wretched borders of Hell," were made the victims of man's greed and gain.

Border States.—The states bordering on the slave states, while not permitting slavery within their borders, yet passed what were called "Black Laws," which left the free Negro but little better off in Ohio, Indiana and Illinois than in the Southern states. Black or mulatto persons were not allowed to reside in the state without having a certificate of freedom. Later, amended laws in Ohio required that a bond be given not to become a charge upon the county in which they settled. They were not permitted to give evidence in any court of record or elsewhere in the state against a white person. Severe penalties were inflicted on all who harbored such as had not given bonds. Thus, being denied the right of citizenship, ruled out of courts, compelled to produce a certificate of freedom, and in many other ways annoyed by laws limiting the rights they were suffered to enjoy, the free Negroes of these states were little better than slaves. That they endured patiently these restrictions which public sentiment threw across their social and political pathway is a matter of record.

Pensioning Old and Feeble Slaves.—This question has been discussed and urged upon our government

LEFT BY SLAVE TRADERS TO THEIR FATE.

repeatedly, but no definite action has been taken. While race prejudice is rapidly disappearing, it may be safe to say that before a sentiment can be obtained that will enact laws favorable to pensioning old and feeble slaves by congress or by any state legislature, every ex-slave will have passed into that life where he receives the recompense of reward for all his deeds, and where he is beyond the reach of the inhumanities of the slave master and needs no pension.

Added Items.—The emancipation of slaves in all the French colonies took place February 4, 1794.

The complete emancipation of slaves in the English colonies occurred in 1838 to 1839, when more than 800,000 men, besides women and children, were liberated.

Sweden emancipated her slaves in 1846, and this was soon followed (in 1848) by the Danish colonies proclaiming the freedom of her slaves.

Holland delivered her American colonies from slavery August 8, 1862.

The African slave trade was closed in this country on the first day of January, 1862.

FALL OF ATTUCKS AND HIS NOBLE COMPANIONS, BOSTON, MARCH 5, 1770

CHAPTER III.

Slave Population.—In 1715 the slave population was about 60,000, but England's policy of crowding her American plantations with slaves increased the number rapidly, so that sixty years after, when the revolutionary war began, the slave population of the thirteen colonies was about 500,000; 50,000 of these were found in the North.

The desire to gain liberty with such a host of beings was not to be despised, and both sides contended for their services.

A Great Mistake.—If the colonists had at once willingly enlisted the Negro in the cause of liberty it can hardly be doubted that the struggle of eight years would have been shortened greatly, but in this case, as in many other instances, their enemy, the mother country, succeeded in using the slaves to a much greater extent than the colonists. Jefferson says: "That 30,000 Negroes from Virginia alone went to the British army." Had the colonies permitted the Negro to enlist, and had the Negro been urged from the first to stand for the cause of liberty, much bloodshed might have been avoided. The selfishness of the colonists, especially in the South where the opposition to the arming of the Negro was much stronger than the love for independence, asserted itself to such a degree that any effort to enlist the Negro in that section seemed useless.

The First Blood for Liberty shed in the colonies was that of a real slave and Negro. On the 5th day of March, 1770, occurred the Boston massacre, which, although not opening the real struggle, yet was the bloody drama that opened the most eventful and thrilling chapter in American history.

Crispus Attucks, a runaway slave, at the head of a crowd of citizens resolved that the conduct of the British soldiers who marched through Boston as through a conquered city could no longer be endured, and led the charge against the British with the cry: "The way to get rid of these soldiers is to attack the main guard. Strike at the root, this is the nest." The troops were ordered to fire, the exposed and commanding person of the fearless Attucks went down first. Three others fell in the same attack, Caldwell, Gray and Maverick. This aroused the people of Boston. The burial of these four men from Faneuil Hall was attended by a large and respectable concourse of people.

"Long as in freedom's cause the wise contend,
Dear to your country shall your fame extend;
While to the world the lettered stone shall tell
Where Caldwell, Attucks, Gray and Maverick fell.'

The following notice appeared in the Boston Gazette twenty years before when Attucks ran away from his master:

"Ran away from his master, William Brown, of Framingham, on the 20th of Sept. last, a Mullato Fellow, about 27 years of age, named Crispus, 6 feet 2 inches high, short curl'd hair, his knees nearer together than common; had on a light colored Bearskin Coat, plain brown Fustian Jacket, or brown All Wool one, new Buckskin breeches, blue Yarn Stockings, and a checked woolen shirt. Whoever shall take up said runaway, and convey him to his abovesaid master, shall have ten pounds, old Tenor Reward, and all necessary charges paid. And all Masters of Vessels and others are hereby cautioned against concealing or carrying off said Servant on Penalty of the Law. Boston, October 2, 1750.''

Hero and Martyr.—Attucks cut the cord and knot that held us to Great Britain. ''From that moment,'' says Webster, ''we may date the severance of the British Empire.'' It touched the people of the colonies as they had never been touched before. Orators poured out upon this former slave, now a hero and martyr, their unstinted praise. At each succeeding anniversary of this eventful day Crispus Attucks and his noble companions were lauded until our National Independence was achieved, when the 4th of July was substituted.

Committee of Safety.—A committee of safety was early appointed after the beginning of the war, and according to its decision no slaves were to be admitted into the army under any consideration whatever. Some free men had already enlisted. Peter Salem was a slave who fought side by side in the ranks with white soldiers. It was he who, on that memorable occasion at Bunker Hill when Major Pitcairn, at the head of the British army made an attack upon the American forces, shouting, '' The day is ours,'' poured the contents of his gun into that officer's body killing him instantly, and checking temporarily the advance of the British.

Of this occasion Mr. Aaron White, of the Massachusetts Historical Society, writes:

'' With regard to the black hero of Bunker Hill, I never knew him personally nor did I ever hear from his lips the story of his achievements; but I have better authority. A soldier of the Revolution, who was present at the Bunker Hill battle, related to my father the story of the death of Major Pitcairn. At the moment when the major appeared, startling the men before him, a Negro stepped forward, and, aiming his musket at the major's bosom, blew him through. I have frequently heard my father relate the story and have no doubt of its truth. Salem was not the only Negro at the battle of Bunker Hill. Others whose bravery has not been recorded participated in the battle, showing valor and fidelity."

Major Lawrence, who fought through the war from Concord to the peace of 1783, and who participated in many of the severest battles, at one time commanded a company of Negroes whose courage, military discipline and fidelity he spoke of with respect. On one occasion, being out reconnoitering with his company, he got so far in advance of his command that he was surrounded and on the point of being made a prisoner by the enemy. The colored men, soon discovering his peril, rushed to his rescue and fought with the most determined bravery till that rescue was effectually secured. He never forgot this circumstance, and ever after took special pains to show kindness and hospitality to any individual of the colored race who came near his dwelling.

Freeing the Slave.—After the committee of safety had excluded slaves from the army many of them were freed by their masters on condition that they join the army. But the prejudice against the Negro asserted itself more and more until the legislative bodies took action and entirely prevented Negroes from enlisting.

Colonial Congress. — Edward Rutledge, of South Carolina, moved that all Negroes be discharged that were in the army.   This proposition was strongly supported by the Southern delegates, but the Northern delegates succeeded in voting it down.   The contest, however, continued until a conference committee was called at Cambridge, at which it was agreed that the Negro should be rejected altogether.

Reorganization.—In the reorganization of the army many officers who had served with Negroes in the militia, and who had been enlisted in the Colonial army, protested against the exclusion of their old comrades on account of color.   Washington saw what might be the result if they were not permitted to enlist, and gave his consent to the enlistment with this proviso—"If this is disapproved by Congress I will put a stop to it."   It could be clearly seen that if a Negro was not permitted in the army the British would gain the advantage over the Colonial forces, and no one could predict what the Negro might do.   Congress reluctantly receded from its position and granted permission to enroll Negroes under certain conditions.

Lord Dunmore, who had charge of the British forces in the South, proclaimed freedom to all the slaves who would repair to his standard and bear arms to the king.   The flocking of slaves to the British standard greatly alarmed the Colonial forces and caused them to utilize the Negro forces, but in this the British had already preceded them.

The Negro Prince.—It is impossible to recite all incidents and circumstances showing the heroism and bravery on the part of the Negro in this war, but a few stand out more prominently than others.   Of these one is the Negro Prince, in Colonel Barton's command, who succeeded in capturing General Prescott in bed. The daring part that this negro took is shown in the following:

" The pleasing information is received here that Lieutenant-Colonel Barton, of the Rhode Island militia, planned a bold exploit for the purpose of surprising and taking Major-General Prescott, the commanding officer of the royal army, at Newport. Taking with him, in the night, about forty men, in two boats, with oars muffled, he had the address to elude the vigilance of the ships-of-war and guard boats, and, having arrived undiscovered at the quarters of General Prescott, they were taken for the sentinels; and the general was not alarmed till the captors were at the door of his lodging chamber, which was fast closed. A Negro man named Prince, instantly thrust his beetle head through the panel door and seized his victim while in bed. This event is extremely honorable to the enterprising spirit of Colonel Barton, and is considered an ample retaliation for the capture of General Lee by Colonel Harcourt. The event occasions great joy and exultation, as it puts in our possession an officer of equal rank with General Lee, by which means an exchange may be obtained. Congress resolved that an elegant sword should be presented to Colonel Barton for his brave exploit."

Major Jeffrey.—Among the brave blacks who fought in the battles for American liberty was Major Jeffrey, a Tennesseean, who, during the campaign of Major-General Andrew Jackson, in Mobile, filled the place of "regular" among the soldiers. In the charge made by General Stump against the enemy the Americans were repulsed and thrown into disorder, Major Stump being forced to retire in a manner by no means desirable under the circumstances. Major Jeffrey, who was but a common soldier, seeing the condition of his comrades and comprehending the disastrous results about to befall them, rushed forward, mounted a horse, took command of the troops, and by an heroic effort rallied them to the charge, completely routing the enemy who left the Americans masters of the field. He at once received from the general the title of "major," though he could not, according to the American policy, so commission him. To the day of his death he was known by that title in Nashville, where he resided, and the circumstances which entitled him to it were constantly the subject of popular conversation.

Major Jeffrey was highly respected by the whites generally, and revered in his own neighborhood by all the colored people who knew him.

A few years ago, receiving an indignity from a common ruffian, he was forced to strike him in self defense, for which act, in accordance with the laws of slavery in that as well as many other of the slave states, he was compelled to receive on his naked person, nine and thirty lashes with a rawhide! This, at the age of seventy-odd, after the distinguished services rendered his country, probably when the white ruffian by whom he was tortured was unable to raise an arm in self defense, was more than he could bear; it broke his heart, and he sank to rise no more, till summoned by the blast of the last trumpet, to stand on the battlefield of the general resurrection.

Re-enslavement.—Many Negroes were induced to enlist in the Colonial army with the understanding that they were to have their freedom at the close of the war. But the re-enslaving of the Negro who fought for American independence by stay-at-homes was a flagrant outrage. In the legislatures of some states they passed acts rebuking the injustice of such treatment.

The Legislature of Virginia ordered that persons in the states who caused the slaves to enlist as free persons could not thereafter force them to return to a state of servitude, so contradictory to that principle of justice and their own solemn vows. Every slave who had enlisted in any regiment, and who had been received as a substitute for any free person whose duty it was to serve in a regiment, was held and deemed free in as full and ample a manner as if each one who came had been especially named in the act.

Simon Lee.—Simon Lee, grandfather of Wm. Wells Brown, was a slave in Virginia and served in the war of the Revolution. Although honorably discharged with the other troops at the close of the war he was sent back to his master where he spent the remainder of his life toiling on a tobacco plantation.

Massachusetts, although having abolished slavery in 1783, it seems was still subjected to slave hunts, and her Negro soldiers were insulted by attempts to re-enslave them.

The British Army.—Not only did the soldiers of the American army receive unjust treatment but the British, who had promised freedom to all who would join their ranks, after enduring·the hardships of the war often committed them back to slavery.

Mr. Jefferson says: " From an estimate I made at that time, on the best information I could collect, I supposed the state of Virginia lost under Lord Cornwallis' hand that year, about thirty thousand slaves, and that of these twenty thousand died of the smallpox and camp fever. The rest were partly sent **to**

the West Indies and exchanged for rum, sugar, coffee and fruit, and partly sent to New York, from whence they went, at the peace, either to Nova Scotia or to England.   From this place I believe they have lately been sent to Africa.   History will never relate the horrors committed by the British army in the Southern states of America.''

The Heroism of the Negro.—The heroism of the Negro has been eulogized by many of our American statesmen, notably Mr. Pinckney and Mr. Eustis.

Mr. Pinckney says: ''It is a remarkable fact that notwithstanding, in the course of the Revolution, the Southern states were continually overrun by the British, and that all Negroes in them had an opportunity of leaving their owners, few did, proving thereby not only a most remarkable attachment to their owners, but the mildness of the treatment from whence their affections sprang.   They then were, as they still are, as valuable a part of our population to the Union as any other equal number of inhabitants.   They were in numerous instances the pioneers, and in all, the laborers of your armies.   To their hands were owing the erection of the greatest part of the fortifications raised for the protection of our country; some of which, particularly Fort Moultrie, gave, at the earlier period of the inexperience and untried valor of our citizens, immortality to American arms.   In the Northern states numerous bodies of them were enrolled into, and fought by the side of the whites, the battles of the Revolution.''

Mr. Eustis, of Massachusetts, said: ''At the commencement of the Revolutionary war there were found in the Middle and Northern states many blacks and other people of color capable of bearing arms; a part of them free, the greater part slaves. The freemen entered our ranks with the whites. The time of those who were slaves was purchased by the states, and they were induced to enter the service in consequence of a law by which, on condition of their serving in the ranks during the war, they were made freemen.''

'' The war over and peace restored, these men returned to their respective states, and who could have said to them on their return to civil life after having shed their blood in common with the whites in the defense of the liberties of their country, You are not to participate in the liberty for which you have been fighting? Certainly no white man in Massachussetts.''

Rev. Dr. Hopkins, of Rhode Island, said:

'' God is so ordering it in his providence that it seems absolutely necessary something should speedily be done with respect to the slaves among us, in order to our safety and to prevent their turning against us in our present struggle, in order to get their liberty. Our oppressors have planned to get the blacks and induce them to take up arms against us, by promising them liberty on this condition, and this plan they are prosecuting to the utmost of their power, by which means they have persuaded numbers to join them. And should we attempt to restrain them by force and severity, keeping a strict guard over them, and punishing those severely who shall be detected in attempting to join our oppressors, this will only be making bad worse, and serve to render our inconsistence, oppression and cruelty more criminal, perspicuous and shocking, and bring down the righteous vengeance of Heaven on our heads. The only way pointed out to prevent this threatening evil is to set the blacks at liberty ourselves by some public act and laws, and then give them proper encouragement to labor, or take arms in the defense of the American cause, as they shall choose. This would at once be doing them some degree of justice, and defeating our enemies in the scheme that they are prosecuting,''

Colonel Laurens.—No man stands out more prominently in the war of the Revolution than Colonel Laurens. He labored earnestly for the South to overcome the prejudices and to raise colored regiments. Although supported by the general government the selfishness of the Southern slaveholder frustrated his plans. In one of his letters to Washington he says: ''The approaching session of the Georgia legislature induces me to remain in these quarters for the purpose of taking new measures on the subject of our black levies. I shall, with all the tenacity of a man, do everything that I can in regaining a last effort on so interesting an occasion.'' Washington's reply showed that he, too, had lost faith in the patriotism of the citizens of the South to a great degree. He said:

''I must confess that I am not at all astonished at the failure of your plan. That spirit of freedom which, at the commencement of this contest, would have gladly sacrificed everything to the attainment of its object has long since subsided, and every selfish passion has taken its place. It is not the public, but private interest which influences the generality of mankind, nor can the Americans any longer boast an exception. Under these circumstances it would rather have been surprising if you had succeeded; nor will you, I fear, have better success in Georgia.''

Negro Soldiers.—George Williams says as soldiers the Negroes went far beyond the most liberal expectations of their staunchest friends. Associated with white men, many of whom were superior gentlemen and nearly all of whom were brave and enthusiastic, the Negro soldiers of the American army became worthy of the cause they fought to sustain. Colonel Alexander Hamilton had said: "Their natural faculties are as good as ours," and the assertion was supported by their splendid behavior on all the battlefields of the Revolution. Endowed by nature with a poetic element, faithful to trusts, abiding in friendship, bound by the golden threads of attachment to places and persons, enthusiastic in personal endeavor, sentimental and chivalric, they made hardy and intrepid soldiers. The daring, boisterous enthusiasm with which they sprang to arms disarmed racial prejudice of its sting and made friends of foes.

Their cheerfulness in camp, their celerity in the performance of fatigue-duty, their patient endurance of heat and cold, hunger and thirst, and their bold efficiency in battle, made them welcome companions wherever they went. The officers who frowned at their presence in the army at first, early learned from experience, that they were the equals of any troops in the army for severe service in camp and excellent fighting in the field.

CHAPTER IV.

Slavery Established in the South.—After the Revolution, when the new nation was recovering from the effects of the long continued war, it was found that slavery had established itself in the Southern States while in the North, slaves were being set free.

Responsibility.—The responsibility of fastening slavery upon the new republic was not the fault of the Declaration of Independence, which stated that all men are created equal and are endowed by the Creator with inalienable rights of life, liberty, and the pursuit of happiness. Southern statesmen proved themselves masters of the situation, and, seeing great gain in the traffic in slaves, labored to establish it more and more in the South. While they could not hide behind the walls of the constitution they took refuge, as they thought, behind the Bible, and urged that the divine origin of slavery was incontrovertible, that slavery was the normal condition of every Negro, and that the white man was God's agent to carry out the prophecy of Noah respecting the descendants of Ham.

Agitation.—While in the slave states there was a determined effort to establish slavery, yet throughout the whole nation, especially in the North, the anti-slavery sentiment was being agitated and increased. Some statesmen, notably Mr. Jefferson, prophesied a dissolution of the Union if the nation were to remain half slave and half free.

The whole commerce between master and slave was

denounced as the most unrelenting despotism on the one part and degrading submission on the other.

Property in Man.—Says George Williams: "When the doctrine of property in man was driven out of Europe as an exile and found a home in this New World in the West, the ancient and time honored anti-slavery sentiment combined all that was good in brain, heart and civilization, and hurled itself with righteous indignation against the institution of slavery the perfected curse of the ages.

The Quakers.—Foremost in the anti-slavery agitation were the good and kind-hearted Quakers, or Friends. In our poor Negro slaves they saw a brother, and very early in the history of the nation emancipated all their slaves and labored to increase the anti-slavery sentiment.

Benjamin Lundy.—One of the first agitators of the anti-slavery movement was Benjamin Lundy, who traveled through a number of states and labored incessantly for the freeing of the Negro. In 1830 he says: "I have within ten years sacrificed several thousands of dollars of my own earnings, I have traveled upwards of 5,000 miles on foot and more than 20,000 in other ways, have visited nineteen states of this Union and held more than two hundred public meetings, have performed two voyages to the West Indies, by which means the emancipation of a considerable number of slaves has been affected, and, I hope, the way paved for the enfranchisement of many more." Considering the extreme dangers to which any one agitating anti-slavery was subjected in these times this was a remarkable work. He was afterwards associated with William Lloyd Garrison. These men, together equally ardent in their efforts to abolish slavery, were, however, not agreed as to the method. Lundy favored gradual emancipation, Garrison immediate and unconditional emancipation.

William Lloyd Garrison.—This young man devoted his life to the cause of freeing the Negro. At an early period he edited an anti-slavery paper and afterwards

WILLIAM LLOYD GARRISON.

united with Mr. Lundy in publishing a paper at Baltimore. Seeing a load of slaves for the New Orleans market, the sundering of families, as well as the harrowing cruelties that attended these scenes, he denounced in his paper in no measured terms, the whole institution, and expressed his determination to cover with thick infamy all who were engaged in the trans-

action. The result was that his paper was destroyed,
he was arrested, tried for libel, and convicted and
imprisoned. The exorbitant fine imposed upon him
was afterwards paid by the benevolent Arthur Tap-
pan. Garrison went forth from the prison if possible
a more inveterate foe to slavery than ever. It was not
popular to denounce slavery and hence this young
orator often encountered great dangers. When cautioned he replied: "I am aware that many object to
the severity of my language, but is there not cause for
severity. I am but as harsh as truth and as uncom-
promising as justice. Tell a man whose house is on
fire to give a moderate alarm; tell him to moderately
rescue his wife from the hands of the ravisher; tell the
mother to gradually extricate her babe from the fire
into which it has fallen; but urge me not to use mod-
eration in a cause like the present. I am in earnest.
I will not equivocate—I will not excuse—I will not
retreat a single inch. And I will be heard." There
never was a more intrepid leader against slavery than
William Lloyd Garrison.

Anti-Slavery Societies.—In 1836 there were 250
auxiliary societies in thirteen states, and eighteen
months later they had increased to 1,000.

Silence of the Pulpit.—It is true that many of the
foremost ministers of the day maintained an unbroken
silence on the slavery question, but all could not be
kept silent. There were notable exceptions in many
parts of the north, while in some parts anti-slavery
men who had been hoping for aid from the church
went out of the church temporarily, hoping that the
scales would drop from the eyes of the preachers ere
long. Dr. Albert Barnes stated: "That there was no
power out of the church that would sustain slavery an
hour if it were not sustained in it."

Leaders of the Anti-Slavery Party.—Among the leaders of the anti-slavery party we may mention Parker Pillsbury, Stephen Foster, James G. Birney and Samuel Brooke. Mr. Pillsbury said: "The anti-slavery movement has unmasked the character of the American church. Our religion has been found at war with the interests of humanity and the laws of God. And it is more than time the world was awakened to its unhallowed influence on the hopes and happiness of man while it makes itself the palladium of the foulest iniquity ever perpetrated in the sight of Heaven."

Theodore Parker was another of the strong men who lent his influence wholly against slavery.

Other Agitators.—Foremost among agitators were such men as E. P. Lovejoy, who afterwards gave his life for the cause, James G. Birney, Cassius M. Clay and John Brown. Of John Brown it may be said that it was given to him to write the lesson upon the hearts of the American people so that they were enabled, a few years later, to practice the doctrine of resistance and preserve the nation against the bloody aggressions of the Southern Confederacy.

Colonization Societies.—These were formed earlier than any other anti-slavery organizations. Their objects were to rescue the free colored people of the United States from the political and social disadvantages and to place them in a country where they might enjoy the benefits of free government with all the blessings which it brings in its train. The American Colonization Society was never able to secure the confidence and the support of the anti-slavery societies of the day nor the Negro in general. It did not oppose slavery in its stronghold, but simply sought to secure a place for freed Negroes. The press, in many cases, lent its aid to the colonization societies, but, notwithstanding the apparent favor which it received, it was readily seen that to send the Negro to Africa or some other favored spot was an impossibility. The society lost strength

WENDELL PHILLIPS.

yearly until all were convinced the race could not be colonized, but that the Negro must be emancipated here and remain here.

Wendell Phillips.—One of Mr. Garrison's most able and earnest supporters was Wendell Phillips. Although

in many respects they strangely differed yet they stood
united for the cause of freedom; one was a self-made
man, the other a product of New England culture.
One was the executive of the anti-slavery movement,
the other the orator spreading the eloquence that melted
the fetters from a race and transformed a nation. Mr.
Phillips was a reformer and early espoused the cause
of anti-slavery. One of his most remarkable addresses
against slavery was made in Faneuil Hall, Boston,
where a number had gathered after the murder of Lovejoy to discuss the subject of slavery. Faneuil Hall was
secured by Dr. Channing. It was crowded at the time
of the meeting, thronged with three factions, some
being for free discussion, some to make mischief, and
others, idle spectators, were swayed to and fro by each
speaker in turn. Resolutions were offered denouncing
the murder of Lovejoy. To defeat the adoption of
these resolutions a popular politician, attorney-general
of Massachusetts, made a captivating speech and
almost succeeded in turning the audience against the
cause for which they had met. The foes of freedom,
through this astute attorney, captured the hall and
were ready to vote down the resolutions. It was at
this important moment, under the very shadow of the
pending catastrophe, that Wendell Phillips claimed
the floor and with his marvelous voice captivated
the ears of his audience. Mr. Phillips soon made himself master of the situation and hurled anathemas at the
previous speaker, and so completely carried his audience with him that at the close, with a whirlwind of
applause, the resolutions were carried by an over-
whelming vote. Oliver Johnson says of this speech:
"I had heard Phillips once before, and my expectations were high, but he transcended them and took the
audience by storm."

It was a speech to which not even the ablest report could do justice, for such a report could not bring the scene and the speaker vividly before the people.   Mr. Phillips, by espousing the cause of anti-slavery, was ostracised from social circles, for caste at that time in New England knew no recognition of true moral worth. It cost Wendell Phillips much when he became an abolitionist.   This speech on Lovejoy's murder in Faneuil Hall, cut him from all social intercourse with previous friends.   No one but those who have endured the persecutions of these days can understand what it cost these men to stand so earnestly for the freedom of the slaves.   Their true moral worth cannot be too forcibly presented to the youth of to-day.   Long live in the memory of the present and future generations men like Wendell Phillips who staked their all and were ready at any cost to stand for the suppression of the slave trade.

Convention of Colored People.—As early as 1831 the freed Negroes throughout the Northern states determined to do what they could for their brethren in bonds.   Several conventions were held.   A college was to be established and no doubt much good might have been done had they been permitted to continue in their work.   Able leaders succeeded in making the convention a power, but the intense hatred of the slavery element succeeded in abolishing these societies composed of persons of color.   These societies were disbanded and their members took their places in white societies.

The Proposed College.—A plan was proposed at one of these conventions that a college on the manual-labor system be established in New Haven.   It seems, however, New Haven resented the idea of having a colored

CHARLES SUMNER.

A staunch anti-slavery man who did more in Congress for the
freedom of the slave than any other man.   He was
Senator from Massachusetts.

college and another site was selected.   The disband-
ing of the colored associations put a stop to this movement which might have brought so much good to the
whole of the colored race.

Anti-Slavery Women of America.—In 1837 the anti-
slavery women met in their first convention in New
York, and the question as to admitting colored women

7 Progress.

was discussed and ably defended. It was finally decided that the society should admit colored members as well. The following lines by a colored member, Miss Sarah Forten, justified the hopes of her white sisters concerning the race:

"We are thy sisters. God has truly said
That of one blood the nations he has made.
Oh, Christian woman, in a Christian land,
Canst thou unblushing read this great command?
Suffer the wrongs which wring our inmost heart,
To draw one throb of pity on thy part.
Our skins may differ, but from thee we claim
A sister's privilege and a sister's name."

Anti-Slavery Orators.—The arguments of anti-slavery orators were often met by rotten eggs and many of them were abused. Mr. Garrison was dragged through the streets of Boston with a halter about his neck. Colored schools were broken up. Public meetings were disturbed by pro-slavery mobs. All this violent opposition added fuel to the flame and made the anti-slavery agitators all the bolder. While the foreign slave trade had been suppressed slave population was increasing at a wonderful ratio. Garrison's voice was not uncertain in those days. In July, 1860, he declared: "Our object is the abolition of slavery throughout the land. I am for meddling with slavery everywhere—attacking it by night and by day, in season and out of season—in order to effect its overthrow. Down with this slave-holding government! Let this 'covenant with death and agreement with hell' be annulled! Let there be a free, independent Northern republic and the speedy abolition of slavery will inevitably follow."

HARRIET BEECHER STOWE.
Author of "Uncle Tom's Cabin."

Literature.—Anti-slavery literature was scattered throughout the nation. Many pamphlets and books were written by eminent Negroes informing the public mind, stimulating the action and touching the heart of the civilized world of two continents. "Uncle Tom's Cabin," however, pleaded the cause of slavery more effectually than the millions of anti-slavery books and pamphlets, presenting the despairing cry of the enslaved, the struggle of fettered manhood, and touched the sympathies of the youth as well as the aged with a pity for the slave and a determination to abolish so hideous an institution.

Harriet Beecher Stowe.—Although Harriet Beecher Stowe was not permitted to take an active and direct part in freeing the slaves, yet her work, "Uncle Tom's Cabin," did more in bringing about the final liberation of the slave than any other agency. This volume has been translated into many languages. Everywhere read it is destined to create a sentiment against the traffic in man.

The Pro-Slavery Reaction.—The agitation of the anti-slavery question brought about a strong opposition to any effort made to free the slaves. Rewards of $10,000 and even $50,000 were offered for the heads of prominent abolitionists. Andrew Jackson in his message to Congress in 1835, suggested the propriety of a law that would prohibit, under severe penalties, the circulation in the Southern states through the mails of publications intended to incite the slaves to insurrection.

Attempts to Stifle Discussions.—The legislatures of the different states, as well as Congress, were next entreated to prohibit discussions of the slavery question. These efforts were generally defeated in the North, but in the South were successful.

Mob Riots.—In many places mob violence was resorted to in breaking up meetings called for the discussion of anti-slavery questions. Philadelphia had a riot lasting three nights and the harmless and powerless blacks were mainly its victims. At Concord, N. H., the mob demolished an academy because colored boys were admitted as pupils. At Northfield, N. H., George Storrs attempted to deliver an anti-slavery lecture, but was dragged from his knees while at prayer. On trial he was acquitted, but soon after was again arrested and sentenced to three months' imprisonment. He appealed and that ended the matter.

At Boston, William Lloyd Garrison was dragged through the streets with a rope around his body, but was finally rescued by the mayor who protected him from further violence. In the same city a women's anti-slavery society was dispersed by a mob while its president was at prayer. In the South there was but one mode of dealing with the abolitionists. "Let your emissaries cross the Potomac and I promise you that your fate will be no less than Haman's," says a Southern writer.

Rifling the Mails.—Anti-slavery literature was not permitted to be sent through the mails in the South and a meeting in Charleston, S. C., unanimously resolved that all mail matter of this kind should be burned. The mails were searched and rifled for the purpose. Attempts were made to bring offenders to justice, but failure met them in every case.

Congress Suppressing Agitation.—Not only in the state legislatures, but in Congress, measures were adopted to suppress the discussion of the slavery question. In 1837 Congress adopted by a vote of 117 to 68 the following resolution: "That all petitions, mem-

orials, resolutions, propositions, or papers relating in
any way to the subject of slavery or the abolition of
slavery shall, without being either first read or referred,

HENRY WILSON.

An anti-slavery agitator and Vice-President in 1872.   While in
Congress in 1862 he introduced a bill for the employment
of Negroes as Soldiers.

be laid on the table." Amazing as it may seem, this
heroic treatment was not successful in arresting agitation and restoring tranquillity to the public mind,

so that each succeeding Congress was necessitated to do the work over again.

John Brown.—One of the most prominent of the agitators of anti-slavery was John Brown of national fame. The story of this man's life is too well known to be repeated here. After laboring for many years and succeeding in aiding the cause of anti-slavery in many ways, he attacked Harper's Ferry in 1859 and, with a number of associates was made a prisoner. It is vain to under-rate either the man or his work. With firmness of will and a purpose unconquerable, he labored for the cause so dear to him and to which he had given most of his years. After the fight at Harper's Ferry he said: "I never intended plunder or treason or the destruction of property, or to excite the slaves to rebellion; I labored only to free the slaves." South Carolina, Missouri and Kentucky each sent a rope to hang him, but Kentucky's, proving the strongest, was selected and used. His last letter, written before his death to Mrs. George L. Stearns, Boston, Mass., follows:

"CHARLESTON, JEFFERSON CO., 29th Nov., 1859.
"MRS. GEORGE L. STEARNS, Boston, Mass.

"My Dear Friend: No letter I have received since my imprisonment here has given me more satisfaction or comfort than yours of the 8th inst. I am quite cheerful and never more happy. Have only time to write you a word. May God forever reward you and all yours.

"My love to ALL who love their neighbors. I have asked to be spared from having any mock or hypocritical prayers made over me when I am publicly murdered; and that my only religious attendants be poor little, dirty, ragged, bare-headed and bare-footed slave boys and girls .led by some old gray-headed slave mother. Farewell. Farewell,

"Your friend,

"JOHN BROWN."

John Brown gave slavery its death wound and his immortal name will be pronounced with blessings in all lands and by all people till the end of time.

JOHN BROWN, THE ABOLITIONIST.

CHAPTER V.

THE FUGITIVE SLAVE LAWS.

UNDERGROUND RAILROAD SYSTEM—SLAVE POPULATION.

Fugitive Slave Laws.—Very severe and stringent laws were passed to prevent anyone from aiding the slaves in attempting to escape to the North. These laws permitted owners to follow slaves and legally claim them in other states. Any one suspected of showing even an act of kindness to a fugitive slave was liable to be flogged, fined or imprisoned. The greater the agitation of the question the more severe were these laws.

Calvin Fairbanks.—Many respected citizens were imprisoned and fined for aiding slaves. Calvin Fairbanks spent nearly eighteen years in a Kentucky penitentiary for the crime of aiding poor slaves in gaining freedom. It is said that during this time he received 35,000 stripes on his bare body. Early in life he had heard of the sufferings and miseries endured by slaves and had resolved then to do all in his power to right the wrongs suffered by the race. He was one of the first in the Underground Railway work along the Ohio. A number of times he was arrested in the act of giving assistance to slaves and committed to prison, where he suffered untold cruelties from the hands of his keeper. "I was flogged sometimes bowed over a chair or some other object, often receiving seventy lashes four times a day, and at one time received 107 blows at one time, particles of flesh being thrown upon the wall several feet away." All this was endured by a white man in order to free the Negro.

Rev. John Rankin, of Ohio, was fined $1,000, besides serving a term in prison.

W. L. Chaplin aided two young slaves of Georgia to escape. Caught in the act, he was imprisoned for five months and released on a bail of $25,000. His friends, knowing that he would be convicted and sent to the penitentiary for a number of years, and perhaps for life, resolved to pay his bail. All his property was sacrificed, and through the liberality of that princely man, Garrett Smith, the sum was raised.

Thomas Garrett, a Quaker of Delaware, one of the most successful agents of the Underground Railway, assisted nearly 3,000 slaves to escape from bondage; he was at last convicted and fined so heavily that he lost all his property When the auctioneer had knocked off his last piece of property to pay the fine he said: "I hope you will never be guilty of doing the like again." Garrett, although penniless at the age of sixty, replied: "Friend, I have not a dollar in the world, but if thee knows a fugitive slave who needs a breakfast send him to me." It is with pleasure we learn Mr. Garrett lived to see the day when the slaves obtained their freedom.

Levi Coffin.—This man of high social position, a Quaker of Cincinnati, was frequently called the president of the Underground Railway. He succeeded in aiding about 25,000 slaves in gaining their freedom.

Captain Jonathan Walker.—Mr. Walker took a contract to build a railroad in Florida and for this purpose employed a number of Negroes. By kind treatment he gained the confidence of these slaves who afterwards persuaded him to aid them in gaining their liberty. They attempted to escape in a boat to an island not far away. Captain Walker was taken violently sick, and the Negroes, not understanding how to manage the boat, were taken up by another vessel and taken to Key West. Captain Walker was tried in the United States Court and was sentenced to be branded on the right hand with the capital letters "S. S." (slave stealer), and to pay as many fines as there were slaves; to suffer

THOMAS GARRETT.

From " Underground Railroad," by permission of Author.

as many terms imprisonment; and to pay the costs and stand committed until the fines were paid. The initials of the words " slave stealer " were branded upon his hand and he was imprisoned, but his friends succeeded in raising money to pay his fines and he was released in 1845. The following lines by Whittier gave quite another meaning to the brand "S. S.,"

making it a badge of honor, signifying the heroism
and self-sacrifice in spirit of these forerunners of
liberty.

" Then lift that manly right hand, bold plowman of the wave,
   Its branded palm shall prophesy Salvation to the Slave;
   Hold up its fire-wrought language, that whoso reads may feel
   His heart swell strong within him, his sinews change to steel;
   Hold it up before our sunshine, up against our Northern air.
   Ho! men of Massachusetts, for the love of God, look there!
   Take it henceforth for your standard, like the Bruce's heart of
     yore;
   In the dark strife closing round ye let that hand be seen
     before."

Underground Railroad.—By this term we designate
the many methods and systems by which fugitive
slaves from the Southern States were aided in escaping to the North or Canada.

After slavery was abolished in the North slaves
frequently ran away from their masters and attempted
to reach the free states of the North, or better still,
Canada, where they were beyond the reach of their
former masters.

These so-called railroads were most useful auxiliaries in giving aid to the Negro. Fugitive slave laws
gave masters the right to pursue the slaves into another state and bring them back. The men interested
in these railways were men who felt they should fear
God rather than man, that the fugitive slave laws
were unjust and that they should not be obeyed.
They were composed of a chain of good men who
stretched themselves across the land from the borders
of the slave states all the way to Canada. Many fugitive slaves were thus permitted to escape. They
were carried by night to a place of safety and then
turned over to another conductor who very often

would load up and convey the fugitives in a covered wagon to the next station. Thus they were carried on from one place to another. As soon as leaders rose among the slaves who refused to endure hardship, the fugitive then came north. George Williams says: "Had they remained, the direful scenes of St. Domingo would have been re-enacted, and the hot vengeful breath of massacre would have swept the South as a tornado and blanched the cheek of the civilized world."

Different Branches.—It would be very difficult to name all the branches of the "Underground Railroad." They extended all the way from New Jersey to Illinois. Probably those on which the greatest number was rescued extended through Pennsylvania and Ohio. Many local branches existed in different parts of the country.

William Still.—One of the most active workers in freeing slaves was William Still. He was chairman and secretary of the eastern branch of the road. It is wonderful what work such men as Mr. Still did in those days when opposition was so great. A part of the work that he has done is recorded in " Underground Railroad." In the preface of this work Mr. Still says: "In these records will be found interesting narratives of the escapes of men, women and children from the present House of Bondage; from cities and plantations; from rice swamps and cotton fields; from kitchens and mechanic shops; from border states and gulf states; from cruel masters and mild masters; some guided by the north star alone, penniless, braving the perils of land and sea, eluding the keen scent of the bloodhound as well as the more dangerous pursuit of the savage slave-hunter; some from secluded

DESPERATE CONFLICT IN A BARN.

From "Underground Railroad," by permission of Author.

dens and caves of the earth, where for months and years they had been hidden away awaiting the chance to escape; from mountains and swamps, where indescribable sufferings and other privations had patiently been endured. Occasionally fugitives came in boxes and chests, and not infrequently some were secreted in steamers and vessels, and in some instances journeyed hundreds of miles in skiffs. Men disguised in female attire and women dressed in the garb of men have under very trying circumstances triumphed in thus making their way to freedom. And here and there, when all other modes of escape seemed cut off, some, whose fair complexions have rendered them indistinguishable from their Anglo-Saxon brethren, feeling that they could endure the yoke no longer, with assumed airs of importance, such as they had been accustomed to see their masters show when traveling, have taken the usual modes of conveyance and have even braved the most scrutinizing inspection of slave-holders, slave-catchers, and car conductors, who were ever on the alert to catch those who were considered base and white enough to practice such deception." Mr. Still says that the passengers on the Underground Railroad were generally above the average order of slaves.

Agents.—As the branches of the railroad were numerous it would be impossible to name any considerable number of the agents of the road. Some of these nobly periled their all for the freedom of the oppressed. Seth Concklin lost his life while endeavoring to rescue from Alabama slavery the wife and children of Peter Still. Samuel D. Burris, whose faithful and heroic service in connection with the underground railway cost him imprisonment and inhuman treatment, at last lost his freedom by being sold from the auction block.

WILLIAM STILL.
See sketch in Chapter XIV.

Stockholders.—Stockholders did not expect any dividends in this road, nor were any reports published.

Indeed, prudence often dictated that the recipients of favors should not know the names of their helpers and vice versa, they did not desire to know others. The slave and his friends could only meet in private to transact the business of the road. All others were outsiders. The right hand was not to know what the left hand was doing. The safety of all concerned called for still tongues. For a long time no narratives were written. Probably the best and most authentic of these thrilling accounts of the struggle for liberty are found in " Underground Railroad."

Methods Pursued.—Different methods were pursued to aid fugitive slaves; some availed themselves of steamboats, railroads, stage coaches, but more frequently a more private method was resorted to, so as to escape detection. A number of cases are reported where colored men were boxed up and shipped by express across the line.

William Jones, from Baltimore, succeeded in having his friends box him up and ship him by express to Philadelphia; for seventeen hours he was enclosed in the box, but friends at the Philadelphia underground station succeeded in getting the box safely, and after a time in sending the slave to Canada.

Mr. Pratt, in his sketches of the underground railway, gives a number of interesting accounts of escapes, among which are a mother and daughter who escaped in a box from Washington to Warsaw, New York. With the aid of a friend they secured a box, put in it straw, quilts, plenty of provisions and water, and their friend carried the box in a spring wagon to the North. This friend, in order to succeed in his efforts, passed himself off as a Yankee clock peddler, and as he drove a wagon and good team, no questions were asked.

When out of sight of settlements he would open the box and give the inmates an opportunity to walk in the night for exercise. The master heard of their whereabouts and sent slave-hunters to recapture them,

A BOLD STROKE FOR FREEDOM.

From "Underground Railroad," by permission of Author."

but the sentiment against slavery was so strong that they were not permitted to take them back.

Henry Box Brown.—The marvelous escape of Henry Box Brown was published widely in papers when the anti-slavery agitation was being carried on. In point of interest his case is no more remarkable than any other; indeed, he did not suffer near as much as many. He was a piece of property in the city of Richmond. He seemed to be a man of inventive mind, and knew that it was no small task to escape the vigilance of Virginia slave hunters, or the wrath of an enraged master, for attempting to escape to a land of liberty.

The ordinary modes of travel, he concluded, might prove disastrous to his hopes, he therefore hit upon a new invention, which was to have himself boxed up and forwarded to Philadelphia by express. Size of box was 2 feet wide, 2 feet 8 inches deep and 3 feet long. His food consisted of a few small biscuits. He had a large gimlet which he intended to use for fresh air if necessary. Satisfied that this would be far better than to remain in slavery, he entered the box. It was

RESURRECTION OF HENRY BOX BROWN.
From "Underground Railroad," by permission of Author.

safely nailed up and hooped with five hickory hoops, and addressed by his friend, James A. Smith, a shoe dealer, to Wm. Johnson, Arch street, Philadelphia, marked "This side up, with care." It was twenty-six hours from the time he left Richmond until he arrived in Philadelphia. The notice, "This side up," did not avail, for the box was often roughly handled. For a while the box was upside down and he was on his head for miles. The members of the vigilance committee of Philadelphia had been informed that he would be started. One of the committee went to the depot at half past two o'clock in the morning to look after the box, but did not find it. The same afternoon he received a telegram from Richmond, "Your case of goods is shipped and will arrive to-morrow morning."

Mr. McKim, who had been engineering this undertaking, found it necessary to change the program, for it would not be safe to have the express bring it directly to the anti-slavery office. He went to a friend who was extensively engaged in mercantile business who was ready to aid him. This friend, Mr. Davis, knew all the Adams Express drivers, and it was left to him to pay a trusty man $5 in gold to go next morning and bring the box directly to the anti-slavery office.

Those present to behold the resurrection were J. M. McKim, Professor C. D. Cleveland, Lewis Thompson, and Wm. Still. The box was taken into the office. When the door had been safely locked, Mr. McKim rapped quietly on the lid of the box and called out "All right." Instantly came the answer from within, "All right, sir." Saw and hatchet soon removed the five hickory hoops and raised the lid of the box. Rising up in his box, Brown reached out his hand, saying, "How do you do, gentlemen." He was about as wet as if he had come up out of the Delaware. He first sang the psalm beginning with these words: "I waited patiently for the Lord, and he heard my prayer." At the home of Lucretia Mott he received a cordial reception, and was entertained for some time, when he went to Boston.

The success of this undertaking encouraged Smith, who had nailed him up in the box, to render similar service to two other young bondmen. But, unfortunately, in this attempt the undertaking proved a failure.

The young men, after being duly expressed and some distance on the road, were, through the agency of the telegraph, betrayed, and the heroic young fugitives were taken from the box and dragged back to helpless bondage. Smith was arrested and imprisoned for seven years in a Richmond penitentiary. He lost all

CHARITY STILL,
Who Twice Escaped from Slavery.

his property, was refused witnesses on his trial, and for five long months, in hot weather, he was kept heavily chained in a cell 4x8 feet in dimensions. Mr. Smith had, by his efforts, aided many to gain their liberty. He received five stabs aimed at his heart by a bribed assassin. But all these things did not move him from his purpose. After his release he went North and was united in marriage at Philadelphia to a lady who had remained faithful to him through all his sufferings.

Amanda Smith, in her autobiography, tells how her

father assisted runaway slaves. "Our house," she says, "was one of the main stations of the underground railway. My father took the Baltimore Weekly Sun newspaper, that always had advertisements of runaway slaves. These would be directed by their friends to our house and we would assist them on their way to liberty. Excitement ran very high, and we had to be very discreet in order not to attract suspicion. My father was watched closely, as he was suspected of aiding slaves. After working all day in the harvest field he would come home at night, sleep about two hours, then start at midnight and walk fifteen or twenty miles and carry a poor slave to a place of security, sometimes a mother and child, sometimes a man and wife, then get home just before day. Thus he many times baffled suspicion, and never but once was there a poor slave taken from my father's hands, and if that man had told the truth he would have been saved.

"One week the papers were full of notices of a slave who had run away. A heavy reward was offered, a number of men in our neighborhood determined to get the reward if possible. They suspected our home as a place of safety for the poor slave. We had concealed the poor fellow for about two weeks, as there was no possible chance for father or anyone else to get him away, so closely were we watched. One day four men came on horseback. As father saw them he called to mother that four men were coming. He met them and they demanded of him to know whether he had a nigger there. Father said, 'If I tell you I have not you won't believe me, if I tell you I have it will not satisfy you, so search for yourself.' Mother had in the meantime concealed him between the cords and the straw tick. The men searched the house, looked under the bed, and satisfied themselves that he was not there; thus we succeeded in saving him from slavery."

William and Ellen Craft were slaves in the state of Georgia. The desire to become free became so strong that they commenced planning to escape. Ellen, being fair, would pass for a white man, and was to act the part of master, while William was to be the servant. She dressed in a fashionable suit of male attire, and was to pass as a young planter. But Ellen was *beardless*. After mature reflection her face was muffled up as though the young planter was suffering from a face or toothache. In order to prevent the method of registering at hotels, Ellen put her right arm in a sling, put on green spectacles, and pretended to be very hard of hearing and dependent upon the faithful servant.

Ellen, disguised as a young planter, was to have nothing to do but to hold herself subject to her ailments and put on the air of superiority. The servant was always ready to explain in case of inquiry. They stopped at first-class hotels in Charleston, Richmond and Baltimore, and arrived safely in Philadelphia, where the rheumatism disappeared, her right arm was unslung, her toothache was gone, the beardless face was unmuffled, the deaf heard and spoke, the blind saw. The strain on Ellen's nerves, however, had tried her severely, and she was physically prostrated for some time. Her husband, William, was thoroughly colored, and was a man of marked ability and good manners, and full of pluck. They were sent to Boston, where they lived happily until the fugitive slave law was passed. Then slave hunters from Macon, Georgia, were soon on their track, but the sympathy of friends in Boston would not permit their being returned to Georgia. It was, however, considered best for them

to seek a country where they would not be in daily
fear of slave capturers, backed by the United States
Government.   They were therefore sent by their
friends to Great Britain.

In England the Crafts were highly respected. After
the emancipation they returned to the United States
with two children, and, after visiting Boston and
neighboring places, William purchased a plantation
near Savannah, and is living there with his family.

Emancipators Tried.—Those who aided slaves in
their struggle for liberty were often tried and imprisoned. Many of them lost all of their property and
suffered much from the hands of slave dealers.

Seth Concklin's noble and daring spirit induced him
to put forth the most strenuous efforts to redeem a
family of slaves.   He learned to know Peter Still and
found that his wife and children were still in Alabama
in bondage.   After considering the hazardous undertaking, he decided to make an attempt to bring the
wife and children of Peter Still to the North. He went
South, laid his plans well, and succeeded in carrying
the family for seven days and seven nights in his skiff,
then traveled hundreds of miles on foot.   They at last
reached Vincennes, Indiana.   By this time the advertisements of the runaway slaves had spread all over the
country, and at Vincennes they were arrested and
taken South to their former owner.

Imagine the state of mind of these enslaved ones,
who, after having endured so many hardships and pain,
so near to freedom's territory, were caught and returned
to slavery.   Seth Concklin was brutally murdered on
the way south.

Thus we might give numerous cases where slaves
were secreted for months and endured the greatest

hardships and were willing rather to meet death than to remain in slavery. Several girls made their escape in male attire, some secreted themselves in woods, traveling at night. Others succeeded in having friends hide them in steamers, but the underground railroad, with all its stations and well-planned schemes, succeeded often in defeating the plans of the slave hunters. As soon as a slave ran away papers were filled with advertisements and rewards were offered for their return. In this way many were looking for slaves so as to secure the rewards, making the escape of some more difficult. One cannot read such books as "The Underground Railroad, by Wm. Still," or the story of Peter Still, the kidnapped and the ransomed, without sincere thankfulness that slavery is ended, and that a man is a man without respect to the color of his skin.

Slave Population.—In 1800 the slave population was over 900,000; in 1830 it had reached about 2,000,000; in 1840 it was estimated to be about 2,500,000; and in 1850 it was about 3,000,000. In 1860 the aggregate Negro population in the United States was about 4,500,000, of which about 4,000,000 were slaves. Nearly 3,000,000 of the slaves were in the rural districts of the South. Southern prosperity depended upon the product of slave labor, which amounted to about $140,000,-000 per year. It can be readily seen that the Civil War, which commenced in 1861, was destined to shake the very foundation of Southern civilization. While both North and South attempted to keep the real cause of the war in the background the maxim, "No question is settled until it is settled right," asserted itself here, and no real progress was made in the war until the Northern leaders acknowledged slavery as the issue, and met the question direct by freeing all slaves.

ABRAHAM LINCOLN.

CHAPTER VI.

THE NEGRO IN THE CIVIL WAR.

The part enacted by Negro troops in the War of the Rebellion is the romance of North American history.

Number Enrolled.—The records of the war department show that there were 178,595 colored men regularly enlisted as soldiers in the Union army during the rebellion who by their good conduct established a commendable record and did efficient service in camp, fortress and field. The first enlistment of Negroes was by Gen. Hunter in the Department of the South in June, 1862. It was made without the authority of the War Department and was due to an emergency. Gen. Hunter needed men.

Ready for Enlistment.—At the sound of the tocsin at the North the Negro waiter, barber, cook, groom, porter, boot-black, and laborer, stood ready at the enlisting office; although the recruiting officer refused to take his name he waited patiently for the prejudice to be removed, waited two long years before the door was opened, but even then he did not hesitate but walked in, and with what effect the world knows.

Opposition to Enlistment.—From the beginning there was great opposition to enlisting the Negro in the army. The Northerners even went so far as to return runaway Negroes to their owners, while the South kept the Negro on the plantation. The Confederates, however, found it no easy task to watch the Negro and the Yankee too; their attention could be given to but one at a time; as a slave expressed it,

"When Marsa watch the Yankee, nigger go—when Marsa watch the nigger, Yankee come."

Objections.—The "New York Times," of February 16, 1863, in an editorial summed up the objections to enlisting the Negroes as follows: "First, that the Negroes will not fight. Second, it is said that the whites will not fight with them. Third, that the prejudice against them is so strong that our citizens will not enlist or will quit the service if compelled to fight by their side, and thus we shall lose two white soldiers for one black one that we gain. Fourth, it is said that we shall get no Negroes—or not enough to be of any service. In the free states very few will volunteer, and in the slave states we can get but few because the rebels will push them southward as fast as we advance upon them. Fifth, the use of the Negroes will exasperate the South. We presume it will—but so will any other scheme we may adopt which is warlike and effective in its character and results. We are not ready with Mr. Vallandinham, to advocate immediate and unconditional peace! The best thing we can do is to possess ourselves in patience while the experiment is being tried."

The President and Secretary of War and a large majority of the generals in the army acted on the theory, "This is a white man's war, and the Negro has no lot or part in it."

They seemed to be ignorant of the fact that slavery was the real cause of the war, and hence held to the principal that all runaway slaves must be returned to their owners by the Union army.

General Hunter.—To General David Hunter, commanding the army in the South, is given the honor of organizing the first southern colored regiment. He could not get white recruits and was surrounded by a

multitude of able-bodied Negroes who were idle, but
anxious to serve as soldiers. In advance of public
opinion he organized a regiment and was called to
account for it by the Secretary of War. He replied
that he had instructions to employ all loyal persons in
defense of the Union and the suppression of the
rebellion, and hence was not limited as to color. He
informed the secretary that loyal slaves everywhere
remained on their plantations to welcome them, aid
them, supply the army with food and information, and
since they were the only men who were loyal, he had
organized them into a regiment and appointed officers
to drill them. He closed with these words: "The
experiment of arming the blacks, so far as I have
made, has been a complete and even marvelous success. They are sober, docile, attentive and enthusiastic; displaying great natural capacities for acquiring
the duties of the soldier. They are eager, beyond all
things, to take the field and be led into action; and it
is the unanimous opinion of the officers who have
charge of them that in the peculiarities of this climate
and country they will prove invaluable auxiliaries."

Mr. Wyckliff created a scene in the house by denouncing General Hunter and declaring that the enlist-
ments of Negroes was an insult to every white soldier
in the army. Nevertheless Congress authorized the President to enlist "persons of African descent," but provided that they should be used as laborers in the camps
and forts, and were not to be allowed to bear arms.

After a Year.—Towards the close of 1862 the war
clouds were still growing thicker. The Union army
had won few victories; the Northern troops had to fight
in a tropical climate, the forces of nature and an arro-
gant, jubilant and victorious enemy, but in the face of

all these discouraging features the President still held
to his views of managing the war without bringing the
subject of slavery to the front.   In reply to a deputa-
tion of gentlemen from Chicago, who urged a more
vigorous policy of emancipation, the President denied
the request and stated: "The subject is difficult and
good men do not agree.   For instance: The other day,
four gentlemen of standing and intelligence from New
York called as a delgation on business connected with
the war; but before leaving two of them earnestly be-
sought me to proclaim general emancipation, upon
which the other two at once attacked them.   You know
also that the last session of Congress had a decided majority of anti-slavery men, yet they could not unite upon
this policy.   And the same is true of the religious people.
Why, the rebel soliders are praying with a great deal
more earnestness, I fear, than our own troops, and
expecting God to favor their side; for one of our
soldiers, who had been taken prisoner, told Senator
Wilson a few days since that he met nothing so discouraging as the evident sincerity of the prayers of those
he was among."

He admitted that slavery was at the root of the
rebellion, but was not willing to act, but just nine days
from that time when he thought a proclamation not
warranted and impracticable, he issued his first Emancipation Proclamation.

Public Opinion Changes.—When the Union men
began to see the worth of the Negro to the Confederate
army in throwing up breastworks that were often
almost impregnable, they began to complain that the
Negro with his pick and spade was a greater hindrance
to their progress than the cannon ball of the enemy;
slowly but surely public opinion changed.   Congress

GENERAL GRANT AND A COLORED GUARD.

The guard, being under instructions, would not permit even General Grant to pass before he had thrown away his cigar.

121

prohibited the surrender of the Negroes to the rebels, the President issued his Emancipation Proclamation and the Negroes were rapidly enlisted.

In the Union Ranks.—Charles Sumner says: "Those who have declaimed loudest against the employment of Negro troops have shown a lamentable amount of ignorance, and an equally lamentable lack of common sense. They know as little of the military history and martial qualities of the African race as they do of their own duties as commanders. All distinguished generals of modern times who have had opportunity to use Negro soldiers have uniformly applauded their subordination, bravery, and power of endurance. Washington solicited the military services of Negroes in the Revolution, and rewarded them. Jackson did the same in the War of 1812. Under both these great captains the Negro troops fought so well that they received unstinted praise."

Confederate Measures.—The enlistment of Negroes in the Northern army changed the policy of the South, and public opinion, now so strongly endorsed in the North, affected the rebels, who soon passed a measure for arming 200,000 Negroes themselves.

In the Navy.—In the navy a different course was pursued from the first. Negroes were readily accepted all along the coasts on board the war vessels, this being no departure from the regular and established practice in the service.

Official Authority.—General Rufus Saxon was the first officer to receive official authority to enlist Negroes as soldiers. On the 26th of August, 1862, the Secretary of War ordered him to proceed to the Department of the South and organize 5,000 troops of "African descent," which were to be designated for service in

garrisons not in danger of attack by the enemy, to
relieve white regiments whose terms of enlistment had
expired. But one of General Saxon's first acts after
recruiting a regiment was to send it on a foraging
expedition into the enemy's country. The result was
entirely satisfactory. The colored men proved to be
remarkably good foragers, and brought in more supplies than three times the number of white men could
have secured.

Recruiting Offices.—Recruiting stations were established throughout the South, and officers were sent out
to enlist slaves. In these journeys through the country
officers often met with strange experiences. Recruits
were taken wherever found, and as their earthly possessions usually consisted of but what they wore upon
their backs, they required no time to settle their
affairs. The laborer in the field would lay down his
hoe, or leave his plow, and march away with the
guard. On one occasion a large plantation was visited
and the proprietor asked to call in his slaves; he com-
plied, and when they were asked if they wished to
enlist replied that they did, and fell into the ranks
with the guard. As they started away the old man
turned and, with tears in his eyes, said: "Will you
take them all? Here I am an old man; I cannot work;
my crops are ungathered, my Negroes have all enlisted
or run away, and what am I to do?" Several recruiting officers were tarred and feathered and others were
shot. Several officers were dismissed from the army
for refusing to command Negro troops; others resigned
in preference to doing so.

Indignation.—Although the Confederates anticipated
the Federal government in the employment of Negroes
as military forces, they exhibited a good deal of indig-

nation when their example was followed, and the
Records of the Confederate Congress show some sensational measures of retaliation threatened against the
government of the United States on this account.
It was proposed, among other things, to raise the black
flag against Negro soldiers and white officers who commanded them, and in some cases this retaliation was
enforced, as at Port Pillow, but finally the Confederate
Congress formally recognized the usefulness of the
Negro as a soldier as well as a laborer, and authorized
President Davis to enlist an unlimited number of colored troops.

Governor Yates.—This fact was commented upon by
Governor Yates, of Illinois, in a message he sent to the
legislature of that state, as a most extraordinary phe-
nomenon in history. He said the leaders of the insurrection had called upon the cause of the insurrection
to save it, and had recognized the intelligence and
manhood of the despised race by lifting it to a level
with themselves. A wise providence, he said, was
directing the destiny of the Confederates, so that they
will terminate the very evil they are fighting to maintain. Slavery was to be the corner stone of their new
Confederacy, but, says Governor Yates, a man who has
been a soldier will never be a slave.

Discrimination.—In the matter of pay there was for
a long time discrimination against the Negro troops.
While the troops of the regular army were paid $13.00
per month, the Negroes received but $10.00, three of
which was deducted on account of· clothing. Some
regiments refused to receive $10.00 per month and
others were paid in full. The injustice done the Negro
soldier in this discrimination was often a violation
of a solemn and written pledge of the govern-

ON PICKET DUTY.

ment that declared that they should receive the same pay and allowances as the white men. In definite terms, Congress and the War Department was denounced as the enemy of the Negro in this discrimination. All honor to the Fifty-fourth colored regiment of Massachusetts that refused to receive the $7.00 per month until the authorities were driven to give equal pay to Negroes and whites.

General Butler.—Nearly all the generals of the army opposed the enlistment of the Negro. General Phelps, stationed at Louisiana, made a bold fight for the Negro, and attempted to enlist them in and around New Orleans, but being so strongly opposed by General Butler, he was forced to resign and return to his home.

The sentiment of the North seemed to admit the right of the South to hold slaves. That General Butler afterwards entirely changed his opinion is seen by his speech on the floor of Congress, when he said: "It became my painful duty, sir, to follow in the track of the charging column, and there, in a space not wider than the clerk's desk, and three hundred yards long, lay the dead bodies of three hundred and fifty-three of my colored comrades, slain in the defense of their country, who laid down their lives to uphold its flag and its honor as a willing sacrifice; and as I rode along among them, guiding my horse this way and that way lest he should profane with his hoofs what seemed to me the sacred dead, and as I looked on their bronzed faces upturned in the shining sun as if in mute appeal against the wrongs of the country for which they had given their lives, and whose flag had only been to them a flag of stripes on which no star of glory had ever shone for them—feeling I had wronged them in the past, and believing what was the future of my country to them

—among my dead comrades there I swore myself a solemn oath: 'May my right hand forget its cunning, and my tongue cleave to the roof of my mouth, if I ever fail to defend the rights of those men who have given their blood for me and my country this day, and for their race forever;' and, God helping me, I will keep this oath.''

President Lincoln, when urged by Dr. Patton, of Chicago, to press the Negro into service said: "If we were to arm them, I fear that within a few weeks, the arms would be in the hands of the rebels.''

In Congress.—In Congress a bill was passed to raise and equip 150,000 soldiers of African descent. Colonel T. Higginson now watched the acts of Congress and ascended the St. John's river in Florida and captured Jacksonville, which had been abandoned by white Union troops.

The New York Tribune said: "Drunkenness, the bane of our army, does not exist among our black troops.'' "Nor have I yet discovered the slightest ground of inferiority to white troops.''

Prejudice Broken Down.—The bravery and excellence of the Negro in the battlefield soon broke down prejudices against the Negro on the part of the white officers, and it was not long before 100,000 Negroes were found in the Union ranks.

Colonel Shaw.—Colonel Shaw commanded the first colored regiment organized in the free states, the Fifty-fourth Massachusetts, and it was this regiment that played such an important part in the attempt to take Fort Wagner. After making a forced effort and march for a day and a night, through swamps and drenching rains, without food or rest, hungry and fatigued they reached General Strong's headquarters on that memorable morning, just as they were forming into line of battle. Colonel Shaw made a thrilling patriotic speech to his men, and, after a most desperate and gallant fight, succeeded in planting the regimental flag on the works. The Negro color bearer, John Wall, was killed. But. Wm. H. Carney seized it, and, after receiving several wounds, one of which mangled his arm, brought the flag to the standard with his own blood on it and shouted, "Boys, the old flag never touched the ground."

Fort Wagner.—M. S. Littlefield, in writing of Fort Wagner says: "Sergeant W. H. Carney, Company C, writes he was with the first battalion, which was in the advance of the storming column. He received the regimental colors, pressed forward to the front rank, near the colonel, who was leading the men over the ditch. He says, as they ascended the wall of the fort, the ranks were full, but as soon as they reached the top 'they melted away' before the enemy's fire 'almost instantly.' He received a severe wound in the thigh, but fell upon his knees. He planted the flag upon the parapet, lay down on the outer slope, that he might get as much shelter as possible; there he remained for over an hour, till the second brigade came up. He kept the colors flying until the second conflict was ended. When our forces retired he followed, creeping upon one knee, still holding up the flag. It was thus that Sergeant Carney came from the field, having held the emblem of liberty over the walls of Fort Wagner during the sanguinary conflict of the two brigades, and having received two very severe wounds, one in the thigh and one in the head. Still he refused to give up his sacred trust until he found an officer of his regiment.

SERGEANT WM. H. CARNEY.

"When he entered the field hospital, where his wounded comrades were being brought in, they cheered him and the colors. Though nearly exhausted with the loss of blood, he said: 'Boys, the old flag never touched the ground.' Of him as a man and soldier I can speak in the highest terms of praise."

Milliken Bend.—"Tauntingly it has been said that Negroes won't fight. Who say it, and who but a dastard and brute will dare to say it, when the battle of Milliken's Bend finds its place among the heroic deeds of this war? This battle has significance. It demonstrated the fact that the freed slaves will fight."

General Grant says of Milliken Bend: "This was the first important engagement of the war in which colored troops were under fire. These men were very raw, perhaps all had been enlisted since the beginning of the siege, but they behaved well."

First Colored Regiment.—The first colored regiment raised in New Orleans under General. Butler, after remaining in camp for about six months, were quite efficient in the use of arms. It was then ordered to report to General Dwight. Its commanding officer, Colonel Stafford, was disabled, and was not permitted to go with the regiment. Before the regiment left the officers assembled at the quarters of Colonel Stafford. The colored guared marched up to receive the regimental flags. Colonel Stafford made a speech full of patriotism and feeling, and concluded by saying: "Colored guard, protect, defend, die for it, but do not surrender these flags." The reply of the sergeant was, "Colonel, I will bring back these colors to you in honor, or report to God the reason why."

Port Hudson.—At Port Hudson, "the deeds of heroism performed by these colored men were such as the proudest white men might emulate. Their colors were torn to pieces by shot, and literally bespattered by blood and brains. The color-sergeant of the First Louisiana, on being mortally wounded, hugged the colors to his breast, when a struggle ensued between the two color-corporals on each side of him as to who should have the honor of bearing the sacred standard, and during this generous contention one was seriously wounded. One black lieutenant actually mounted the enemy's works three or four times, and in one charge the assaulting party came within fifty paces of them. Indeed, if only ordinarily supported by artillery and reserve, no one can convince us that they would not have opened a passage through the enemy's works.

"**Captain Callioux**, of the First Louisiana, a man so black that he actually prided himself on his blackness, died the death of a hero, leading on his men in the thickest of the fight. One poor wounded fellow came along with his arm shattered by a shell, and jauntily swinging it with the other, as he said to a friend of mine: 'Massa, guess I can fight no more.' I was with one of the captains, looking after the wounded going to the rear of the hospital, when we met one limping towards the front. On being asked where he was going, he said: 'I have been shot bad in the leg, captain, and dey want me to go to the hospital, but I guess I can gib 'em some more yet.' I could go on filling your columns with startling facts of this kind, but I hope I have told enough to prove that we can hereafter rely upon black arms as well as white in crushing this infernal rebellion. I long ago told you there was an army of 250,000 men ready to leap forward in defense of freedom at the first call. You know where to find them and what they are worth."

"Although repulsed in an attempt which, situated as things were, was all but impossible, these regiments, though badly cut up, are still on hand, and burning with a passion ten times hotter from their fierce baptism of blood. Who knows but that it is a black hand which shall first plant the standard of the republic upon the doomed ramparts of Port Hudson."

In the Mississippi Valley.—In many engagements of the Mississippi valley the colored soldiers won for themselves lasting glory and golden opinions from the officers and men of white organizations.

The Battle of Wilson's Wharf.—The following account is given: "At first the fight raged fiercely on the left. The woods were riddled with bullets; the dead and wounded of the rebels were taken away from this part of the field, but I am informed by one accustomed to judge, and who went over the fields today, that from the pools of blood and other evidences, the loss must have been severe. Finding that the left could not be broken, Fitz-Hugh Lee hurled his cavalry—dismounted of course—upon the right. Steadily they came on, through obstruction, through slashing, past abattis without wavering. Here one of the advantages of the colored troops was made apparent. They obeyed orders, and bided their time. When well tangled in the abattis the death warrant, "Fire," went forth. Southern chivalry quailed before Northern balls, though fired by Negro hands. Volley after volley was rained upon the superior by the inferior race, and the chivalry broke and tried to run."

Petersburg.—This was a stronghold of the Confederacy. To dislodge them tons of powder were buried near their lines. It was to be exploded and in the consequent confusion in the Confederate ranks a charge

FIERCE ENCOUNTER WITH BLOODHOUNDS.

In October, 1862, the Confederates attacked the 1st South Carolina Regiment with bloodhounds. The hounds, so long a terror to the Negro, rushed fiercely upon the troops. The troops, equal to the occasion, quickly shot or bayonetted them, and triumphantly held up the beasts speared with their bayonets.

was to be made and capture their forces. Four thousand four hundred Negro braves were on hand to do this work. The refusal to allow them to do so, many believe, lost the day to the Union army. Ah! but the black braves that day proved that they were willing to fight, bleed and die for their kindred in chains so cruelly forged. Black men fell on the very parapet of the enemy's works, in a hand-to-hand fight with their white antagonists. The soil was saturated in the blood of the colored valiants. When Petersburg did fall into Federal hands, and Richmond followed later, Negro soldiers were among the first to enter the field and claim these cities in the name of the Federal government. Close on the fall of these Confederate cities Lee surrendered at Appomatox under the shade of the old apple tree. Thus ended the war, leaving our brave black heroes covered with glory crowned with imperishable laurels. When, therefore, the last drum shall beat, the last bugle note shall sound, and the roll call of nations shall be heard, and the names of Phillips, Leonidas, Alexander, Hannibal, Caesar, Napoleon and Wellington are sounded on the lips of the worshipers of heroes, with equal praise shall be heard the name of Attucks, Peter Salem, Captain Cailloux, Colonel Shaw the talented, and Toussaint L'Overture. A race with such indomitable courage, under such discouragements, must have under God a future inspiring and glorious.

General Smith on Petersburg.—"The hardest fighting was done by the black troops. The forts they stormed were the worst of all. After the affair was over General Smith went to thank them, and tell them he was proud of their courage and dash. He said: 'They cannot be exceeded as soldiers, and that hereafter he will enter them in a difficult place as readily as the best.' ''

"The charge on the advanced works was made in splendid style, and as the 'dusky warriors' stood shouting upon the parapet, General Smith decided that 'they would do,' and sent word to storm the first redoubt. Steadily these troops moved on, led by officers whose unostentatious bravery is worthy of emulation. With a shout and rousing cheers they dashed at the redoubt. Grape and canister were hurled at them by the infuriated rebels. They grinned and pushed on, and with a yell that told the Southern chivalry their doom, rolled irresistibly over into the work. The guns were speedily turned upon those of our 'misguided brethren,' who forgot that discretion was the better part of valor. Another redoubt was carried in the same splendid style, and the Negroes have established a reputation that they will surely maintain.

"Officers on General Hancock's staff, as they rode by the redoubt surrounded by a moat with water in it, over which these Negroes charged, admitted that its capture was a most gallant affair. The Negroes bear their wounds quite as pluckily as the white soldiers."

Adjutant General L. Thomas pays the following tribute to the Negro soldiers: "On several occasions when on the Mississippi river, I contemplated writing to you respecting the colored troops, and to suggest that, as they have been fully tested as soldiers, their pay should be raised to that of white troops, and I desire now to give my testimony in their behalf. You are aware that I have been engaged in the organization of freedmen for over a year, and have necessarily been thrown in contact with their orders.

Strict Obedience.—"The Negro, in a state of slavery, is brought up by the master from early childhood to strict obedience and to obey implicitly the dictates of the white man, and they are thus led to believe that they are an inferior race. Now, when organized into troops, they carry their habits of obedience with them, and their officers, being entirely white men, the Negroes promptly obey them.

Important Addition.—"A regiment is thus rapidly brought into a state of discipline. They are a religious people—another high quality for making good soldiers. They are a musical people, and thus readily learn to march and accurately perform their maneuvers. They take pride in being elevated as soldiers, and keep themselves, as their camp grounds, neat and clean. This I know from special inspection, two of my staff officers being constantly on inspecting duty. They have proved a most important addition to our forces, enabling the Generals in active operations to take a large force of white troops into the field; and now brigades of blacks are placed with the whites. The forts erected at the important points on the river are nearly all garrisoned by blacks—artillery regiments raised for the purpose, say at Paducah and Columbus, Kentucky; Memphis, Tennessee; Vicksburg and Natchez, Mississippi, and most of the works around New Orleans.

Heavy Guns.—"Experience proves that they manage the heavy guns very well. Their fighting qualities have also been fully tested a number of times, and I have yet to hear of the first case where they did not fully stand up to their work. I passed over the ground where the First Louisiana made the gallant charge at Port Hudson, by far the stronger part of the rebel works. The wonder is that so many have made their

GENERAL EDWARD JOHNSON AND G. H. STEWART AS PRISONERS
IN CHARGE OF A FORMER SLAVE.

137

escape. At Milliken's Bend, where I had three incomplete regiments—one without arms until the day previous to the attack—greatly superior numbers of the rebels charged furiously up to the very breastwork. The Negroes met the enemy on the ramparts, and both sides freely used the bayonet, a most rare occurrence in warfare, as one or the other party gives way before coming in contact with the steel. The rebels were defeated with heavy loss. The bridge at Moscow, on the line of railroad from Memphis to Corinth, was defended by one small regiment of blacks. A cavalry attack of three times their number was made, the blacks defeating them in three charges made by the rebels.''

General S. C. Armstrong, who for years was at the head of Hampton Institute, says: "Two and one-half years' service with Negro soldiers (half a year as captain and major in the One Hundred and Twentieth New York Volunteers) as lieutenant-colonel and colonel of the Ninth and Eighth regiments of the United States colored troops, convinced me of the excellent qualities and capacities of the freedmen. Their quick response to good treatment, and to discipline, was a constant surprise. Their tidiness, devotion to their duty and their leaders, their dash and daring in battle, and ambition to improve, even studying their spelling books under fire, showed that slavery was a false, though doubtless for the time being an educative, condition, and that they deserve as good a chance as any people.

A Cavalry Force.—"A cavalry force of three hundred and fifty attacked three hundred rebel cavalry near the Big Black with signal success, a number of prisoners being taken and marched to Vicksburg.

Forrest attacked Paducah with 7,500 men. The garrison was between 500 and 600, nearly 400 being colored troops recently raised. What troops could have done better? So, too, they fought well at Fort Pillow till overpowered by greatly superior numbers. The above enumerated cases seem to be sufficient to demonstrate the value of the colored troops."

Few of Many Tributes.—These are but few of the many tributes that generals and white leaders have cheerfully given to the loyalty, valor and bravery of the colored troops during the war. George Williams truly says: "No officer, whose privilege it was to command or observe the conduct of these troops, has ever hesitated to give a full and cheerful endorsement of their worth as men, their loyalty as Americans, and their eminent qualifications for the duties and dangers of military life. No history of the war has ever been written without mentioning the patience, endurance, fortitude, and heroism of the Negro soldiers who prayed, wept, fought, bled and died for the preservation of the Union of the United States of America."

Items of Interest.—History records the fact that during the late rebellion the Negro soldiers participated in more than four hundred engagements.

There were between four and five hundred Negro soldiers who were engaged in the battle of New Orleans.

About 6,000 Negroes were connected in different ways with the Confederate army.

The first colored regiment to enter the services of the rebellion was the Fifty-fourth Massachusetts Volunteers.

In Present Service.—At present time there are four regiments of colored men in the regular service, two of cavalry and two of infantry. They are commanded by white officers and have done very good service in Indian warfare. Their constitutions endure the heat of the Southern states much better than those of the white men, and they have been particularly valuable along the Mexican border.

In Military Academy.—James Smith, of Columbia, S. C., was the first colored student to enter the U. S. military academy at New York. Up to date there were ten colored cadets admitted, of whom three graduated.

Colored Soldiers of Georgia.—The colored soldiers of the state are pleading for proper aid from the state they have enlisted to defend. They deserve help, if the following letter be true, which was written by one of the oldest colored soldiers in the state.

"The colored soldiers of Georgia have maintained their military organizations for twenty-six years. At the re-organization of the state militia in 1888, there were forty-seven colored companies of infantry uniformed and equipped by themselves at a cost of not less than $25,000. Besides this, they furnished their own armories, fuel and lights, the cost of which, added to the above, would make the amount spent by the colored soldiers themselves for their support and for an opportunity to assist in defending the state for a period of twenty-six years, more than $95,000. This money has come from the poor or average colored citizen, as the majority of colored soldiers come from that class of our people. Though these men are Georgians, they love their name, they love their honor, and they are willing to lay down their lives in the defense of her soil. All they ask at the hands of those in power is to treat them as citizens and as soldiers.

CHAPTER VII.

Hon. Frederick Douglass once said in a great public meeting in New York: "The colored race will not crawl in the dirt forever. It is honorable to do whitewashing, but there is no reason why my people should do that and nothing else. The day will come in which they will be found in all pursuits, achieving distinction and showing capabilities which they were never supposed to possess. The destiny of the colored race is in their own hands, they must bear and suffer, they must toil and be patient, they must carve their own fortunes, and they will do it."

Statement Verified.—Thirty-five years have gone since the shackles of the slave were broken. Is the truth of Mr. Douglass' statement being verified? Look at the colored race of that time, grossly ignorant, destitute of clothing, without homes, without name, persecuted, forced to bear much on account of the prejudices against color. This despised race to-day after so few years has made progress such as history nowhere else records. Although much remains to be done, yet to-day we find the Negro recognized as a man, having the sympathy and respect of all, filling important and honorable positions throughout the land; greatly improved and exalted in his home life; recognizing that he has a part to do in the elevation of his race, aiming at the highest success, and determined to stand among the best citizens and the most useful members of society. He is determined that there shall be no better schools than his own, no grander statesmen, **no more success**

141

ful business men, none better known in the professional life, no happier homes, no more cultivated women, none better, more moral, upright and righteous than his own. Look at that picture and then at this, and the fact that the Negro is rapidly rising will dawn at once upon the most skeptical of minds.

Hopeless Condition.—Prof. Bowen says: "When the famous edict of freedom went forth on January 1, 1863, the Negro, instead of being born into a state of liberty and freedom, was damned into it. For well-nigh eight generations he had been worked like dumb, driven cattle and punished like a brute, crushed with the iron hoof of oppression and repression; whipped, torn, bleeding in body, mind and soul; day after day, year after year, he had toiled, sweated, groaned and wept, but there had been no hope of reward to lighten his burdens. He had no wife, no children, no altar; no home, no hope, no purpose; no motive, no aspiration, no thought, no life, but he had a God. He was a thing, a dog, a brute, an animal. His notions, even among his preachers, were crude; he had seen her whom he had desired to call his wife torn from his side, insulted, degraded, banished; he had looked upon his fondlings with an indescribable heartache as they were sold from under his eye; he had been trained in theft, dishonesty and duplicity; he had drank deeply from the bitter waters of crime and lewdness. He was ignorant of the duties, and even privileges of Christianity, and of the responsibilities and possibilities of the family life. Thus he walked forth on that famous morn, out from the tomb of his living and torturing death, with absolutely nothing in his hands, his head, his heart, his pocket, and he went forth to try his fortunes in a new world.

Freedom Gave Him His Hands.—Freedom gave him his hands and his wife to start with, two great boons; with the hand to chip out his place and to work with a royal will, and with a wife to build his altar and weave his destiny, he is endowed as never before. Hence the Negro at the close of the war, was all that American slavery would make any people, viz., bestialized and animalized; ignorant, poor, crude, rude, helpless, moneyless and thoughtless. American slavery was not a blessing; it was a curse. The good that came to the Negro (and there was good even in so baneful contact) came in spite of slavery. "Endeavor, then, to combine the whole in one view—to take in the full idea of this mighty mass of evil, in all the suffering of mind and body which it inflicts, in all its brutalizing effects and demoralizing tendencies on the slave and on his master—the misery which it entails on man, and the guilt which incurs in the sight of God—and you will have some conception of the multiplied and horrifying evils of slavery."

Not Surpassed in History.—This view represents the status of the Negro at the close of the war. No other slavery in all history has ever succeeded to so great an extent as has this American slavery in degrading the women of a race and in corrupting the fountain of every virtue; and were it not that the gospel is all conquering and all purifying, we would be hopeless.

Degraded by Compulsion.—"The slave Negro," says Professor Bowen, "was taught by precept and authoritative commandment, as well as trained by example and driven by the merciless lash, to commit adultery and fornication, and to live in the murky and unrestrained passions of the flesh that rush on through the open sluices of libertinism and shame down through the

gates of hell.   Who dare deny it, and will buttress that
denial with fact?   A thousand trustworthy witnesses
will confirm it, who carry in their minds and souls the
imprint of that lustful period, and who can speak that
which they do know and testify to what they have seen
and felt."   President Dewey, of William and Mary
College, in Virginia, speaking of the slave trade, says:
"It furnishes every inducement to the master to attend
to his Negroes, to encourage breeding and to cause the
greatest number of slaves to be raised."   "Virginia is,
indeed, a Negro-raising state for other states."   "The
noblest blood of Virginia," says Paxton in a letter to
Jay, "runs in the blood of her slaves."   The slave had
no marriage or family rights.   Dr. Taylor, in his
"Elements of the Civil Law," says: "Slaves were not
entitled to the condition of matrimony, and therefore
had no relief in cases of adultery, nor were they the
proper objects of cognation or affinity, but of quasi
cognation only."   And the Louisiana reports quoted
by Wheeler in his "Law of Slavery," page 199, declare:
"It is clear that slaves have no legal capacity to assent
to any contract.   With the consent of their masters
they may marry, but while in a state of slavery it can
not produce any civil effects."   "No slave," says Jay,
"can commit bigamy, because the law knows no more
of marriage of slaves than it does of the marriage of
brutes.   A slave may indeed be formally married, but,
as far as legal rights and obligations are concerned, it
is an idle ceremony."

Slave Breeders.—The cruelties of the lash did not in
any measure equal in degradation the action of the gain-
greedy and conscienceless slave breeders, who sold
wives into separation from their husbands and compelled them to accept new partners in order that the
fruitfulness of the plantation might not suffer.

Well Known to Slave Holders.—Professor Bowers says, "The deplorable condition of the slaves was well known to the slave-holders and abolitionists. The legally closed school house and church, and the cupidity of master, as well as his inhumanity and brutality, were bringing forth fruit of the blackest kind and in prodigious quantities. Human reason hesitates to accept, without convincing proof, the horrible tale of woe, and when this tale is well authenticated it sits dumb and speechless in its presence. These are not the fancies of verdant youth, nor are they the ravings and discolorations of an unbalanced brain, neither are they the highly colored tales of the Arabian Nights; but they are the statements of honorable slaveholders, the careful compilations and observations of the white ministry in the South during slavery, and the unvarnished accounts of the actual sufferers themselves.

Why Stated.—Let it be borne in mind that these facts are not written to feed the almost quenchless fires of prejudices. I would walk, face forward, in the presence of that harrowing and nameless shame and cover it with the garment of Christian charity; but my only apology for uncovering this pit of seething, reeking and nauseating corruption is to show from whence we came, and to refute the statement that slavery was the halcyon days of purity and moral power for the Negro, and to show the absurdity of the claim that the slave-driver's whip and bloodhounds are superior moral teachers for a man to sympathetic, consecrated and humanity-loving teachers with a spelling book in one hand and the Bible in the other. And again these words are written to show the Negro himself the black heritage he has brought with him from slavery, and to impress with him the thought that heroic treatment, patiently and persistently administered, will ultimately develop in him those moral qualities that are necessary to a happy life.''

Heathenism.—On the 5th of December, 1833, a committee of the Synod of South Carolina and Georgia, to whom was referred the subject of the religious instruction of the colored population, made a report, which has been published, and in which this language is used:

"Who would credit it that in these years of revival and benevolent effort in this Christian republic there are over 2,000,000 of human beings in the condition of heathens, and in some respects in worse condition? From long continued and close observation, we believe that their religious and moral condition is such that they may justly be considered the heathen of this Christian country, and will bear comparison with the heathen of any country in the world. The Negroes are destitute of the Gospel, and ever will be under the present state of things. In the vast field extending from an entire state beyond the Potomac to the Sabine river, and from the Atlantic to the Ohio, there are, to the best of our knowledge, not twelve men exclusively devoted to the religious instruction of the Negroes. In the present state of the feeling in the south, a ministry of their own color could neither be obtained or tolerated. But do not the Negroes have access to the Gospel through the stated ministry of the whites? We answer, No; the Negroes have no regular and efficient ministry; as a matter of course, no churches; neither is there sufficient room in white churches for their accommodation. We know of but five churches in the slave-holding states built expressly for their use; these are all in the State of Georgia. We may now inquire if they enjoy the privileges of the Gospel in their own houses and on plantations? Again we return a negative answer. They have no Bibles to read by their own firesides; they have no family altars; and when in affliction, sickness or death, they have no minister to address to them the consolations of the Gospel, nor to bury them with solemn and appropriate services.

Humane Masters.—In every state there were masters who were kind-hearted and genuinely sympathetic, who treated their slaves with consideration, and some of them taught their slaves to read; had them to marry according to the requirements of the church; did not allow them to violate with impunity, nor did these masters themselves violate, the marriage vows of the slaves; took them to their churches and had them to share the benefits of the pulpit ministrations, and thus acted towards them in the capacity of fathers and mothers towards their children. There was genuine affection between them, and these slaves were the favored ones in the South, and the ex-slaves of to-day who had such masters, never cease to sing their praise.

Few in Number.—But it must be borne in mind that such slave-masters were exceedingly few and far between, and what is still more remarkable, such moral, intellectual and spiritual care of the slave by these few noble spirits was contrary to the letter and spirit of the law in every slave state.

The law of certain states forbade the use of the Bible or any other book, and also religious meetings of the Negroes, unless a majority of whites were present. All prohibited the impartation of instruction, while Virginia unequivocally forbade all evening meetings. "In the House of Delegates of Viginia, in 1832, Mr. Berry said: 'We have, as far as possible, closed every avenue by which light might enter their (the slaves') minds. If we could extinguish the capacity to see the light our work would be completed; they would then be on a level with the beasts of the field, and we should be safe! I am not certain that we would not do it if we could find out the process, and that on the plea of necessity.'"

Defending Slavery.—Dr. Blyden, in his "Christianity, Islam and the Negro," says: "The highest men in the South, magistrates, legislators, professors of religion, preachers of the gospel, governors of states, gentlemen of property and understanding, all united in upholding a system which every Negro felt was wrong. Yet these were the men from whom he got his religion, and whom he was obliged to regard as guides. Saints, no doubt, there were among the bondmen, but they became so not in consequence, but in default, and often, we may say, in defiance, of instructions." The sacredness of the marriage relation, the punishments for fornication and adultery, ethical integrity, the glories and rewards for faithful service, and the duties, privileges, and opportunities of the Christian life, were never discussed before and unfolded to the slave. Where he was permitted to hold meetings he was trained in the most grotesque types of worship; his emotions and wildest eccentricities were cultivated, and his motives for life were drawn from no higher source in the main than this temporary, enthusiastic and emotional worship.

Financial Consideration.—He was trained in certain handicraft for financial consideration. The lash was his taskmaster, and from him he received no view of the dignity of labor. A man may learn mechanics by force, but not ethics. The last may make (?) a good blacksmith, but not a good conscience. There was no thought among the slaveholders of improving the slave in any element for the slave's sake.

A Struggling Race.—President Wright says: "Extremely interesting must such a task be when it is understood that the history of the American Negro is the history of a race struggling amid environments and against difficulties such as no similar nation in all history has had to meet. It is pretty generally agreed that the Negro in America introduces a problem without a parallel. His history is unique. Properly given in all its phases, the narrative would teem with incidents and achievements almost romantic.

"The surrender of General Lee was the occasion of the total collapse of the social and industrial features of the old Georgia progress. Society among the white people for the time was thrown into almost chaotic condition, but it was for the moment only. They understood how to cover a rout, to gather the demolished fragments and reform.

"But how was it with the Negro? Had he ever any conception of society, of voluntary order? Had one-tenth of one per cent of them ever looked into a book or saved a dollar?

Ignorance Equaled by Poverty.—Their ignorance was equaled only by their poverty. Improvident and totally helpless, the freedman was well nigh friendless. Considered by many as property illegally taken from those among whom his lot was to be cast hereafter as a citizen, he was looked upon as an intruder in the body politic. Hindered, rather than helped, by those whom he knew best; confused by his new surroundings, and with his intellectual and moral abilities subjects of misunderstanding and doubt on the part of his friends, the Negro of Georgia was sent forth in 1865 to develop character, to get education and money, and to prove himself worthy the freedom which was thrust upon him. In short, he was to maintain himself as a freedman and citizen in the midst of his old masters, who had enjoyed centuries of civilization. That it was a great task all will acknowledge; that under its environments it was a feat fraught with much doubt, few will deny. But while this condition was pitiable, it was not hopeless. Under slavery, he, though a simple child of the shovel and hoe, had developed a faith in God which was abiding, and had obtained a working knowledge of the English tongue. These were his sole stock in trade, but they were very valuable. To understand, then, the difficulties which the Negro has overcome and to estimate the progress which he has made in the past thirty years, his condition at emancipation must be borne steadily and faithfully in mind.

Difficult to Comprehend.—It is difficult to comprehend the utter poverty and disheartening ignorance which enveloped the colored people at the beginning of the period under discussion. They began without any adequate amount of food, clothing or shelter; a vast majority without the least conception of a school or a home. Their exertions to obtain food, clothing, and shelter, certainly greatly retarded their efforts for book learning. They did not know how to make contracts or agreements for wages. Consequently they worked the first year for a bare subsistence; with a few exceptions their first possessions outside of food and clothing were bought during the second year, and consisted of oxen and mules and farming implements. They began to rent lands in the third year, and in the fourth to buy land. This was the rule; there were exceptions. To fully understand the educational development of the first decade would require a thorough knowledge of the colored man's progress and achievements as a free laborer; for the labor question and educational problem are, as Siamese twins, inseparable.''

Moral Improvement.—''Talks for the Times'' says: ''To estimate fairly their improvement in this direction it would be necessary to realize, if possible, the depth of degradation to which two hundred and fifty years of thralldom had sunk them, and to take into consideration at the same time the fact that the moral nature of man everywhere and among all people is by far the most difficult to train. This being so, what must be the task to repair it, after it has been bruised and maimed and twisted and gnarled and distorted? A crooked limb, by proper appliances, may be straightened. A bone of the body may be broken and set, and become even stronger in the fractured parts; but man cannot sin and be strong. The violation of the moral law means, in every instance, the sapping of moral foundations, the weakening of the moral nature. When, therefore, I consider by what processes, during two centuries, the moral groundwork of my people was undermined and shaken, it is no wonder that to-day many of them are found immoral. The greater wonder is that their moral perception has not been entirely swept away. Many people, however, and those, especially, who stigmatize us as a race peculiarly immoral, do not reason in this way. They do not seem to realize that slavery was a school ill adapted to the producing of pure and upright characters. Can you rob a man continually of his honest earnings and not teach him to steal? Can you ignore the sanctity of marriage and the family relations and not inculcate lewdness? Can you constantly govern a man with the lash and expect him always to speak the truth? If you can do these things, then, verily, are my people dishonest, impure and untruthful. But our enemies demand of us perfection. They are unreasonable. They require among us in twenty short years a state of moral rectitude which they themselves, with far more favorable opportunities, have not realized in one hundred times twenty. They are unphilosophical, for they do not perceive that diseases are more quickly contracted than cured.

Negro Immoralities.—"Very amusing, too, it is to listen to the hue and cry sent up every little while against Negro immoralities; such a cry and howl as went up but recently from the swamps of the Mississippi, and are still reverberating through the country with a jarring sound. Very amusing, I say, it is to listen to these cries against Negro immoralities, when the same immoralities are continually cropping out among the white people, professedly our superiors. How many times within the last two decades, has this nation had to hang its head in shame because of the dishonesty of its public men! What about Credit Mobilier and the Tamany frauds? What about whisky rings? What about cipher dispatches? What about Star Route trials? What about the stuffing of ballot boxes? What about the defalcation and impeachment of high state officials? And so on, and so on, *ad infinitum*.

In Proportion to Opportunities.—"We have not had a fair chance in this country; but, in proportion to our opportunities we can show as many good, virtuous, law-abiding citizens as any other race on this continent. Wherever, in the South, Christian education has reached the freedmen it has awakened in them a taste for the true and beautiful. This may be seen in the changed manner of living of many of them. The dirty shanty and clumsy log cabins in which, formerly, so many were accustomed to be huddled together, are retreating, step by step, before the steady advance of neat and cozy cottages. Christian homes, the strength of any nation, are being built up, decorated with the beauties and improvement of modern art.

Negro Domination.—"Old civilizations die hard, and old prejudices die harder. They have nine lives, like a cat. For this reason, therefore, you may expect for many a year yet to find those who are still living in the dead past, and who feel it their duty to champion the old order of things, and to throw stumbling blocks in the path of progress. I entertain no ill will toward this class of persons. I have for them no word of censure or reproach. I give them the credit of even being sincere; but I assure them from every page of history and human experience they are mistaken. They are at war with the spirit of the age and the sermon on the mount. Nor are they even consistent. They advocate the theory of repression. They say the Negro must be kept down for fear of Negro domination. On the other hand, they hold that he is an inferior race, fundamentally inferior, created so by almighty God. Why, in the name of righteous heaven should it be necessary to keep down a race that is naturally inferior? Why should there be any fear of its ever becoming dominant? There is something crooked in this philosophy. To say the least, there is something in it exceedingly incongruous. Nevertheless it is this kind of philosophy that is sending armed ruffians into first-class cars to drag them from their seats, for which they have honestly paid their money, the best men and women of our race. It is this kind of philosophy that is shutting everywhere in our faces the doors of public accommodation. It is this false philosophy, I say, by which it is made to appear that every advancement of the Negro is a menace to the interests of the white man; and it is this philosophy that will ever keep alive in the South race antagonism.

Inconsistent, Incorrect and Narrow Views.—"The men who advocate this philosophy are not only inconsistent, but incorrect, and exceedingly narrow in their views as to the nature of this government. They claim that it is not only a 'white man's' government, but an Anglo-Saxon government, thereby robbing of their merit and glory the noble-minded foreigners who helped fight for American independence, and the hundreds of thousands more who were not Anglo-Saxons, but who, during four years of a terrible civil war fought as bravely and as heroically as any Anglo-Saxon to save this nation from dissolution and ruin. Did not Lafayette, that gallant Frenchman, fight for American independence? Let the battle of Brandywine tell. Did not Count Pulaski, the noble Pole, fight for American independence? Let the same battle of Brandywine tell. Did he not afterward even fall in an attempt to capture Savannah? Did not Kosciusko, another Pole, and even far more distinguished than the other, cast in his fortune with the cause of American independence? And what shall we say of the hundreds of thousands who were not Anglo-Saxons, but who poured out their life blood at Gettysburg and the Wilderness and Chickamauga, and around the defenses of Richmond and Vicksburg? Indeed, it is my belief, that if all the blood that is not Anglo-Saxon could be drawn off from the great stream supplying our national life, that which remained would be conspicuous for the insignificance of its quantity.''

Look Not for Greatness.—Senator Logan once said: If there is any one thing that will clog the wheels of your material progress it is the fact that some of you are trying to overreach yourselves. Do not become dazzled at the splendor and magnificence of those who had hundreds of years to make this country what it is today. No man is a success who has not a fixed object as a sign-post—an aim in life to attain unto. A man should get that kind and that amount of education that will best fit him for the performance and the attainment of his object in life. Too much Greek will do you no good; what does a man want with Greek around a table with a white apron on? I do not say that you should not study Greek if you intend to fill a chair in some institution of learning; I do not say that you should not read medicine if you desire to become a physician, or law if you wish to follow that profession. But I tell you our white people are fast growing indolent and lazy. If you watch your chance and take timely advantage of the opportunities offered you, your race will be the wage workers, the skilled artisans, and eventually the land owners and the wealthy class of this country. I advise you to learn trades, learn to become mechanics. You have the ability and the capacity to reach the highest point, and even go further, in the march of progress than has yet been made by any people.

Labor to Become Great.—It takes labor to become a great man, just as it takes centuries to become a great nation. Great men are not fashioned in heaven and thrown from the hand of the Almighty to become potentates here on earth, nor are they born rich. I admit that there is, in some parts of this country, a prejudice against you on account of your color and former condition. In my opinion the best way to overcome this is to show your capability by doing everything that a white man does, and do it just as well or better than he does. If a white man scorns

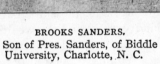

BROOKS SANDERS.
Son of Pres. Sanders, of Biddle
University, Charlotte, N. C.

DAUGHTER OF
BISHOP C. R. HARRIS,
Salisbury, N. C.

you, show him that you are too high bred, too noble hearted, to take notice of it; and, the first opportunity you have, do him a favor, and I warrant that he will feel ashamed of himself and never again will he make an exhibition of his prejudice. The future is yours, and you have it in which to rise to the heights or descend to the depths.

In America.—I believe that the future of the Negro race is to be found in the segment of that race providentially lodged on this soil. Say what we may about this or that, these United States have given us the most advanced, the most progressive Negro to be found on the face of the globe. And this is true for the reason that she is giving him the largest all-round opportunities, the highest civil ideals, and the steadiest aims. The troubles we suffer here in our day are only a part of the old, old conflict that has raged so long.

> "Must we be carried to the skies
> On flowery beds of ease,
> While others fought to win the prize
> And sailed through bloody seas?"

No, we cannot be, and will not be, though we may wish to ever so much. "Through conflict to the skies," is as true for dark humanity as for any other variety of men. Had we then not better learn this lesson and cease our shameful grumbling, as if the Almighty had done us some special wrong? God has given us minds to think, hands to work and hearts to love. Let us subject these God-given powers to the regimen of a severe discipline, and, walking with hope to the future, work out a noble destiny for ourselves and our children.

Change During Years of Bondage.—Said Rev. A. D. Mayo, at the Mohonk conference in 1890: "It has never been realized by the loyal North what is evident to every intelligent Southern man, what a prodigious change has been wrought in this people during its years of bondage, and how, without the schooling of this era, the subsequent elevation of the emancipated slave to a full American citizenship would have been an impossibility. In that condition he learned the three great elements of civilization more speedily than they were ever learned before. He learned to work, he acquired the language, and adopted the religion of the most progressive of peoples. Gifted with a marvelous aptitude for such schooling, he was found in 1865 farther out of the woods of barbarism than any other people at the end of a thousand years."

In Twenty Years.—The scholastic education of the Negro began in earnest only about twenty years ago, 1876 being the date of the complete inauguration of the public school system of the South. This is too short for us to expect great results. The educated generation are not yet fairly out of school, but there have already appeared some isolated cases which show signs of promise. In the class of 1888 at Harvard University were two Negroes, one of whom was selected by the faculty to represent his class on commencement day, as being the foremost scholar among his two hundred and fifty classmates; the other was elected by the class for the highest honor in their gift, by being made their orator on class day. The circumstance reflects honor, not merely on him, but on the democratic spirit of our oldest university, which recognized merit without regard to color. Boston University has also yielded first honors to a Negro. A Negro professor of theology at Straight University, at New Orleans, is a graduate of Vermont University, who afterwards took the prize for traveling scholarship from Yale Theological Seminary, and spent a year in Germany upon it. Professor Bowen, of the Gammon Theological Seminary, delivered at the Atlanta Exposition opening an address which in classic finish will bear comparison with the best orations of Edward Everett. The principal of one of our auxiliaries, Mr. E. N. Smith, a perfect gentleman and an excellent teacher, is a full blooded Negro, a graduate of Lincoln University and Newton Theological Institution, and pronounced by Dr. Hovey one of the best scholars that have been educated there.

False Hopes.—The most obvious hindrance in the way of the education of the Negro has so often been presented and discussed—his origin, history and environment—that it seems superfluous to treat it anew. His political status, sudden and unparalleled, complicated by antecedent condition, excites false hopes and encourages the notion of reaching *per saltum*, without the use of the agencies of time, labor, industry, discipline, what the dominant race had attained after centuries of toil and trial and sacrifice. Education, property, habits of thrift and self-control, higher achievements of civilization, are not extemporized nor created by magic or legislation. Behind the Caucasian lie centuries of the educating, uplifting influences of civilization, of the institution of family, society, the churches, the state, and the salutary effects of heredity. Behind the Negro are centuries of ignorance, barbarism, slavery, superstition, idolatry, fetishism, and the transmissible consequences of heredity.

Charitable Judgment.—Nothing valuable or permanent in human life has been secured without the substratum of moral character, of religious motive, in the individual, the family, the community. In this matter the Negro should be judged charitably, for his aboriginal people were not far removed from the savage state, where they knew neither house nor home, and had not enjoyed any religious training. Their condition as slaves debarred them the advantage of regular, continuous, systematic instruction. The Negro began his life of freedom and citizenship with natural weaknesses uncorrected, with loose notions of piety and morality, and with strong racial peculiarities and proclivities, and has not outgrown the feebleness of the moral sense which is common to all primitive races.

Thrift.—Professor Greenwood says: "Twenty-five years ago the colored people of Missouri were uneducated, poverty-stricken, dependent, and helpless creatures. To-day they number 200,000. The value of their real and personal property is more than $30,000,000.

"Thousands of them live in comfortable homes.

"Of the 50,000 children of school age, seventy per cent. are now in attendance. They are as neatly and cleanly clad as the average white child, and many of them much better. Those who were the boys and girls in school a few years ago are the leaders among their people now. The self-denial practiced by parents to educate their children is one of the strongest evidences of parental affection that the world has ever beheld. When the schoolhouse doors were opened for the admission of colored pupils, they rushed in to get an education, and the influx is unabated. I have seen old white-haired men and women studying the first reader and spelling book so as to be able to read the Bible, the newspapers, and to write letters to relatives and friends. Have you seen white people doing these things?"

A Loyal American.—But let us look at these people from another standpoint, and see what progress they have made. In Missouri there are 45,000 of them church communicants; more than 450 ministers of the gospel; 400 church edifices and 60 parsonages. Do these evidences of prosperity indicate the wretchedness of this race? The Negro must be treated as a man, neither cajoled nor despised. He is here to stay, and it is our duty to help him make the most of himself as an industrious, intelligent, law-abiding and faithful citizen. Whether educated or uneducated, he is not a dangerous element in our civilization. A thousand-fold is he to be trusted when compared with those dangerous elements which have swept in upon us from European countries, and are now a standing menace to our social and political institutions. The Negro is thoroughly and loyally American.

Thrift and Self-Respect.—The thrift and self-respect of the Negro has removed him from the dark and cheerless abode in which he lived, and has placed him in neat and well-kept homes.

Negro Homes, The Contrast.—The Negro whose soul is free, like every other man, appreciates the sacredness and beauty which must be inseparable from a happy home. On the other hand, the Negro, debased and brutified by a servitude of centuries, has no desire for home in any exalted sense.

Legacy Bequeathed by Slavery.—Perhaps the least respected legacy left by slavery to the children of its victims is the disintegrating and nomadic tendency to a homeless and non-familied people. There are among the Negroes those whom no wretchedness can impel, no opportunity inspire to alter or make tolerable the places in which their families exist, and many an old Negro lives for years in a one or two room cabin, declining to build another room "Kase he won't be g'wine to leave."

Happy and Comfortable Homes.—The influences that are at work in transforming the women of the race, making a generation of virtuous, clean, industrious women, though they may not shine in society and speak but one language, though they may be ugly in features and unsophisticated in manner, though their names are never heard outside of the limits of their own state, these influences, I say, will improve the homes

REV. W. W. LUCAS, A. M., B. D.

Secretary of the Stewart Missionary Foundation for Africa, graduate of Clark University and Gammon's School of Theology of Atlanta, Ga., and Boston University, of Boston, Massachusetts.

of the race more speedily than any other aspiration, after the empty honors and applause of the multitude.

Do Something.—Booker Washington says: "We expect too often to get things that God did not mean for us to have in certain ways. At one time an old colored man was very anxious to get a turkey, and prayed and prayed for the Lord to send him a turkey. The turkey did not come, and finally the old man changed his prayer somewhat and said, 'O Lord, send dis nigger to a turkey,' and he got it that night. God means for us to get many things in about that same way, that is, by working for them rather than by depending on the power of mouth."

There are multitudes who are willing to accept honors and advantages who are not ready to work for them. It is necessary for all who would succeed to put forth strenuous efforts in that direction. The days of chance are gone, it is only the man who does not wait for things to turn up, but turns up something, that succeeds. Young man, do something; attempt something that will be a benefit to your race. Something ennobling, something enduring; something to elevate manhood and win men to noble, virtuous, upright lives, and your life will not have been lived in vain.

These thoughts must be impressed upon the humblest of the race. Success comes not by waiting for it. If the Afro-American race is to continue to rise, and is to hold a prominent place in this nation, there must be an effort. Empty wishes carry us nowhere. Without an earnest effort on the part of those of the race who hold the key to circumstances the race may as well yield to the prejudice still existing, and hold forever an inferior position, but with a determination that surmounts the obstacles and with a corresponding effort to stand first in the industries of our nation, we may well expect that the past achievement in this line is nothing compared to the progress of the future.

Cast Down Your Bucket.—"At one time a ship was lost at sea for many days, when it hove in sight of a friendly vessel. The signal of the distressed vessel was at once hoisted, which read: 'We want water; we die of thirst.' The answering signal read, 'Cast down your bucket where you are,' but a second time the distressed vessel signaled, 'We want water, water,' and a second time the other vessel answered 'cast down your bucket where you are.' A third and fourth time the distressed vessel signaled, 'We want water, water; we die of thirst;' and as many times was answered, 'Cast down your bucket where you are.' At last the command was obeyed, the bucket was cast down where the vessel stood, and it came up full of fresh and sparkling water from the Amazon river. My friends, we are failing to cast down our buckets for the help that is right above us, and spend too much time in signaling for help that is far off. Let us cast down our buckets here in our own sunny South, cast them down in agriculture, in truck gardening, dairying, poultry raising, hog raising, laundering, cooking, sewing, mechanical and professional life, and the help that we think is far off will come and we will soon grow independent and useful.''

In Our Stead.—In a speech before a National Council of Colored Men, Bishop Turner made the following excellent points: ''I am willing to accord to the white man every meed of honor that ability, grit, backbone, sagacity, tact and invincibility can entitle him to. For this Anglo-Saxon, I grant, is a powerful race; but put him in our stead, enslave him for two hundred and fifty years, emancipate him and turn him loose upon the world, without education, without money, without horse or mule or a foot of land, when passion engendered by war was most intense, to eke out a subsistence from nothing beyond the charity of an indignant people on the one hand, and a cold shouldering and proscriptive people on the other, and I do not believe he would have equaled us in respect, obedience, fidelity, and accomplished the results and maintained the pacific equilibrium we have. For our nation freed the black man as a war measure, I grant, but that freedom entailed and left upon us a mendicancy that the unborn will ask the reason why. Even the usufruct claim, guaranteed to the serfs of Russia—a nation at that time regarded as semi-civilized—was denied the freedmen by this so-called enlightened and Christian nation.

The Mule and Forty Acres.—The mule and forty acres of land, which has been so often ridiculed for being expected by the black man, was a just and righteous expectation, and had this nation been one-fiftieth part as loyal to the black man as he has been to it, such a bestowment would have been made, and the cost would have been a mere bagatelle, compared with the infinite resources of this republic, which has given countless millions to foreigners to come into the country and destroy respect for the Sabbath, flood the land with every vice known to the ends of the earth, and form themselves into anarchal bands for the overthrow of its institutions and venerated customs.

Freedom.—Nevertheless, freedom has been so long held before us, as man's normal birth-right, and the bas-relief of every possibility belonging to the achievements of manhood, that we received it as Heaven's greatest boon, and nursed ourselves into satisfaction, believing that we had the stamina, not only to wring existence out of our poverty, but also wealth, learning, honor, fame and immortality.

Rape.—But, through some satanic legerdemain,

within the last years, the most fearful crimes have been charged upon the members of our race known to the catalogue of villainy, and death and destruction have stalked abroad with an insatiable carnivoracity that not only beggars description, but jeopardizes the life of every Negro in the land, as anyone could raise an alarm by crying rape, and some colored man must die, whether he is the right one or not, or whether it was the product of revenge, or the mere cracking of a joke.

An Awful Charge.—The civilized world has been informed through Christian Advocates and through the public daily papers that Negroes have raped white women in such numbers that the charge is undoubtedly the most revolting and blood-curdling ever presented against the people since time began. Without affirming or denying this monstrous imputation, we owe it to ourselves and posterity to inquire into this subject and give it the most patient, thorough and impartial investigation that ever befell the lot of man.

No Attribute to Side with Us.—If the charges are true, then God has no attribute that will side with us. Nature has no member, no potential factor, that will defend us; and while we may not all be guilty, nor one in ten thousand, it nevertheless shows, if true, that there is a libidinous taint, a wanton and lecherous corruption, that is prophetic of a dreadful doom, as there must be a cardinal blood poison in the precincts of our race that staggers the most acute imagination in determining its woeful results.

Counter Charge.—Nor can we excuse it, palliate it, or manifest indifference upon the postulation that it is a righteous retribution upon the white man for the way he treated our women for hundreds of years. For if the counter-charge is true, we certainly did not visit swift vengeance upon the white man, as he is doing upon us by his lawless mobs.

One Recourse Left.—There is but one recourse left us that will command the respect of the civilized world and the approval of God, and that is to investigate the facts in the premises, and if guilty, acknowledge it, and let us organize against the wretches in our own ranks. Let us call upon the colored ministry to sound it from the pulpit, our newspapers to brand it with infamy daily, weekly, monthly and yearly. Let us put a thousand lecturers in the field, to canvass every section of the land, and denounce the heinous crime.

Heathen Africa.—Among the heathen Africans, whatever else may be said about them, the world will have to admit that they are the purest people, outside of polygamy, in their connubial and virgin morals, upon the face of the globe. White women, to my personal knowledge, hundreds of miles interiorward in Africa, can remain in their midst and teach school for years without being insulted, which proves to a demonstration that where our natures have not been distorted and abnormalized we are the most honorable custodians of female virtue now under Heaven. I have been told by white ladies in Africa, from Louisiana, South Carolina, New York, Nebraska, England, and Ireland, that no white lady could be improperly approached in Africa in a lifetime unless she made herself unusually forward.

Not the Nature of the Black Man.—It is not the nature of the black man to outrage white women, unless it is one of our American retrogressive abnormalities, which has possibly grown out of the degradation entailed upon us by the singular prejudice and degrading conditions under which we exist. The whole range of West India islands show by their records that only one rape has been charged upon a black man since 1832, and that occurred twenty years ago, while eleven rapes were charged upon white men, nine of which were perpetrated upon black women and two upon white women.

Like Begets Like.—It may, however, be due to the fact that there the laws and institutions recognize the black man as a full-fledged citizen and a gentleman, and his pride of character and sense of dignity are not degraded, and self-respect imparts a higher prompting and gentlemanly bearing to his manhood, and makes him a better citizen and inspires him with more gallantry and nobler principles. For like begets like.

A Degraded Condition.—While, in this country, we are degraded by the public press, degraded by the courts of the country from the United States Supreme Court down, degraded on the railroads after purchasing first-class tickets, degraded at the hotels and barber shops, degraded in many states at the ballot-box, degraded in some of the large cities by being compelled to rent houses in alleys and the most disreputable streets. Thus we are degraded in so many respects that all the starch of respectability is taken out of the manhood of millions of our people, and as degradation begets degradation, it is very possible that in many instances we are guilty of doing a series of infamous things that we would not be guilty of if our environments were different.

The World's Fair.—Think of it! The great World's Fair, or exposition, in Chicago, out of more than ten thousand employes, gave no recognition to the colored race beyond taking charge of the toilet rooms.

Half Free and Half Slave.—I would not have you understand that I am denying, condoning or excusing the crime of rape, as is being charged to a greater or less extent upon the members of our race; nor must we jump at a hasty or rash conclusion; but I fear much of it, if true, is due to our natural and immethodical environment and ignoble status, nor do I, for one, believe that we will ever stand out in the symmetrical majesty of higher manhood, half free and half slave.

The Great Desideratum.—The one great desideratum of the American Negro is manhood impetus. We may educate and acquire general intelligence, but our sons and daughters will come out of the college with all their years of training and thrift to the plane of the scullion, as long as they are restricted, limited and circumbounded by colorphobia. For abstract education elevates no man, nor will it elevate a race. What we call the heathen African will strut around in his native land, three-fourths naked, and you can see by the way he stands, talks, and acts that he possesses more manhood than fifty of some of our people in this country, and any ten of our most distinguished colored men here.

A Dwarfed People.—Until we are free from menace by lynchers, hotels, railroads, stores, factories, restaurants, barber shops, machine shops, court houses and other places where merit and worth are respected, we are destined to be a dwarfed people. Our sons and daughters will grow up with it in their very flesh and bones.

Gratitude.—As one, I feel grateful for many things that have been done for us within the last thirty years. I am thankful for Mr. Lincoln's manumitting proclamation, for its ratification by Congress, for the thirteenth, fourteenth and fifteenth amendments to the Constitution, which were placed there by the American people for the benefit of our race, even if the United States Supreme Court has destroyed the fourteenth amendment by its revolting decision.

Millions for Education.—I am thankful to our generous-hearted friends of the North who have given voluntarily millions upon millions to aid in our education. I am thankful to the South for the school laws they have enacted, and for the generous manner in which they have taxed themselves in building and sustaining schools for our enlightenment and intellectual and moral elevation.

Full-Fledged Men.—But, if this country is to be our home, the Negro must be a self-controlling, automatic factor of the body politic or collective life of the nation. In other words, we must be full-fledged men. Otherwise we will not be worth existence itself.

God Hates Cowardice.—To passively remain here and occupy our present ignoble status, with the possibility of being shot, hung and burnt, not only when we perpetrate deeds of violence ourselves, but whenever some bad white man wishes to black his face and outrage a female, as I am told is often done, is a matter of serious reflection. To do so would be to declare ourselves unfit to be free men or to assume the responsibilities which involve fatherhood and existence. For God hates the submission of cowardice.

Physical Resistance.—But, on the other hand, to talk about physical resistance is literal madness. Nobody but an idiot would give it a moment's thought. The idea of eight or ten millions of ex-slaves contending with sixty millions people of the most powerful race under Heaven! Think of two hundred and sixty-five millions of dollars battling with one hundred billions of dollars. Why, we would not be a drop in the bucket. It is folly to indulge in such a thought for a moment.

Debt of Our Nation.—This nation justly, righteously, divinely, owes us for work and service rendered billions of dollars, and if we cannot be treated as American people, we should ask for five hundred million dollars at least, to begin an immigration somewhere, if we can not for service rendered receive manhood recognition here at home. Freedom and perpetual degradation are not in the economy of human events.''

Bishop Gaines on Lynching.—''The better class of colored people all over the South are unanimous in the condemnation of the wretches who are guilty of this unmentionable crime. They recognize the fact that the whole race is suffering in the eyes of the world through the conduct of the vile scoundrels who perpetrate these crimes. In many places the white people regard a Negro with detestation and suspicion, believing him to be capable of any criminal act where he is left unrestrained. From experience and observation I know this to be true.

Not in Sympathy with Crime.—I for one am not willing to be thought in sympathy with crime or criminals, and especially those cf the character I am now considering. If the colored people, as a race, expect to gain the confidence and respect of their white neighbors and to elevate themselves in the scale of civilized life, they must emphasize in no uncertain way their detestation of that most brutal of the race, who commit the horrible offense of rape, arson and the like. There must be no maudlin sympathy for such characters who disgrace their own race and bring the Negro into shame and contempt.

Innocent Men Victims.—While I say these things I would not be understood as favoring lynch laws. Could the real criminal suffer it would not be so bad, but when innocent men are frequently the victims of excited and infuriated mobs, who take the law into their own hands, the necessity of legal conviction is apparent. Lynch law, too, no matter how justly administered, is bad in its tendency, working a disregard for all laws and educating the people in the lawlessness it is intended to prevent.

Justice.—All our people ask is that justice be done—that before the law the same evidence be required to convict a Negro that is required to convict a white man, and that the same punishment be meted out to the one as to the other. Wherever the proof is conclusive let the guilty suffer, though the heavens fall. Lynching is not a race question but a national question, as is proven by the fact that of one hundred and forty-one persons lynched in 1896, fifty-four were white men."

Temperance, Soberness Increasing.—"Remembering the circumstances," says Rev. J. C. Price, "in which the Negro was placed by the dreadful institution of slavery, it is not to be wondered at that he now cultivates a taste, even a love, for alcohol. Yet it is remarkable to note the progress towards sobriety that the race has made in the latter years of its emancipation. A colored total abstainer is not a rare person in any community nowadays. The various temperance societies, and nearly all the other secret organizations supported by the Afro-American race, uniformly require those who seek admission to pledge themselves to be sober men and women, and in most cases to be total abstainers. The drift is more and more in this direction, and hence soberness in the race is constantly on the increase.

Total Abstinence.—It is remarkable, too, to observe the steadfastness and persistency with which the colored teachers, as a rule, hold to the idea that the race is to be uplifted morally, as well as materially and religiously improved, through total abstinence as a chief instrument. It is the rare exception, not the rule, to find a colored teacher who does not hold to this doctrine. The result is that many boys and girls in the school-room all over the South and other sections as well are being trained to habits of temperance, and will in all probability develop into consistent temperance men and women. And it must not be forgotten that the true and most influential leaders of the race, the ministers, are molding and shaping the opinions of both old and young in favor of soberness and total abstinence.

Leaders Temperate.—I have watched closely the men who are recognized as the race leaders in various states and localities. It is acknowledged that they are generally shrewd, calculating, and hard to circumvent when they attempt political maneuvers. It is my observation that these leaders are strictly reliable and trustworthy when confided in, and—however surprising the statement may be to some—that they are generally sober, upright and honest. I confess that in some localities this rule does not apply, but on the whole a more sober class of leaders does not exist in any race than in the Afro-American.

Cross-Roads Grocery.—One of the evils against which our people have to contend is the cross-roads grocery store, to be found all over the Southland—the bane of this section. Here, with no city or town ordinance to make drunkenness an offense, and to threaten certain punishment, they congregate and drink their fill, carouse, engage in free fights, and do other hurtful and equally unlawful things, while no one dares molest or make afraid, and the grocery keeper, finding his trade benefited, encourages the debauchery. This evil, instead of becoming less, increases. The business of many prosperous towns and villages is being injured seriously by the competition at the cross-roads, and the resulting vice, violence and impoverishment.

Crime Traceable to Liquor Habit.—The records of the courts show that crime among our people is traceable in a large majority of cases to a too free exercise of the liquor habit. Of the men belonging to the race who were hanged, I think it entirely reasonable to say that at least four-fifths committed their offenses while under the influence of liquor. But speaking of the race broadly, and duly allowing for all the unusual circumstances that ought to be taken into consideration, I think it cannot fairly be charged with anything like gross intemperance.

Delirium Tremens.—It is something out of the usual order to come upon a case of delirium tremens among the Negroes. Comparatively few of them drink anything of consequence during the week, but excessive imbibation is mostly indulged in on Saturdays.

Not a Race of Drunkards.—Therefore this is not a race of drunkards, and there is abundant reason for believing that with proper education and training it may be made a race of sober people and abstainers.

Reliable Allies.—In order to strengthen the cause of temperance in the South, nothing is more important than to treat the Negro fairly, and to keep faith with him, to permit no pledge to be broken. Once won, the colored man is the most faithful and reliable of all allies. It is, of course, needless to add that the supply of temperance literature should be kept up and increased."

Educational Institutions.—Especially valuable is the work of arousing total abstinence enthusiasm among the students in the various educational institutions—young men, and women too, upon whom the future of the race and its influence for good or evil so largely depends. I am indeed hopeful for the future of the Afro-American race, and particularly hopeful that it will become a positive and influential contributor to the triumph of the temperance reform.

The Shame of a Christian Nation.—It is estimated that Christendom has introduced 70,000 gallons of rum into Africa to every missionary. In the great Congo Free State there are one hundred drunkards to one convert. Under the maddening influence of intoxicating drink sent from New England two hundred Congoans slaughtered each other. One gallon of rum caused a fight in which fifty were slain.

A Sad End.—A generation since there lived in a western city a wealthy Englishman who was what is called a high liver. He drank his toddy in the morning, washed down his lunch with champagne, and finished a bottle of port for dinner, though he complained that the heavy wines here did not agree with him, owing to the climate. He died of gout at fifty years, leaving four sons. One of them became an epileptic, two died from drinking. Called good fellows, generous, witty, honorable young men, but before middle age miserable sots. The oldest of the brothers was a man of fixed habits, occupying a leading place in the community from his keen intelligence, integrity and irreproachable morals. He watched over his brothers, laid them in their graves, and never ceased to denounce the vice which had ruined them; and when he was long past middle age financial trouble threw him into a low, nervous condition, for which wine was prescribed. He drank but one bottle. Shortly after his affairs were righted and his health and spirits returned, but it was observed that once or twice a year he mysteriously disappeared for a month or six weeks. Nor wife, nor children, nor even his partner, knew where he went; but at last, when he was old and gray-headed, his wife was telegraphed from a neighboring obscure village where she found him dying of *mania a potu.* He had been in the habit of hiding there when the desire for liquor became maddening, and when there he drank like a brute."

Temperance Resolutions Adopted by the A. M. E. Church.—The African Methodist Episcopal Church, at its General Conference, held in Indianapolis, Indiana, adopted the following resolutions:

"*Resolved:* 1. That we discourage the manufacture, sale and use of all alcoholic and malt liquors.

"2. That we discourage the use of tobacco by our ministers and people.

"3. That we discourage the use of opium and snuff.

"4. That we endorse the great prohibition movement in this country, also work done by the Woman's Christian Temperance Union, and will use all honorable means to suppress the evils growing out of intemperance.

"5. That it shall be a crime for any minister or member of the A. M. E. Church to fight against temperance, and if convicted of this crime he shall lose his place in the conference and the church."

The bishops at this same conference said in their address: "We should allow no minister, or member who votes, writes, lectures or preaches to uphold the rum trade to retain his membership, either in the conference or in the church. And those who are addicted to strong drink, either ministers or laymen, should have no place among us. Visit our station houses, bridewells, jails, almshouses, and penitentiaries, and you will there witness the effects of this horror of horrors. Rum has dug the grave of the American Indian so deep that it will never be resurrected. If we would escape the same fate as a church and race, we must be temperate.

"Some of the loftiest intellects have been blasted and blighted by this terrible curse. The use of wine at weddings should never be encouraged by our ministers; it is often the beginning of a blasted life."

Woman in Temperance. — Mrs. McCurdy, corresponding secretary of the Georgia W. C. T. U. for colored women, says: "The call for 'God and home in every land,' is growing to be more popular than in former years. Ministers all over the Southland are taking hold of the temperance question and are agitating it as never before. They see that

"Mental suasion for the thinker
Moral suasion for the drinker
Legal suasion for the drunkard maker
Prison suasion for the statute breaker "

are not virtues and therefore will not bring about the desired end. We are growing in numbers and are believing that among the Christian races temperance is a cardinal virtue, upon which physical strength, moral worth, social happiness and political tranquillity depend."

Evils of Alcohol as a Beverage. —The shackles of strong drink are more galling than were the shackles of slavery. In saying this we do not discount the horrors of the slave pen and the auction-block. The slave-master could not put shackles on the *man*, the immortal. President Lincoln, with the aid of General Grant and his mighty host, could proclaim liberty to the captive; but in the war against King Alcohol, each man must be his own emancipator.

The horrors of intemperance are known to the most thoughtless. Every intelligent person knows the awful effects of alcohol on the intellectual, moral, and religious nature of man. But, strange as it may seem, "the multitude" believe that alcohol has the power to give life, vitality, energy, force to the *body;* that it is needful in heat or cold. But, listen! The following statements are made by the president of one of the largest life insurance companies in America: "A group of total abstainers, aged 20, will, on the average, live 44.2 years apiece; a group of moderate drinkers, aged 20, will, on the average, live 15.6 years apiece. A group of total abstainers, aged 30, will, on the average, live 36.5 years apiece; a group of moderate drinkers, aged 30, will, on the average, live 13 years apiece. A group of total abstainers, aged 40, will, on the average, live 28.8 years apiece; a group of moderate drinkers, aged 40, will, on the average, live 11.6 years apiece."

It will be seen by the above testimony that total abstainers between the ages of 20 and 40 have 23 years' advantage over the users of alcoholic beverages in the expectancy of life. This, of course, has reference to the average man of his class.

Smoking a Crime.—Tobacco was early introduced into Europe. Its use, however, was condemned, and the Sultan of Turkey declared smoking a *crime*, and death of the most cruel kind was fixed as the punishment. In Russia, the "noses of the smokers were cut off in the earlier part of the seventeenth century." Its use was described by King James I of England, as "a custom loathsome to the eye, hateful to the nose, harmful to the brain, dangerous to the lungs, and in the black, stinking fume thereof nearest resembling the horrible Stygian smoke of the pit that is bottomless."

Tobacco a Poison.—Dr. J. H. Kellogg, M. D., in Health Science Leaflet, No. 216, says: "Chemists, botanists and physicians unite in pronouncing tobacco one of the most deadly poisons known. No other poison, with the exception of Prussic acid, will cause death so quickly, only three or four minutes being required for a fatal dose to produce its full effect.

Nicotine.—"The active principle of tobacco, that is, that to which its narcotic and poisonous properties are due, is nicotine, a heavy, oily substance which may be separated from the dry leaf of the plant by distillation or infusion. The proportion of nicotine varies from two to eight per cent. A pound of tobacco contains on an average 380 grains of this deadly poison, of which one-tenth of a grain will kill a dog in ten minutes.

Killed in Thirty Seconds.—"A case is on record in which a man was killed in thirty seconds by this poison. Hottentots use the oil of tobacco to kill snakes, a single drop causing death as quickly as a lightning stroke. It is largely used by gardeners and keepers of greenhouses to destroy grubs and noxious insects (its proper usefulness)."

Habit of Smoking.—The habit of smoking was discovered on the island of Cuba. Two sailors who were

sent by Columbus to explore the island report that:
"Among many other strange and curious discoveries,
the natives carried with them lighted fire brands, and
puffed smoke from their mouths and noses, which they
supposed to be the way savages had for perfuming
themselves.   They afterwards declared that they 'saw

ROBERT H. BONNER,   ORISHANTKEH FREDREMAS.
New Haven, Conn.   Grad. Theol. Dept.,Ceylon,West Africa.
CHAS. H. BOYER,   HENRY H. PROCTOR.
Maryland Academical Dept.   Graduate Theological Dept.,
Yale University.

the naked savages twist large leaves together and
smoke like devils.' "

Filthy and Pernicious.—The use of tobacco is both
filthy and pernicious.   "Keep thyself pure," was
Paul's injunction to Timothy; and again he says, "Let

us cleanse ourselves from all filthiness of the flesh and spirit." "If any man defile the temple of God, him shall God destroy; for the temple of God is holy, which temple we are."

Leaders Needed.—Since the death of Dr. J. C. Price, of Livingstone College, Rev. J. H. Hector, of York, Pa., is the most popular temperance lecturer of the race. The race sadly needs a great leader in the temperance work, a leader who will inspire the hosts to active and progressive measures.

Moral Status.—President Wright says: "One who does not know the character of the moral lives of the colored people at the emancipation is incapable of rendering an opinion as to the Negro's moral status now. It is extremely difficult to measure the distance of the advancement or to estimate the weight and quality of the good that has been done. No people have made further advancement in moral and Christian character. The schools have given them eyes to see. Eyes to see themselves as others saw them, and year after year vice and ignorance have become odious. In 1865 there was scarcely any Negro homes in all Georgia. In 1870 they could be easily counted. Who but the census taker would undertake such a task to-day? There is taxable property of some sixteen millions of dollars, and thousands of comfortable homes in the city and rural districts. None have become very rich but many have made a good start in life. There are over five hundred good business establishments whose affairs are conducted wholly by colored men.

Business World.—The Negro is taking a reliable, useful, and honorable place in the business and industrial world. He is becoming an intelligent producer and developer of the resources of this great state.

Under the benign influence of private and public schools he is becoming patriotic; he is purchasing land and fixing himself to the soil.

Discourtesies and Insults.—He is becoming more sensitive with regard to discourtesies and insults. His restiveness is the natural result of his increased intelligence and love for his country in common with others. He may even grow defiant in the face of these outrages, if continued. The intelligence and means among the colored people inspire confidence and respect on the part of the whites. There is practically no trouble or possibility of trouble between the intelligent and upright colored people and the same class of white people. This is what Christian and industrial education has done. The Negro, or Southern problem, finds its key in the education of the race. The Negro should not only be given every opportunity the state can afford for elementary education, but should be urged to avail himself of these opportunities.

Criminals.—There are in Georgia more than five thousand Negro criminals; about twice the number of colored teachers. Very few of these criminals can read or write. Here is found the connection between crime and ignorance. Education is not a panacea for crime, but, in proportion to the intelligence of the colored people of a given community, the number of actual and alleged crimes among that class of citizens has decreased.

Professions.—There are in Georgia some twenty-five physicians, two pharmacists, seven lawyers, and half a dozen newspaper editors. Some of these, however, have not been broadly educated. What Georgia needs most is men who can clearly and wisely state the needs of the colored people.

Trade Education.—While the work in the schools has included industrial training, yet very little legitimate and genuine trade teaching has been done until within the last few years. The entire number of persons who have learned, in all these schools, enough of a trade to make them as safe in following it as it would in attempting to teach school, is very small. This is the natural result of the beginnings. There is, however, an awakening on these lines, and a demand for abler and better teachers and advantages in industrial work. The colored people are at a point in their natural and material development when everybody recognizes the pressing need of more attention to the teaching of trades. The march of the Negro race towards the better day will not be only along the class of classic learning, but its pathway of victory must be as well through the physical sciences and along the avenues of industrial and business enterprises. The demands of the times are for genuine industrial teaching, which sends a young man into the world with an industrial bent that fits him for his life work; that gives him a trade by which he may support himself and benefit the world.

Patents.—The colored patentees of the Union are credited with more than sixty useful inventions. This clearly shows that the Negro has genius and skill, and the means and opportunities now presented aid in the development and training of their genius. Perhaps no other school can come nearer to filling the demands than the industrial school well equipped and with a liberal curriculum.

Debt of Gratitude.—The colored people of the South are under an everlasting debt of gratitude to the philanthropists of the country, north and south, who have done so much to raise them from their low estate. While it is difficult to estimate the amount of money spent by the states and different benevolent institutions for the education of the colored people, the fact remains that a great and grand work has been done, and is being done, for their education.

Our Country.—There are many and almost ancient ties that bind the Negro to the United Stats. There are numerous reasons why he should feel as much at home on the American soil as any man of any other nation that treads our shores. Among America's earliest explorers and discoverers, some of the boldest and bravest, and most successful of our citizens, as early as 1529, were woolly-haired Negroes. From then until now, whether he is happy and prosperous in his Southland, or fighting the battles of the nation, the Negro, by sweat and blood, identified himself with every phase and fiber of the American history and life. The pathway of the race has not been strewn with flowers, but it has steadily led towards the light. And to-day the Negro stands upon higher ground, where the light of liberty shines upon him more steadily. Standing here, new duties, new responsibilities, await him. In this broader day the demand is for more men of thought and action.

Does Not Crave Domination, but Equality.—The Negro craves not domination. He simply asks for equalization of rights and privileges, such as belong to American citizens under the fundamental law of the land. As an American citizen he cannot ask less nor be contented with less."

Prejudice.—"Talks for the Times" says: "There are but very few white people in this country who are capable of passing fair judgment upon us as a race, for the large majority of them do not associate with us. The Jews have no extensive communion with the Samaritans. Now, it is a law in optics that the size of the visual angle varies with the distance of the body, and an object looks smaller as we recede from it. On this principle it is easy to account for the absurd and strange opinions of many of our white friends concerning us. They stand off at so magnificent a distance from the Negro that they either lose sight of him altogether, or what they do see of him seems insignificant and contemptible.

Corruption of Public Men.—I am proud, too, to know, that in this transition period of ours we have among us a few public men of unimpeachable character. When Oscar Dunn was lieutenant-governor of Louisiana a certain white man, interested in a bill before the legislature, endeavored by the use of money, to secure Mr. Dunn's influence in favor of that bill. The reply of that noble Negro was as withering as it was laconic: 'Sir,' said he, 'my conscience is not for sale.' In that memorable presidential election when Messrs. Hayes and Tilden were candidates, a colored man in one of those Southern states, at that time a member of the electoral college, was approached by a white man and offered fifty thousand dollars for his vote for Mr. Tilden, being informed, at the same time, that it was a 'graveyard secret,' and that if he ever exposed the offerer of that sum death would be the penalty. I am proud to say that brave and faithful man rejected with scorn the proffered bribe. Would Anglo-Saxon morality have stood a better test against gilded corruption?"

Toward the Light.—Professor Bowen says: "Before the war the Negro was a dumb driven and a dumb used cattle for work and for breeding. Shame, the virtue that Eve brought out of the Garden with her, that belongs alike to heathen and to Christian, was mocked, insulted and trampled under the merciless hoofs. The women were the tools for lechery. The whole head of the race was sick and the heart was faint; bruises and putrefying sores covered the body of the race. To-day, in education, in morals, in spiritual power, the Negro is far superior. He marries according to law, rears his family in a home of culture and morality, and reaches up with divine aspirations to the ideal perfections of human nature. The women are women. And while it is true that, as a mass, the race has not yet attained unto all perfection, yet they press with vigor toward the mark and are far removed from that dark age. They are purer, their preachers have improved and are still improving in all the elements of moral power.

Progress Since Freedom.—Says E. A. Johnson, in his history of the Negro race: "Through a century and a half we have traced our ancestors' history. We have seen how they performed the hard tasks assigned them by their masters; followed the hoe and the plow with a laugh and a song; making magnificent estates, building mansions, furnishing them with the splendor of the times; so eager in patriotism as to be the first to shed their blood on the altar of their country's liberty. All this they did with no other hope of reward than a slave's cabin and a life of bondage for themselves and children. Scarcely have they ever sought revenge in riot and bloodshed. Stolen from a home of savage freedom, they found themselves in straitened circumstances as slaves in America, but the greatness of the Negro's nature crops out plainly in the wonderful way in which he adapted himself to his new conditions. The fact that he went to work willingly, worked so long and faithfully, and rebelled so little, marks him as far superior to the Indian, who never accepts the conditions of labor, either for himself or another; and universally enjoys the rank of a savage rather than that of a civilized being. A plant placed in the window of a dark chamber gradually bends its foliage towards the sunlight; so the Negro, surrounded by the darkness of slavery, bent his life toward the light of his master's God. He found Him. In Him he trusted, to Him he prayed, from Him he hoped for deliverance; no people were ever more devout according to their knowledge of the word, no people ever suffered persecution more bravely, no people ever got more out of the few talents assigned them; and for this humble devotion, this implicit trust and faithfulness, God has now rewarded them. The race comes out of slavery with more than it had before it went in. But there was no need of any slavery at all. Jamestown, New England, and other colonies might have held the Negro long enough to serve out his passage from Africa, and then given him his freedom, as they did their white slaves imported from England. The mistake was made then; the mistake became a law which the people were educated to believe was just. Many did not believe it, and some slave holders sought to make the condition of their slaves comfortable. The affection arising between the slave and his master often governed the treatment. The Negro, being largely endowed by nature with affection, affability and a forgiving spirit, generally won for himself good treatment. Then, too, the master had some soul, and where that ingredient of his make-up was deficient, a selfish interest to the slave as his property somewhat modified the venom that might have more often visited itself upon the unfortunate slave in lashes and stripes.

Many Affections and Friendships formed between master and slave exist to the present day. Some slaves are still at the old homestead, conditions entirely reversed, voting differently at the polls, but friends at home; and in death the family of one follows that of the other to the grave.

When the War Ended the whole South was in an unsettled condition, property destroyed, thousands of her sons dead on the battlefield, no credit, conquered. But if the condition of the whites was bad, that of the blacks was worse. They were without homes, money, or learning. They were now to feed, clothe and protect themselves in a government whose treasury they had enriched with two and a half centuries of unrequited labor, and a country whose laws they must obey but could not read.

It Was Natural that they should make mistakes. But they made less mistakes than the bummers who came south for plunder during reconstruction times, and with the false promise of "forty acres and a mule," led the unlettered race into a season of idleness and vain hopes. But this condition did not last. The Negro inherited the ability to work from the institution of slavery. He soon set about to utilize this ability. I ask, what race could have done more. And this the Negro has done, though virtually ostracised from the avenues of trade and speculation. His admission to a trades union is the exception rather than the rule in America. A colored boy taking a place as a porter in a store at the same time with a white boy, may find the white boy soon promoted to a clerkship, then to a partnership in the firm, if he is smart; but the colored boy remains, year after year, where he first commenced, no matter how worthy, no matter how competent.   His lot is that of a menial; custom assigns him there, and in looking for clerks and partners he is not thought of by the white business man; and thus, by the rigid laws of custom, he has continually lost golden opportunities to forge his fortune; yet he has prospered in spite of this, and it bespeaks for him a superior manhood."

Best Specimens of Physical Manhood.—Under the influence of civilized customs and habits, they have improved in form and feature, until they have become strong, well proportioned, and can furnish some of the finest specimens of physical manhood in the world. They have improved equally in mental and moral traits.   From naked barbarians they have become civilized Christians.   From groveling and stupid savages they have become intelligent and industrious workmen, skilled in many of the arts and all of the handicrafts of civilized life.   By this vast progress in so short a period, the Negroes have demonstrated a capacity, an aptitude for improvement, which should make us hesitate to predict that they cannot finally ascend, under favorable conditions, to the highest heights of human development.   In that event the argument based on the inferiority and the color of the Negro must vanish.

Not in Color.—Dr. Haygood truly says: "The Negro cannot rise simply because he is black; the white man cannot stay up simply because he is white.   A man rises, not by the color of his skin, but by intelligence, industry and integrity.   The foremost man in these excellencies and virtues must, in the long run. be also the brightest man."

Remarkable Advancement.—It should be remembered that less than thirty years ago the Negro started with less than nothing, having, as a slave, acquired habits of thriftlessness and wastefulness, unfitting him for the accumulation of property. In one generation he has managed to accumulate and pile up an aggregate of wealth that is simply enormous.

Still in Idleness.—It is true that a considerable percentage of the race still retain their habits of idleness which characterized them as slaves. It is true that a large percentage exhibit talents for accumulation, but are content to earn from day to day the wages of the day before, trusting to providence for the future. But there is a rapidly increasing number of those who exhibit decided financial ability.

Honored Mention.—Starting in the most humble way, with limited intelligence and exceedingly circumscribed knowledge in a manner in which economy is to be practiced, they have gone on from year to year accumulating a little until the savings, as represented by their property, have built churches, erected schools, paid teachers and preachers and greatly improved the home and home life. These results, coming through the humble earnings of day labor deserve honorable mention.

Just Judgment.—It is frequently the case that in contemplating the race as a mass it is judged by its worst representatives. This is unkind and unjust. The colored people of the South cannot justly be judged by the criminals among them, who have become conspicuous for their evil deeds. They should rather be judged by the honest, hard-working men and women, who, beginning with nothing, in the course of one generation accumulated an amount of property that even in our magnificent wealth forms no inconspicuous portion.

CHAPTER VIII.

THE COLORED WOMAN OF TO-DAY.

"Above all let the Negro know that the elevation of his race can come only, and will come surely, through the elevation of its women."

Womanhood.—It is but a generation ago that the colored woman had no stand, and the term womanhood was not broad enough in this Christian republic to include women of African descent. Her birthright was supposed to be that of banishment from high social circles. In spite of the prejudice against her she has, in a remarkable way, emerged from obscurity and overcome the prejudice so that to-day she stands on such a level that no one would have supposed her to have had any relationship with slavery in the recent past.

Appreciative.—That the colored women of to-day are appreciating the value of culture and industries is shown in their readiness to enter all open doors in this direction. Universities and professional industries of this country and Europe find the colored women ready as soon as permission is granted. There are very few professions and callings into which they are not winning their way in spite of the prejudice that would restrict them to the lower walks of life. There are physicians and dentists, lawyers and linguists, musicians, stenographers and nurses, in this rising race that are an adornment to the position they hold.

Good Wives.—Make it your highest aim to be good wives; the race needs you and must depend upon you. When we come to calculate the forces that decide the destiny of nations it must be confessed that the

MRS. MARY RICE PHELPS, AUGUSTA, GA.
See sketch in Chapter XIV.

mightiest and grandest come from home, good homes, the very salt of society, the strength and joy of any nation. Then banish from your minds, I pray you, that labor in itself is harmful and degrading.

National Association of Colored Women.—That the Afro-American woman appreciates her position is shown by the federation of women of that race. The second annual convention in 1896 was a representative body, many of the states having appointed delegates.

In response to the address of welcome, Mrs. Sprague,

only daughter of the late Frederick Douglass, in behalf of the federation said: "It is with gratification that I respond in behalf of the colored women of the United States to the gracious words just spoken."

False Impressions.—We are weary of the false impressions sent broadcast over the land about the colored woman's inferiority, her lack of virtue, and other qualities of noble womanhood. We wish to make it clear to the minds of your fellow countrymen and women that there are no essential elements of character that they deem worthy of cultivating that we do not desire to emulate; that the sterling qualities of purity, virtue, benevolence and charity are not any more dormant in the breast of the black woman than in the white woman. While the white race has chronicled deeds of heroism and acts of mercy of the women of pioneer and other days, so we are pleased to note in the personality of such women as Phyllis Wheatley, Margaret Garner, Sojourner Truth, and our venerable friend, Harriet Tubman, sterling qualities of head, heart and hand."

Wants.—Our wants are numerous. We want homes in which purity can be taught, not homes that are police court feeders. We want industrial schools, we want the dram shops closed, we want the pool rooms and gambling dens of every variety swept out of existence. We want kindergartens largely established, we want reform schools for our girls in such cities where the conscience of the white Christian is not elastic enough to take in the Negro child. Our progress depends in the united strength of both men and women. This is indeed the woman's era, and we are coming."

Papers Read.—The enthusiasm, as well as the merit, of papers read before this convention is worthy of a place in any woman's convention in our land. That these representatives of the race are awake to the interest of their people is shown in the following

Resolutions.—Whereas, The social conditions of the Afro-American race render home-making and home-getting questions of supreme importance;

Resolved, That we heartily endorse the movement lately inaugurated in this city looking to the establishment and maintenance of industrial schools, wherein our youth may, by the co-ordinate training of hand, heart and head, thoroughly equip themselves for the great battle of life.

Resolved, That we commend to the race the work being done at all institutions whose purpose it is to give our youth the higher and more truly practical education.

Whereas, It is customary in some portions of this country for whole families to live in one room; and,

Whereas, The mothers of our people are sadly in need of appreciating the value of good homes; be it

Resolved, That we use our influence throughout the country to have mothers' meetings held, where the mothers of our race may be taught the necessity of pure homes and lives and privacy in home apartment.

Provident Hospital.—The Provident Hospital and Training School for Nurses, in Chicago, recently organized, has opened a field for the colored ladies, and they are availing themselves of opportunities and showing to the world that they are efficient and capable of filling positions where the highest ideals of womanhood are needed. The colored women of to-day are proving themselves progressive, and are fully alive to their responsibilities, showing full well that out of "The social disorder of a bondaged race there shall arise a womanhood, strong, spirited, and chaste, in all the things that make for social uplifting and refinement."

Womanhood Insulted.—Dr. Crummell says: "In her girlhood all the delicate tenderness of her sex has been rudely outraged. In the field, in the rude cabin, in the press-room, in the factory, she was thrown into the companionship of coarse and ignorant men. No chance was given her for delicate reserve or tender modesty. From her childhood she was the doomed victim of the grossest passion. All the virtues of her sex were utterly ignored. If the instinct of chastity asserted itself, then she had to fight like a tiger for the ownership and possession of her own person, and ofttimes had to suffer pain and lacerations for her virtuous self-assertion. When she reached maturity all the tender instincts of her womanhood were ruthlessly violated. At the age of marriage—always prematurely anticipated under slavery—she was mated as the stock of the plantation were mated, not to be the companion of a loved and chosen husband, but to be the breeder of human cattle for the field or the auction block."

Purity.—"From a recent careful survey of every Southern state through nearly one hundred trusty observers," says Professor Bowen, "I have the testimony that the young women are pure in large numbers, and are rapidly increasing in an intense desire and determination to preserve themselves chaste and pure from the lustful approaches of the sinner; and that the number of legally and lovingly married families purely preserved in domestic and social virtues among husbands and wives, sons and daughters, is so far beyond the days of slavery that a comparison would minify the difference. The marvel is that the Negro had sufficient moral vitality left to make his way through the whirlpool of licentiousness to the solid rock of Christian character. From the harem life of the promiscuous and unnameable sins of slavery, some of which were the natural and fatal growth of pagan vices, others the fruit of prostitution, to the making of one clean, beautiful, noble and divine family and home, covers a period of intense moral, spiritual and intellectual development, more magnificent than the geologic transformation of ages. Be it known that this one family can be duplicated a hundred thousand times and more.''

High Sense of Womanhood.—My experience has taught me to advise the race to cultivate a high sense of the womanhood of the race. This must begin with the mother. There is little of the family idea. Here the race is sadly deficient. The mother should teach the boy to honor his parent, his mother, to respect his sister, and, as a result, other men's sisters. To reverence the seat of the family. In this way alone will the marriage relation which becomes less sacred year by year, be the power and ennobling agency for the salvation of our people.

Character.—Learning, culture and wealth must not be sought for as an end to existence, but as a means to the only true purpose of life.

Unity of Race.—We must have a greater solidarity of race. There are some individuals, but no classes, of the white race in this country who love us. Some of them give us money, but it is out of pity. With no one to love us, we must love ourselves. Until the Negro race is more united we can have no real and lasting success.

Virtue.—Fear of God, love of true devotion to righteousness must possess us. The principal virtues to be maintained by the industries of families, by the assiduity of teachers, and by the discipline of fathers, by the tears, entreaties and prayers of the mothers, by the devotedness of churches, by the zeal and purity of the ministers, by the modest chastity of maidens, by the morality and self-control of youths and young men, by the piety and beauty of obedient children.

Ebb and Flow.—I have no fear of the ultimate triumphs of these principles. Great evil is manifest on every side; once in a while it looks as though the devil were going to be the charioteer of the race-course of life, but you will notice that these abnormal things are only phases of the ebb and flow of the great river of life—the central current flows to God.

> "A wiser spirit is at work for us,
> A greater hand than ours."

The Mother of Douglass—Douglass, who, as many able judges hold, was one of the most remarkable men America has produced in this century—this Douglass had a mother, who, though sold off from her boy on a distant plantation, would walk, after her day's work, in the darkness of the night, a number of miles and back before the driver's call in the morning—and all this that she might spend just one hour with her little Fred. Who can love like a mother? Who can tell how much that mother's love contributed toward the greatness of the man? The exaltation of a race depends largly upon the mothers of the race. Is the Negro mother of today conscious of the fact that the ennobling and elevating of the race is largely to be decided by her influences?

Woman a Teacher.—Mrs. Mary Rice Phelps says: "To what extent does woman teach, and where does her tutorage begin? Every woman is a teacher,

whether she be worthy or unworthy; whether educated
or ignorant.   In the home circle, and around the fireside, her teaching begins with the first dawn of intelligence.   This is her inalienable right, the charter
given by the Almighty hand.   It is she who first points
out those paths which are so full of pleasantness and
peace, and directs the innocent minds to a Heavenly
Father.   She makes her own life a daily example (we
speak of the true woman) of all that is pure and ennobling.   She it is who teaches those qualities that are so
essential to any race or tribe of beings—morality, the
corner stone in the building of any race; Christianity,
the thread that must make the warp and woof of a prosperous people; economy, one of the foundations stones
that cannot be dispensed with.

Responsibility.—It is a woman's responsibility to
teach the coming generations to live inside of their
means, and to reserve extra pennies for rainy days
(they will be sure to come), and secure a home for old
age.   How many are paid large salaries, "live high,"
unmindful of the future, and end their existence in
the almshouse?

Ignorance and Poverty.—The time is fast approaching, so near that we can hear his footsteps in the distance, when nobody will care for that class of persons
who are content to live in poverty.   Such have neglected opportunities, misused means and wasted time.
They are content to know little, and possess less, a
universal sentiment, because it is a universal experience.

Woman's responsibility is great, and its importance
vast, when we analyze it.   She alone has the power to
set at naught the monster "ignorance," uproot "base
desire," break down the barrier, "prejudice," and

MISS ANNA JONES.

Is an alumnus of the University of Michigan, a brilliant linguist, and a very successful teacher in the Kansas City high school.

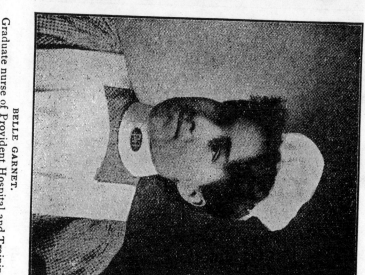

BELLE GARNET.

Graduate nurse of Provident Hospital and Training School, now a medical student in the Chicago Medical College.

198a

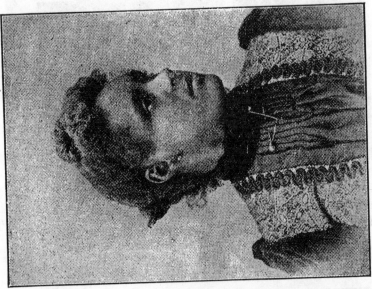

MISS SARAH A. BLOCKER.

Principal of Normal Department of Florida Baptist College, Jacksonville, Florida.

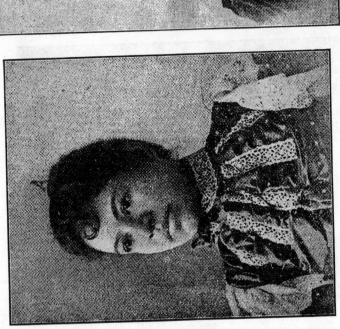

IDA GRAY NELSON, D. D. S.

The only colored lady dentist in the country. Graduate of Ann Arbor, Michigan, and now enjoys a lucrative practice in Chicago.

bury the race problem under the black pall of oblivion, beyond the possibility of a resurrection. Why should she fill a position as a public teacher? Why, because our educated men are needed for so many vocations that the work of teaching is left almost wholly to women.

Great and Multifarious.—Woman's work in the world is great and multifarious. It is a work which she alone can do. We do not mean to compare her with man, but compare woman with woman. Judge of what I can do by what I have done; of what women can do by what they have done. She can inspire when man fails. 'Tis hers to uplift, purify and adorn. What great cause of the world has brought about the desired result without woman's help. She did not bring down the lightning and connect electricity with thought, that different countries could talk to each other; but what did not the Reformation owe to the clear, womanly insight of Catherine Von Bora? Does not American independence owe much to the courage and steadfast resolution of the women of the Revolution?

Power Given Woman.—'Tis woman's responsibility to teach the young men what it is to be true men; what it is to be a loyal man; 'a man' in every sense of the word. To teach the young woman to be womanly; that it is honorable to work; that fashionable and frivolous women, who live only in self-indulgence and to have a 'good time,' are a dead weight upon their parents and a blot in society. In the age of chivalry and knighthood the laws of human nature were expressed when the crowning of the victor was assigned to woman's hand. As on the knightly fields, so it is on the great battlefield of life, contestants and combatants are animated and encouraged by woman's approval and cheering words.

Drudge of the Nation.—In the dark ages of the world's history she was the drudge of the nation, and considered only capable of doing menial work. But with the birth of Christianity she broke the manacle of society and conventionalism and came forth full-fledged, exerting power in every sphere of life. There is no home where her power is not felt, from the lowliest cabin to the king's palace.

The Center.—Woman's power is very great. She was not the first to pry with microscopic eyes and discover the startling truth that a single drop of water is crowded with a million living forms playing their part in the great drama of life. But she may be styled the axle on which the great wheel of society turns. If you ask of her devotion, behold Rizah defending her dead. If you would know of her stern training we have the words of the Spartan mother to her son as she buckles on his shield and bids him 'Return from the battlefield either with your shield or upon it.' If you would know of her military ability, we point to 'Joan of Ark,' as she clads herself in the warrior's apparel and is victorious in battle.

There are hosts of women we might name of our day, but suffice it to say, she is to mankind what the sun is to the universe. She is the center around which society moves and the light by which they are guided.

Young Women, did it ever occur to you that you had a great and awful responsibility resting upon you, and that you in part hold the destiny of our race in your hands?

If you have never thought, I beg of you, in the name of all that is pure and right, to think now. If you have never been factors in the upbuilding of the Negro race, begin now to do your part. It has been said,

'Whatever the women are the men will be sure to be.' Knowing this, fit yourself for the great emergency about you.

Prepare Yourself to raise those about you to a higher standard of all that goes to make a true man and woman. Educate yourself. Don't be contented with mere smattering. 'A little learning is a dangerous thing.' Educate your heads, your hearts and your hands. Let your thought be as pure and your character as spotless as the snow upon the summit of the loftiest mountain where the feathered songsters have never plumed their wings for flight nor the sweet sound of their notes have ever been heard.

Do Not Fail.—If you fail, young woman, to use this power, you fail positively, not negatively; so fail that you will drag down instead of elevate. This power is yours, and you cannot change it. It belongs to you as women.

Begin Now.—If you have never been a factor in the upbuilding of your race, count up the cost and begin to do your part. If you have never thought of your race pride, think now. Not only think, but act well your part. Without the ennobling power of the woman we can never be a great and noble race. If young men aspire to reach the highest pinnacles of fame, they rise but to fall lower, unless the women are pure and will demand respect. Learn to resent insults, young women. Learn to respect and defend tne women of your race, young men.

The World Will Feel It.—I would that I had a thousand tongues, and every tongue a thousand voices, and every voice a thousand echoes, that could reach from America to the utmost parts of Africa, and I would speak in loudest tone, with animating voice, to every Negro woman, and bid her take up woman's responsibility. Let colored women begin to act, begin to do, and exert their power in the right direction, and the world will feel it. Not as it would feel an earthquake shock, but as the globe feels the grand cohesive power which cements its heterogeneous masses and binds them into one harmonious band.''

A New Era.—Mrs. Fannie Barrier Williams says: ''A whole race of women, whose only heritage has been ignorance and isolation, needs no philosophers to lead them into a higher state. Their needs are elementary, and the duties of Christian women in their behalf are near, direct, and easy of comprehension. If the colored women who are sufficiently intelligent and warm-hearted to share in the responsibilities of helping where help is needed could be aroused from their do-nothing, unsympathetic and discouraged condition, and could be conscious of their opportunities for accomplishing good deeds, there would at once come the dawning of a new and better era for the American Negro. We would then understand that the question is not what we ought to demand, but what we can do; not what are our rights, but how we can best deserve them; not so much how to condemn prejudice, but how to remove its cause. The hour is not for the lamentations of Rachel, but for the hopes, courage and duty becoming women who are called by large opportunities to noble work. If we would have the public interested in us and our needs, we must become interesting, and we will become interesting just as soon as we begin to help ourselves to the utmost extent of our opportunities.

Home Life.—The one thing that should appeal most strongly to our hearts is the need of a better and purer

MRS. J. W. E. BOWEN,
President of the W. C. T. U., Georgia, No. 2.
Formerly Professor of Music in Clark University, Atlanta, **Ga.**

FANNIE BARRIER WILLIAMS,
Lecturer, Chicago, Illinois.

home life among our people in many parts of the South. I scarcely need tell you that our most embarrassing heritage from slavery was a homelessness and a lack of home ties. All the sanctities of marriage, the precious instincts of motherhood, the spirit of family alliance, and the upbuilding of home as an institution of the human heart, were all ruthlessly ignored and fiercely prohibited by the requirements of slavery. Colored people in bondage were only as men, women and children, and not as fathers, mothers, sons and daughters, brothers and sisters. Family relationships and home sentiments were thus no part of the preparation of colored people for freedom and citizenship. It is not agreeable to refer to these things, but they are mentioned merely to suggest to you how urgent and immensely important it is that we should be actively and helpfully interested in those poor women of the rural South, who, in darkness and without guides, are struggling to build homes and rear families. When we properly appreciate the fact that there can be no real advancement of the colored race without homes that are purified by all the influences of Christian virtues, it will seem strange that no large, earnest, directed and organized effort has been made to teach men and women the blessed meaning of home.

One - Room Cabins.—The first thing that should interest us is the fact that thousands of colored families in the South are still living in one-room cabins. Though the South is filled with our professors, ministers and smart politicians, yet few have attempted to teach these people the difference between a slave cabin and a Christian home.

Booker T. Washington, who has done more for the practical education of the colored people in all things than any other one man in America, tells us that the one-room cabin is the very root of all social evils in the South. It also appears that this indiscriminate huddling together of a whole family, large or small, in one room, is due more to ignorance of a better way than to poverty. The reform so earnestly needed in the mode of living in a large part of the South should not be left to a few chance individuals who are struggling to effect it.

Organization.—Colored women in every part of this country, who know what good homes mean to the well being of the colored race, should come together inorganization to study the situation, and earnestly put in motion every possible agency for reform. Such organization would learn at once, to their surprise and shame, how many things they could do that are not being done. They will learn that those who need our hearts, hands and advice are not suffering so much for want of equal rights, and political rights, and some easy escape from prejudice, as they are for the simplest necessities that make for decency, order and the sanctities of home making. Thousands of our women in the South are eager to learn some of the primary lessons of household sanitation, moral guides, mental stimulants, and the purifying environments for the children of their hearts; yet these yearnings are not heeded by those who can help and comfort them.

System.—Thousands of capable young women and men, who are eager for enlightenment and culture, are without books, papers and pictures, yet good literature and art of all kinds are prodigally wasted under our feet, because there seems to be neither sense nor sympathy enough to know where to send them as rays of light into dark places. In short, there are a thousand sources of plenty and helpfulness for our fellow-men and women, if we could but organize agencies to command and use them.

Prejudice.—Do you know that thousands of our bright young women, comely and capable, are without employment partly on account of American prejudice, partly on account of their own timidity, and especially because no effort is made to suggest or to show them the many new fields of employment that they know not of? Do you know that the tendency of our time is to make all work respectable and honorable that is well and honorably done? And that our girls who can do housework better than anything else should be as much respected for doing it as they would be if making less wages as clerks? Do you know that thousands of our young men are reckless and unworthy of their privileges because they have no inspiration to better things, and no rebuke from young women? Do you know that our ministers would be nobler in all things, in all the best attributes of their calling, if our women were to insist upon it? Do you know that all things that are pure, healthful and sacred, in the relations of husband and wife and child, depend primarily upon worthy women? All these things and many more of like nature are suggested to women who come together in a spirit of reform. Surely, we have something more than sorrow, complaint and tears.

Work Left to Colored Women.—Colored women of culture and force of character can do much to urge this thought upon women of the dominant race. If I may be pardoned a personal reference, I will say that my best reward in meeting and talking to representative white women, at all times and places, is that they are so susceptible to the idea that they need us to some extent in the same way that we need them. All state-ments to them concerning our wrongs and how we suffer under all forms of injustice are received with startling surprise. I have been happily repaid for all my efforts by fewest assurances of many of the women in the country that they have been converted to right thinking concerning us. We may feel safe in the belief that the women who are strong enough to resist the domination of fashion's nonsense and the snobbery of caste are ever ready to lay aside their false presump-tion against us, and accept the truth of our cause if we would but put ourselves more in evidence in their efforts to benefit humanity.

Self Respect. —I would also appeal to the hearts of our women for a stronger sense of self-respect. I believe that it is an infallible rule that people are weak who believe themselves weak. We help to make ourselves unimportant and underestimated by the habit of confessing our inferiority. We are everywhere hampered by the false and cringing notions that certain positions and achievements are beyond our reach. Hundreds of young men and women graduate with high academic honors from schools and colleges and pass at once into obscurity, as much because of their own low sense of self-importance as from the resisting force of popular prejudice.

In Bondage.—Thirty-five years ago we alone were in the wilderness of bondage, crying aloud for freedom. Our happy release from that condition thrilled men and women everywhere with a most exalted sense of the value and sweetness of liberty. To-day we are not alone in any of our claims, disabilities, wants and hopes. That large number of wretched women who are stitching their lives out in the sweat shops of our large cities in order to get a crumb of bread for their children, the toiling men and women of the land who groan and smart under the oppressions of wealth, women of all kinds and conditions who are restive under the restraint imposed by senseless customs and unjust laws, in fact all our countrymen who are conscious of being forced to live short of a complete enjoyment of life, liberty and the pursuit of happiness, are with us in our every contention.

No Monopoly.—We as surely have no monopoly of misery as we have no monopoly of fortune; there is somewhere and somehow a compensation for every difficulty we meet and complain of. Our poetry has opened the floodgates of philanthropy, prejudice has multiplied our friends and has tended to sharpen the mettle of our character, and all forms of injustice against us react in terms of justice for us. Indeed, our advantages and opportunities are large, exalting, and a part of the very constitution of things.

How to Win.—We are women claiming, yearning and aspiring for rights at a time when woman's winsome voice of supplication, of stern command, is heard and heeded above the din and clamor of the times. Would you win the interest and confidence of the world? The answer comes from a thousand sources: Be brave in the consciousness of your own worth, be beautifully graced with all that virtue asks in woman and you shall in time remove from all laws, ways and customs the darkening blight of woman's prejudices against woman."

A True Lady.—Mrs. M. A. McCurdy says: "A true lady is, to a great extent, judged by her conversation and behavior when on the street or in any public conveyance. To hear a woman or a girl talk loudly on

GRADUATING CLASS, 1900—ACADEMIC DEPARTMENT, SPELMAN SEMINARY

A CORNER IN MILLINERY ROOM, TUSKEGEE NORMAL AND INDUSTRIAL INSTITUTE.

208b

the street or in a street car, is a practice quite unbecoming and disagreeable, because it is common.

Company.—Our girls should beware the company they keep, for "on the choice of friends our good or evil name depends," and the girl who is seen with common, ill-bred, or rude companions, no matter how ladylike she herself may be, will, as a rule, be judged by them.

Books and Papers.—The books and papers that a girl reads have much to do in forming her habits and character of conversation. If she reads the poor and trashy books which she finds exposed for sale on many newspaper stands, her mental life will, of necessity, partake of the character of the poor, unwholesome food with which she feeds it. If, on the other hand, she reads instructive and interesting books and papers, which she may obtain at no greater cost, she will be laying the foundation of a good, useful and happy life in the future.

Amusements.—The question of girls' amusement is a very important one at the present time, because of the silly and vicious attractions that are being offered on every hand, and mothers should see that their girls are not present on all occasions, regardless of the fact that they are accompanied by some intimate gentleman friend, because true enjoyment is not to be found in continually attending places of amusement, but rather in living a quiet, wholesome life, doing one's duty from day to day, reading useful and inspiring books, doing our daily work, striving to do service for Christ on any and all occasions. Then let the girl be modest in her dress, careful as to what and to whom she talks, choice in her selection of books and companions, moderate as to her indulgence in amusements, and she will find that she will not only win the approval of all who casually come in contact with her, but the Lord will greatly bless her, and open ways for her to fit herself for usefulness in honored positions in the ranks of true ladies.''

Homes.—The following paragraph from ''Talks for the Times'' is pertinent: ''Young ladies, there is a vast and important field open to you. You are to build up the homes of a race. Having enjoyed the blessings of one for several years in your school life, it is expected that you will go forth to give deeper meaning to home life among the people. It will devolve upon you to teach them that home life does not mean kenneling together like wild beasts, nor does it mean costly furniture and rich tapestry, for there may be more moral worth upon homespun than under silk, and more real happiness in a Christian log cabin than in a Godless mansion, whose floors are spread with English velvet, and whose windows are draped with lace curtains. It will devolve upon you to teach them that a home means mutual respect and mutual affection, mutual confidence and harmonious co-operation. May it never be said of the young ladies who graduate in colored schools that they were found standing before the temple of fashion, while their ignorant and degraded sisters were perishing for lack of Christian instruction.''

Good Taste Displayed in Dress by the young colored women of the South is noticeable. The girls who earn money spend it to suit their own tastes, display good discrimination in the harmony of colors and the use of ornamentation, and a choice for delicacy of fabric. Their scorn for high colors, especially red, and for bizarre effects, is amusing, and at the same time most suggestive, for here, too, we see the influence of tradition and a rebound from previous conditions.

The Negroes are an emotional people; the emotions are the roots from which the esthetic sentiments spring, and in their education the development of the esthetic sensibilities should receive its full share.

Duty to Perform.—"Young women, there is a duty for you to perform, also. It has been well said that "it is easy to judge what the men are when you know what the women are." Oh, the word woman! We pause to think of the purity and innocence which existed in her when first placed in the garden of Eden. Make society good by your Christian character, live so that the world will be better for your having lived in it. The path of duty in this world is not all gloom or sadness or darkness, and it is only when we turn to the right or left that we are lacerated by piercing thorns and concealed dangers. When we learn that doing our duty will help some poor, weak one, it will strengthen us and we will do more in the interests of our brothers and sisters. When we have a task to perform, we should go about it with a cheerful heart, with an eye single to doing our best; then duty becomes a pleasure.

Topmost Round.—Now, having attained womanhood, let us aim to be first in the pursuit of our life's work; we cannot reach the topmost round at once, and if we get there at all there must be something in us worthy of the upper rounds. Can we ask Him to be our guide who noticed the falling of a sparrow to the ground? Do so; then we will not choose the wrong path, we will not stumble in our darkest hours. We will not think solely of our slavery, of our closing hour, or how we will spend the evening, but will put our mind on our duties and resolve that they shall have the best that is in us; and, by and by, we shall enjoy the reward which is laid up for the finally faithful.''

Possibilities.—Her possibilities for usefulness are great. She is not less capable than other women, she is endowed with the same emotions of love and of hate, joy and sorrow, of fear and faith. Why may she not be fired with the same ambition and have the same sense of right and wrong, the same regard for humanity and love for God as her sister in white? Look at the host of noble, worthy women that have already written their names high. Early in the history of the race in this country Phyllis Wheatley, by her extraordinary intellectual power moved the hearts of men, and to this day stands out prominently as a literary genius. The posssibilities of the colored woman are great. What she has done she can do again. Yea, can increase in manifold ways.

Difficulties.—That there are great difficulties to encounter in the work must not be overlooked; that the negro woman is less fortunate than her white sister, is a fact. Poverty and prejudice prevail on every hand, but even this cannot quench her ambitions. Seeing the need of help to a race rising from degradation nothing should prevent her from overcoming these great obstacles.

Great Need.—The condition of homes in the South, languor and apathy of the many who have not yet realized their true condition and the possibilities of improvement, suggests the great need of labor in brain, help and information to those so sadly in need of it.''

Our Homes.—While it is true that our homes should be models, that Christian character is most largely built there, here more than elsewhere should the power of woman exert itself in beautifying and cheering homes and in cultivating a taste for the true, the beautiful, and the ennobling. It is not necessary that wealth be ours, but even a humble home may be made beautiful and cheerful.

Not Confined to Homes.—Although the work of the woman is largely in the homes, yet it is not confined entirely to the homes. Woman's sphere is anywhere where she may do good. Negro women are needed in the school room, where, next to the home, is found the place of character building, engraving on the tables of the useful mind that which will brighten through all eternity one of the noblest of occupations.

Social Purity Among Our Girls.—The young girls of our race, especially those that throng larger cities, and who have no home influences to hold them, are being dragged down in numbers year by year. Here is a great work for leaders. The work done in the larger cities of the North in this line suggests to the colored women something of what may be done for their race. Be up and doing. Raise the fallen, and so fulfill the law of Christ.

Industrial Schools. — Then again, the industrial schools where dressmaking, cooking, and the work of the home in general are taught, present a large field of usefulness among the women of the race. The work of Miss Lucy Laney, of Augusta, Ga., suggests what might be done in these lines, were more to realize the possibilities of so great a harvest.

Professional and Literary Workers.—Why should not women of the race, as well as their sisters in white, prepare to fill the professions of medicine, law, etc. What a great field for usefulness is open! The young ladies cannot too early enter this field, where there is so great a need of work, and where such happy results are attained.

Path of Duty.—The women of the race should then, in whatever sphere their lot is cast, follow the plain path of duty. Some may ask what recompense they are to receive for years of self-denial and toil? Man's ingratitude is not limited by race or color. Much may be accomplished in lifting up humanity, we may not be recognized, but we are not living with a view of notoriety, but what we desire to accomplish is something in the elevating and ennobling those around us. With this end in view, let us follow closely in the path of duty and we shall, in due time, receive recompense and reward.

Retrospective and Prospective View.—"Take a retrospective view of the condition of the colored women a generation ago; the advancement in all times is certainly remarkable. The home has been elevated and home and family ties have ennobled many lives, and the work of those who have so faithfully labored in this field is crowned with blessing on every hand. Let us not suppose that all has been done that can be done. There are many that are living only a little, if any, above the life of slavery, where true homes were unknown. It becomes the colored woman's duty of today to take courage from what has been done and seek in all the various avenues means and organizations to continue the work of raising and elevating the people of the race. We may not always realize our desires, but be sure that the united efforts of our women will, in time, demand the respect of every race on the face of the earth."

We take the following extracts from an address on "Enlightened Motherhood," given by Mrs. Frances

E. W. Harper, before the Brooklyn Literary Society:
Thirty Years.—"It is thirty years since an emancipated people stood on the threshold of a new era, facing an uncertain future—a legally unmarried race, to

MRS. F. E. W. HARPER,
Author and Lecturer, Philadelphia, Pa.   See sketch of Life in
Chapter XIV.

be taught the sacredness of the marriage relation; an
ignorant people, to be taught to read the book of
Christian law, and to learn to comprehend more fully
the claims of the gospel of the Christ of Calvary.
A homeless race, to be gathered into homes of peace-

ful security and to be instructed how to plant around
their firesides the strongest batteries against the sins
that degrade and the race vices that demoralize.
A race unversed in the science of government and
unskilled in the just administration of law, to be translated from the old oligarchy of slavery into the new
commonwealth of freedom, and to those men came the
right to exchange the fetters on their wrists for the
ballots in their right hands—a ballot which, if not
vitiated by fraud, or restrained by intimidation, counts
just as much as that of the most talented and influential man in the land.

Christian Women.—While politicians may stumble
on the barren mountain of fretful controversy, and
men, lacking faith in God and the invisible forces
which make for righteousness, may shrink from the
unsolved problems of the hour, into the hands of
Christian women comes the opportunity of serving the
ever-blessed Christ, by ministering to his little ones,
and striving to make their homes the brightest spots on
earth and the fairest types of Heaven. The school
may instruct and the church may teach, but the home
is an institution older than the church and antedating
the school, and that is the place where children should
be trained for useful citizenship on earth and a hope of
holy companionship in Heaven.

Home.—The home may be a humble spot, where
there are no velvet carpets to hush your tread, no
magnificence to surround your way, nor costly
creations of painter's art or sculptor's skill to please
your conceptions or gratify your tastes; but what
are the costliest gifts of fortune when placed in the
balance with the confiding love of dear children or
the true devotion of a noble and manly husband, whose

heart can safely trust in his wife? You may place upon the brow of a true wife and mother the greenest laurels; you may crowd her hands with civic honors; but, after all, to her there will be no place like home, and the crown of her motherhood will be more precious than the diadem of a queen.

Marriage.—As marriage is the mother of homes, it is important that the duties and responsibilities of this relation should be understood before it is entered on. A mistake made here may run through every avenue of the future, cast its shadow over all our coming years, and enter the lives of those whom we should shield with our love and defend with our care. We may be versed in ancient lore and modern learning, may be able to trace the path of worlds that roll in light and power on high, and to tell when comets shall cast their trail over our evening skies; we may understand the laws of stratification well enough to judge where lies the strain of silver, and where nature has hidden her virgin gold; we may be able to tell the story of departed nations and conquering chieftains, who have added pages of tears and blood to the world's history—but our education is deficient if we are perfectly ignorant how to guide the little feet that are springing up so gladly in our path, and to see in undeveloped possibilities gold more fine than the pavements of Heaven and gems more precious than the foundations of the holy city. Marriage should not be a blind rushing together of tastes and fancies, a mere union of fortunes or an affair of convenience; it should be a 'tie that only love and truth should weave and nothing but death should part.

Foundation Stones.—Marriage between two youthful and loving hearts means the laying of the foundation stones of a new home, and the woman who helps erect that home should be careful not to build it above the reeling brain of a drunkard, or the weakened fibre of a debauchee. If it be folly for a merchant to send an argosy, laden with the richest treasures, at midnight on a moonless sea, without a rudder, compass, or guide, is it not madness for a woman to trust her future happiness, and the welfare of the dear children who may yet nestle in her arms and make music and sunshine around her fireside, in the unsteady hands of a characterless man, too lacking in self-respect and self-control to hold the helm and rudder of his own life; who drifts where he ought to steer, and only lasts when he ought to live?

A Good Character.—The moment the crown of motherhood falls on the brow of a young wife, God gives her a new interest in the welfare of the home and the good of society. If hitherto she has been content to trip through life a light-hearted girl, or to tread amid the halls of wealth and fashion the gayest of the gay, life holds for her now a high and noble service. She must be more than the child of pleasure or the devotee of fashion. Her work is grandly constructive. A helpless and ignorant babe lies smiling in her arms. God has trusted her with a child, and it is her privilege to help that child develop the most precious thing a man or woman can possess on earth, and that is a good character. Moth may devour our finest garments, fire may consume and floods destroy our finest homes, rust may gather on our silver and tarnish our gold, but there is an asbestos that no fire can destroy, a treasure which will be richer for its service and better for its use, and that is a good character.''

A Single Standard.—''I hold that no woman loves

social purity as it deserves to be loved and valued, if she cares for the purity of her daughters and not her sons; who would gather her dainty robes from contact with the fallen woman and yet greet with smiling lips and clasp with warm and welcoming hands the author of her wrong and ruin. How many mothers to-day shrink from a double standard for society which can ostracise a woman and condone the offense of the man? How many mothers say within their hearts, 'I intend to teach my boy to be as pure in his life, as chaste in his conversation, as the young girl that sits at my side encircled in the warm clasp of loving arms?' How many mothers strive to have their boys shun the gilded saloon as they would the den of a deadly serpent? Not the mother who thoughtlessly sends her child to the saloon for a beverage to make merry with her friends. How many mothers teach their boys to shrink in horror from the fascinations of women, not as God made them, but as sin has degraded them?

Ruined Manhood.—If you and I could walk through the wards of various hospitals at home and abroad, perhaps we would find hundreds, it may be thousands, of young men awaiting death as physical wrecks, having burned the candle of their lives at both ends. Were we to bend over their dying couches with pitying glances, and question them of their lives, perhaps numbers of them could tell sad stories of careless words from thoughtless lips that tainted their imaginations and sent their virus through their lives; of young eyes, above which God has made the heavens so eloquent in His praise, and the earth around so poetic in His ideas, turning from the splendor of the magnificent sunsets or glorious early dawns, and finding allurement in the dreadful fascinations of sin, or learning to gloat over impure pictures and vile literature. Then, later on, perhaps many of them could say, 'The first time I went to a house where there were revelry and song, and the dead were there and I knew it not, I went with men who were older than myself; men who should have shown me how to avoid the pitfalls which lie in the path of the young, the tempted, the inexperienced, taught me to gather the flowers of sin, that blossom around the borders of hell.'

Wise Mothers.—Suppose we dared to question a little further, not from idle curiosity, but for the sake of getting, from the dying, object lessons for the living, and say, 'God gave you, an ignorant child, into the hands of a mother. Did she never warn you of your dangers, and teach you how to avoid them?' How many could truthfully say, 'My mother was wise enough to teach me and faithful enough to warn me'? If the cholera or yellow fever were raging in any part of this city, and to enter that section meant peril to health and life, what mother would permit her child to walk carelessly through a district where pestilence was breathing its bane upon the morning air and distilling its poison upon the midnight dews? And yet, when boys go from the fireside into the arena of life, how many ever go there forewarned and forearmed against the soft seductions of vice, against moral conditions which are worse than 'fever, plague and palsy, and madness *all* combined?'

Ante-natal Life.—Among the things I would present for the enlightenment of mothers are attention to the laws of heredity and environment. Mrs. Winslow, in a paper on social purity, speaks of a package of letters she received from a young man of talent, good education, and a strong desire to live a pure and useful life.   In boyhood he had ignorantly ruined his health, and, when he resolved to rise above his depressed condition, his own folly, his heredity and environment, weighed him down like an incubus.   His appeals, she says, are most touching.   He says: 'If you cannot help me, what can I do?   My mother cursed me with illegitimacy and hereditary insanity.   I had left only the alternative of suicide and madness.'   A fearful legacy!   For stolen money and slandered character we may make reparation, but the opportunity of putting the right stamp on an ante-natal life, if once gone, is gone forever; and there never was an angel of God, however bright, terrible, or strong he may be, who was ever strong enough to roll away the stone from the grave of a dead opportunity.

Heredity.—Would it not be well for us women to introduce into all of our literary circles, for the purpose of gaining knowledge, topics on this subject of heredity and the influence of good and bad conditions upon the home life of the race, and study this subject in the light of science for our own and the benefit of others?   For instance, may we not seriously ask the question, Can a mother or a father be a habitual tippler, or break God's law of social purity, and yet impart to their children, at the same time, abundant physical vitality and strong moral fibre?   Can a father dash away the reins of moral restraint, and, at the same time, impart strong will power to his offspring?

Aristocracy.—Men may boast of the aristocracy of blood; they may glory in the aristocracy of talent, and be proud of the aristocracy of wealth, but there is an aristocracy which must ever outrank them all, and that is the aristocracy of character.

"The work of the mothers of our race is grandly

constructive. It is for us to build about the wreck and ruin of the past more stately temples of thought and action. Some races have been overthrown, dashed to pieces and destroyed; but to-day the world is needing, fainting, for something better than the results of arrogance, aggressiveness and indomitable power. We need mothers who are capable of being character builders, patient, loving, strong, and true, whose homes will be an uplifting power in the race.

Need of the Hour.—This one of the greatest needs of the hour. No race can afford to neglect the enlightenment of its mothers. If you would have a clergy without virtue or morality, a manhood without honor, and a womanhood frivolous, mocking and ignorant, neglect the education of your daughters. But if, on the other hand, you would have strong men, virtuous women, and good homes, then enlighten your women, so that they may be able to bless their homes by the purity of their lives, the tenderness of their hearts, and the strength of their intellects.

Science of a True Life.—From schools and colleges your children may come well versed in ancient lore and modern learning, but it is for us to learn and teach, within the shadow of our own homes, the highest and best of all sciences, the science of a true life. When the last lay of the minstrel shall die upon his ashy lips, and the sweetest numbers of the poet cease to charm his death-dulled ear; when the eye of the astronomer shall be too dim to mark the path of worlds that roll in light and power on high; and when all our earthly knowledge has performed for us its mission, and we are ready to lay aside our environments as garments we have outworn and outgrown: if we have learned the science of a true life, we may rest assured that this acquirement will go with us through the valley and shadow of death, only to grow lighter and brighter through the eternities."

MRS. MARGARET WASHINGTON, TUSKEGEE, ALA.

Mrs. Washington is one of the ablest leaders of woman's meetings of her race. See sketch, Chapter XIV.

National Meeting for 1897.—The National meeting of the colored women for 1897 was held September 15, in Nashville, Tennessee. The meeting was the most representative and enthusiastic yet held. All sections of the country were represented by the best, brightest and most intellectual women of the race. We are glad to see that even in this city of the South the whites took more interest in this convention than in any previous convention held.

Fourth Meeting.—This is the fourth national assembly of women of African descent for the purpose of improving their social condition. It is estimated that the Association has a membership of ten thousand. Previous meetings have excited a widespread interest in the work. At a meeting a year ago the following five points were discussed: Improvement of the home life among the colored people; industrial improvement of the girls; better and more practical schools for girls; temperance; abolishment of the convict lease system. There is not a phase of the many questions and reforms that are of special interest to women that has not commanded the earnest attention and support of the colored women's organizations. There has been a stirring and quickening among colored women of a sense of responsibility for whatever evil there is in the social life of the race.

Finding One's Place.—It is certainly no unimportant .ning to witness how readily the colored women of the country find their work and are going about it with the directness and single heartedness of true apostles of reform. They have faith in themselves and the sure and virtuous outcome of all for which they pray, plan and work.

President's Address.—The able address of the President of the National Association, Mrs. Mary Church Terrell, should be read by every colored woman. We have space for but a few short extracts:

Not Discouraged.—It is not because we are discouraged at the progress made by our people that we have uttered the cry of alarm which has called together this band of earnest women assembled here tonight. In the unprecedented advancement made by the Negro since his emancipation, we take great pride, and extract therefrom both courage and hope. From a condition of dense ignorance but thirty years ago, we have advanced so far in the realms of knowledge and letters as to have produced scholars and authors of no mean repute.

Progress.—Penniless as a race but a short time ago, we have among us today a few men of wealth, and multitudes who own their own homes and make comfortable livings. We therefore challenge any other race to present a record more creditable, and show a progress more wonderful than that made by the ex-slaves of the United States of America, and that, too, in spite of prejudice, proscription and persecution against the like of which no other people has ever had to contend in the history of the world.

Weakness and Defects.—And yet, while rejoicing in our steady march onward and upward to the best and highest things of life, we are nevertheless painfully mindful of our weaknesses and defects. While we know the Negro is no worse than other races equally poor, equally ignorant and equally oppressed, we would nevertheless see him lay aside the sins that do so easily beset him, and come forth clothed in all those attributes of mind and graces of character that stamp the real man. To compass this end through the simplest, swiftest, surest methods, the colored women have organized themselves into this association, whose power for good, let us hope, will be as enduring as it is unlimited.

A Mission to Perform.—Believing that it is only through the home that a people can become really good and truly great, the N. A. C. W. shall enter that sacred domain to inculcate right principles of living and correct false views of life. Homes, more homes, pure homes, better homes, is the text upon which our sermons to the masses must be preached. So long as the majority of a people call that place home in which the air is foul, the manners bad and the morals worse, just so long is this so-called home a menace to health, a breeder of vice, and the abode of crime. Not alone upon the inmates of these hovels are the awful consequences of their filth and immorality visited, but upon the heads of those who sit calmly by and make no effort to stem the tide of disease and vice will vengeance as surely fall.

Mothers' Congress.—If the women of the dominant race, with all the centuries of education, culture and refinement back of them, with all their wealth of opportunity ever present with them, if these women recently felt the necessity of calling a mothers' congress, that they might be enlightened as to the best method of rearing children and conducting their homes, how much more do the women of our own race, from whom the shackles of slavery have just fallen, need information on the same subjects? Let us have a mothers' congress in every community in which our women can be found.

Self-Respect.—Among other practical suggestions as to their duty in the home, let us urge upon our mothers the necessity of increasing the self-respect of our children. Let the reckless, ill-advised, and oftentimes brutal, methods of punishing children be everywhere condemned. Let us teach our mothers that by punishing children inhumanely, they destroy their pride, crush their spirit, and convert them into hardened culprits whom it will be impossible later on to reach or touch in any way at all.   More than any other race at present in this country, we should strive to implant feelings of self-respect and pride in our children, whose spirits are crushed and whose hearts are saddened enough by the indignities from which, as victims of an unreasonable, cruel prejudice, it is impossible to shield them.''

MRS. MARY CHURCH TERRELL,
President National Association of Colored Women, 1896-97.

Colored Youth.—"The colored youth is vicious, we are told, and statistics showing the multitude of our boys and girls who fill the penitentiaries and crowd the jails appall and discourage us. Side by side with these facts and figures of crime, I would have presented and pictured the miserable hovels from which these youthful criminals come. Crowded into alleys, many of them the haunts of vice, few if any of them in a proper sanitary condition, most of them fatal to mental or moral growth, and destructive of healthful, physical development as well, thousands of our children have wretched heritage indeed.

Work in Homes.—"It is, therefore, into the home, sisters of the association, that we must go, filled with all the zeal and charity which such a mission demands. To the children of the race we owe, as women, a debt which can never be paid, until herculean efforts are made to rescue them from evil and shame, for which they are in no way responsible. Listen to the cry of the children, my sisters. Upon you they depend for the light of knowledge, and the blessing of a good example. As an organization of women, surely nothing can be nearer our hearts than the children, many of whose lives, so sad and dark, we brighten and bless."

CHAPTER IX.

PROGRESS IN INDUSTRIES.

FARMS AND HOMES—SKILLED LABOR.

Progress in Industries.—When we remember that thirty-five years ago the Negro was in slavery it is certainly remarkable to note the progress made in all lines of industry. Keeping in mind some of the difficulties the Negro has had to strive against the progress made in industries is commendable. All throughout the South are found men who stand at the head in the various lines of business. Be it said to the credit of the colored people, and greatly to their benefit, that the race has in its possession a sound means of displaying its progress.

United Efforts.—While much has been done in all lines of business, yet very much more remains to be done before the Negro holds that place in business to which he is entitled. In order to accomplish what should be done in this respect it is necessary that there be united efforts on the part of the race to assist one another in every business enterprise. Wherever men of the Negro race attempt to increase the advantages of the race there should be found those who stand by them and support them. With the full confidence and patronage of the people the Negro race will have rich merchants and capitalists carrying on rich business enterprises in every section of the country, that will demand the respect and recognition of the world.

No More Speedy Remedy.—Let the race continue in the progress that it has made the last thirty years; let the Negro push out into different enterprises and

ALLEN UNIVERSITY, COLUMBIA, S. C.

assist in controlling large business enterprises, and this alone will be worth more than any other remedy in suppressing and eradicating prejudice on account of color and blotting out the iniquitous legislation against the race in the South, wiping every unjust law from the statutes.

A Progressive Age.—We live in a progressive age; here we are in the evening of the nineteenth century with all the modern inventions and discoveries of the telegraph, telephone and electricity. There is no reason why the race should remain any longer in the dark. In unity there is strength, and when the colored people stand shoulder to shoulder, advancing the standard of the race in all industries, then will the colored man's prospects in business be as bright as those of the Anglo-Saxon.

Race Pride.—In order that progress in these lines shall be made it is necessary that the colored men everywhere encourage one another, and when a colored man progresses in business not to envy his prosperity, but rather to be proud of him and his success, throwing away envy, jealousy and race hatred. Race pride must be cultivated. As the different nationalities, Irish, Jews, Germans and other people are recognized and respected only as they are united and held together, so it is essential that the Negroes should stand united in helping one another by their speech, by pen, by vote, and by money.

Consumers.—The Negro race is a race of consumers, and it is essential that it be a race of producers. When it reaches this point, that the colored man is able to manufacture as well as consume, he will have the respect of all. The industrial schools of the South are doing more in this respect, in bringing up the masses to a realization of their privileges, than any other agency.

Brains and Labor.—If the Negro is to succeed it is essential that in the first place he dignify labor, and in the second place that he put brains into labor.

Thrift and Industry.—Rev. J. E. Edwards, D. D., a white man of learning and exalted character, says: "Hand in hand with the progress of education among the Negro population of Petersburg, Virginia, there has been a corresponding progress in industry, thrift, morals and manners of the race. Their ability to live at less expense than the poor whites has enabled the more provident of them to lay by a larger surplus from their earnings, and, as a result, they are buying lots, and in some instances putting up comfortable and tastefully constructed residences. The marriage relation is recognized by them as of more binding obligation than formerly, both in its civil and moral respects. The family idea is a healthful growth. Self-respect and self reliance are on the advance.

Improving in Morals.—They are property owners, shop keepers, manufacturers, contractors, master builders, mechanics and laborers, competing fairly and with out let or hindrance with the whites. They are constantly improving in morals, in thrift and industry, and are rapidly advancing in civilization, refinement and learning.

Peaceable Community.—The present population of Petersburg may be put down in round numbers at 22,000 —say 10,000 whites and 12,000 colored—giving the Negroes 2,000 majority in the whole population. At the ballot-box the Negroes can poll a larger number than the whites. But with this predominance of the

Negro population we have the most gratifying spectacle presented of one of the most orderly, quiet and peaceable communities anywhere to be found in all these broad lands. There is, comparatively, but little litigation in the civil courts of the corporation; and the police record will compare favorably with that of any city of the same population in the whole country. The Mayor's court is often held without a case, even of misdemeanor. Felonies are infrequent, and of those that do occur, which are sent up to higher tribunals, the parties are quite as often white as colored. Disturbances of the peace are not more common among the Negroes than among the whites. Life, limb and property are as secure and as well protected in Petersburg by day and night as in any city of 22,000 population in the United States of America.

No Idle Boasting.—The appeal from any question of these facts is to our records—police, civil and criminal; and when it is remembered that there are 12,000 Negroes and only 10,000 whites in the city, the record is as creditable as it is really wonderful. It is very much questioned whether a parallel can be found in all this country.

Testimonials of Hampton Students.—The following items taken from "Twenty-two years' work at Hampton," being the testimony of graduates of that school, are worthy of consideration. If any one is unable to judge whether the Negro is rising or not, the reliable testimony of these graduates ought to decide the question:

James A. Fields, Hampton, Virginia.—"All things considered, the condition of the colored people is good. They are rapidly improving in religion, intelligence, and morals. My property consists mostly of land and house, in value six thousand dollars. I have only one child, the finest boy in Christendom."

David D. Weaver, Philadelphia, Pennsylvania.—"I employ more help and do more work than any other colored shoemaker in Philadelphia, and have had the lead for five years. I am doing as much for my people as I could in the school room. The colored people are progressing; they work. The money is made and the money is spent. The greatest barrier is that they do not look beyond to-day. They expect every day to take care of itself. With such short calculations they are often found wanting. There are many exceptions to this rule. There are men here who are doing good business and making great headway in the world."

Lewis Peyton, Wabash, Indiana.—"The intellectual religious, moral, industrious and economical status of the people varies much in different sections of the country. Where they are settled down and have their homes and regular pursuits, they are prosperous, and every way in a prospering condition."

George F. Calloway, Halifax County, Virginia.—"In this section of the state our people show a decided improvement. As a rule, they are farmers. Some own their homes, and a few own large tracts of land varying from forty to twelve hundred acres."

William P. Henry, Berlin, Maryland.—In this community, which I believe was one of the worst places below Mason's and Dixon's line for prejudice and Negro persecution, the Negro people are grasping every effort that will lift them higher in the intellectual, moral and social scale. They are generally sober and industrious, and they adhere strictly to economy, through which the rude hut and log cabin are rapidly being transformed into neat cottages, with their domestic improvements."

L. L. Ivy, Danville, Virginia.—"The colored people in this vicinity are improving slowly but surely, getting little homes, and making great sacrifices to do as other people."

NEGRO FARMER'S ONE-ROOM LOG CABIN.

William B. Weaver, Sassafras, Virginia.—"The colored people in this neighborhood are industrious and temperate. Some accumulate property and have good homes, and are interested in the work of education."

R. H. Matthews, Pensacola, Florida.—"On account of the large number of dram-shops and the tendency of our people to patronize them, their condition is not what we might desire. They are badly divided and will seldom unite for any public good; this is on account of the narrow and ignorant spirit engendered in our churches by ignorant ministers. Notwithstand-

ing, there is gradual progress.   Hard work, honesty
and frugality are the means by which we are to rise.
I own property in Columbus, Georgia, and in Pensacola worth three thousand dollars."

**Robert H. Hamilton, one of the Hampton Student
Singers, now Assisting in the Normal at Tuskegee.**—
"To the thoughtful Negro there is a great deal in the
condition of his people to make him sigh.   Such a
dense mass of humanity steeped in ignorance!   Who
can foresee the danger and bloodshed that may yet
overtake this sunny land?   While these men and women
have the minds of children, they have the passions of
age.   However, as dark as things may be, they are not
so bad as they were.   It is fair to say the Negro of the
South is rising."

Mrs. William Day, Greensboro, North Carolina.—
"The general condition of our people in Greensboro is
good.   There are few renters now among good mechanics.   We have good schools and churches; one
colored doctor.   Our people have certainly improved
themselves and are second to no other town in this
respect."

Mrs. F. Calloway, Lynchburg, Virginia.—"When I
first came to this place there were not many people
owning property.   They were renting from their masters or from some other white man, paying as much
for a cabin a year as it would take to buy an acre of
land.   Some of the houses, actually, were not good
enough for horses to stay in.   Today for two or three
miles around you will find colored people owning
from two to twenty acres of land, horses, cows, farming implements, and raising their own bread.   When
we were married we did not own anything; now we

have two and one-half acres of land and a comfortable little house to live in."

Mrs. George E. Rumsey, Thomas Run, Maryland.— "The majority of the colored people at Thomas Run are property-holders, and are improving their lands considerably. My husband has a farm, and owns thirty-three acres of land."

C. R. Creekmur, Deep Creek, Virginia.—"I own a house and lot with four and one-half acres of land, farming utensils, etc. The people are poor and ignorant. There are, however, signs of improvement. Several have purchased homes and they are working nicely in that direction."

Mrs. Mary Owen, Warrentown, North Carolina.— "Large numbers of Negroes here own homes. Some have nice large houses, others have small but neat ones. They are, as a rule, making rapid progress."

Mrs. Briscoe, Mecklenburg, North Carolina.—"The general condition of the Negro people is improving. There are many who do not take as much interest in bettering their condition as they should, but there are many who have made marked progress in business and intellectual matters."

E. D. Stewart, Farmville, Virginia.—"The condition of the colored peope is hopeful. They are accumulating property and educating their children."

J. B. Tynes, Smithville, Virginia.—"The colored people in the main are financially embarrassed, but here and there are signs of improvement."

Mrs. Martin, Carlisle, Ohio.—"We own property valued at about three thousand dollars. I do not find the majority of the colored people so far advanced as I expected, considering the advantages they have had compared with the colored people of the South."

Frances L. Butt, Germantown, Pennsylvania.— "The colored people are improving financially, but the young girls are not doing well. Their standard is low."

C. E. Vanharler.—"The people are slowly climbing the ladder of prosperity."

Julia E. Coles, Halifax County, Virginia.—"In some places the people are very well situated, owning a small tract of land with a good house on it. In ——— they are in a worse condition than in any other place. The people are very poor, living in houses no better than sheds, and with the poorest kind of food. This is true of the whites as well as the colored."

J. W. Brown, Winchester, Virginia.—"The Negroes in this section are industrious and independent, and, although some spend the greater part of their hard earnings foolishly, they have money enough to secure for themselves comfortable homes, which the majority have. The homes differ with the ambition of the owner. Their cost ranges from one hundred dollars up into the thousands. Some own farms of from fifty to two hundred acres. The richest colored man in the county is said to be worth more than fifty thousand dollars. I do not think you will find a dozen beggars in our town, and the Negro population is over two thousand."

Hope and Progress.—The best hope of the South is in the manufacture of her raw material. The best hope of the Negro is in his application to the various callings of industry. The future commercial greatness of the South depends upon the measure in which she manufactures her iron, wood, and cotton into articles of merchandise, and the happiness and well being of the Negro depend upon the part that he elects to play in this drama of industrial progress. Will he, by careful training, fit himself as an artisan and thus contribute to his country's progress and to his own uplifting, or will he scorn the homely callings of industry and devote himself to college lore and starvation? The South will one day be the nation's workshop. Whence will come her workmen? In the solution of this problem is wrapped up the hope and progress of the Negro.

Dignity and Nobility of Manual Labor.—When the colored citizen can demonstrate his usefulness as a member of society, his rise to a higher plane of liberty and independence is assured. Industrial training will help students to appreciate the dignity and nobility of manual labor; will make them self-reliant, competent to lay out work for others, to oversee the erection of a dwelling house, a school house, a meeting house; will make them industrial leaders, and, in a modest way, capitalists, enabling them to own a house, a farm, working with the hands in the intervals of preaching or teaching; and all this not for themselves alone—they should never lose sight of the idea of service, that he who would be first must become the servant of all.

In the Business World.—If the Negro is to maintain his place in the business world as an industrial and commercial factor, it behooves him to put on his thinking cap; no force without will help him. He must rise, if he rises at all, through his own efforts. He is not wanted in many of the avenues of opportunity and will be shut out if he does not get to thinking for himself. The politician has no use for him excepting before election. If he would maintain his place, he must, of necessity, think for himself.

Half Free.—Booker T. Washington, that wise leader

SAW-MILL MEN OF TUSKEGEE INDUSTRIAL INSTITUTE.

of the colored race, never spoke more truly and pithily than when he said: "The black man who cannot let love and sympathy go out to the white man is but half free. The white man who would close the shop or factory against a black man seeking an opportunity to earn an honest living, is but half free."

Negro Labor.—Although the Negro is practically barred from the great trade alliances of the land, and denied a place in the industrial army which he would so naturally and capably fill, the race is slowly edging into labor equalities and must, ere long, be counted a factor. The latest movement serving to bring Negro labor to a permanent stage of discussion is the introduction of black labor into the cotton mills of the South. Charleston Cotton Mills have recently introduced Negro labor with excellent results. The Negro hands are proving entirely satisfactory. It seems that colored operators were employed successfully in several mills before the war, but since then the Negro was denied an entrance. This will open a new field for the Negro. Besides this, all over the South colored men are being employed in mechanical pursuits, as carpenters, masons, wheelrights, engineers, while colored women are employed as cooks, dressmakers, etc. This predicts a brighter day for the colored race, and if the race is true to its calling and exhibits true merit by rising and showing proficiency in all these lines, the day is not far distant when Negro labor in the South or in any other section of our country will be in as great demand as the labor of any other race.

Fears Aroused.—The danger that is feared by some who have given any thought to the Charleston experiment is that the colored operators will succeed so well there that they will gradually supplant the white opera-

tives in Southern mills, and that their success in Charleston will result in the establishment of many Negro cotton
mills in the South by New England capitalists. We
believe that the Charleston "experiment" will succeed
—we are told that it is succeeding; but we do not
believe that its most substantial success will greatly
interfere with the labor problem in the Southern mills.
It probably would result in the establishment of many
cotton mills in the black belt of the South, but it would
not, for years, if ever, result in the displacement of
white labor.

They will work the kind of hands they can hire at the
lowest wages and get good results. The agitation of
the Negro-in-the-cotton-mill question began among the
Southern mill managers. No Northern owned and conducted mill has been mentioned in connection with
Negro help.

Capable.—There is little reason to doubt that Negroes
will prove capable of performing the work required of
them in the cotton mills. With white superiors to
direct they can easily perform the duties of mill hands
in the manufacture of the coarser goods of cotton
cloth. Negro slaves, it is alleged, were successfully
employed in the cotton mills.

Prospect.—What a field is presented for speculation
as to the possibilities in this contrast! What if the
success of the experiment should give such an impetus
to the cotton mill industry in this city that soon not
only the spindles of the old mill would be humming
night and day under the inspiration of a happy, contented and economic labor, but other mills would start
up, giving hope, ambition and employment to thousands
more of our at present idle and non-productive surplus
colored population, who are a burden upon the com-

PICKING COTTON.

munity instead of a blessing! Does it not follow, as the night the day, that more money would be put into circulation; more stores would be given patrons; more business men and clerks would be needed, as well as that increase of forces in every other of the departments of life preferred by white men which necessarily follows an increase in the volume of business and of the productive population of the community? The prospect is a pleasing one. Let us hope that at last we have found the true philosopher's stone, that with its magic touch will bring about the renewed prosperity and business revival which we have so long hoped for in vain.

A Business Education.—Rev. A. A. Whitman says: "We need to begin in a business way right at the bottom and grow up from the ground. We need to know how to make a living. That education which fails to fit one to do this fails to educate. He who has not the business parts and qualifications in him to earn a living is a dependent—a pauper, as it were—and undesirable as a citizen, regardless of any amount of useless information that may be found lying around loose in his cranium. The Negro, the masses, must come back to the ground. Business is the root and the bottom of the education he needs now. The Negro must be found taking a helping part—lending a helping hand in the exercises and business of his day; thus making himself needed by the state. This is the root of the whole matter."

Tilling the Soil.—Man's independence grows up out of the soil. It is never a fungus. The Negro must be trained to know how to intelligently and successfully till the soil; and, what is more, he must learn to love the occupation. He must know the farm, the orchard

and the vineyard.   He must see that his farm is a duke-
dom.   He must find that stalwart independence comes
up with his cotton and corn.   The landscape, beautified and ennobled by the touch of care and endeared by
the fond and exalted idea of possession, must be to him

PARKER MODEL HOME.
Made by Tuskegee Students.

the rallying point for his patriotism.   Cincinnatus,
Washington, Lincoln, Grant, mightiest of earth, dignified their lives by tilling the soil.   The Negro must
see this.

Way-Marks.—Pastures filled with horses and cattle; ample barns and great farm houses are grander way-marks for civilization than all the monuments ever reared on the fields of battle. Back to this idea the Negro must come and make a start. It must be taught into his brains to see this truth.

Waiting for Something to Do.—The man who reads Greek and Latin while he sits in idleness waiting for something to do is an inferior man; while he who tills the soil is a sovereign, though he knows little of books. The Negro must not be afraid of the clouds; he must come out of the shade. He must learn that there is more music in a hand saw than in a guitar, and a great deal better pay. He must feel that it is no disgrace to go to work after he has gone to school. He must understand that a liberal education is as valuable to him who tills the soil as it is to the professions.

Skilled Mechanics.—Next to tilling the soil, the Negro must learn the value of being skilled in mechanics. He must learn to mingle his thoughts with his labor. He must be taught to see that if he can chop wood and earn one dollar per day, he may, by using saw and chisel, earn twice that amount and work no harder than before; and again by using steam and lathe and scroll he can earn ten times that amount and still work no harder.

Practical Education.—This, we understand, is practical education, to enlighten the citizen first concerning his nearest environments—earth, air, water, wood, stone, metal—first become acquainted with these and then come on with your theorems, your hypotheses, your abstractions and such. First the dinner pot and the loom, and then the beatitudes—poetry, painting and the like.

Higher Education.—After a moral and industrial training those who have the talent, the means, and the leisure, may pursue their studies into the province of higher education, language, literature, the arts and the sciences. All hold out brilliant inducements for such as strive to find "room at the top."

What the South Especially Needs is Negro farmers who study the best methods of tilling the soil, and are alert to find the most improved method and best implements the market can supply. No profession is higher or more honorable than that of farming. A farmer supports the people.

Go to the Farm.—As Horace Greeley advised young men to go west, so we would advise young people in cities and towns who cannot find anything to do, often compelled to beg or to steal in order to live, we would advise such to go to the farm, for there they can make an independent living for themselves.

Buy a Farm.—By saving a little money a small farm at least, can be bought, and by cultivating it carefully more can be added from time to time.

The European emigrants come to this country and settle on homestead lands and soon become independent. Why should not the Negro do the same if he is willing to lay aside extravagance and expensive habits and devote himself to industry, economy and frugality. There is no reason why the average Negro should not have a home of his own. Young men, aim to have a home of your own.

Sound Advice.—A typical Louisa county, Va., Negro tobacco raiser was asked very lately how he managed to beat all his neighbors making tobacco, as was evidenced by his having always led them in prices on the market. Here is the secret in his vernacular:

"What I does make, I makes de bes' de lan' will fotch. I keeps puttin' back de manure on de same lan'. I makes dat manure myself, en I don't spread out none like some folks does, who ain't never satisfied 'ceptin' dey allers plants more'n dey can ten' to. No matter how terbarker is sellin' I gits to de top price—it's allus $10 to $12 roun'. Noc, sah, I ain't neber studyin' 'bout spreadin' out like some folks, 'case I dun seen um try dat, an' my four acres beats der'n all de time. Dey plant more'n double as much agin as me—an' more, too. In course I know how to make fine sun-cured terbaker, and I ain't trustin' dat to nobody else, nuther.

"Nor, sah, I ain't nuver grumble 'bout de price yit—do I see plenty uv dem what duz, an' I ain't never spec' to crap more'n dem four acres—sometimes a little less dan dat. I ain't nuver hear nobody complain 'bout my terbaker yit—allus 'pear to suit dem what buys it, an' dey want more. Yas, I got 150 akers size dese four, but dese four is dat rich as when I fust started, and richer, too."

We wish we could emphasize this good advice still more strongly. What the market wants is *quality*, not *quantity*. This applies to everything that the farm produces. The way to get the prices that are paying ones is to follow the old "darky's advice, to make the best the land will make, by heavy and appropriate fertilization, on only such an area of land as can be properly prepared and carefully and constantly attended to, and then to give the greatest attention to the crop, so as to make a type that the market calls for. You must please the market, and the market will then please you.

Advancement.—Professor Glenn, state school commissioner of Georgia, in an able address before the State Teachers' Association, at Macon, recently said, in

RESIDENCE OF ALBERT NASH, BARBER, ATLANTA, GA.

speaking of the advancement of the colored people in America, that in improvement along all lines, in the same length of time, they stood without a peer, either in or out of history. He spoke of how they had reduced their illiteracy more than forty per cent in thirty-two years, etc. He told how Georgia's colored citizens alone had made returns for $16,000,000 worth of property, and, said he: "If they are as sharp about giving in property as the white man, and they may be, instead of owning $16,000,000, they really own in this state alone about $32,000,000 worth of property." What is true of Georgia is true of the colored people in all parts of the United States.

Worth of Property.—The colored people in the United States own today more than $325,000,000 worth of property. They have about 27,000 school teachers, more than 1,000 lawyers, and nearly 2,000 physicians that have graduated from some of the best schools in this and other countries. They have 3,068,822 members of the church, scattered among the various denominations, including the Catholic church. These are led by thousands of able and well-educated ministers, including about twenty or twenty-five bishops. About 5,000,000 of the people can read. These, I think, are worthy achievements for the colored people during one generation, when we remember that they started empty-handed, empty-headed and with empty pockets.

Looking Upward.—Of course we have had our trials, tribulations and hindrances, and our many drawbacks. These have come from all directions—from within as well as from without—but by God's help, and with the steady efforts of a few we find ourselves today far up the hill toward the city of success.

A Changed Man.—The time was when, if you should

meet a colored man on the streets, you could soon place him, so far as his business and intellectual capacity was concerned, without asking a single question. But that is by no means the case to-day. When you pass down the street to-day and meet a colored man, he may be a wealthy merchant, a retired business man with his thousands of dollars; he may be a prosperous farmer owning his plantation, horses, mules and cattle; he may be a banker, a bishop, an educated minister of the gospel, with all the degrees that belong to that high calling; he may be principal of a city school, professor of Greek, Latin, Hebrew, German, French, mathematics, or science, in some college, or he may be president of some great university or president of a young republic in some part of the world; he may be a lawyer, dentist, physician, pharmacist, or a telegraph operator; he may be a man such as I have named here —a man that is both an honor and a help to his city, country and state.

At Progressive Door.—This is the colored man that is standing at the progressive door of American civilization today and asks for a man's chance—for an American citizen's chance in the race of life—this is the colored man that asks for, and should have, a first-class railroad ride for a first-class railroad ticket. I hope Christian civilization, right and justice will soon permeate the hearts of all the American people to the extent that they may see the ten millions of colored American citizens as they really are today and not as they were a generation ago.

Atlanta's Colored Representatives.— Dr. Butler says: "Atlanta has two oil dealers, one laundry, several good coal and wood yards, seven or eight tailoring establishments, one creamery, one real estate

17 Progress.

dealer, one insurance agent, four undertakers, one hotel, and restaurants and ice-cream saloons innumerable. We have a large number of grocery stores, well stocked and well patronized. It is impossible for me to call to mind all of our contractors, blacksmiths, carpenters, brick-masons, and stone-masons. We have several owners of hack lines. We have a large number of railway mail clerks and letter-carriers. We have one clerk in a white jewelry store. He is well thought of by everybody and draws a large trade to that firm from his people. This is a good example for others to follow. We have one first-class artist who has been working for one white firm for more than fifteen years. We have one sewing-machine representative, one plumber who has passed the required examination and received his license; we have two cleaning and dyeing establishments; we have five public schools, with forty teachers; we have six colleges and seminaries, in which are many colored professors; we have four well-stocked and well-equipped drug stores, several pharmacists, seven physicians and two dentists. Besides, there are many dressmakers, milliners, slaters, tinners, and hundreds of other good professional businesses that I have not the time to mention. These are the accomplishment of a colored population of about forty thousand. I came near forgetting our three lawyers, who are doing a good practice. We also have a Young Men's Christian Association in the city and one in each of our colleges; we have eight organizations of the Woman's Christian Temperance Union, all doing much good work. We also have the Atlanta Woman's Club, of colored women, one of the best and most active of its kind in the country. We have the United Friendly Society, an

RESIDENCE OF JOHN T. SCHELL, ATLANTA, GA.

organization that is doing much good work among our people, and our women have an industrial club which is turning in an excellent profit to its members. This is only a bird's-eye view of what our people are doing. In conclusion, I would say, that Atlanta is the home of the following newspapers: The Southern Age, The Voice of Mission, The Gospel Trumpet, The Southern Christian Recorder, The Social Gleaner, and The Paris Visitor. I refer to these things to show our friends that we are up and doing for ourselves, our children, and our country.

'Forest Home' is the name of D. T. Howard's country home, eight miles from Atlanta, on the Peach-tree road. It is indeed a beautiful place, with groves, lakes, and fruit trees of all kinds. There are five springs on the property, and one of them is very valuable. The lakes have been stocked with fish. He has ordered 5,000 more fish from Washington, D. C., to place in his lakes. He also has a number of fine Jersey cattle and many fine fowls out there. D. T. Howard has quite an interesting family, and all of them take a special interest in their country home. This is what I have often advised my people to do—get homes in the country and raise country produce and furnish this and other markets. The money we spend for a small 25x100 foot lot here in the city, or any city, for that matter, would buy from ten to fifty acres of good land in the country. Talking about gold and silver, there is plenty of it out in the country, under the soil—all we have to do is to dig for it. It is there for the truck farmer; it is there for the florist; and it is there for the scientific farmer; and our people can do all of these things if they will only apply themselves.''

Items of Interest.—The city government of Philadelphia employs nearly 1,000 colored men. In the bureau of health is David Brown, the oldest employe in the service of the city. He was appointed in 1837, and has held the position ever since. These men receive salaries ranging from $800 to $1,000 and more. There are sixty-one in the police department, one in the fire department, and several clerks, among whom is James F. Needham, a clerk in the tax office. He has held the position twenty-five years at a salary of $1,500. The inspector of gas meters is a colored man. C. J. Perry, the colored councilman, is a clerk in the sheriff's office. He is also editor of the Philadelphia Tribune. This is another proof of how the colored people are laboring for the welfare of their country and for the honor of themselves, by faithfully discharging every duty placed upon them.

The largest silkworm grower in the South is a colored man, S. R. Lowry, near Huntsville, Ala. He took a premium at the New Orleans exposition over several foreign competitors from China, France, Japan and Italy. Mr. Lowry is of the opinion that the culture of silk in the South will supersede that of cotton.

Wiley Jones, of Pine Bluff, Arkansas., is one of the wealthiest colored men in his state, and is said to be the largest blooded-stock breeder of his race. Besides his herds of Durham and Holstein cattle, he has a stable of trotting horses valued at $50,000.

Granville T. Woods, the electrician, mechanical engineer, manufacturer of telephone, telegraph and electrical instruments, was once a day laborer in Springfield, Ill.

There are more than fifty Negro establishments in Atlanta, Ga., representing $100,000 invested in business, giving employment to not less than one hundred persons of the race, and affording them an opportunity to acquire a thorough knowledge of business.

Mr. John W. Wilson is the leading colored clothier of Baltimore, Maryland. He has a good trade, and keeps on hand a full supply of the latest goods.

Mr. Madison Short is one of the most prominent farmers of Surry county, Virginia. He owns a beautiful farm and has some of the finest horses in the state.

There are over 2,000 colored people employed in the executive departments of the government at Washington.

The increase of colored population in the last decade is greater in Arkansas than that of any other state.

Thirty-five Afro-Americans are employed on the police force in Pittsburg, Pa.

Mrs. Alpha V. Miner, of Kansas City, Missouri, has the reputation of being one of the most successful business women of her race in the west. She is quoted at $10,000 and free from debt. She commenced business several years ago as a dressmaker. She now has a dozen or more employes.

Gilchrist Stewart, the great colored creamery man, and dairy scientist of Wisconsin, has just been chosen dairy editor of the Dakota Field and Farm, and elected one of the editorial contributors for the coming year of the Wisconsin "Agriculturist," one of the leading agricultural papers in the country. Mr. Stewart is a graduate of Tuskegee and of the Wisconsin Dairy school. He is rapidly achieving fame and prominence in the agricultural and dairy worlds. He is yet a very young man and the son of T. McCants Stewart of New York.

H. D. Smith is the wealthiest colored man of Greensville county, Virginia. He owns a valuable farm.

At one time he represented his people in the state legislature.

Mr. D. Rowen, a merchant of Texas, after having passed through varied scenes and hardships, finds himself a prosperous merchant of Dallas. He paid taxes on real estate in 1896 valued at $41,000. Mr. Rowen has shown what can be done by a poor boy who is determined to let the world know that he is living in it.

A colored planter now owns one of Jefferson Davis' old plantations in Mississippi.

John T. Schell, one of Atlanta's progressive and assiduous business men, has met with success by facing adversity. Through poverty he has pushed his way, working wherever he was able to find employment. Upon reaching Atlanta he could find no work, but at last succeeded in obtaining employment that hardly paid his expenses, but, continuing this work, he was soon offered a better position. At last he succeeded in gathering enough cash to open a small grocery store, with shoe shop attached. From this time forth success seemed to attend him, until he is to-day one of the wealthiest citizens of that city. A cultured and amiable wife presides over his comfortable and beautiful home, in which four happy children mingle their glad voices. Besides a vast amount of real estate, he owns a well-stocked dry-goods establishment. His residence is, beyond doubt, the largest and handsomest and most complete residence of any colored man in the state. Such houses as these are the monuments the thoughtful men and women of the race are erecting for their children. They are accumulating property and improving themselves along all lines.

W. H. Councill was born in Fayetteville, N. C., in 1848. When nine years old he was carried by slave-

traders to Alabama, where he worked in the cotton
fields until set free as a result of the Civil war. He
attended one of the first schools opened by Northern
teachers at Stevenson, Ala., in 1865.

PROF. W. H. COUNCILL, PH. D.

He was founder, and editor of the *Huntsville Herald*
from 1877 to 1884. He is now president of the Agricultural and Mechanical College, Normal, Ala., which
he organized a quarter of a century ago.

He is an active church-worker and a temperance
advocate.

At his Normal school he is educating native Africans as missionaries to the "Dark Continent."

C. H. Jackson is a very successful grocery and dry goods merchant in Nashville, Tennessee.

Hon. Henry A. Rucker has been appointed collector of internal revenue for the state of Georgia.   Mr. Rucker

HON. H. A. RUCKER, ATLANTA, GEORGIA.

is comparatively a young man, and his appointment gives the greatest satisfaction to his friends. He is one of the ablest men in the state and has the full con-fidence of all who know him. He has had considerable experience as a revenue official and will make a most efficient collector.

Henry Allan Rucker was born in Washington, Wilkes county, Georgia, November 14, 1852. Three months after his birth his parents moved to Kensington, Georgia, residing there for five or six years, and from there to Atlanta, Savannah, Macon, and back to Atlanta in 1866, where he has ever since lived. Soon after returning to Atlanta he entered a school which was opened in the A. M. E. Church on Jenkins street by Northern teachers. This school was afterwards moved to a car box near what was then the famous Walton springs, and again into the building on Houston street, which, ever since its establishment, has been known as Storrs' school. On account of the inability of his parents to maintain him in a day school, he had to seek employment and attend school by night, and finally was compelled to lay aside his books, which he had no opportunity of taking up again, until, by steady application to whatever he could get to do, and by strict frugality, he was again able to take them up in Atlanta University in 1876. By teaching country schools during the summer months and by economizing, he kept himself in this school until 1880, leaving off after finishing his sophomore year to take up the study of homeopathy, which he pursued for one year. During this year he also entered national politics and made a successful race as a Blaine delegate to the national convention which met in Chicago, Illinois, in 1881. He was given an appointment as storekeeper and gauger in the Internal Revenue Service in Georgia. In 1883 he was promoted to a clerkship in the office of the collector, where he remained until shortly after the inauguration of President Cleveland, when a new collector was appointed.

This Democratic collector, on assuming charge of the office, asked Mr. Rucker, "How long have you been in the service?" On being told about four years, he simply said, "You have been in long enough." Four years later, on the inauguration of President Harrison, Mr. Rucker appeared before Secretary Windom, and, in his speech urging a change in the Collector's office of Georgia, repeated this little circumstance and wound up by saying, "Now, Mr. Secretary, this Democratic collector has been in a little over four years, and I, with other Republicans of Georgia, believe he has been in long enough to be removed without delay." At this the Secretary smiled and said: "While this is not poetic language, it is politic, and I'll see that the change is made." In 1880, Mr. Rucker met Major McKinley at Salt Springs, Georgia, where, while shaking hands with the major after his Chautauqua address, he said, "Major, I hope I may have the pleasure of shaking your hand when you are president of the United States." In 1890, in September, large mass meetings of a non-partisan character were being held in Atlanta to nominate a reform city ticket, as municipal officers were getting in a confused condition and taxation was exorbitant and the city's credit was suffering. These mass meetings resulted in a city convention, where Mr. Rucker made the platform the reduction of taxation from one and one-half per cent to one and one-third per cent, and since that time this measure of reduced taxation has become a law and the burdens of the people relieved and the city's credit raised. During the same year Mr. Rucker was called back to an important position in the Internal Revenue Service, discharging his duties honorably until he was again released in consequence of the fortunes of politics by another Democratic collector. In 1895, Mr. Rucker again met Major McKinley in Atlanta. The Major was holding a reception at the time, and as one man after another was introduced to the Major, one of them holding his hand, inquired, "Are you Governor McKinley of Ohio?" and on being modestly informed that he was said, "Well, Governor, you want to be president, and I want to tell you that Georgia is against you." Mr. Rucker, who was standing on the right of the Governor, spoke up at once and said, "Governor, pay no attention to that fellow, you shall have Georgia." He was himself elected one of the delegates to the St. Louis convention, and introduced a resolution condemning lynching and mob violence, which became a plank in the Republican platform upon which President McKinley was elected. After the inauguration of President McKinley, Mr. Rucker was appointed Collector of Internal Revenue for the District of Georgia, and on the eve of the 5th day of August, 1897, had the pleasure of succeeding the man who, four years before, had relieved him from clerkship in the same office.

In 1889, Mr. Rucker was joined in marriage to Miss Annie, the younger daughter of Hon. Jefferson Long, the only colored man to represent a Georgia district in the United States Congress. To them four children have been born. Mr. Rucker is sober, honest and intelligent, enjoying the respect and confidence of the best people among whom he lives, as well as that of many of the leading men of the country. When asked to what he attributed his success, he emphatically says: "To the faithful, patient training and earnest prayers of a devout Christian mother."

The following is taken from the Atlanta Constitution, and may suggest to some young men the advantage to be gained in not hurrying from the country to the city. What these men have done can be done again by others, if industry, economy and good management are not wanting.

Bartow F. Powell was born a Negro in Bainbridge, Georgia, under all the weight which must ever depress a black race living in the midst of a dominant and all-conquering white. Worse than that, there was added to the natural disqualification of skin the stigma of recent slavery, with the jealousy, as yet unabated, of those who have been deprived of their ownership. A more unpropitious beginning is beyond conception, and, before the record which this man has achieved, is there a man in Georgia who will idly fold his hands and say that there is no room for him in the band wagon of progress?

"Born in Bainbridge thirty-two years ago, Bartow F. Powell ran the gauntlet through which all the boys of his race have to go, but he had one quality not common to all—and that was that a dime once reaching his pocket stayed there. This qualification and the thoroughness of his service secured for him constant employment. Drifting from stores about town into the government service in the dredge boats clearing out the Flint river, his resources increased, and with the interest savings on money already acquired, he found himself at the age of twenty the owner of $2,000, $100 for each year of his life. That, as stated, was twelve years ago, and the event was celebrated by a trip to Albany, where a white landowner was committing the usual mistake of parting with five hundred acres of Baker county pine land. The white man got the $2,000, which has most likely taken wings long ago, whilst the Negro got the five hundred acres, which are to-day worth three times the money.

BARTOW F. POWELL.

" 'I hired ten men,' describing his first year's work, 'for the year round, paying them $8 a month and board, and put eight mules to work. It was during Christmas week that I bought the land, so I started in with my force on the first day of January, because they say whatever you do that day you will do the year round. It proved to be so in my case, for it was not until the Christmas week of the next year that I saw a day off. We started clearing and tearing up in January, and reached planting by March, which took up two months. We then cultivated the crop regularly till August 1st, after which, gathering and ginning and marketing took up our time.

" 'When I had sold my cotton, corn and sugar cane I had $2,500. Besides that I had raised hogs and made provender, potatoes and peas sufficient to offset the running expenses of the farm. I found that the best way to succeed is to hire men by the month, paying them regular wages, and planning ahead for the work that they must do the year round. You can command their work better.

" 'Well, I just kept on the next three years, not doing so well the second year. The fifth year I bought a second farm of three hundred acres in the oaky woods, for which I paid $3,000 cash, and the next year I added a five hundred and sixty acre place in the ninth district of Baker for $2,500 cash. I ran along two years more this way, when I had some more money to spare, when I took in another oaky woods farm of four hundred and forty acres for $3,200 cash. My land, for which I gave $10 an acre, has paid me fully twenty per cent. in cotton returns, not to speak of my gains from other sources. While I have been saving all this money and buying land, I have freely stocked all my places out of the proceeds which I do not count.   I have now 2,100 acres of land, a town house and lot, forty-four head of horses and mules, one hundred Jersey and scrub cows, one hundred and fifty head of improved hogs, besides wagons, buggies, plows and all kinds of machines used on a big farm.   I now run a public gin on my home place, as well as a grist mill.

" 'If I were to sell my land I could not make as good use of the money as I can of my land.   You see you are always getting principal as well as interest back from your land, and after you get it all back the land still remains more valuble than it was at first.   In money you can only get the interest, and principal is always likely to disappear.   Every other kind of property wears away, but constant use improves land. There is no such thing as wearing out land—it must be kept at work, but rested by different crops.   It is like resting from walking 'by running a little, but never sit down, because if you do you are sure to be left behind.' "

Mr. Powell generally sells his cotton at the beginning of the market season.   Concerning the raising of cotton, Mr. Powell says:

"There's money in cotton all the time, said Powell, only don't be paying this money for other things you can raise at home.   Five cents pays well and seven cents is bushels.   I can always make the difference good by living at home."

Powell is not the only man of his race who has made what is called "big" money.   As he is a mulatto, inheriting, as will be seen from his picture, the phrenological cast of the Caucasian, it may be argued that his success springs from that strain.

Mr. Billingslea is as black and full-blooded a Negro

as ever disported himself in the jungles of Africa, with
a greasy coal face, great lips, which, when parted, display almost wealth enough of ivory for an elephant.
He has come right out of slavery itself, and is now the
owner of two thousand acres of land, from which he
markets four hundred bales of cotton annually. Besides
his success on the farm, he has developed the country
supply store idea, and thus rakes in thousands of dollars a year.

Deal Jackson is another typical "before the war"
Negro, who owns six hundred acres of land worth
$10,000, and who has money to loan at all times.

Joe Jeffis, still another full-blooded African, living
on the east side of the river, owns 1,500 acres of
superb land, out of which he makes equally good returns
with those already mentioned.

No white man should be afraid to do as well as these
men have done, and here is their greatest possibility;
the ownership of property makes good citizens of the
Negroes. The influence of these men is great with
members of their race.

And they, in turn, help to preserve the good relationship between the races, which has removed all the
rancor of former times. We always work together and
for the common good. You can go to these men at any
time and make suggestions as to proper lines upon
which to work, and they have the good sense to comply,
so that racial troubles never occur. Whenever you
hear of such trouble it is between a no-account white
man and a mean Negro, and we are then just as certain
to get rid of the one as the other. These men command the highest credit in our banks and commercial
houses.

Altogether these incidents furnish one of the best

lessons as to the possibilities of the South, and now we are talking, not in the interest of Northern immigrants, but of our own Southern boys. Go to the commercial college in our big cities; go to the stenographic schools; go to the dry goods and other business houses, and see the hundreds and thousands of bright young men stunting their youth in the fever of exertion for callings which will not bring them a livelihood in their maturity, but out of which they will be crowded by a fresh influx of boys. While these young men have turned their backs upon the old homes, their patrimony is being taken possession of by strangers, who are making the waste spots bloom in luxuriance. In the days to come, when these young men will have grown older, they will seek a season's vacation, called up by a bubbling of the old home feeling, and going there the very face of nature will have changed, but the greatest change, the one most cutting and heart-rending, will be to see the face of the stranger peering out of the old window, and the hand of the stranger holding, not ajar, but firmly closed, the gate which once led to home, with its smiles and tears which are now recalled through the vista of time and adversity.

Look upon these broad and smiling acres, young men of the South. There is more wealth concealed beneath their carpeted green than all the eldorados ever afforded; there is more joy and comfort clustering around that old house; there is more of heart in the handclasp, the more of Heaven in the prospect than ever city, with its promises fulfilled, has been able to give you.

Go to the country, young man, go!

Cotton States, Industrial Exposition, 1895.—The Negro building of this exposition was erected by Negro hands and supervised by Negro skill and brain.   Much of the success which was realized is due to the chief commissioner, Professor Crogman, who traveled throughout the Southern states in the interest of the Negro building.   Those who are able to judge assure us that this exhibit was by far the best yet made by the Negro race.   The educational, business and industrial development of the race during thirty years of emancipation was shown here in practical form.   It was in all respects a success.

The commissioner of education says of the exhibit: "The very creditable exhibit made at the Atlanta exposititition in 1895 by the more progressive element among the Negroes aroused new interest in all parts of the country in their educational advancement."   There arose a very general demand for information on the subject, and this resulted in a special effort on the part of the Educational Bureau to furnish more extended information and statistics than ever before given. Thus the Atlanta Negro exhibit was an occasion for better information on the subject.   The commissioners who labored so faithfully to make that exhibit a success, it is safe to say, had hardly hoped to make their influence and work felt throughout the nation, and yet this was the case.

The Negro Exhibit at Nashville, 1897.—The one hundredth anniversary of Tennessee as a state was celebrated by the Centennial exposition at Nashville, from the first day of May until the last day of October, 1897. This occasioned for the Negro in particular an opportunity to demonstrate to the world his capabilities in everything that appertains to development of the mental, moral and physical powers.   To the Negro this opportunity meant a reward of patient industry and

honesty. The Centennial exposition in general was a
great credit to the state. The Negro building in particular attracted the attention of visitors. The people
of Tennessee generously erected, at a cost of twelve
thousand dollars, a handsome and imposing building,
known as the "Negro building." It was three hundred
feet long by one hundred feet wide, and the architectural plans were not surpassed by any other building on
the grounds. All the lines of progress were here
noted, but, as it is along educational lines that the
Negro race has made its greatest progress, the exhibit
of schools devoted to Negro education necessarily
occupied much space. Although the time since emancipation has been only a little more than that devoted to
the eduation of a single generation, the race has made
considerable progress in the arts, sciences, trades and
professions, commerce, agriculture, and all other callings of the world, as a people, making creditable showings in these lines. The display of talent in art by the
Negro surprised and delighted the visitors to the
Atlanta exposition. At Nashville, this department surpassed every other exhibit of the work of Negro artists
yet given. Miss E. Lewis, a talented young lady of
Tennessee, who is now studying in Europe, forwarded
some of her best paintings to the exposition. Mr.
Tanner, whose work recently received favorable attention at Paris, also sent some of his pictures. Portraits
of famous men and women adorned the walls. On the
whole, the Negro building at the Tennessee exposition
was a decided success, and the works therein contained
have proved that the Negroes, as a race, have made
more progress in civilization since their emancipation
than any other race similarly situated has in the same
length of time.

CHAPTER X.

Property Owners.—It is said that the colored population of Georgia pay taxes on about $40,000,000 worth of property; the amount of mortgage on lands is not stated, but even if it should be one-half the value of the real estate the result would be the possession by these people of $20,000,000 worth of land, accumulated since the war. It is probable from the estimates that the Negro of the South owns, free of incumbrances, from $250,000,000 to $300,000,000 worth of real estate. Is not this result really unprecedented in the history of our civilization?

The Negro of the South pays taxes on over $300,000,000 worth of real and personal property, indicating that the true value of the race holdings in 1890 was not less than $650,000,000. Practically, every dollar of this has been accumulated in the last thirty years, about the period of a single generation of our colored race; and it shows, as nothing else can show, that the spirit of thrift and enterprise is being acquired by the Negro, from his white neighbors.

The race has in its possession, certainly, a sound and strong basis of means for displaying its progress, objectively, to the high credit of the colored people and greatly to their benefit.

Wealthy Men; Examples.—Among the property owners of Jackson ward, Richmond, Va., the following are the most prominent: Mrs. Bettie T. Lewis, $150,000; Mrs. Fannie C. Thompson, $15,000; W. I. Johnson, $13,000; A. Hayes, $12,000; William Lyons,

$10,000; John Oliver, $10,000; Dr. S. H. Dismond, $8,000; J. B. Harris, $7,000; William Tennant, $7,000; W. H. White, $7,000; Rev. W. W. Browne, $6,000; Rev. J. E. Jones, $5,000; B. F. Turner, $5,000; Dr. R. E. Jones, $5,000; S. W. Robinson, $5,000.

Many other colored men of wealth in Richmond deserve to be mentioned in this connection, but time and space forbid. The above are only examples of what can be done by the industrious, economical colored men in every city.

Much Property is owned by the colored people of the North and West. Some of their estates run high into the hundred thousands. Many of them, though shut out almost entirely from the trades and business avenues, have accumulated handsome homes, and live in elegance and refinement.

Rev. A. G. Davis, of Raleigh, North Carolina, in an address at the North Carolina Colored Agricultural Fair, in reference to the Negro's progress, says that among other things: "Scan, if you will, the long line of eight million Negroes as they march slowly but surely up the road of progress, and you will find in their ranks such men as Granville T. Woods, of Ohio, the electrician, mechanical engineer, manufacturer of telephones, telegraph and electrical instruments; William Still, of Philadelphia, the coal dealer; Henry Tanner, the artist; John W. Tarry, foreman of the iron and fitting department of the Chicago West Division Street Car Company; J. D. Baltimore, engineer, machinist and inventor, of Washington, D. C.; Wiley Jones, of Pine Bluff, Arkansas, the owner of the street railroad and park; Richard M. Hancock, foreman of the pattern shops of the Eagle Works and Manufacturing Company, and draughtsman; John Black, the inventor, whose inventions are worth tens of thousands; W. C. Atwood, the lumber merchant and capitalist.'' To this we might add the following list of names of a few wealthy colored people in the United States, as given by Prof. E. A. Johnson, of Raleigh:

Amanda Eubanks, of Georgia	$400,000
Mrs. M. Carpenter, San Francisco	300,000
John McKee, Philadelphia	300,000
W. Q. Atwood, Baltimore	300,000
Fred Douglass Estate, Washington, D. C.	300,000
William Still, Philadelphia	200,000
Robert Purvis, Washington, D. C.	150,000
Mr. Smith, New York	150,000
Ex. Gov. P. S. B. Pinchback, Louisiana	150,000
John Thomas, Baltimore	150 000
Mr. D. C. White, New York	130,000
The Morrisettes of South Carolina	130,000
Mrs. Mars, New York	100,000
Mr. W. C. Coleman, North Carolina	100,000
Bowers Estate, Philadelphia	80,000
Mr. Avery Smith, Florida	80,000
Mr. J. H. Lewis, of Boston, formerly of North Carolina	70,000
Bishop Beebe, North Carolina	50,000
Several in Alabama	50,000
Fifty in North Carolina	10,000
Fifty in Georgia	10,000
One hundred in Louisiana	10,000
Twelve in Mississippi	10,000
Sixty in Texas	10,000
Fifty in Virginia	10,000

Wealthy Colored New York Men.—There are many wealthy colored men who live in New York City. Several who were formerly slaves count their money by the hundred thousand. Four or five physicians in this great metropolis have a practice of many thousand dollars a year.

Mortgaged Property.—One of the notable showings of the last census is the low percentage of mortgaged property in the South. In Georgia this percentage is 3.18; in Tennessee, 3.87; in Florida, 3.63; in Alabama, 3.98, and in Louisana, 3.94. The census of 1890 also gives another evidence, that is more direct, of the improved condition of the Negroes in the South. In 1890 there were 12,690,152 homes and farms in the United States, and of this number 1,186,174 are occupied by pure blacks and 224,595 by Mulattoes. Of the Negroes, 207,616 own their own homes or farms, and 978,558 rent them. Of the Mulattoes, 56,662 own and 167,923 rent. The percentage of mortgaged property owned by Negroes is only 10.71, while the percentage of mortgaged property for the whole country is 38.97. Of the property held by Negroes, 88.58 per cent is owned without encumbrance. In the North Atlantic states there are 5,808 homes and farms owned by Negroes free from mortgage, and 3,921 that are mortgaged; in the North Central states there are 20,060 homes and farms owned by Negroes free from incumbrance, and 9,691 that are mortgaged; in the South Central states there are 100,591 homes and farms owned by Negroes free from incumbrances, and 7,608 that are mortgaged; in the Western states there are 1,204 farms and homes owned free by Negroes, and 289 that are mortgaged. In the whole country there are 234,747 homes and farms owned by Negroes free from all incumbrance, and 29,541 mortgaged. In the South the percentage of home owners is larger than in the North, and the proportion of these owners on farms of their own is larger than that of those who have homes in cities and villages. With the white race the condition is just the opposite, the large percentage of owners having homes in cities and villages rather than farms.

Twenty-five Years' Accumulations. — Alabama, $9,200,125; Arkansas, $8,010,315; Florida, $7,900,400; Georgia, $10,415,330; Kentucky, $5,900,010; Louisiana, $18,100,528; Mississippi, $13,400,213; Missouri, $6,600,343; North Carolina, $11,010,652; South Carolina, $12,500,000; Texas, $18,010,545; Tennessee, $10,400,211; Virginia, $4,900,000.

The Colored Churches in the United States own $16,310,441; the total amount of property owned by the colored people in *all* the states is rated at over $263,000,000.

Jacob McKinley.—Jacob McKinley, of Atlanta, Ga., was a man of worth and character. He was a man of perhaps more than thirty years when Sherman captured Atlanta and marched to the sea.

With many others of his race he came to Atlanta at that time, having neither education nor money; but he did have an enviable reputation as a Christian and an honest man, and also had a good trade as a stone mason.

With this capital he set to work to help rear Atlanta from the heap of ashes in which he found her to the great and prosperous city of more than a hundred thousand inhabitants of today.

In this work he made both friends and money, and when he passed from labor to reward in 1896 his friends were found among both races and all classes of men.

*At his death his estate was valued at $40,000, all of which he left to his wife and children, except a lot on which he had erected a Baptist church, known as "McKinley's Chapel." This he gave to his race and left it as a monument to his name.

Robert Thomas Taylor was born a slave in Georgia.

He has shown what determined will and energy might reveal to many others. Soon after he was freed, he, with his wife and five children, moved to Texas, and in a few years, through industry and economy, was the owner of 100 acres of land. Mr. and Mrs. Taylor are honored more for what they have made of their sons than for what they are themselves. One of them, after taking a course in a college, is principal of a school in Texas; a second is pastor of a Baptist church in Corsicanna, Texas, one of the largest Baptist churches in the state. The third has completed a course in the Meharry Medical College, and is now a practicing physician in a city in Texas. The fourth, who has completed a course in Shaw University, Raleigh, North Carolina, is teaching in Texas. Mr. Taylor may well be proud of the success of his sons. He has, since freedom, learned to write and transact his own business. He has accumulated property to the amount of about $6,000, besides having paid out about $4,000 for the education of his sons.

Lewis Bates is probably the wealthiest colored man in Chicago, being rated at nearly $500,000. He is entirely uneducated, dresses poorly, and lives like a poor man. He was born a slave nearly seventy years ago. In 1861 he reached Chicago by the "Underground Railroad," and began working in a foundry. He soon became an expressman, and at once began investing his savings in real estate. In this he has shown excellent judgment, and nearly all his investments are gilt-edged. Though he spends little money on himself, he is open hearted and kind. He has no family, and his only heirs are a few very distant relatives.

Encouraged.—Dr. Butler says: "Our people should feel greatly encouraged when they learn that in 1894 their aggregate wealth, including church property, was estimated at more than $325,000,000. At that time there were many thousand men and women of the race with fortunes ranging from $5,000 to $1,000,000. Besides, they have many lawyers, preachers, teachers, bishops, business men and women, and more than one thousand physcians. They also have authors of poetry and music, and over three hundred newspapers and magazines. All this has been accomplished in one generation. While it is a wonderful stretch, yet, if we had started right, we might have been much further on the road of success. Therefore, I say, every member of the race, old and young, great and small, poor and rich, learned and unlearned, let us start out with the year of 1898 to do all in our power to better our condition—morally, mentally, spiritually, and financially. Let us acquire intellect, morals and wealth, and in the meantime, let us not fail to lay up for ourselves treasures in the kingdom of God."

The Negro in Politics.—While the emancipation brought many blessings to the colored people of the United States, it also brought with it many disappointments. When the chains of slavery were broken many colored people pictured to themselves a life of ease and pleasure, as they had seen their masters living, but instead they met stern responsibilities which compelled them to provide for themselves. It became necessary for the race to learn, through the struggles and persecutions, through want and poverty, how to provide for themselves and become independent citizens.

Greed for Office.—Of course, there were a number who expected to be promoted to offices at once. While there were some of the colored race who held public positions and acquitted themselves nobly, yet, this greed for office has been detrimental to the advancement of the Negro in general. It is the general opinion that the Negro, in many cases, has had too much to do with politics. The greed for office has often occasioned distrust and dread in the minds of the whites, and thus the whole cause has been hindered.

Politics Should Follow.—Carl Schurz very aptly says: "The wiser heads among the colored people themselves can hardly fail to see that their political preferment must not precede but follow their advancement in the other walks of life. A goodly number of Negroes achieving distinction as lawyers, or as physicians, or as ministers, or as educators, or as business men, will, by the impression produced upon public opinion, effect far more for the political advancement of their race than ever so many Negro politicians getting themselves elected to Congress or appointed to other offices, and infinitely more than the horde of colored place hunters who besiege party committees for "influence" or appointing officers for favors in the name of the colored vote, and who thus intensify the repulsiveness of one of the most baneful features of our political life. In this respect nothing more helpful can happen to the colored people than that all the government employments be put under civil service rules, so that every colored citizen who gets an appointment be known to have obtained it on account of his own individual merit, in free competition on an equal footing with other citizens, white or black, and that he is, therefore, fairly and honorably entitled to it. Places so won will indeed be marks of real proficiency and distinction, and raise the colored people in that public esteem which above all things they need."

CHAPTER XI.

The Colored Race in Nashville.—Prof. Harris, of Fisk University, recently completed a canvass of the colored people living in a certain district of Nashville. He gives us the following striking and important facts:

Birth Rate.—I visited 145 families containing 649 people, or an average of something over four to a family. In other words, each family contains on an average between two and three children. This falls far below what former literature on the rapid increase of the Negro might lead us to expect. If one may generalize from so limited a canvass, the Negro is not the "prolific animal" that he has been termed. His birth rate is considerably less than it ought to be.

Mortality.—This fact in connection with the excessive mortality among them is, to all thoughtful colored men, an occasion of some alarm. The Negro population of Nashville is probably only half as great as the white; yet they sometimes have not only relatively but absolutely, a greater number of deaths. The excess of deaths among the colored people is due largely and perhaps altogether, to constitutional diseases. During a short period of time some years ago the colored death rate was far ahead of the birth rate; I estimated that if emigration and immigration were shut off, and the vital statistics were to continue right along as they did that period of time, in less than one hundred years there would not be a colored man, woman or child living in the city of Nashville.

Homes.—Of the homes I canvassed in the territory

279

described, 77 are rented, 61 are owned by their occupants, and 7 are being bought in monthly payments, averaging $8.00 per month; that is, nearly 47 per cent. either own or are buying their homes. This is a very good showing, when we remember that thirty years ago they hardly owned even the clothes on their backs.

Of the 77 who rent, 12 pay above $6.00 per month, 18 pay $6.00; 20 pay $5.00, and 27 pay less than $5.00 The highest monthly payment made by those who are buying is $12.00; the lowest $5.00.

Deaths.—Within the last five years there have been 92 deaths in this community, 19 of which were due to consumption, and 8 to pneumonia. The other 65 deaths were due to 34 different causes. It would seem as if pulmonary consumption is the "destroying angel" among us, and yet I am told that before the war this dread disease was virtually unknown among the slaves. During the year 1896, the people suffered from 43 different diseases, seven dying from consumption. Thirteen suffer from scrofula, occasioning the loss of an eye in the case of six and rendering four others quite deaf.

Children in Public Schools.—Eighty-seven per cent. of the children of scholastic age are in the public schools. Many, perhaps most, of the 13 per cent. who are out, have applied for admission to the schools, but have been turned away because of lack of room.

Use of Educational Advantages.—The colored people are making splendid use of their educational advantages, and however unfavorably their vital and social statistics may compare with those of another race, in educational progress they have equaled any, and surpassed most other people.

Occupation and Earnings.—Among the colored people of this community there are represented 51 different occupations: For the year 1896 the total weekly income of the families investigated, including all that was earned by every member of the family, was $1,321.65, or a weekly average of only $9.11 per family. When we remember that more than one-half of these families pay rent, and that some support a large number of children, it is a true saying that "one-half of the world does not know how the other half lives." But of 133 families visited, 33 earned less than $6 a week, 49 earned $6 or more, but not $10; 43 earned $10 or more, but not $20; 8 earned $20 or more, but not $30, and 2 earned $30 or more, but not $40. It is worthy of a remark that among the 649 people canvassed, in spite of their poverty, I found only four pro fessional beggars.

Enforced Idleness.—During the last year 61 colored people, 21 years old and above, who are habitually employed, underwent a period of enforced idleness aggregating 749 weeks, or an average of three months per capita. When we remember how scanty is the average income earned by the whole family, being only $9 per week, three months of enforced idleness must have intensified greatly their already hard battle for life.

Constitutional Diseases.—The slow rate of increase among the colored people is due to two causes, constitutional diseases and the crimes of mothers. More white people die from contagious diseases than colored. More white people die from local diseases than colored; while more colored people die from constitutional diseases than white. In other words, the excess of colored deaths over white is due to constitutional diseases.

Crimes of Mothers.—I also found by personal investigation that year that a large number of colored washerwomen, finding it hard to get the husks to feed and the rags to clothe their already large family of little ones, living in one room like stock, rather than to add to their burdens, resort to crime. This is also a fruitful reason of the slow rate of increase in the colored population. This state of affairs is not confined to Nashville. It is true of nearly all our large Southern cities; and whether we like it or not, the hard fact remains that the enormous death rate among us, together with our small birth rate, is one of the signs of the times that, unless our home life be radically changed, the Negro problem in America may be ultimately solved by the extinction of the Negro.

Lack of Stamina.—Anglo-Saxons are exterminating the inferior races more rapidly and more surely than shot and shell and bayonet. Before the advancing march of the Anglo-Saxon, the New Zealanders, the Tasmanians, the Pacific Islanders, the Negroes of South Africa, and the aborigines of Australia have all gone down to the grave; and, be it remembered, brethren, that these races have all perished, not because of destructive wars and pestilence, but because they were unable to live in the environment of a nine-teenth century civilization. Their destruction was not due to a persecution which came to them from without, but to a lack of stamina within. Their extermination was due to the inexorable working out of a law as natural as the law of gravitation. And be it remembered, that these races perished in spite of the human-itarian and philanthropic efforts that were put forth to save them. They perished because they had not power of resistance within.

Keep Up, or Get Out of the Way.—If the fate of

these races teaches me anything, it teaches me that in the onward march of the nations the colored race in America has got to keep up with the procession, or else, like them, it has got to get out of the way. Now, this may seem hard to you, but hard as it is, it is a hard fact, and we might as well face it. The social, intellectual, and scientific world is moving as fast in its orbit as the earth beneath our feet; and those of us who cannot keep up with it are bound to be crushed to pieces by it. Our white friends could not retard the world's progress to accommodate us, even if they would; and, men, I believe, that we are too manly to ask them to do so, even if they could.

Social Regeneration.—We are apt to look to business and to politics to bring about our social regeneration, to give us civil standing and political recognition; we are apt to look solely to business and to politics to do away with the old order of things among us, and bring in the new. We are looking to business and to politics to give us a new home life, to give us new social status— to give us a new earth—and we neglect Christian work because we forget in a measure that before we can have the new earth we must have the new heaven. First, we must have the new heaven; then we can have the new earth. First, new ambitions, new purposes, new motives, new ideals; then the new home life, the new social status, the new civil and business standing, and the new political conditions. First, the new heaven, then the new earth.''

Mortality.—In 1896 a convention on the mortality among the Negroes in cities was held at Atlanta University, and widespread interest was exhibited. From the proceedings of this convention we cull the following items from papers read by eminent men through the nation:

A Problem.—The rapid growth of our great cities within recent years is one of the phases of modern life which brings with it problems whose solution calls for the best efforts of the leading men in the city communities, whether white or black. Special courses for the study of these problems have been established in the Northern colleges, and it is felt that the time has come when Atlanta University must take up the study of these problems of city life which its graduates are called upon to meet and solve. It is none too soon to begin this work, for each year a larger proportion of the colored race are concentrated in the cities.

In Cities.—In 1860 only 4.2 per cent. of the colored population of the United States were living in the cities. By 1880 the number had increased to 8.4 per cent. of the whole colored population, while by 1890 it had increased to 12 per cent. This process of concentration in the cities has been relatively much more rapid among the colored people than among the whites, the figures for whites during the same period being 10.9 per cent. in 1860, and 15.7 per cent. in 1890, or an increase of 4.8 per cent., against 7.8 per cent. colored. How rapid this increase in the city population really is may be illustrated by the growth of the colored population of Atlanta, where the increase has been at a rate three times as great as for the country at large. For decade 1870-1880, the increase was 64 per cent.; for 1880-1890, 72 per cent.; while the average increase of colored population for the whole country during the same period was only 20 per cent. in each decade.

Five Cities.—From the United States census for 1890, we have the mortality for the white and colored population of five of our largest cities—Washington, Baltimore, New Orleans, Louisville and St. Louis—as given in a paper published by the trustees of the Slater Fund:

	⌒Rates per 1,000⌒	
	White.	Colored.
Washington	19	36
Baltimore	22	36
New Orleans	22	37
Louisville	18	32
St. Louis..........................	17	35

The excess of colored over white is 100, 63.6, 68, 77 and 106 per cent.

Twenty-one Families in Washington.—Dr. Evans has furnished the information in regard to one group of twenty-one families, and although it is impossible for us to make from this one group any generalization in regard to the colored population of the city of Washington, a community of 86,000 persons, the information is very interesting as representing the generally well-to-do character of the twenty-one families represented.

The neighborhood in which they live is reported as being fair or good, and this is confirmed by the following figures deduced from this report, thus:

Thirteen of the twenty-one families own their own houses. The houses for the most part are supplied with modern conveniences, nineteen having city water, nine sewer connections, etc. The average number of rooms occupied by the family is between five and six, the smallest number being four, while over half have six or eight.

The average number of persons occupying the same sleeping room is two, although in four instances there are four to a room, and in one instance five. There are only four cases of sickness reported, while twelve families report no sickness at all.

Income.—Only ten families report as to income, but

the average for the ten is high, being $664 a year, and in seven families out of the ten the husband entirely supports the family by his sole labor. It is interesting to note the occupation of these seven men. The largest income is earned by a carpenter, who reports his earnings as $780; next comes a barber, earning $720 a year; a teacher, earning $650; a janitor, $560; a laborer, $480; a steward, $390; and laborer, $250.

Largest Income.—The largest income of one family is that of a family of nine, the father and mother both dead, and the eldest brother and two sisters supporting the family. The brother is an expressman, earning $500 a year; the two sisters are teachers, earning $450 each, making a total of $1,400 a year. This family owns its own house, having eight rooms, with city water, sewer connections and other conveniences. Five of the families report savings averaging $123.52 per family.

Negligence a Cause of Mortality.—The average laborer is exceedingly neglectful. He will drive or walk all day in the rain or snow, come home and go to bed with his wet clothes on, with the belief firmly fixed in his mind that unless he lets these clothes dry on him he will contract a cold, and no argument we might use will convince him otherwise. Again, since the colored people here compose the majority of the laboring classes, it stands to reason that they are more exposed than the whites, and are therefore more susceptible to those diseases that may be caused by exposure. The colored man sweeps the streets and fills his lungs with the dust and dried bacteria expectorated on the streets a few hours since from the lungs of some consumptive; he drives the garbage carts, he digs the sewers, drives the hacks and drays, and, in fact, does the most of work involving exposure, which naturally makes him more liable to contract such diseases as pleurisy, bronchitis, pneumonia and consumption.

Charitable Institutions.—The city has neglected, and is still neglecting, the colored people, and especially that class of them which is dependent upon its charity in times of sickness. It has millions to build prisons with, but not a dollar with which to build charitable institutions. It allows money grabbers to build small huts and crowd into them five times the number of people that should be allowed; it has no law by which the owner of this property can be made to keep it clean. The houses are never painted, the wells are filled with the filth of the neighborhood, and the fences are never whitewashed, and the city is powerless to interfere. Family after family move into these places, and often only one or two are left to tell the story. My friends, it is one thing to stand here in this clean, well-lighted hall and read papers on this subject, but it is altogether different to go down into those dark, poor and humble homes and see death going through destroying the old and young because of the negligence on the part of those in authority.

Physicians.—Some of the white physicians neglect the colored people. I wish it to be understood, however, that I mean some, not all, for there are some honorable exceptions to the statement just made. I say they neglect our people, and we cannot blame them. Doctors can no more afford to work for nothing than a teacher or any other person who is working for an honest living. Hence, he refuses to go to these people; first, because they are not able to pay, and secondly, because the city has appointed physicians whose duty it is to attend the poor in their various wards. These physicians are paid from $500 to $800 a year to do that work, and then they neglect it, especially such cases as diphtheria.

Dispensaries.—While this city has furnished physicians, it has furnished no medicine. It has no free dispensaries, as it should, nor does it pay the physicians money enough to furnish medicines applicable in every case, and at the same time care for himself and family. Hence, when he is called to see a patient, it matters not what the disease may be, it is either compound cathartic pills, calomel, epsom salts, blue mass, or castor oil. Any case these remedies don't reach is left to get well if it can, or die if it must. I ask, then, in all candor: Is it any wonder that we die so fast when we get such attention, doctors, such excellent nursing, such fresh medicines, applicable in every case of our diseases?

Hospitals.—Here in Atlanta, a city of push, pluck and Christian progress, there is not a decent hospital where colored people can be cared for. At the Grady hospital, which takes about $20,000 of the city's money annually to run it, is a small wooden annex down by the kitchen, in which may be crowded fifty or sixty beds, and that is all the hospital advantages 40,000 colored citizens have. But, on the other hand, our white friends, with a population of about 70,000, have all the wards and private rooms in the entire brick building at this hospital, together with a very fine hospital here, known as St. Joseph's Infirmary. Hence, my friends, you can see that one of our greatest needs is a first-class, up-to-date hospital, where the colored people can not only get proper treatment, but can also have all necessary operations performed.

Intemperance a Cause of Mortality.—To ascertain the truth of this subject concerning the relation of intemperance to mortality, it is necessary not only to enumerate the deaths due to acute alcoholism, such as delirium tremens and the various sudden congestions and paralyses consequent upon the taking of excessive quantities of strong drink, together with the great majority of homicides, suicides and accidental deaths, which may be traced directly to the use of alcoholics; but it is necessary, also, to inquire into the real cause of the deaths ascribed to the ordinary acute and chronic diseases, the contagious and the infectious diseases— indeed, the whole category of classified diseases.

Contagious and Infectious Diseases.—With reference to death from contagious and infectious diseases, it is the unanimous testimony of the leading authorities that during the scourges of cholera, yellow fever and smallpox, it is the drinker who falls victim, the moderate drinker being no exception to the rule, while the total abstainer is less liable to contract the disease, and if affected, is far more likely to survive. The fact holds good in such diseases as scarlet and typhoid fevers, when there are unknown antidotes to the specific poison, and the quality of the tissues is relied upon to resist or survive the disease.

Heredity.—Alcohol, as a remote cause of death, is none the less effective in cases in which the victim is not himself addicted to the use of strong drinks, but inherits from drinking parents a weak constitution, which renders him an easy prey, an inviting field for disease. To inherited weakness is due a large per cent of the alarming rate of infant mortality resulting from cholera infantum, measles, scarlet fever, diphtheria, etc. Says our own Dr. Orme: "If it were possible to separate deaths due to alcohol from the classified diseases to which they are ascribed, the facts would be astounding."

Principal Factors.—That intemperance is one of the principal factors in the terrible death-rate among the Negro population in the cities, there can be no question. It is in the cities that intemperance prevails. I believe that no one at all informed would hesitate to assert that ninety-nine per cent of the city population are addicted to some extent to the use of strong drinks. No one will deny that the Negro is no exception to this rule. It is well known that that class of the Negro population which furnishes the excessive death rate is that class addicted to the use of whisky and beer in their vilest forms. It is this ignorant, drunken class of Negroes which furnish 90 per cent. of the criminals which crowd our jails and penitentiaries, and who, poorly clad and fed, exposed to the great extremes of heat and cold, working rain or shine at most laborious tasks, while serving terms in the chain-gangs, contract diseases and die by hundreds annually. Those who live to be released flock to the cities to furnish their remaining weeks or months, and add their quota to the death-rate. If this were the end alone of men and women, old and hardened criminals, it would not be so serious, but this is the end of hundreds of boys and girls arrested for misdemeanors.

Poverty a Cause of Mortality.—Slavery left the colored man the rich inheritance of a log cabin and a patch of turnip greens. This log cabin is a piece of architecture that will soon be entirely relegated to the barbarous past. Peace be to its ashes! It has disappeared in the towns and cities, and is found only in the poverty-stricken rural districts. Can not you recall the picture of that poor family who worked hard all day in the field while their little ones, almost nude, played around the door until the sun dropped behind that hill studded

with beautiful trees? See the mother return and prepare her evening meal; the fire is lighted, the children
hungry and crying; behold the repast—fried bacon,
poorly-cooked bread and black molasses. A pine
torch illuminates the room that serves as a kitchen,
dining-room, bed and bath-room. After supper the
little ones are off to bed without being properly bathed
and dressed, and after the usual chair-nap, the father
and mother retire. There they are in a row, and only
one small window and door to let in nature's life-giving
air that keeps them from suffocating.

Mortality Among the Children of the Poor.—We
find great mortality among the children of the poor.
Even before they can make their wants known, the
mother is compelled to leave them daily, and a surprising number are burned to death. The older children are taught to go out and pick up trash to burn,
rags, bones, and iron to sell, thereby inviting disease
and death. It is a strange fact, yet true, that all work
that is obnoxious, dangerous and laborious is given the
poor Negro at pay that would kill some people even to
think of having it to do for a living. These people, in
buying food etc., always seek quantity and not quality;
hence the butcher, fisherman, fruiterer, dairyman and
merchants are careful to anticipate their wants.

Ignorance.—Among the many causes which produce
death in our large cities, it is by no means an easy
matter to distinguish beween ignorance, poverty and
negligence. However, it is safe to assert that no few
of the deaths which occur in our large cities are the
result of ignorance, either directly or indirectly.

It will be seen from the outset that city life requires
a more accurate observance of the laws of health than
country or village life. With this fact in mind, all

cities have established their boards of health to look after and remove any and all causes which in their minds produce sickness or death.   These boards are usually composed of the best informed physicians who, from time to time, make and publish rules which are to be observed and obeyed by all citizens.   These rules the ignorant classes do not obey, not because they are willfully disobedient, but because they are ignorant.   They cannot read, they have no interest in public affairs; they know but little about the causes which bring sickness and disease among them, and hence are the easy prey of epidemics and contagions.

Improper Ventilation.—Many suffer on account of improper ventilation, not knowing that impure air is the parent of every lung trouble known to the human family.   Pure air is one of the freest and best gifts bestowed upon man by our beneficent Father; but alas! how many thousands in our large cities die every year from failing to use this gift!   Man and woman, through ignorance, shut the doors and windows of their houses, thus barring out God's life-giving atmosphere, and inviting consumption and death.   Pure air gives life, foul air gives death.

General Condition.—"Birds of a feather flock together."   In Augusta, as in most cities of America, there are parts of the city occupied exclusively by Negroes, except a few whites, usually German or Irish, keepers of small stores, who live among the Negroes for the sake of their trade.   Although some do not believe it, yet it is true that there are grades of society among Negroes, as among other races, and the lines of distinction are drawn for as wise and as silly reasons as are those among the more favored people.   As in other things, this grading is seen in the choosing of a locality for a home. The poorest, most untidy and the most ignorant seek each other. They always find homes in the same neighborhood, if not in adjoining houses. As each city has its Negro settlements, and as the great rank and file of the race belong to the grade or class called the poorest and most ignorant, the largest settlements are of this kind.

Wages.—These people have small wages, many with nothing to do a great part of the year, and the majority have no steady employment. For food, rent, fuel and clothing they are dependent upon the odd jobs that pay not more than fifty cents per day for two or three days in a week. To eke out a living on such an income requires, they know, the strictest economy, but how to economize they know not, yet, thinking they know, in their way they set about it. The first step is to cut down the expense of living by taking no more house room than barely enough in which to turn around. A small family, parents and two or three children, take one room.

Contents of a Room.—In this room, 15x15, sometimes smaller space, are placed a bedstead, a three-quarters bed, sometimes two (but in these days of cheap furniture and installment sales, a folding lounge very often takes the place of the second bedstead), one or two tables, a trunk, bureau, not less than four chairs, tubs, boards, etc., for laundering, cooking utensils, and a lot of odds and ends. These, with the family, give breathing space scarcely sufficient for one, yet by some means it is hoped to get enough for the whole family. It is not long before hypostatic pneumonia or tuberculosis visits them, and finding the atmosphere congenial abides with the family.

Infants.—The high rate of mortality among infants

is a subject well worthy the consideration of all thoughtful men and women, and naturally leads one to enquire as to causes and possible remedies. Prominent among the causes of this high rate must be mentioned bad heredity and injudicious and harmful management of these little ones by their parents. As a result of these two causes, many children are ill-prepared to meet and battle with the acute diseases almost inevitably before them; they are more apt to contract disease than a healthier child; they are more apt to die from it, when once contracted, as their resisting power is weakened by their heredity and their management since birth.

Sociological Condition.—For a number of years I have thought that the greatest danger to the real progress of the colored people lies in this sociological condition in the large cities. It is difficult, however, to get the facts. There is very little attention given in the South to the vital statistics of Negroes. In fact, the census is neither full nor altogether reliable. The facts, if gotten at all, must be searched out by conscientious persons specially interested in this kind of work. Nevertheless, any one who will give the least observation to this matter will see that the cities are the hotbeds of crime, misery and death among the colored people. Here the people are huddled together, with often two or three families in one room. Without employment for more than half the time, they are consequently insufficiently fed and poorly clothed. When sick they are unable either to employ a physician or to buy medicine. At least 25 per cent. of them die without medical aid.

Savannah.—In the city of Savannah, during the year 1894, 251 colored persons died without medical attention. This is 33⅓ per cent. of the total number of deaths among these people for that year. About 60 per cent. of this number of deaths were children under the age of ten. Twenty-four thousand of the 52,000 population of Savannah are Negroes. Hence, it will be seen that whatever affects these people affects at least nearly half the population of our chief seaport. What is true of Savannah I judge to be approximately true of all the cities of Georgia and most of the cities of the South.

Crime.—The city colored people drift into crime because they are idle and hungry far oftener than because they are purposely vicious. All cities furnish far too large a proportion of crime, ignorance and misery of the colored people. Any movement, therefore, that will bring to light the facts, lay bare the causes, and suggest the remedies in relation to this crime, misery and death which affects our people in the cities will merit universal applause.

REV. WM. H. FURNESS,
One of the foremost Abolitionists of Pennsylvania.
'Death is the worst that can befall us, if so, be that we are faithful to the right."

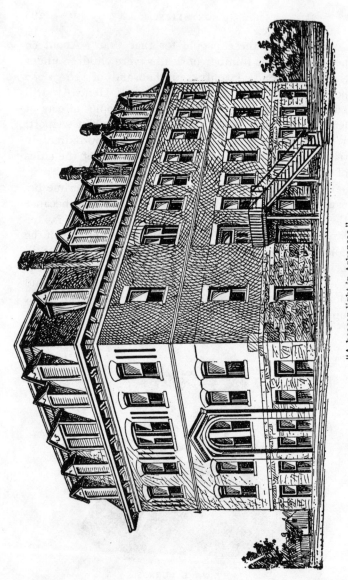

"A beacon light in Arkansas."

ARKANSAS BAPTIST COLLEGE, LITTLE ROCK, ARK.

Arkansas Baptist College, Little Rock, Ark., has made rapid strides during the first twelve years of its existence. The attendance has increased from year to year till the last matriculation register shows nearly two hundred names who attended some of its departments during the past year. Consequently, it now wields a wide-spread influence over the entire state and adjacent states. During the summer vacation (1899) the president has had applications from Georgia, North Carolina, Mississippi, Louisiana, Texas, Missouri, Alabama, Indian Territory, and Oklahoma.

Besides the increased attendance and the consequent growth of influence ever strengthening and ever widening, its property values have enhanced and its improvements have moved steadily on in spite of the hard times. The great brick structure has been nicely finished on the inside, with a chapel large enough to accommodate five hundred, with an elegant suite of office rooms, and ample recitation rooms.

The property is located in the southwest part of the city, between two of the most popular street railway lines, fine electric cars passing every twelve minutes.

The printing department also has a handsome building 25x60, in which there is placed a large Prouty power press, operated either by hand or mechanical power, a small job press and six racks or stands fitted with a great variety of news and job type. From this department the students issue the *Baptist Vanguard*, most of the denominational minutes, college catalogues and smaller jobs for local patrons. A small beginning has also been made in the line of carpentry and shoe mending, fashionable and plain sewing, cooking and laundry work.

GIRLS' INDUSTRIAL SCHOOL, CLARK UNIVERSITY.

CHAPTER XII.

Educational Institutions — Industrial Schools — The Press.

Next in importance to freedom and justice, is popular education, without which neither justice nor freedom can be permanently maintained. —Garfield.

Bishop Atticus Haygood says: "The most unique and altogether wonderful chapter in the history of education is that which tells the story of the Negroes of the South since 1865."

Education.—The great end of education is to prepare one for usefulness in life, and the education that does not accomplish this is worse than useless. This age calls for practical men and women. The man who will continue to sit at his desk, the young woman who will go butterfly chasing and then look for the fulfillment of dreams and visions, will awake and find that the procession of progress has passed without a discovering of the true essentials of practical living.

It is vain to seek knowledge simply for the sake of being smart, but this practical age needs practical men. Casting a boy adrift with a mind stored with classic lore, but not able to find an honorable means of support, is, as Julia Hook says: "nothing less than a crime, he is a miserable failure as a breadwinner." Idleness and uselesness naturally follow, crime and poverty come next in the train, crowding our penitentiaries and swarming our houses of prostitution. Ignorance of industries and idleness are what cause our people to lose their patriotism. The perpetuity of our national life depends upon our knowledge and the usefulness of industrial pursuits. We have more need of carpenters than athletes, of educated farmers than professionals. Industry is the bright ray of hope. The industrial schools of the south are bringing us out of ignorance and vice and make us a blessing to society and posterity.

Not in Question.—The intellectual development of the race is no more in question. The revelations of history are indeed a reflective commentary upon the so-called intelligence of those who went so far as to affirm the impossibility of the intellectual improvement of the Negro. Today there may be found many brilliant scholars in all the disciplines of learning. Ignorance of the historical and present day facts is inexplicable, except it be that American prejudice has decreed what should be known and what left unknown. These adverse views must be treated with the deference that extreme antiquity, without the adjunct of intelligence, deserves. The truth remains, seen or unseen, that the Negro has a right and title to the citizenship of the republic of thought.

No Higher Duty.—Gov. Atkinson says: "There is no higher duty resting upon the governors of the Southern states than to advance the education of the people of the state without regard to color. If any doubt that the colored man can be educated exists, it will all be dispelled by attending the commencements of the colleges for the colored."

Education Improves.—Every one competent to speak and honest enough to be candid knows that education benefits and improves the Negro. It improves his morals, his character, and his usefulness. It makes him a better man and a better citizen, a better neighbor and a better workman, no matter what you put him at. The slave-owners learned that it paid to take good care of their slaves and the people of the South will learn that it pays to educate their Negro employes. Above all things, education of the Negro diminishes if it does not totally banish all danger of race conflict and trouble.

Knowledge Not a Substitute for Virtue.—Hear what Dr. Haygood says: "No theory of universal education entertained by a rational people proposes knowledge as a substitute for virtue, or virtue a substitute for knowledge. Both are necessary. Without virtue knowledge is unreliable and dangerous; without knowledge virtue is blind and impotent." "I must say a word in defense," says the same authority, "of the Negroes, particularly those living in the Southern states. Considering the antecedents of the race in Africa, in those states before the emancipation, and their condition today, the real surprise is that there is so much virtue and purity among them. Above all things, let the white people set them better examples. Since progress has already been made in this direction, we are permitted to hope that education will continue its beneficent work in this moral reformation of the people. Education will certainly afford a better knowledge of the duties of the home, a keener appreciation of the obligation of the marriage state, a more consistent regard for the rights and the property of others, and a clearer conception of what virtue in womanhood signifies, and, therefore, a more determined purpose and means of defending that honor from the assaults of any man, even at the very risk of their lives."

Color Blind.—President Ware, of the Atlanta University, was one of the early workers in the educational field among the Negroes. On one occasion, being seriously asked by a Southern white man how, with all his culture and qualifications, he could content himself to live and labor among the blacks, he tersely replied: "Oh, I can easily explain that. I'm simply color-blind."

Appreciating Advantages.—"Talks for the Times" says: "Last year, in the four institutions of higher learning, established in Atlanta by Northern benevolence, there were, in round numbers, twelve hundred students. Of these, Atlanta University enrolled 310; Clark University, 222; the Baptist Seminary for Males, about 140, and the Baptist Seminary for Females, 500. But Atlanta is only one of the great centers of education in the South. There is Nashville, literally girdled by institutions; there is New Orleans—in fact, you will find today, in every Southern state, one or more institutions for the higher training of Negro youth; and the very fact that all these institutions are more or less crowded yearly, and the very fact that frequent appeal goes out from them to Christian philanthropy for more buildings, for increased accommodations, are proof conclusive, I think, that the Negro not only appreciates the advantages held out to him, but is also exerting himself to enjoy them."

Civilization Progressing.—Dr. Ruffner, for many years superintendent of public instruction for the state of Virginia, in one of his reports a few years ago, bore this testimony to the credit of the Negro: "He wants to do right and is the most amiable of races. The Negro craves education, and I believe his desire has increased; it certainly has not diminished. He makes fully as great sacrifices to send his children to school as the laboring classes of the whites. The civilization of the race is progressing, and even faster than his thoughtful friends anticipated."

Trained Minds.—At the 250th anniversary of Harvard College, a profound student of public affairs, James Russell Lowell, in a famous address, said: "What we need more than anything else is to increase the number of thoroughly trained minds, for these, wherever they go, are sure to carry with them, consciously or not, the seeds of sounder thinking and of higher ideals. The only way in which our civilization can be maintained, even at the level it has reached—the only way in which that level can be made more general and be raised higher—is by bringing the influence of the more cultivated to bear with greater energy and directness on the less cultivated, and by opening more inlets which make for refinement of mind and body." This is the testimony that runs along the history of education. Our New England fathers cherished sound learning for Christianity's sake.

Wisdom.—But if this is wisdom, and continues to be an ever-present necessity for people who have cherished higher education for centuries, not less is it wisdom and necessity for a race undeveloped, where the need of this affiliation of learning and religion is absolute. No people can rise who are shut in to limited and partial privileges.

Higher Institutions.—Indeed, except for higher institutions, the public school system of the South for the colored people could not be carried on with any degree of worthiness. But the public schools did not exhaust our reasons for our higher institutions. Our reasons are in our pulpits. They are in necessary professions. They are found among the bankers and builders and editors and printers. They are rapidly raising the rank of their race. This is very practical; for, when we consider the question of practicability in the salvation and elevation of a people, we realize that our fathers were right to conclude that the idea of education is short-sighted and bad which considers knowledge to be practical only as it can be made at once to grind corn, or can be measured by merely materialistic values.

Practicability.—Accepting the fact of the decrees which decide the capacities of men and their limitations, so that the rank and file must be prepared for and engage in manual labor of some kind, it remains true that those who can impregnate the minds of people about them, who can quicken their thoughts, who can rouse lower intellects and energize them, who can change their low views to higher ones and give larger and truer ideas of life and the world, here and hereafter, and make their lives more vital with thought for daily wants and uses, will be found to have a very practical education.

Thinkers.—Moreover, by forces not material are the material forces penetrated and stirred. When we see how the thoughts of men are harnessed into service in the places of industry then we understand that there is no arithmetic with figures enough to compute the mere money-value of the thoughts which are the secrets of materialistic accomplishment. In education we cannot forget that the world's advance in wealth, as in everything else, comes from those who know how to think, and that those who develop the thinkers develop the workers. The greater the intellectual wealth of a people, the greater will be the aggregate of materialistic wealth, and the developed material prosperity will come more rapidly and surely with better developed men.

Needs of Today.—Low-grade men are content with low-grade things. Along all the lines of materialistic development the great need of the Negro people today is men of trained thought, thinking men, men of larger vision, and more comprehensive minds, who can and will uplift and establish the material as well as the intellectual and spiritual standard of the race. Therefore we are confident that the shortest path in the development of the colored people is in the more perfect development of their intelligence, in the more complete command of their mental powers. With this there comes a better industry in their habits, for ignorance and indolence are twins. We know also that all experience stands back of this knowledge—that a low mental life tends to a low moral life, and that both of these conditions are a natural prey for oppressors and for all who do not wish to do justly.

Equal Opportunities.—The African has a right to an equal opportunity with every other man to show what his competence is. This seed will not sprout, you say. Of course it will not sprout if you leave it in the drawer. Put it in the same soil with that other seed; let the same sun shine upon it; let the same rain fall upon it, and then see whether it will sprout or not. What we demand for the colored man is that all doors shall be opened to him, all opportunities freely offered to him, the right and the liberty of industry given to him. We protest against a system which puts the wall of reservation about the Negro, which denies him the fundamental rights of a free man, the right of locomotion, the right to buy in the cheapest market and sell in the highest market, the right to dispose of his goods wherever he can. We protest against a system which builds a wall around any portion of our American people and confines them as paupers and classes them with other paupers. If we were to take a dozen young men and women under twenty-one years of age out of Boston and shut

CLASS IN CHEMISTRY, ATLANTA BAPTIST SEMINARY.

them up in some great wilderness and were to say to them, "You shall not own the products of your industry, you shall not sell them in the markets of the world, you shall not have free access to the telegraph and the press, you shall not know what is going on in the world; but we will put a mission chapel and a mission school here and there, and if you do not work we will feed you." How long would it take for them to become tramps and paupers. We claim for the African absolute and equal opportunities with the white man—the same door as widely open, the same avenues as free, the same wages for the same labor, the same chance to prove his manhood in industrial relations.

Equal Political Rights.—This does not mean universal suffrage, but it does mean the same conditions of suffrage to the man of one color as to the man of another color. The question whether there shall be a property qualification or not is a very fair question, but if there be such a qualification it must be, under any just and equitable system of government, the same for one race as for another. The law which says to a thrifty Negro, "You shall not vote," and to a thriftless white man, "You shall vote," is unjust and inequitable. The law which provides one kind of educational qualifications for one because his skin is tanned, and another for the man whose skin is not tanned, is unfair and unjust. We stand for equal rights in this republic of republics.

Equal Facilities and Stimulus.—The Negro race must have the same educational and religious facilities and the same stimulus to intellectual and moral growth, and any scheme of education which purposes to furnish the Negro race only with manual and industrial education is a sly contrivance for putting him in serfdom; it tacitly says that the Negro is the inferior of the white race, and therefore we will educate him so as to serve us. The race must have an education which in its final outcome shall be complete, and which shall open opportunities for the highest culture of which any individual of that race is capable.

Duty of the Government.—Judge Gunby says: "The failure of the Federal government to educate the slaves they made freemen is a shame and a disgrace, a scarlet letter on the garb of our history, a stigma which, like the damned spot that soiled the little hand of Lady Macbeth, will never wash out until the wrong has been repaired."

Slavery at the Bottom.—President Price says that slavery, as a system, degraded the Negro to the level of the brute, because it denied him the untrammeled exercise of all the instincts of a higher and better manhood. It recognized no moral sensibility in man or woman, regarded no sacred and inviolable relation between husband and wife, sundered at will or caprice the tenderest ties that the human heart is capable of forming or the human mind is able to conceive. Such a system had the support of the highest tribunal of men, and even the representatives of the church of God came to its rescue and defense, with all the weight of its divine authority and power. From the maternal knee, the table, the family altar, the forum, and the pulpit was the lesson taught that the person of sable hue and curly hair was a doomed, and therefore an inferior, race—not entitled to a place in the brotherhood of men. This impression, made on childhood's plastic nature, grew with his growth, and strengthened with the power of increasing years.

Power of Law.—To deepen the blot, and intensify

the damning heresy, the law of the land wrote him down a chattel, that is, cattle, and forbade the training of the mind and the culture of the heart, by making learning, on his part, and teaching on the part of others, a crime. It is not surprising, then, that men brought up in the face of such a system for two hundred and fifty years should be skeptical as to the real manhood of the Negro, and hesitate to give him a place in the one-blood family.

Prejudice.—The feeling against the Negro which helps to make our race problem is called prejudice, and it is not without some grounds. For two hundred and fifty years the white man of the South saw only the animal, or mechanical, side of the Negro. Wherever he looked, there was degradation, ignorance, superstition, darkness, and nothing more, as he thought. The man was overshadowed and concealed by the debasing appetites and destructive and avaricious passion of the animal; therefore, the race problem of today is not an anomaly, it is the natural and logical product of an environment of centuries.

Key to Problem.—Now, if ignorance, poverty and moral degradation are the grounds of the objection against the Negro, it is not difficult to discover that the knotty elements of the race problem are the intellectual, moral, and material conditions of the Negro race. It is reasonable, therefore, to suppose that if we can find the means that will change these conditions, we have found a key to the problem, and gone a great distance towards its satisfactory solution. Of course, none of us would dare argue that intelligence, or even education, is a panacea for all the ills of mankind; for, even when educated, a Nero, a Robespierre, a Benedict Arnold, an absconding state treasurer, or a New York sneak-thief, would not necessarily be impossibilities.

Not by Magic Spell.—I do not argue that increased intelligence or multiplied facilities for education will, by some magic spell, transform the Negro into the symmetry, grace and beauty of a Grecian embodiment of excellence. It is certainly not my humble task to attempt to prove that education will, in a day, or a decade, or a century, rid the black men of all the physical peculiarities and deformities, moral perversions and intellectual distortions which are the debasing and logical heritage of more than two and a half centuries of enslavement.

Education the Best Means.—It is, nevertheless, reasonable to presume that, admitting the ordinary human capabilities of the race, which no sane and fairminded man will deny, it can be readily and justly predicted that if the same forces applied to other races are applied to the Negro, and these forces are governed by the same eternal and incontrovertible principles, they will produce corresponding results and make the Negro as acceptable to the brotherhood of men as any other race laying claims to the instinct of our common humanity. I believe that education, in the full sense of the term, is the most efficient and comprehensive means to this end, because in its results an answer is to be found to all the leading objections against the Negro which enter into the make-up of the so-called race problem.

Good Government Implies Intelligence.—Dr. A. G. Haygood, of Georgia, in his "Pleas for Progress," says: "Good government implies intelligence, and universal suffrage demands universal education." It cannot now be said, as it was fifty years ago, that a Negro cannot be educated. The history of education among the colored people for a quarter of a century does not confirm the statement. The noble men and women who went into the South as missionaries, and felt their way through the smoke of battle and stepped over crimson battle-fields and among the wounded and the dying to bring intelligence to the Negroes, were taunted as going on a fool's errand. But the tens of thousands of young men and women in the schools of high grade established by Northern service and philanthropy—a million Negro children in the public schools in the South—are an imperishable monument to the wisdom of their action. I again quote from Dr. Haygood, who is an authority on this subject: "All told, fully fifty millions of dollars have gone into the work of their (Negroes') education since 1865." Of this fifty millions, more than half has been Southern money. The Negroes have made more progress in elementary and other education during the twenty-three years than any other illiterate people in the world, and they have justified the philanthropy and public policy that made the expenditure.

Whites Must Also Be Educated.—President Price aptly says that it must be remembered, however, that more is to be done than the education of the blacks, as a solution of the race problem; for much of the stubbornness of the question is involved in the ignorant, lawless and vicious whites of the South, who need education worse that many of the blacks. To educate one race and neglect the other is to leave the problem half solved, for there is a class in the South to some extent more degraded and hopeless in their mental and moral condition than the Negro. This is the class to which many of the actual outrages are more attributable than to any other class. Educate these as well as the blacks, and our problem is shorn of its strength.

When we call to mind the fact that 70 per cent. of the colored vote in the South is illiterate, and 30 per cent. of the white vote is in the same condition, it is not difficult for one to discern that education of the blacks and whites as well is not only necessary for the solution of the race problem, and for good government, but for the progress and prosperity of that section where such illiteracy obtains. For the safety of the republic, the perpetuity of its glory and the stability of its institutions are commensurate, and only commensurate, with the intelligence and morality of its citizens, whether they be white men or black men. It is sometimes harder to educate out of prejudice than out of ignorance.

Wealth-Producer.—The Negro is a wealth-producer now. Whether he reaps all the benefits of his labor or not, it is clear that he is the prime element in the growing and boasted prosperity of the South. The late Henry W. Grady said, just before his death, that the Negroes in his state (Georgia) paid taxes on twenty million dollars' worth of property, and that the Negroes in the South contribute a billion dollars' worth of products every year to the material prosperity of that section. The Atlanta Constitution, speaking of the Negroes in Texas, said recently that they own a million acres of land and pay taxes on twenty million dollars worth of property, have 2,000 churches, 2,000 benevolent associations, 10 high schools, 3,000 teachers, 23 doctors, 15 lawyers, 100 merchants, 500 mechanics, 15 newspapers, hundreds of farmers and stockmen, and several inventors. Now, these two states are but samples of the wealth-producing results of twenty-five years' labor. If this has been their progress when it is admitted they have been under the hampering and retarding influences of ignorance, not to speak of other disadvantages, it is fair to assume that under the stimulus of intelligence they will do a hundredfold more, and year by year and decade by decade change their poverty-stricken state, and thus remove another element in the problem, and thereby hasten its solution.

Race Pride.—There seems to be quite as strong an affinity for their own race developed among the colored people, as a result of the improvement in their condition, as among the whites. This improvement of both implies purity of race blood, combined with the recognition of legal and political equality.

This is manifest, not in the relations alone, but in almost everything. Probably it would be found quite as difficult to bring the colored people to consent to the substitution of mixed for separate churches and schools in the South as to reconcile the other race to the change.

The Question.—The "race problem" in our country includes not merely the question, What shall the white man do with the Negro? There is another, still more serious: What shall the Negro do with the white man?

The colored people number nearly, if not quite, ten millions—one-sixth of our population. They are possessed with a certain form of independence, which is beyond the reach of adverse laws and unkindly surroundings, and which cannot be taken from them without their consent to it—the independence which comes of subjection to fewer wants than press upon the white people who are about them, and who compose the balance of the nation. If they get but little, they have the advantage of being able to go without. Their mental, spiritual and physical wants are few, because of their lack of development. If they are ignorant,

MORRIS BROWN COLLEGE, ATLANTA, GA.

they are accustomed to the consequences of ignorance; and if they are deprived of their rights, they have the advantage of having been slaves from the beginning.

But, on the other hand, it does not go so easy with the white race, who compose the larger factor of the American people. If the wants of the Negro are few, on the contrary, those of the white man are many; and, as in the struggle for life the opportunity to labor and to produce is the opportunity to live—for only by producing something to sell can any one buy and thus procure the means of satisfying wants—it follows that if the man with few wants can get the work, he has the advantage of the man with many wants, who must suffer in being deprived of his purchasing power.

Power of Education.—"The same light lighteth every man that cometh into the world." Says Henry W. Blair: "Education is the solution of the Southern problem; education is the solution of the Northern problem; education is the solution of the problem of all human advancement. Right education of the physical, mental and spiritual powers of each individual will perfect society, and nothing else will do it.

"Five hundred thousand teachers, who constitute the great profession in our country, are solving the difficulties which environ the nation.

"True, there be other agencies—the church, the press, and the influences of the daily contact of life.

"But the work of the teacher is fundamental, and is necessary, in order that intelligence may criticise creed and prevent religion from degenerating into superstition; in order that the press may perform its work at all, and that daily contact with others may not simply reproduce in coming generations the imperfect environment of the present.

"The public school system is the only hope, in the sense that it is the great creative and saving institution of the republic. The general diffusion of knowledge, intelligence and virtue made us a republic."

The Public School System.—The public school system is the army which wages everlasting war upon ignorance and all whose victories are peace.

Taxation by the public must be for the general good, and of necessity results in the public school, without which at least one-half of the property of the country would escape its just contribution to the education of the people, and not less than one-half the children would grow up in ignorance, by reason of the poverty of those who, while they have produced life, may not have made money.

The Outlay of Money and means for the education of the Negro during the last twenty-five years has exceeded that of all the centuries of his enslavement. It is estimated that the Southern states have expended for his education $55,000,000, and the Northern states $20,000,000, making a total from the states of $75,000,000.

Number of Institutions.—Among the public and private institutions set apart for this purpose, there were, in 1891, 52 normal and industrial schools maintained by the states and by various religious denominations, having 10,000 students; 25 denominational and non-denominational universities and colleges, having 8,000 students; 47 institutions for secondary instructions, having 12,000 students; 25 schools in theology, having 700 students; 5 schools of law, with 100 students; 5 schools of medicine, with 240 students; all, with two exceptions, located in the states formerly known as slave states. Besides these, there are in the South 16 schools receiving both state and federal aid, and offering to the colored youth industrial and agricultural training, having about 2,500 students.

Twenty-five Years.— Said the Honorable William B. Webb, District Commissioner, having in charge the schools of the District of Columbia, in presenting the certificates of graduation to the graduating class: "Twenty-five years ago colored men were not allowed upon the streets of the city of Washington after sundown without passes. Twenty-five years ago I, myself, as Superintendent of Metropolitan Police, issued passes permitting colored persons to be found on the streets after sundown in the city of Washington. Tonight I am permitted, and I assure you it is no small pleasure to me, to give young colored people, not unlikely the sons and daughters of those to whom I issued passes twenty-five years ago, certificates showing that you have completed a course of instructions, including that of the high school, provided for the young people of the District of Columbia, white and colored alike."

Profitable Work.—Prof. W. B. Powell says: " The colored people should be educated as other people are educated, but the beginnings of such education should be wisely determined. They must be made industrious. I have said they are not idle, but to be made industrious they must be taught to work profitably. They must be made provident; to do this they must be trained in the arts and processes of economy. They must be taught the meaning and value of thrift; to accomplish this they must learn to work intelligently, to plan economically, and patiently to wait. They must learn the value of the investment of labor, and patience and faith, and waiting.

Practical Training.—These valuable qualifications come not through books or letters alone; they come by doing.   So while I would say, teach the colored youth in and of books, I say, emphatically, train him also in the arts and processes of agriculture and gardening, and train him in these while he is learning to read; thus will he learn to do both better.   Train him in the process of the most useful mechanical arts, and let him get this training contemporaneous with the acquirement of his primary scholastic education; train him in the arts and processes of barter and sale, and let this be done while he is taking his first steps in reading and arithmetic; thus, becoming a man of affairs, his scholastic training will be intelligible to him.

A supervisor (a colored man, graduate of the Vermont State Normal School), having in charge a hundred schools, when asked what he would do to educate the colored race if he were given authority to act and the disposition of the money now expended on their education, replied, that he would foster the lower graded schools, but instead of the colleges and high schools he would establish agricultural and trade schools, and perhaps more normal schools.

Academic Instruction.—Academic instruction alone never reached such results; it never can.   I am not discussing the question of manual training; I am talking about the education of a people who know how to do a very little in harmony with the governing civilization on this continent.   Our civilization represents, in the process of its growth, all the qualifications for which I plead.   They cannot be omitted in the growth of any people.   They cannot be transmitted from one people to another by any process of philanthropic endeavor or legal enactment.   The people who would have the growth must themselves do the growing.

The Great Danger of academic education for the

colored youth as now given by the schools in their developed condition, successful and brilliant as it is, is that it leads them away from the bread-winning pursuits of life, which must necessarily be the lot of the great mass of them as it is of us all. This must be so while their manual pursuits are so rude and uninteresting. Unless the colored youth are made to know and feel that successes in manual labor are respectable and honorable, as honorable as purely scholastic successes, and unless they are made acquainted with, and given skill in, modern industrial arts and appliances, their education will be to them a source of restlessness and discontent, and may be to the community a source of danger. This is not true because of their color.

The New England Farmer Boy did not learn to despise his home work by attending school three or four months in the winter. He was learning, under the skillful management of the father, more and more rapidly, at home than he learned at school. What he learned at school was only an additional acquisition that helped him in his home work. His chief learning was at home. The daughter of the colonial days made her chief acquisitions at home under the skillful management of the mother, where she learned to spin and weave and darn and patch. Her school life added accomplishments to these useful arts, and made her more intelligent and useful.

Only Means of Growth.—The school is to the colored youth of whom I speak his only place of learning. He learns nothing at home; nobody is competent to teach him advantageously; he learns nothing from his neighbors; nobody with whom he associates does anything better than he finds it done in his own home. He comes to look on the school, therefore, as the only means of growth, as the only means of bettering his condition; he comes to look on school and scholastic acquisition as the only means by which he can become

PROF. J. L. MURRAY.
Principal Normal School, Albany, Georgia.
(Graduate of Fisk University.)

respectable and grow to be like the white man. Will he not learn to despise labor? This is a new view of life, its possibilities and opportunities, that means defeat to the race that holds it, that is fraught with danger to the community. This may all be avoided by training the hand and the mind simultaneously and proportionally. If the colored man has not been so trained, it is not his fault; it is the fault of those who gave him the schools, the fault of those who builded for him. He knew not how to build for himself.

Useful and Independent.—The colored youth can be educated to usefulness, respectability and honor. The education that the colored man receives, however, should be so directed as to make him useful and independent at the earliest possible moment. The philanthropist will give alms to the unfortunate, will feed the man temporarily out of employment, but he will not give employment to the unskilled man when one who is skilled can be found. Not many years ago it was found that skilled persons from foreign lands were occupying the most lucrative positions in the factories of America. Aroused by this fact and further awakened by the Centennial Exposition of 1876, the public schools of the nation began in earnest the training of hand and eye. Polytechnic schools sprang up in all parts of the land. These things were done for the benefit of America's bread-winners.

America's Prosperity is due less to her agricultural interests than to her making powers. She has made herself wealthy, respected, and powerful, by transforming raw material into valuable and useful things. There is more of this to be done in the future than there has been in the past, and skilled hands will do it. The colored man should be made to appreciate this fact.

If the colored man is not trained in the useful arts of life, in those arts that have made the best citizenship of America, in those arts that have given the greatest wealth to America, in those arts that have given the greatest dignity to America, in those arts that have

brought the greatest renown to America, in those arts
that have made it possible for the people to preserve a
united interest and a common pride, under one government, the skilled white laborer will occupy the paying
positions, leaving the unskilled colored laborer the poorly paid places of helpers and assistants.   I wish only to
see things as they are.''

In One Generation.—It is only thirty years since all
the learning of his race was embodied in its folklore,
when the written literature of the white man among
whom he lived was sealed to him by the compulsory
ignorance in which he was kept.   The Negro in the
old days must spend his time thinking and talking, where
the white man by his side spent it in learning through
the medium of books; and thoughts and beliefs must
be perpetuated by him in stories, songs, rhythmic utterances and rites and ceremonies which could by the
whites be committed to paper, to survive or be forgotten as the case might be.   In consequence of this short
distance in time that lies between the Afro-American
and the unwritten learning that belongs to the childhood of his past, he may look back with ease and gather
up for himself and his future history the small beginnings of learning which preceded literary attainment.

School Population.—The report of the Commissioner
of Education for 1895 gives the following reliable information and statistics for the colored schools for that
year.   In the sixteen slave states and the District of
Columbia, the estimated number of persons five to
eighteen years of age, the school population, was 8,297,-
160.   Of this number 5,573,440 were white children
and 2,723,720, or 32.9 per cent., colored.   The total
enrollment in the white schools was 3,845,414, and in
the colored schools 1,441,282.   The per cent. of white

school population enrolled was 69, and the per cent. of the colored school population enrolled was 52.92. The whites had an average daily attendance of 2,510,907, or 65.30 per cent. of their enrollment, while the average attendance of the blacks was 956,312, or 58.41.per cent. of their enrollment. There were 89,276 white teachers and 27,081 colored teachers in the public schools of the South in 1895.

Money Expended.—An accurate statement of the amounts of money expended by each of the Southern states for the education of the colored children cannot be given, for the reason that in only two or three of these states are separate accounts kept of the moneys expended for colored schools. Since 1876 the Southern states have expended about $383,000,000 for public schools, and it is fair to estimate that between $75,-000,000 and $80,000,000 of this sum must have been expended for the education of colored children.

Illiteracy of the Colored Population.—What have the Negroes themselves accomplished to justify the generosity of the white people of the South and the benevolence of the people of the North? It may be said that in 1860 the colored race was totally illiterate. In 1870 more than 85 per cent. of the colored population of the South, ten years of age and over, could not read and write. In 1880 the per cent. of illiterates had been reduced to 75, and in 1890 the illiterates comprised about 60 per cent. of the colored population ten years of age and over. In several of the Southern states the percentage is even below 50 per cent. In the states where the colored population is greatest in proportion to the total population, or where such colored population is massed, as in the black belt" of South Carolina, Georgia, Alabama, Mississippi and Louisiana, there the per cent. of illiteracy is highest.

ALLEGHENY UNIVERSITY

Illiteracy Disappearing.—In thirty years 40 per cent. of the illiteracy of the colored race had disappeared. In education and in industrial progress this race had accomplished more than it could have achieved in centuries in a different environment, without the aid of the whites. The Negro has needed the example as well as the aid of the white man. In sections where the colored population is massed and removed from contact with the whites, the progress of the Negro has been retarded. He is an imitative being, and has a constant desire to attempt whatever he sees the white man do. He believes in educating his children, because he can see that an increase of knowledge will enable them to better their condition.

Secondary and Higher Education.—There are in the United States 162 institutions for the secondary and higher education of the colored race. Six of these schools are not located within the boundaries of the former slave states. Of the 162 institutions, 32 are of the grade of colleges, 73 are classed as normal schools, and the remaining 57 are of secondary or high school grade. While all these schools teach pupils in the elementary studies, they also carry instructions beyond the common school branches. State aid is extended to 35 of the 162 institutions, and 18 of these are wholly supported by the states in which they are established. The remaining schools are supported wholly or in part by benevolent societies and from tuition fees. In these schools were employed 1,549 teachers, 711 males and 838 females. The total number of students was 37,102; of these 23,420 were in elementary grades, 11,724 in secondary grades, and 1,958 were pursuing collegiate studies. Of the 13,682 students in secondary and higher grades, there were 990 in classical courses,

811 in scientific courses, 295 in business courses, and 9,331 in English courses.

Teachers.—There were 4,514 colored students studying to become teachers, 1,902 males and 2,612 females. Many of these students were included among those pursuing the English and other courses.

High Schools.—The number of students graduating from high school courses was 649, the number of males being 282 and the number of females 367. There were 844 graduates from normal courses, 357 males and 487 females. The number of college graduates was 186, the number of males being 151 and the number of females 35.

Professions.—There were 1,166 colored students studying learned professions, 1,028 males and 138 females. Of the professional students 585 were studying theology, 310 medicine, 55 law, 45 pharmacy, 25 dentistry, and 8 engineering. The 138 female students were receiving professional training for nurses. There were 42 graduates in theology, 67 in medicine, 21 in law, 2 in dentistry, 16 in pharmacy, and 25 in nurse training.

Industrial Training.—The importance of industrial training is almost universally recognized by teachers of the colored race, and the Negroes themselves are beginning to see its value. There are about 13,000 pupils receiving industrial training in the schools.

Industrial Schools.—"Talks for the Times" says: "The wisdom and foresight in the establishment of these industrial departments are apparent. We cannot all be teachers and preachers and lawyers and doctors. This has never been the condition of any people, and the colored people are no exception. Somebody must push the saw and drive the plane. Somebody must plow.

There must be somewhere among us a strong, intelligent, virtuous middle class, the salt of society in all ages. Moreover, the demand for skilled labor becomes more and more imperative, and, unless the ranks of the colored mechanics and artisans can be recruited from these schools, or some other schools, if you please, with workmen of higher intelligence, the South will be flooded with foreigners to meet the demand. This, of course, would be bad for the Negro, but perhaps worse for the South and the nation; for, with Europe in her present condition, an influx of foreigners may be accompanied by an influx of dangerous isms—Fenianism and Socialism and Communism and Nihilism, and all those isms whose arguments in the settlement of social questions are dynamite and assassination. Surely, then, it is as politic as it is provident in the leaders of our educational work in the South to guard against this train of evils by educating and training for the management of our ever-increasing industries a people born to the soil, a people whose characteristics, tested during two centuries and a half, have been found to be love, affection, gentleness, fidelity, forgiveness, and whose only crime has been the color of their skin. This, then, in brief, is what the Christian church has done and is doing for us.''

Industrial Education.—Industrial education is gaining many friends all through the Southland, and while there are multitudes who speak in praise of the industrial schools of the South there are others who object to the methods pursued.

"Industrial training," says President Mitchell, of the Leland University, New Orleans, "is good and useful to some persons if they can afford time to take it, but in its application to the Negro several facts should be clearly understood. It is a mistake to suppose that industrial education can be applied to the beginning of school life; it is not possible or desirable to train large bodies of youth to superior industrial skill without a basis of sound elementary education. You cannot polish a brickbat, and you cannot make a good workman of a plantation Negro or a white ignoramus until you first wake up his mind, and give him the mental discipline and knowledge that come from a good school. Industrial training is expensive of time and money, as compared with its results as a civilizer. When you have trained one student you have simply fitted one man to any ordinary living. When you have given a college education to a man with brains it is sending forth an instrument that will fit hundreds and thousands. Again, industrial training is liable to divert attention from the real aim and end of education, which is manhood. Lastly, the industrial schools of the South seem to show that even their students are not proficient. Of 18 colored schools in which industrial instruction is given, such as carpentry, tinning, painting, plastering, shoemaking, tailoring, blacksmithing, farming, gardening, etc., having 1243 graduates, there are found to be only 12 farmers, 2 mechanics, 1 carpenter.

The employments of the graduates were: Teachers, 693; ministers, 117; physicians, 163; lawyers, 116; editors, 5; merchants, 15; U. S. government service, 36, etc.

We take the following extracts from an address delivered by Booker T. Washington, principal of the Tuskegee Normal and Industrial Institute:

Advantages.—Industrial training, combined with the mental and religious training, has several emphatic advantages. Few of the young men and women who came to us were able to remain in school during the nine months and pay in cash the $8 per month charged for board. Through our industries we give them the chance of working out a part of their board, and the remainder they pay in cash.

Respect for Labor.—Industrial training gives to students the respect and love for labor, helps them to get rid of the idea so long prevalent in the South that labor with the hands is rather degrading, and this feeling is not altogether original with the black men of the South. The fact that a man goes into the world with the consciousness that he has within him the power to make a wagon or a house gives him a certain moral backbone and independence in the world. At the head of each industrial department there is a competent instructor, so that the student is not only learning the practical work but is taught as well the underlying principles. When the student is through with brick masonry he not only understands the trade in a practical way, but also mechanical and architectural training to such an extent that he can become a leader in this industry.

Leaders.—In everything done, in literature, religion and industrial training, the question kept constantly before us all is that the institution exists for the purpose of training a certain number of picked leaders who will go out and reach the masses, and show them how to lift themselves up. It must be remembered that 85 per cent. of the colored people in the South live in the country districts, where they are difficult to reach except by special effort.

Importance.—The question is often asked me, why is it important to emphasize industrial education in the South, especially among the colored people? Let me try to give the answer. For three hundred years the influence of slavery had the effect to educate the white man and black man away from loving labor. The white man's aim was to have the Negro perform the labor, and the Negro's aim was to escape as much of it as possible. Then all the conditions that surrounded slavery made intelligent labor impossible. Under such circumstances no class in the South was trained to dignify labor, to look upon it as something ennobling, but the reverse. In addition, slavery left 4,000,000 slaves and twice as many whites practically empty handed so far as material and industrial possessions were concerned.

Not Limited Mental Development.—Confining the discussion now to the nearly 8,000,000 of Negroes in the South, let any one come into the South and go into the country districts especially, where 85 per cent of our people live, and a few cardinal needs will at once become evident—ownership of land, proper food, shelter, clothing, habits of thrift, economy, and something provident for a rainy day. Since these are emphatic needs, is it not common sense as well as logic to direct a large proportion of our educational force along lines that soonest cure these very needs? Too often when the object of industrial education for the black man is mentioned, some get the idea that industrial education is a synonym for a limited mental development. This is not true. This important question should not be befogged by any such argument. It requires as much brain power to build a Corliss engine as to write a Greek grammar. I would say to the Negro boy what I would say to any boy—get all the mental development possible; but I would also say to a large proportion of the black boys and girls, and would emphasize it for the next fifty years or longer, that, either at the same time that the literary training is being got, or after it is got, they should devote themselves to the mastery of some industry.

Look at Facts.—Praise is good for a race as for an individual, but flattery is not good for either. To tell us as a race that our condition is now the same as that of any other race, and that our training at present should not differ from that of other races, is to tell us something that makes the average black man feel good, but it is not telling him that which is true, nor that which on the long run will benefit him most. It is far better for us as a race to look facts honestly in the face —to recognize that three hundred years of slave labor and ignorance have left our condition far from being the same—and apply the remedy accordingly. In our education of the black man so far, we have failed in a large degree to educate along the very line in which most of the colored people especially need help. At least 85 per cent. of our people in the South depend on agriculture in some form for their living, and yet, aside from what has been done at the Hampton Institute in Virginia, the Tuskegee Institute in Alabama, and two or three other institutions, almost no attention has been given to providing first-class training in agriculture, dairying, horticulture, poultry raising, and stock raising. We have given colored men the highest training in theology, medicine, law, oratory, the classics, etc., and this is right. The colored boy has been taken from the farm and taught astronomy; how to locate Jupiter and Mars, how to measure Venus—taught about everything except that which he depends upon for daily bread. The great problem now is, how to get the masses to the point where they can be sure of a comfortable living and be prepared to save a little something each year.

TRAINED NURSES, SPELMAN SEMINARY.

This can be accomplished only by putting among the masses as fast as possible strong, well-trained leaders in the industrial walks of life.

Ennobling Labor.—Objection is sometimes waged against pushing industrial education for the Negro, on the ground that the Negro has had a training in work for three hundred years, and does not need help along that line. Right here the mistake is made. Industrial education, so far from teaching an individual how to work, teaches him how not to work—teaches him how to make the forces of nature work for him, to lift labor up out of toil and drudgery into the atmosphere where labor is ennobled, beautified and glorified. Industrial education is meant to take the boy who has been following an old mule behind a plow, making corn at the rate of ten bushels an acre, and set him upon a machine, under an umbrella, behind two fine horses, so that he can make four times as much corn as by the old process, and with less labor. Without industrial education, when the black woman washes a shirt, she washes it with both hands, both feet and her whole body. An individual with industrial education will use a machine that washes ten times as many shirts in a given time, with almost no expenditure of physical force—steam, electricity, or water power doing the work. It is safe to say that 90 per cent. of the colored people, as is perhaps true of most races, depend for their living on the common occupations of life. Since this is true, it seems to me that it is part of wisdom to give much attention to fitting these masses to do an ordinary task in an extraordinary way.

High Forms of Labor.—For want of the highest intelligence and skill, the Negroes' labor is confined to what is termed the lower forms of labor. We must not only teach the Negro to improve the methods of performing what is now classed as the lower forms of labor, but the Negro must be put in a position, by the use of intelligence and skill, to take his part in the higher forms of labor, up in the regions where the profit appears. When it comes to the production of cotton, for example, the Negro is the main factor; when it comes to the working of this cotton up into the finer fabrics, where the profit appears, the Negro disappears as a factor. This defect can be remedied only by teaching the Negro that a man with the highest education can make his life useful by giving the race the benefit of his training along the lines of agriculture, dairying, horticulture, laundering, and manufacture in its various forms. If the educated men of the race do not come to the rescue of the masses along these industrial lines, the. Negro, instead of being the soul and the center of important industries, will be relegated to the ragged edge. Slowly the colored mechanics, who received their training in slavery, are dying, and their places are being filled with white men of skill and intelligence. At present, the colored man in the Gulf states has a monopoly of the skilled labor, but he will not hold it many years unless he has men of his own race who can not only perform the mechanical work, but can draw the plans and make estimates on large and complicated jobs.

Value of Culture.—In thus pleading the importance of industrial training for our people, I have often been criticised and misunderstood, because I seem to overlook the ethical, religious side, or seem to underestimate the value of culture. I do not overlook the value of these elements, for they are as valuable for the Negro as for any race; but it is a pretty hard thing to give a man much culture when he has no house to live in, and it is equally hard to make a good Christian of a hungry man. I claim for the Negro all the rights and privileges enjoyed by any other race, but also maintain that we must have a foundation on which to rest our claims. Nothing will so soon cause prejudice against the Negro to disappear as industrial or commercial development, ownership of property; the production of that which others must buy, soon results in an individual's securing all his rights; and the same is equally true of a race.

Here at the Tuskegee Institute, with its 25 industries, 800 students, 78 instructors, we are doing all we can to send out a constant stream of young men who go as leaders to put in force the very ideas that I have tried to mention. Had we the means we could make our work 50 per cent. more potent. Any American who wants to do the most toward producing good citizenship should see that such a movement as is now on foot at Tuskegee does not suffer, as it is now suffering, for want of money.

Friction.—Whatever friction exists between the black man and white man in the South will disappear in proportion as the black man, by reason of his intelligence and skill, can create something that the white man wants or respects; can make something, instead of all the dependence being on the other side. Despite all her faults, when it comes to business pure and simple, the South presents the opportunity to the Negro for business that no other section of the country does. The Negro can sooner conquer Southern prejudice in the civilized world than learn to compete with the North in the business world. In field, in factory, in the markets, the South presents a better opportunity for the Negro to earn a living than is found in the North. A young man educated in head, hand and heart, goes out and starts a brickyard, a blacksmith shop, a wagon shop, or an industry by which that black boy produces something in the community that makes the white man dependent on the black man for something—produces something that interlocks, knits the commercial relations of the races together, to the extent that a black man gets a mortgage on a white man's house that he can foreclose at will; well, the white man won't drive the Negro away from the polls when he sees him going up to vote. There are reports to the effect that in some sections the black man has difficulty in voting and having counted the little white ballots which he has the privilege of depositing about twice in two years, but there is a little green ballot that he can vote through the teller's window three hundred and thirteen days in every year, and no one will throw it out or refuse to count it. The man that has the property, the intelligence, the character, is the one that is going to have the largest share in controlling the government, whether he is white or black, or whether in the North or South.

Privileges of the Law.—It is important that all the privileges of the law be ours. It is vastly more important that we be prepared for the exercise of these privileges. Says the great Teacher: "I will draw all men unto me." How? Not by force, not by law, not by superficial glitter. Following in the tracks of the lowly Nazarene, we shall continue to work and wait, till by the exercise of the higher virtues, by the products of our brains and hands, we make ourselves so valuable, so attractive to the American nation, that instead of repelling we shall draw men to us because of our intrinsic worth. It will be needless to pass a law to compel men to come into contact with a Negro who is educated and has $200,000 to lend. In some respects it is already acknowledged that as a race we are more powerful, have a greater power of attraction, than the Anglo-Saxon race. It takes 100 per cent. of Anglo-Saxon blood to make a white American. The minute that it is proved that a man possesses one one-hundredth part of Negro blood in his veins it makes him a black man; he falls to our side; we claim him. The 99 per cent. of white blood counts for nothing when weighed beside 1 per cent of Negro blood.

Mistakes.—None of us will deny that immediately after freedom we made serious mistakes. We began at the top. We made these mistakes, not because we were black people, but because we were ignorant and inexperienced people. We have spent time and money attempting to go to congress and state legislatures that could have better been spent in becoming the leading real estate dealers or carpenters in our own country. We have spent time and money in making political stump speeches and in attending political conventions that could better have been spent in starting a dairy farm or truck garden, and thus have laid a material foundation, on which we could have stood and demanded our rights. When a man eats another person's food, wears another's clothes, and lives in another's house, it is pretty hard to tell how he is going to vote or whether he votes at all.

Men may make laws to hinder and fetter the ballot, but men cannot make laws that will always bind or retard the growth of manhood:

"Fleecy locks and black complexion
Cannot forfeit Nature's claim;
Skins may differ, but affection
Dwells in white and black the same."

Progress.—We went into slavery Pagans, we came out Christians. We went into slavery a piece of property, we came out American citizens. We went into slavery without a language, we came out speaking the proud Anglo-Saxon tongue. We went into slavery with the slave chains clanking about our waists, we came out with the American ballot in our hands. Progress is the law of nature; under God it shall be our eternal guiding star."

A New Nation.—A new nation, says President Mitchell, has now come upon the stage. Eight millions of people have been thrust into the center of our civilization. They have been endowed with citizenship, with all its responsibilities, with all its possibilities for good or evil. They constitute about one-eighth part of our body politic. Among them is over one-third of the Baptist denomination of this country. Shall they be educated? Can we afford to leave one stone unturned, one agency unemployed, which might lead this mighty force out of the slough of ignorance and poverty and vice and into the plane of Christian manhood and useful citizenship? There can be but one answer to this question. If we have any regard for our brethren in Christ Jesus; if we have any loyalty to our great Baptist brotherhood, we can not withhold any possible facility for that self-improvement of which, through no fault of their own, they have for centuries been deprived. It goes without saying that education is what they need—education, moral, intellectual, physical.

Primary, Industrial and Higher Education.— Mr. Fortune says: "I do not hesitate to say that if the vast sums of money already expended, and now being spent, in the equipment and maintenance of colleges and universities for the so-called higher education of colored youths, had been expended in establishing and maintaining primary schools and schools of applied science, the race would have profited vastly more than it has, both mentally and materially, while the result would have operated more advantageously to the states, and satisfactorily to the munificent benefactors. I do not inveigh, against higher education. I simply maintain that the sort of education that the colored people of the South stand most in need of is elementary and industrial."

Normal Schools for colored teachers must be established and maintained, until all schools can be provided with colored teachers who are thoroughly trained, and who will live in the communities for whom they teach, and who will in every way be united in interest with the pupils and patrons whom they serve. Aside from these peculiarities, the school education of the Negro in the South seems to me to present no new or difficult educational problem. In like manner I see no reason why he may not be allowed or required to construct for himself, apart from the white race, his family, church and civil society; but it is well to be remembered that he can do these well only after he has had guaranteed to him his privileges as component part of the state. The property of the state—of the white man and the black man alike—must be pledged to the equal education of the children of both; and I myself should not in the least object if this principle should be interpreted to have a national application.

The State Superintendent of Mississippi reports there is not a white teacher in the colored schools of the state, and this is substantially true of every state in the South. The entire public school system for the Negro is carried on by Negro teachers In Mississippi there are over 600 colored teachers who hold first grade certificates; these teachers are examined by a white board, and have just the same questions that the white teachers have. Virginia reports 700, North Carolina 761, Arkansas 500; Texas, with a different method of classification, reports 1,900. Of 19 colored teachers in an institute, 18 were found to be college graduates, while in an adjoining county, in a white institute, with 37 in attendance, there were only about one-fourth of them college graduates.

Color-Intellect.—If color has anything to do with intellect, it should appear when the two colors or races are brought into contact and competition. After a careful inquiry the almost universal opinion is that there is no difference of mental ability between the races where the same privileges have been enjoyed. If they have come from ignorant districts and dark surroundings, their intellect is inferior to those who come from cultivated homes, although it is frequently found the greatest ignorance of the former counterbalances this ability.

One-Room Cabins.—The Southern Negroes are not all living in one-room cabins, of which we have heard much recently. There are beautiful and pleasant homes owned by Negroes in New Orleans. There are plenty of ex-slaves in Louisiana that are richer now than their former masters. There are over 300,000 homes and farms owned by Negroes in the South. Six years ago Southern Negroes were paying taxes on nearly $300,000,000. The white Baptists of the South had church property worth $18,000,000, the accumulation of 200 years. The Negro Baptists at the same time (only twenty-six years out of slavery) had acquired church property of over $9,000,000.

President Gates says: "My observation leads me to believe that the proportion of truly successful men, tried by the highest standards of success, among the colored men who study in our Northern colleges is quite as great as is the proportion of successful men among the whites who have the same, or equally good, opportunities for an education."

Industrial Training.—Since industrial training has become so prominent in some of the schools of the South, it seems that other educational circles are not in sympathy with the idea of making industrial schools the prominent school of the South. A crisis in the progress of Negro education has been reached. A new generation of educated youth, wiser than their parents, wiser than their ministers, approaching manhood and womanhood, are ready to take control of affairs and of public sentiment. They already know the difference between learning and ignorance, between religion and superstition. They have no knowledge of slavery. The fact that less than one thousand of the whole South are in collegiate study is to be accounted for not by want of capacity for higher studies, but for want of motive. Education costs them a great deal. Nearly every one earns every dollar which he pays for his learning. With most it has been a great struggle to reach the point of normal graduation, and then the best salary for teaching at present available is open to them. Every influence urges them to stop here and reap the fruits of their hard-earned attainment. Some have brothers and

sisters to educate, annd some must stay at home to earn
the money.   Others have mothers and fathers who are
struggling with poverty and debt.   All this tends to

REV. D. J. SANDERS, D. D.
President of Biddle University, Charlotte, N. C.

keep them from finishing a course in a higher institution.

Economic Condition.—Dr. J. M. Curry, Secretary of Trustees of Slater Fund, says: "The economic condition is a serious drawback to mental and moral progress. Want of thrift, frugality, foresight, skill, right notions, of consumption of property, right to acquire and hold property, has made the race the victim and prey of usurers and extortioners. The Negro rarely accumulates, for he does not keep his savings, nor put them into permanent and secure investments. While it is true that a limited number of colored people are becoming wealthy, it is equally true that the masses have made but little advancement in acquiring property during their thirty years of freedom. On the great plantations the majority live in one-room cabins, tabernacling in them as tenants at will. The poverty, wretchedness, hopelessness of the present life are sometimes in pitiable contrast to the freedom from care and anxiety, the cheerfulness and frolicsomeness of ante-bellum days."

Mr. Bryce, the most philosophical and painstaking of all foreign students of our institutions, in the last edition of his great work, says: "There is no ground for despondency to any one who remembers how hopeless the extinction of slavery seemed fifty or even forty years ago, and who marks the progress the Negroes have made since their sudden liberation. Still less is there reason for impatience, for questions like this have in some countries of the old world required ages for their solution. The problem which confronts the South is one of the great secular problems of the world, presented here under a form of peculiar difficulty. And as the present differences between the African and the European are the products of thousands of years, during which one race was advancing in the temperate, and the other remaining stationary in the torrid, zone, so centuries may pass before their relation as neighbors and fellow-citizens have been duly adjusted. It would be unjust and illogical to push too far the comparison and deduce inferences unfair to the Negro, but it is an interesting coincidence that Japan began her entrance into the family of civilized nations almost contemporaneously with emancipation in the United States."

A Colored Teacher says: "I can do my people more good than I am doing now, if you will let me devote two afternoons of the week teaching them to sew. They come to school untidy; their garments are torn; their sleeves are out at the elbow; they represent the condition of their homes largely. Now, if you will let me teach these young girls to sew, I can teach them to be ashamed to come to school with torn clothes, and I believe that by doing this I will influence the lives of these people at their homes, and thereby do much more than I am now doing."

"Well, this is the key to it. The young woman who teaches the country school should be something more to the community than a teacher of letters to the children. She should be a person who would teach the entire community, either directly or indirectly, in many of the simpler home arts, those arts that are taught in all cultivated homes, white or colored. A school thus presided over would do much more good than is now done by the ordinary school of letters, and would accomplish, I believe, at the same time better scholastic results; for who does not know that, other things being equal, the best scholastic results are reached by men of affairs.

Many-Sided.—T. Thomas Fortune says: "There are so many sides to a race problem nearly 300 years old, only thirty-two years of which has been worked out under conditions of freedom, that a reasonable amount of conservatism should govern all those who undertake to discuss any phase of it.   The Afro-American problem is such a one.   Slavery was a hard school in many respects; freedom is a harder one.

Effects of Slavery.—Slavery destroys entirely the self-dependence and reliance of the slave; and when he has had 255 years of slave education and only thirty-two of freedom education to offset it, it is not ease to determine just what is best for him, to prepare him for the responsibilities of manhood and citizenship.

Poor and Ignorant.—When slavery was abolished the 4,000,000 people who came out of the house of bondage possessed, in the main, no book education whatever.   They were equally destitute of moral and spiritual education.   They possessed no self-reliance.   They were poor in head and heart and purse.   They were compelled to begin at the bottom and build from the ground up in all the essentials that make for character and worth.   They had no leaders, no teachers, to guide them out of the shadows into the sunlight of freedom.   If they had been left to their own devices, they would have gone to pieces; they would have justified the doleful predictions of those who insisted that they were destitute of the common attributes of human kind.

Not Left Alone.—But they were not left to their own devices.   The friends who had fought their battles when they were slaves remained constant to them when they were turned loose upon the land with freedom as their whole stock in trade.   As the flower of the Northern manhood had poured out its life's blood on the battlefield to save the Union and crush the slave power through four years of war, making desolate thousands upon thousands of homes, so, in the wake of the vanishing Northern army, there followed an army of Northern women, and a few men, imbued with the finest missionary spirit that ever actuated human beings, who planted schools and seminaries and colleges on the ruins of the war, and began the completion of the work where their brothers and fathers and husbands had left it off at Appomattox Court House, when

'The war drums throbbed no longer, and the battle flags
     were furl'd,
   In the Parliament of man, The Federation of the world.'

Tribute to Northern Women.—Without the work of these Northern women in the schoolhouses and the churches and the homes of the freed men, the sacrifices of their male relatives in the war would have been in vain. The brave soldier laid the foundation when he achieved the freedom of the blacks; his sister built upon the foundation a superstructure of mental and moral training which will abide and influence the destinies of the republic as long as the Afro-American shall remain an indivisible factor of our national life. The public school systems of the Southern states owe their origin to the devoted efforts and sacrifices of the Northern men and women who flocked into the South when the war closed, and who remained there as long as their services were needed.

Imperishable Monuments.—All the colleges and seminaries scattered all over the South, devoted to the higher education of the manumitted slave, were founded and fostered by the same devoted spirits. They will stand through the ages as imperishable monuments, living witnesses that selfishness is not always the controlling influence in the conduct of mankind. The vast volume of energy and wealth lavished by the North upon the education of the freedmen of the South was a service to humanity and to the republic which can yield no return to the benefactors save the satisfaction of having done their duty."

Opinions.—Dr. Curry truly says: "Whatever may be our speculative opinions as to the progress and development of which the Negro may be ultimately capable, there can hardly be a well-grounded opposition to the opinion that the hope for the race in the South is to be found not so much in the high courses of university instruction or in schools of technology as in handicraft instructions.

Conclusions.— 1. It follows that in addition to thorough and intelligent training in the discipline of character and virtue, there should be given rigid and continuous attention to domestic and social life, to the refinement and comforts and economies of home.

2. Taught in the economies of wise consumption, the race should be trained to acquire habits of thrift, of saving earnings, of avoiding waste, of accumulating property, of having a stake in good government, in progressive civilization.

3. Besides the rudiments of a good and useful education there is imperative need of manual training, of the proper cultivation of those faculties or mental qualities of observation, of aiming at and reaching a successful end, and of such facility and skill in tools, in practical industries, as will insure remunerative employment and give the power which comes from intelligent work.

4. Clearer and juster ideas of education, moral and intellectual, obtained in cleaner home life and through respected and capable teachers in schools and churches. The ultimate and only sure reliance for the education

of the race is to be found in the public schools, organized, controlled and liberally supported by the state.

5. Between the races occupying the same territory,
possessing under the law equal civil rights and privileges, speculative and unattainable standards should be
avoided, and questions should be met as they arise, not
by Utopian and partial solutions, but by the impartial
application of the tests of justice, right, honor, humanity,
and Christianity."

Evolution, not Revolution.—The emergence of a
nation from barbarism to a general diffusion of intelligence and property, to health in the social and civil
relations; the development of an inferior race into a
high degree of enlightenment, the overthrow of customs
and institutions which, however indefensible, have their
seat in tradition and a course of long observance; the
working out satisfactorily of political, sociological and
ethical problems, are all necessarily slow, requiring
patient and intelligent study of the teachings of history
and the careful application of something more than mere
empirical methods. Civilization, freedom, a pure
religion, are not the speedy outcome of revolutions and
cataclysms any more than has been the structure of the
earth. They are the slow evolution of orderly and
creative causes, the result of law and pre-ordained
principles.

Five Great Institutions.—Now, there are, as we
well know, five great institutions that are so distinctively
educational that they must be taken into consideration
in every attempt to educate the Negro. They are the
family, the church, the state, civil society, and the
school. The Negro needs the influence of the responsibilities and the privileges of all these five institutions.
He must be taught the sacred character and educational

value of the family, and his ideals of this institution must be elevated and refined. No community—North South, East or West—having the Negro to educate, can afford to neglect this important matter, or so to treat him in any way that he shall fail of its high civilizing influence. So of the church. Its theory of life, its view of the world and of the destiny of man, its method and practices, must all be made plain to him, and he must be taught to organize the church and must be allowed to carry it on in accordance with its sacred character. In like manner he must be taught to construct and carry on a civil society whose public opinion shall stand for purity, honesty and morality. Again, he must be allowed to take his rightful part in the responsibilities and the privileges of the state; for the institution of the state is little less educational than is the school itself. The state cannot afford to practice injustice upon even its poorest subject, lest it thus give him the ideal and the excuse for the practice of injustice himself. In all these respects the Negro is susceptible to the same general action and reaction of institutions as is the white man, and those who have his education in charge will succeed well or ill in proportion as they regard in these respects his human characteristics.

Prof. Spence.—The following is taken from an address delivered at an annual meeting of the American Missionary Association, by Prof. A. K. Spence, Dean of Fisk University, after an experience of twenty-five years in Negro Education.

Need and Fitness.—I am asked how the work of colored education looks to me after being engaged in it a quarter of a century. Just twenty-five years ago, after teaching twelve years in the University of Michigan, I went to Nashville, Tennessee, to help build up

Fisk University, the first established Negro college in the world, as far as is known. The venture seemed to many great, to most, perhaps, even rash. What need had a people just out of bondage of a college—what fitness for it? One little girl in the school could read eight or ten lines of easy Latin in a day. Nearly all the pupils were in primary grades of English studies. These studies still went on with the mass, while the few were carried toward college, and, in time, through it.

No Mistake.—Was that early effort a mistake? Certainly it was one of intense interest to those who made it. Like early navigators we were out on new seas of discovery. Would we come to the charmed circle beyond which the Negro mind could not go? We would try, and when we came to that fatal place we would stop, not sooner. There may be some question of relative speed in advancement, but we never came to that stopping place. For twenty years now college classes have been graduated with a fairly high standard of scholarship, making in all a total of nearly one hundred and fifty, not to mention an equal number of graduates from the normal course, and several in theology and music. Three hundred graduates as the result of thirty years of labor, beginning at the zero point in 1865, seems to me a large result. Besides this, great numbers have been educated in the institution who do not complete a course, but have been fitted to do much good among their people.

Question Settled.— By this experiment certainly one thing has been settled—the ability of a goodly number of those of the colored race to receive what is called a liberal education. A person who denies that shows a lack of intelligence on the subject.

But the possibility granted, the utility of this education is doubted both as to the individual and as to the race. First, then, as to the individual, aside from the mere mercantile advantage derived from education, does not the hunger of the Negro mind for knowledge prove its right to know, its capacity show that it should be filled, its longing that it should be satisfied? And as to the race at large, does it not need within it men and women of education? How would it be with us of the white race if we had none such with us—no educated ministers, doctors, lawyers, teachers, professors, writers, thinkers? All the preaching to eight millions of people in the United States is done by colored preachers, with the merest exceptions here and there. Do these Negroes not need preparation for their vastly responsible calling? The entire work of instruction in the colored public schools of the South is done by colored teachers.

These teachers cannot be prepared in the white schools and colleges of the South. Where, then, shall they be prepared, if not in special higher institutions of learning open to them? What is to become of the millions of colored people in the United States.

Leaders.—Who are to be their leaders? Doubtless persons of their own race. Do they need less preparation for their calling than do members of the white race for theirs? Is not their task even more difficult? Have they not questions of greater intricacy to solve? Did not Moses when leading ex-slaves out of Egypt need special wisdom? Are not the colored people of today "perishing for lack of knowledge"?

Education Required.—But the objector will say, Why have these long courses, these colleges for colored people? Would not shorter courses be as well or even better?

The following is my belief on this point, after twenty-five years of thought and experience: If the Negro is equal to the white man in heredity and environment, he needs an equal chance in education; if he is superior, he can get on with less; if he is inferior, he needs more. The education required is not simply that of books, but of life in Christian homes, such as are supplied in nearly all our missionary schools for that people, and of religion through the Christian church and its influences.

Changed Condition.—In the city of Nashville we have now many most encouraging examples of the new colored South, not only in schools, but in neat and commodious houses, with the appointments of modern civilization in which refined manners prevail; libraries and instruments of music are found, and children are growing up like those in the better white families. There are already among the graduates of our colored institutions of learning and others educated in them, able doctors, lawyers, ministers, teachers and men of business, who form a society but little known among many, who speak as by authority and say that the case of the Negro is hopeless. There was a club formed recently of men of that race who gather to discuss sociological questions as to health, thrift and general welfare pertaining to their people. It is in these things that the men who think are the men who do. Colleges and schools and churches are the nerve centers of the race.

Meharry Medical College.—There is in Nashville a very successful colored medical college, the Meharry Medical, a department of the Central Tennessee College. A number of Fisk graduates have gone there for their medical education. The dean has informed me that they stand especially well because of their "college training." Many Fisk graduates choose the medical profession, to which there is a great call in the needs of the colored people. Several of them have attended Northern medical colleges. One of these stood first in scholarship in a class of one hundred in the medical department of Harvard University. A few are succeeding in law, but with greater difficulty. A dozen or more are ministers of the gospel, mostly in Congregational churches. The girl whom I found in 1870 reading daily a few lines of easy Latin, is now, after many years of teaching and having the care of a family, "Field Missionary" for a large part of Tennessee under a board of Baptist women.

Homes.—I wish I could take you to many homes in Nashville and elsewhere occupied by our graduates and former students. Say what you will as to the new white South, there certainly is a new colored South, one very interesting and hopeful, and much needing both our sympathy and aid.

Slave Pen, Fort, College.—Where Fisk now stands in its beauty, a beacon of hope to a race, stood once a frowning fort, and before that a slave pen. When the Union troops took possession of Nashville, they girt it about with a series of fortifications filled with men and bristling with cannons, that swept the whole field of vision. Vast forces were concentrated in these forts. Areas outside were taken and retaken by the enemy, but these, never. Rejecting any idea of hostility, except to ignorance and sin, let us in our turn, at all hazards, hold these school fortifications; hold these forts with men and women, and sympathy and prayer. Let this work of Christian patriotism go on. If we do not, God will require it at our hands or those of our children.

Life Work.—I entered this work young. I come back to report upon it, old. If I had many lives, I would

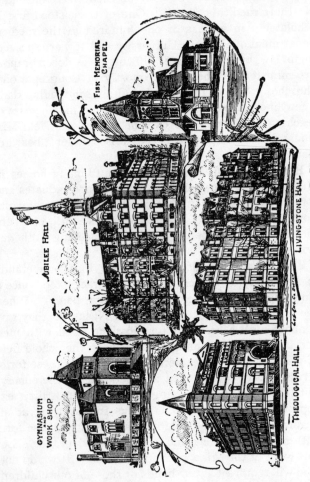

GYMNASIUM AND WORK SHOP.

JUBILEE HALL.

FISK MEMORIAL CHAPEL.

THEOLOGICAL HALL.

LIVINGSTONE HALL.

FISK UNIVERSITY, NASHVILLE, TENN.

give them over again to this cause. It is yet in its infancy, as human history goes. Already from the altars of our schools and churches many have lit their torches and carried them into the darkness, which now twinkles with its stars. The full day is not yet. We will not see it. But it will come. Let us be patient and full of courage. In one of the quaint songs of my people, for myself I can say, 'I ain't got weary yet.' "

Early Schools.—As soon as any part of the seceding states was occupied by the Union army, efforts were at once begun to give the Negro some schooling. September, 1861, under the guns of Fortress Monroe, a school for the "Contrabands of War" was opened. In 1862 they were extended south to the Carolinas. The Proclamation of Emancipation in 1863 gave freedom to all slaves reached by the armies, increased the refugees, and awakened an enthusiasm for meeting the physical, moral and intellectual needs of those suddenly thrown upon charity. The first public school for Louisiana was opened in October, 1863.

General Eaton.—As early as 1861 schools were opened at Hampton, Virginia, near the spot where the first slaves were landed in 1619. In 1863 there had collected in one place in Mississippi so many colored people eager to be taught that General Grant called to the charge of this work General John Eaton, who afterward was made United States Commissioner of Education. General Eaton served the freedmen from 1863 to 1865. He had under him at one time as many as 770,000 people. The work which General Eaton did for the colored people was truly wonderful. One of the most creditable and noteworthy features of his work was the fact that the colored people paid out of their own earnings for their education under him nearly a quarter of a million dollars.

The Freedmen's Bureau.—By act of Congress, March 3, 1865, the Freedmen's Bureau was created. Its work extended far beyond education, embracing abandoned lands, and supplying the Negroes with food and clothing. General Hôward was appointed Commissioner, with assistants. The Bureau founded many schools in localities which had been in the line of the Union armies, and these with the others established by its agency, were placed under some systematic supervision. In some states schools were carried on entirely by aid of the funds of the Bureau, but it had the co-operation and assistance of several religious and benevolent societies. A full history of the Freedmen's Bureau would furnish an interesting chapter in Negro education. But it seems that no complete report can be given on account of the disordered state of the records.

Assisting Agencies.—The Freedmen's Bureau was authorized to act in co-operation with religious and benevolent societies in the education of the Negro. A number of these organizations had done good service before the establishment of the Bureau, and continued their work afterwards. The teachers earliest in the field were from the American Missionary Association, Western Freedmen's Aid Commission, American Baptist Home Missionary Society, and the Society of Friends. After the surrender of Vicksburg others were sent by the United Presbyterians, Reformed Presbyterians, United Brethren of Christ, Northwestern Freedmen's Aid Commission, and the National Freedmen's Aid Association. The first colored school in Vicksburg was started by the United Brethren in the basement of a Methodist church.

American Missionary Association.—The American Missionary Association was the chief body apart from the government in the great enterprise of meeting the needs of the Negroes. It did not relinquish its philanthropic work because army officers and the Federal government were working along the same line. Up to 1866 its receipts were swollen by "the aid of the Free Will Baptists, the Wesleyans, the Congregationalists, and Friends in Great Britain." From Great Britain it is estimated that "a million dollars in money and clothing were contributed through various channels for the Freedmen." The third decade of the association, 1867-1876, was a marked era in its financial history. The Freedmen's Bureau turned over a large sum, which could be expended only in buildings. A Congressional report says that between December, 1866, and May, 1870, the association received $243,753.22. Since the association took on a more distinctive and separate denominational character, because of the withdrawal of other denominations into associations of their own, it, along with its church work, has prosecuted, with unabated energy and marked success, its educational work among the Negroes.

Control and Support.—It has now under its control or support 78 schools, consisting of: Chartered institutions, 6; normal schools, 29; common schools, 43. In these schools are 389 instructors and 12,609 pupils. The pupils are classified as follows: Theological, 47; collegiate, 57; college preparatory, 192; normal, 1,091; grammar, 2,378; intermediate, 3,692; primary, 5,152.

Two-fold Work.—The work of the association is among all kinds of people, from Florida to Alaska, education and evangelization going hand in hand.

Its educational work stretches all the way from elementary teaching in small schools through the various grades to large institutions for higher education. It always emphasizes self-help and self-education. It everywhere provides for the industrial training of both boys and girls.

Teachers.—A great share of its work consists in supplying hundreds of teachers every year for tens of thousands of pupils all through the needy rural communities of the South. It also has in training ministers who are rapidly developing churches and church missions. During the last year forty new churches have been organized with over a thousand members. At the present time great demands come to it for mission work among the country districts of the South. Both our pastors and its teachers in the mountain fields report growth and a still more rapid increase of opportunities for service. Indian schools and missions are being carried on with severe self-denial on account of the lessened resources. The woman's work continues its activities in co-operation with forty-two state organizations whose increased contributions last year amounted to over $29,000.

Freedmen's Aid and Southern Society.—In 1866 was organized the Freedmen's Aid and Southern Society of the Methodist Episcopal Church. Under that compact, powerful, well-disciplined, enthusiastic organization more than $6,000,000 have been expended in the education of the Negroes. Dr. Hartzell, said before the World's Congress in Chicago, that Wilberforce University, at Xenia, Ohio, was established in 1857 as a college for colored people, and "continues to be the chief educational center of African Methodism in the United States." He reports, as under various branches of Methodism, 65 institutions of learning, for colored people; 388 teachers; 10,100 students; $1,905,150 of property, and $652,500 of endowment.

Baptist Home Missionary Society.—This society supports Spelman Seminary, Shaw University, Atlanta Baptist Seminary, and other schools, and has done a good work among the Negroes.

Peabody Fund.—On February 6, 1867, George Peabody gave to certain gentlemen $2,000,000 in trust, to be used "for the promotion of intellectual, moral or industrial education among the young of the more destitute portions of the Southwestern states of our Union." The fund now acts exclusively with state systems, and continues support to Negroes more efficiently through such agencies. To realize what it has accomplished is difficult—impossible unless we estimate sufficiently the obstacles and compare the facilities of today with the ignorance and bondage of a generation ago when some statutes made it an indictable offense to teach a slave or free person of color. The results have truly been remarkable.

John F. Slater Fund.—In his letter establishing this trust is the following clause: "The general object which I desire to have exclusively pursued is the uplifting of the lately emancipated population of the Southern states and their posterity, by conferring on them the blessings of Christian education." This fund has been the potential agency in enlightening public opinion and in working out the problem of the education of the Negro. In view of the apprehensions felt by all thoughtful persons, when the duties and privileges of citizenship were suddenly thrust upon millions of lately emancipated slaves, Mr. Slater conceived the purpose of giving a large sum of money to their proper education. After deliberate reflection and much conference, he selected a board of trust, and placed in their hands $1,000,000. This unique gift, originating wholly with himself, and elaborated in his own mind in most of its details, was for "the uplifting of the lately emancipated population of the Southern states and their posterity, by conferring on them the blessings of Christian education." "Not only for their own sake, but also for the sake of our common country," he sought to provide "the means of such education as shall tend to make them good men and good citizens."

Reflex Influence. — The reflex influence of Mr. Slater's beneficence, we are persuaded, has been great. We cannot estimate the good we do when we do good. The effect of this splendid beneficence in stimulating philanthropic enterprise, passing as it has into the currency of popular thought as a quickening inspiration, its impetus to the noble army of workers for the uplifting of the race, has been enormous. Its inspiration and influence upon this greatest decade of giving in all the history of the world has been immense, we are confident. Other millions have gotten into the wake of this one; and we believe that other men to whom God has given wealth, and into whose hearts the passion of the cross has been poured, are to be moved by it to the breaking of their costly boxes of alabaster in the presence of the world's Christ. Such men are, and are to be, the saving and enduring forces of the world.

The following article, taken from the Independent of August 19, 1897, is commended to the reader. Its author's ability is well known. His opinions deserve consideration:

THE PRIME NEED OF THE NEGRO RACE.

BY ALEX. CRUMMELL, D. D.

Late Rector of St. Luke's Protestant Episcopal Church, Washington, D. C.

Incidents for Problems.—Unfortunately, men often misconceive some of the larger *incidents* of life for its *problems*, and thus, unconsciously, they hinder the progress of the race.

Just such a mistake, if I err not, has arisen with regard to the solution of the "Negro Problem" in the South. It may be seen in the divergence of two classes of minds: the one maintains that industrialism is the solution of the Negro problem; and another class, while recognizing the need of industrial skill, maintains that culture is the true solution.

Civilization.—The thing of magnitude in the South, all must admit, is the civilization of a new race. The question is, then, how is this civilization to be produced? Is industrialism the prime consideration? Is the Negro to be built up from the material side of his nature?

Industrialism.—But industrialism is no new thing in Negro life in this country. It is simply a change in the old phase of Southern Society. It is, in fact, but an incident; doubtless a large, and in some respects, a vital one. It would be the greatest folly to ignore its vast importance. Yet it is not to be forgotten that the Negro has been in this "school of labor" under slavery in America, fully two hundred and fifty years; and every one knows that it has never produced his civilization. That it was crude, previous to emancipation; that it is to be enlightened labor now, in a state of freedom, is manifestly but an alteration in the form of an old and settled order of life.

MIDDLE CLASS, 1899—GAMMON THEOLOGICAL SEMINARY.

New Problem.—When the Negro passed from under the yoke he left a state of semi-barbarism behind him, put his feet for the first time within the domain of civilization, and immediately there sprang up before him a new problem of life. But that problem is not industrialism. That is simply the modification of an old condition; for it is but the introduction of intelligence into the crudeness of the old slave-labor system.

A Question.—The other question, then, presents itself—is not the Negro's elevation to come from the quickening and enlightenment of his higher nature? Is it to come from below or from above?

Higher Culture.—It seems manifest that the major factor in this work for the Negro is his higher culture. There is not dispute as to the need of industrialism. This is a universal condition of life everywhere. But there is not need of an undue and overshadowing exaggeration of it in the case of the Negro.

A Result, not a Cause.—And, first of all, industrialism itself is a *result* in man's civilization, not a cause. It may exist in a people and with much excellence for ages, and still that people may "lie in dull obstruction," semi-barbarous and degraded. We see in all history large populations moving in all the planes of industrial life, both low and high, and yet paralyzed in all the high springs of action, and for the simple reason that the hand of man gets its cunning from the brain. And without the enlightened brain what is the hand of man more than the claw of a bird or the foot of a squirrel? In fine, without the enlightened brain, where is civilization.

A New Factor.—The Negro race, then, needs a new factor for its life and being, and this new factor must come from a more vitalizing source than any material condition.   The end of industrialism is thrift, prosperity or gain.   But civilization has a loftier object in view. It is to make men grander; it is to exalt them in the scale of being; and its main energy to this end is the "higher culture."

Greatness Comes from Altitudes.—Observe, then, just here, that "every good gift and every perfect gift comes from above."   I have no hesitation in using this text (albeit thus abbreviated) as an aphorism.   And what I wish to say in its interpretation is this, viz., that all the greatness of men comes from altitudes.   All the improvement, the progress, the culture, the civilization of men come from somewhere above.   They never come from below!

Culture of Human Society.—Just as the rains and dews come down from the skies and fall upon the hills and plains and spread through, the fields of earth with fertilizing power, so, too, with the culture of human society. Some exalted man, some great people, some marvelous migration, some extraordinary and quickening cultivation, or some divine revelation, "from above" must come to any people ere the processes of true and permanent elevation can begin among them.   And this whole process I call civilization.

A Heritage.—If a more precise and definite meaning to this word is demanded, I reply that I use it as indicative of letters, literature, science and philosophy. In other words, that this Negro race is to be lifted up to the acquisition of the higher culture of the age.   This culture is to be made a part of its heritage; not at some distant day, but now and all along the development of the race.   And no temporary fad of doubting or purblind philanthropy is to be allowed to make "industrial training" a substitute for it.

Leaders.—For, first of all, it is only a dead people who can be put into a single groove of life. And, next, every live people must have its own leaders as molders of its thought and determiners of its destiny; men, too, indigenous to the soil in race and blood.

Thought Makes the World.—It is thought that makes the world—high, noble, prophetic, exalted and exalting thought. It is this that makes races and nations, industries and trades, farming and commerce; and not the reverse of this, i. e., that these make thought and civilization. And without thought, yea, scientific thought, peoples will remain everlastingly children and underlings, the mere tools and puppets of the strong.

From the Schools.—And such thought, in these days, comes from the schools. The leaders of races must have wisdom, science, culture and philosophy. One such man has often determined the character and destiny of his race for centuries.

Opened to the Negro Mind.—This does not mean that noodles and numbskulls shall be sent to college; nor that every Negro shall be made a scholar; nor that there shall be a waste of time and money upon incapacity. No one can make a thimble hold the contents of a bucket! But what it does mean is this, that the whole world of scholarship shall be opened to the Negro mind; and that it is not to be fastened, temporarily or permanently to the truck-patch or to the hoe, to the anvil or to the plane; that the Negro shall be allowed to do his own thinking in any and every sphere, and not to have that thinking relegated to others. It means that when genius arises in this race and elects, with flaming torch, to push its way into the grand arcanum of philosophy or science or imagination, no bar shall

VIRGINIA HALL.—HAMPTON INSTITUTE.

be raised against its entrance; albeit it be incarnated in a form deeply tinged with

"The shadowed livery of the burnished sun."

Conclusions.—I submit:

1. That civilization is the foremost, deepest need of the Negro race.

2. That the "higher culture" is its grandest source.

3. That the gift to the Negro of the scientific mind, by Fisk and Clark and Lincoln, and Oberlin and Howard and Yale, and Harvard and other colleges, is of the most incalculable value to the black race.

United Action.—There is probably no dissent from the above opinion of Dr. Crummell. Even the leaders in industrial education have repeatedly declared themselves in favor of the broadest culture possible. While there may be differences of opinion in the practical working, yet all are laboring diligently for the one great end—the elevation of the race.

Educational Institutions.—It is impossible in the brief space allotted to us to make special mention of many of the excellent schools for the colored race. Some that are not mentioned· we would have been glad to mention, but were unable to secure the needed information. This chapter is prepared at a time when the schools are closed. No doubt when the forms are closed much of the desired information will be at hand, too late to use. We have done the best with the facts at hand.

In the last chapter will be found statistics of all schools of the colored race.

Hampton Normal and Agricultural Institute.—This institution was opened in April, 1868. In 1870 it was chartered by special act of the General Assembly of Virginia. It is not owned or controlled by state or government, but by a board of seventeen trustees, representing different sections of the country, and six religious denominations, no one of which has a majority.

Object.—The object of its founders was to train selected Negro youth so that they could go out and teach and lead their people, first, by example, and by getting land and homes, to give them not a dollar they could earn for this, to teach respect for labor, to replace stupid drudgery with skilled hands, and to these ends to build up an industrial system for the sake not only of self-support and intelligent labor, but also for the sake of character. From the first it has been true to the idea of education by self-support. Nothing is asked for the student that he can provide by his own labor.

Annual Cost.—The school is maintained at an annual cost of about $175,000; deducting the labor payments of Negro students, say $55,000, $120,000. This is provided for in part by one-third of the amount allowed the state of Virginia under the Land Grant Act and the Morrill Act in aid of agricultural schools, by an appropriation from Congress to pay the board, etc., of 120 Indians, with aid from the Slater and Peabody funds. The large balance is met by contributions from friends of the Negro and Indian races.

Valuation of Property.—The cost or the valuation of property owned by the institution is about $600,000. There are about fifty buildings. The home farm consists of 150 acres, the grass and dairy farm, four miles distant, 600 acres. Both are cultivated by students, and the products used or sold.

Enrollment.—The enrollment for the years 1896 and 1897 is as follows: Negro young men, 305; Negro young women, 187; making a total of 492. Indian young men, 87; Indian young women, 51; total, 138. Besides these there are 320 children in the Whittier School, or primary department, making a total of 950 students, representing twenty states and territories.

Teachers and Officers.—There are 80 teachers, officers, assistants and managers, about half of whom are in the industrial department.

Girls' Industries.—Housework, laundering, sewing, tailoring, dressmaking, cooking, and training in the use of carpenter's tools.

Boys' Industries.— Farming, carpentering, house painting, wheelwrighting, tailoring, harness making, printing, engineering, machine knitting, floriculture, and the machinists' trade.

Graduates.—Nine-tenths of the 909 Negro graduates, besides many undergraduates, have done good work in teaching, and about three-fourths have made it their life work. They are also earnest workers in the Sunday school, and in behalf of temperance.

The thirty-thousand free Negro schools of the South need nothing so much as well-trained teachers. Virginia's twenty-five hundred colored schools are not nearly supplied. No harvest field in the land, or in the world, is more urgent than this.

Trade Schools.—The need of a trade school to equip young men who could not only do good work themselves but also reach others has long been felt, and in the fall of 1896 a large and thoroughly equipped building was opened, followed by a very successful term, and another building of similar size is now going up in which the young men receive a like training in domestic science.

Field Missionary.—One of the colored graduates is employed as field missionary, whose work is to visit graduates and ex-students, their homes, schools, farms, shops, and also to keep the school informed as to what they are doing, to assure them of continued interest in their welfare and usefulness, and to encourage and help them to be in their communities ministers of Christ, cultivating industrious habits and intelligent labor. He visits schools for the purpose of selecting good student material for Hampton.

Negro Education.—The North and South are working together for the Negro for whose education no less than $4,000,000 annually in taxation and donations are raised.

Agriculture.—The need of developing and improving agricultural work in the school, always a prominent feature, has taken new impetus and a thoroughly organized system for teaching agriculture scientifically and practically has been introduced. Seventy-five per cent. of the Southern Negroes are still renters of land held under a mortgage system in a very real sort of slavery.

Outgrowth of Hampton.—Tuskegee, Calhoun, Mt. Meigs, Gloucester, Kittrell, Laurenceville, and other outgrowths of Hampton are showing what can be done toward helping the people to get land for their own and making them self-respecting citizens.

"The Southern Workman."—This is the paper published by the school and is a great help in bringing to the country a knowledge of the true condition of the Negro. It probably gives fuller and juster information regarding the condition and wants of the Southern colored people than any other periodical.

A Record of Its Work.—If any one should doubt as to the advisability of educating the Negro we would recommend the reading of the volume, "Twenty-two Years' Work of Hampton Normal and Agricultural Institute." This certainly must satisfy every one that

COBURN HALL, UNION UNIVERSITY, RICHMOND, VA.

370à

MARTIN LUTHER GRAVES HALL, UNION UNIVERSITY, RICHMOND, VA.

370b

the colored people are improving both in morals and intelligence; that they are becoming less dependent upon the charities of the white race, and that they now see that it is no disgrace to work.

A Remarkable Record.—This volume gives a remarkable record of more than nine hundred graduates of Hampton. A large number of them are engaged in teaching, others are in the ministry, a number are merchants, and not a few are cultivating farms. Most of them have homes of their own and property worth from five hundred to five thousand dollars. Not the least benefit that Hampton is to the race is the influence that these graduates exert in the communities in which they live.

Fisk University is now in the thirty-second year of its existence. From its incipiency until today it has been under the auspices and fostering care of the American Missionary Association. The school was formally opened January 9, 1866, in the old army hospital west of the Chattanooga depot. In the year 1871 the university sent out a concert troupe, known as the Jubilee Singers. For seven years they sang with great acceptance both in this country and in Europe, and realized the sum of $150,000, with which the present site of the university was bought and Jubilee Hall was erected. There now stand upon the university grounds five beautiful brick buildings, the Memorial Chapel, built of stone, and one frame building. The present plant of the university could not be replaced with $350,000. The campus comprises thirty-five acres of land, and the site is universally conceded to be one of the most beautiful about Nashville. From the beginning the university has stood for the higher education of the colored race; and, although it embraces departments of domestic science and industrial training, the emphasis is laid upon its classical course of study. Since 1875 there have been graduated 163 from college and 150 from the normal department, making a total of 313, or an average of ten alumni for each of the thirty years of the university's existence. This is a good showing of the work done by the school, when we remember that it started thirty-two years ago with freedmen who had not more than the barest elements of primary education. In addition to the college and normal alumni, there have been graduated five from the theological department, which is only four years old, and six from the department of music.

Work of the Alumni.—The excellence of the work done in Fisk University has elicited again and again the warmest praise of the friends of higher education. Nearly all the alumni are holding positions of honor and trust. Eight of the teachers at Tuskegee are graduates from Fisk University. For a number of years the presidents and most of the faculty of Alcorn Industrial College, at Rodney, Mississippi, have been alumni from Fisk. The same thing is true of the State Normal School at Hempstead, Texas. An alumnus of Fisk, who was recently professor of Greek and Latin at Wilberforce University, then had a fellowship in the University of Pennsylvania, is now professor of economics in Atlanta University. Another alumnus is instructor in Greek in Howard University, in Washington; and still another is instructor in Hebrew and Old Testament literature in his Alma Mater. Eight of the alumni have done missionary work in Africa. The young woman who is in charge of the musical department in Booker T. Washington's School at Tuskegee is a graduate in music from Fisk. The reputation of the school for broad and thorough scholarship has gone throughout the South, and the president, E. M. Cravath, D. D., often receives applications for teachers from school superintendents and principals in different sections of the South. The character of the work done in Fisk University has gained for it the confidence of the people in the North as well as in the South; and, as a consequence, from twenty-three to twenty-five states are annually represented among the students.

Berea College.—The founder of Berea College, Rev. J. G. Fee, was convinced of the evil of slavery while taking a course at Lane Seminary, Ohio. On account of his anti-slavery views his father disinherited him. Before he became an abolitionist his father had given him a farm in Indiana, which he sold for $2,400 and spent the whole of it in buying and liberating a female slave, raised and married on the plantation, to prevent her being sold away. Mr. Fee early began his work of teaching and preaching, but was frequently interrupted by disturbances from slave holders. In 1858 the first charter for Berea was drawn up. It opposed sectarianism, slave holding, and every other wrong institution or practice. On account of the persecution of all men holding anti-slavery views, Mr. Fee and his associates were compelled to flee from the state. Some of them endured much from the hands of the mob. John G. Hanson, one of the trustees of the college, and for a short time a teacher, was almost miraculously protected from a mob. Several efforts were made to return to the state, but nothing could be done until the close of the war. In 1865 the school was opened, and a charter for the college was obtained. Three colored youths asked admission, and but one decision was possible to men like Mr. Fee and his associates. The

morning that these three harmless youths walked in,
half the school walked out. But these brave teachers kept on with their work. The vacancies made by
the white deserters were soon filled with colored students, and eventually all who left returned and became
fast friends of Berea. At no time have the colored pupils
exceeded two-thirds of the school. The evils which
were predicted have never appeared. There is no school
in the state more easily governed than this. The question whether the colored pupils are not necessarily a
drag upon the school would never be asked by one who
had any fair criterion by which to judge. A certain
amalgamation which was to follow is all in the future.
The school regulations make no distinctions whatever
on account of color. They recite in the same classes,
eat at the same table, room in the same buildings,
attend the same meetings, and meet in all general social
gatherings. In 1869 E. H. Fairchild was called to
the presidency of Berea College. Besides the buildings, which are estimated at $82,000, the college owns
three acres of land, not including the ground about the
buildings, worth about $15,000. It has an endowment
of about $100,000 besides the land. In 1892 Professor
W. G. Frost, of Oberlin, was called to the presidency.
The following paper, signed by such men as George
Cable, Herrick Johnson, Frederick Douglas, Josiah
Strong, Cassius Clay, M. D. Mayo and others, will
suggest Berea's work and influence.

"The peculiar work and opportunity of Berea College place it quite apart from all other institutions, and
give it a special claim upon the attention of every
Christian and patriot. Situated near the center of population, and furnishing an education of the best type—
industrial, normal, collegiate—to multitudes who would

KINGSLEY HALL, UNION UNIVERSITY, RICHMOND, VA.

374a

LECTURE HALL, UNION UNIVERSITY, RICHMOND, VA.

374b

otherwise fail of such advantages, it exerts a potent influence in favor of progressive and Christian ideas. But beyond this, having been founded by anti-slavery Kentuckians before the war, and having shown a courage that compels respect, Berea is in a position to do an unparalleled service in opposing the spirit of caste and effacing sectional lines. Berea is distinctively Christian, but controlled by no sect, and there is no denominational school which has before it this providential opening. Until larger endowments can be secured, about $12,000 must be procured each year from friends of the cause. We not only seek the large benefactions of the rich, but earnestly invite every one who approves of this work to contribute, according to his ability, any sum from $5 to 5,000.''

SPELMAN SEMINARY.

Work of a Generation.—The contrast between a slave pen of a generation ago, with its chain-gang, its auction block, its profanity, vulgarity and other accessories, and a modern school for Negro girls, like Spelman Seminary, with its beautiful buildings, its attractive rooms, its chapel and Bible, its corps of Christian workers, the smiling faces of hundreds of pupils budding into strong and useful womanhood, is wonderfully suggestive of the new era that has dawned for the Negroes of the South. Surely, we have reason to thank God and take courage.

Beginning.—The evolution of Spelman Seminary is one of the marvels of the age. Beginning in a damp, dark, desolate basement of a colored Baptist church, without any of the accessories needed for successful work, with two teachers and less than a dozen pupils, it has, within the last fourteen years, grown to be the largest, best equipped school for colored girls in the

STUDENTS OF SPELMAN SEMINARY, ATLANTA, GA.

world. It has a most choice location, with a magnificent outlook over the surrounding country; has buildings specially suited for its need; has a large and able faculty of devoted teachers; an attendance of pupils numbered by the hundreds; a constituency of friends and patrons rapidly extending in numbers and interest; and has made for itself a large place in the educational forces of the South, and established a reputation of the very highest order.

Opening.—Spelman Seminary was opened on the 11th of April, 1881, in the basement of Friendship Baptist church. Two ladies, Miss S. B. Packard and H. E. Giles, journeyed south that they might have a better knowledge of the condition of the freedmen. This visit opened their eyes to the appalling need of help for the colored women and girls. They came north and, after many discouraging efforts, they succeeded in raising funds to start the school. Arriving at Atlanta, they at once called on Pastor Quarles, the leading colored Baptist minister of the state. When he learned their mission, he said: "While I was praying, the Lord answered." For fifteen years I have been pleading with God to send teachers to the Baptist women of Georgia, and now you have come."

Rev. Frank Quarles.—The enthusiasm of this man to establish the work among the colored women was great and he was anxious lest the teachers should become discouraged. He went North to enlist the sympathies of the people and to get further support for the school. His last words to the school were: "I am going North for you. I may never return. Remember, if I die, I die for you and in a good cause." To his people he said: "Take care of those ladies who have come to us as angels of mercy. Don't let them suffer." The northern climate was too severe for his Southern constitution, and he died in New York at the home of his son.

The Second Year.—During the second year 175 were enrolled, one-third of them were of ages ranging from twenty-five to fifty years, and had known and felt the evils of slavery. Touching were the incidents showing the eagerness and perseverance of these women. Often were they laughed at and even persecuted, because they showed a determination to get a little light. Some walked seven and eight miles to and from school, hardly missing a day, even in the severest weather.

The Coal Bin.—In January, 1882, the school was so large two of the recitations were already heard in the main room; a third teacher, Miss Champney, took as her recitation room the coal bin, in which there was one small window.

Rockefeller Hall.—Miss Packard and Miss Giles went North in 1882 to secure funds for the school. When some thousands had been raised, Mr. John D. Rockefeller came to their relief and gave a large sum, and the school was named Spelman Seminary in honor of Mr. Spelman, the father of Mrs. Rockefeller. Rockefeller Hall was dedicated in 1886. It contains recitation rooms, dormitories, and a beautiful chapel, on whose walls is inscribed the motto: "Our whole school for Christ."

Giles Hall.—In 1892 Mr. Rockefeller again presented the institution with a building 170 feet long and four stories high, and requested that it should be called Giles Hall. On the first floor are a large school room and ten class rooms for the use of the primary department; on the second floor are similar rooms for the intermediate department; the third floor contains a laboratory and science lecture room, commodious recitation rooms for the normal and training and missionary training classes, and dormitories for the students of these departments. The building was dedicated in December, 1893.

Buildings.—Spelman Seminary now has six brick buildings, four frame dormitories, and a frame hospital for the sick, and about fourteen acres of land. The property is now estimated at about $150,000.

Enrollment.—The aggregate enrollment for fifteen years has been about 6,500. Fifty-one certificates have been given in the nurse training department. Ninety-two have gone out from the academic department, a majority of whom are teachers. Two are on the Congo as missionaries; one, a Congo girl, was sent to be educated, and returned in 1895 as an appointed missionary from the Woman's Baptist Missionary Society of Boston.

Success.—The success which has attended this work has proved how valuable and important normal training is. There are hundreds whose circumstances would not allow them to remain longer in school who have gone out to do efficient services and become centers of influences for good in the communities where they live.

Teachers.—The number of teachers has greatly increased, until at present there are 38. The Women's American Baptist Missionary Society provided for a number of these; the Slater Fund for others, while some of them labor unselfishly and faithfully with only a meager salary.

Influence.—Spelman Seminary is a power for good. It is to the colored women of the South all that Vassar is to the white women of the North. It is an enterprise of quick growth and phenomenal proportion.

Prof. Wm. E. Holmes.—The Negro Baptists of the

South show their appreciation of the school by the hundreds who have already enlisted as members. The intelligent interest and co-operation of Prof. Holmes, formerly of the Baptist Seminary, from the very commencement have been of inestimable value, a means of elevating the race. The colored people more and more appreciate the worth and work of this noble seminary. They feel they have now a training home for their daughters where correct discipline is administered by consecrated Christian women, who give their lives, while many give their money, to prepare toilers for service as a means in the elevation of the race. Spelman is invaluable and indispensable.

Nora A. Gordon.—Nora A. Gordon was born in Columbia, Georgia, in 1866. Her parents were formerly slaves, belonging to the well-known General Gordon, from whom they received their name. She attended the public schools of La Grange, Georgia, where she resided. In the fall of 1882 she entered Spelman Seminary. She was ignorant and superstitious, and had many mistaken ideas about religion. She soon became a Christian, and joined the Baptist Church of Atlanta. She then

NORA A. GORDON,
Missionary in Africa.

began organizing temperance societies, Sunday schools, and caused family altars to be erected in the homes of her pupils. She was a diligent student, completing the course in Spelman in 1888, and at once accepted the position as teacher in one of the Atlanta public schools, but in 1889 an urgent call came for her to go to Africa. She said: "Christ's preciousness to me makes me feel that I wish my feet had wings, that I might hasten to take the Bread of Life to the poor heathen. I have counted the cost of missionary service, and my love for Christ makes me willing to bear the many' peculiar trials through which I am confident I must pass." At the farewell services in Atlanta she said: "This has been a peculiar day to me, the happiest of my life, as I am so soon to realize a long cherished hope. I feel that perfect peace which passeth understanding.

> "Some friends have asked me why I go,
>   What may my reason be;
> You have my answer in these words,
>   'God's love constraineth me.'"

Miss Gordon labored in Africa until 1893, when broken-down health compelled her to return to America, but in 1895, her health being restored, she was married to Rev. S. C. Gordon, of Stanley Pool, and again returned to the Congo.

Bishop Hapgood says: "No money apportioned by me from 1882 till 1891 was ever better used than that I gave to Spelman. Whatever concerns bodily, mental or spiritual health is considered and provided for at Spelman. The houses and premises are clean; the discipline and instruction are of the very best; the atmosphere is religious."

Clara Howard.—Clara Howard was born in Greenville, Georgia. At nine years of age she entered a little

ATLANTA BAPTIST SEMINARY.

private school and afterwards Atlanta University, where she remained nearly three years. Afterwards she entered Spelman Seminary, and graduated in 1887, and was at once appointed teacher in the Atlanta public schools. She was appointed missionary to the Congo, in 1890, where she remained until 1894, when she was compelled by ill health to leave her work, and returned to Spelman. She hopes again to take up her chosen work after regaining health.

Atlanta Baptist Seminary.—The work of this seminary was begun in 1871, and carried on for some years at Augusta, Georgia, but in 1879 it was removed to the capital of the state and buildings erected at a cost of $12,500. The special aim of the school is the education of preachers and such teachers as can be classed with them profitably. A strong sentiment in favor of education of young women was soon developed after the removal of the school to Atlanta. The Spelman Girls' School and Atlanta Baptist Seminary are located on almost the same grounds. The site contains about eight acres. The colored people of the state have taken a deep interest in the work, and have succeeded in raising money for the purpose. The future work of the school is great, the developing of thought among the 100,000 colored Baptists in the Empire State of the South. In 1888 a new site of eighteen acres was purchased in West Atlanta. The new buildings cost $30,000. The value of the property at present is $40,000.

Clark University, like most schools of its kind, had an humble beginning. Starting as an ordinary grade school, in the city of Atlanta, in the year 1869, it has come, through various changes of fortune, to be what it is today—the largest and best located of the schools of the Freedmen's Aid Society of the Methodist Epis-

CLARK UNIVERSITY, ATLANTA, GEORGIA.

copal Church. Confined for many years to narrow quarters in the city, it was moved to its present spacious site in the year 1880, when its first new building, Chrisman Hall, was erected.

Its charter was secured in 1877, and the first meeting of the trustees took place on the fifteenth day of February of that year.

The land, 450 acres, was secured through the untiring efforts and far sightedness of Bishop Gilbert Haven, and its first building owes its existence chiefly to the generosity and benevolence of Mrs. Eliza Chrisman, of Topeka, Kansas.

From 1880 to 1884, Bishop Henry W. Warren made his home at the institution, and rendered to it the most substantial aid it has had since its foundation. It was in this period that the industrial department, under the patronage of Bishop Warren, came into being—departments that had steady and rapid growth, and continued in operation until two years ago, when, because of the great financial stringency, they were closed—yet with the hope of opening again. In these departments were taught carpentry, blacksmithing, carriage making, carriage painting, harness making, and printing. Simultaneously with the establishment of the shops, was also established the "Model Home," for the instruction of girls in all domestic arts and duties. This home accommodates twenty pupils. No department of the institution has been richer in good results.

In the year 1883, the Gammon School of Theology was founded in connection with Clark University, by Rev. Elijah H. Gammon, of Batavia, Illinois. This school remained a department of the university until the year 1888, when it became a separate institution under the corporate name of Gammon Theological Seminary.

The property of the university, situated just outside the city limits, is at present valued at $400,000. Its value will be enhanced, probably, twice that sum, as the city pushes out around and about it. With proper management, the school has unlimited possibilities for good.

Atlanta University, originally under the auspices of the American Missionary Association, but now independent and unsectarian, was organized in the year 1869. Its organization was largely due to the energy and foresight of Rev. Edmund Asa Ware, who became its first president, and continued in that position twenty years, or up to the time of his death. The school had phenomenal growth during those twenty years, and became, perhaps, the best known institution of its kind in the South. It offers its advantages to both sexes, without regard to race, color, or nationality.

The property of the school is valued at about $200,-000, and is situated on a commanding elevation in the city, easily accessible by the street cars, which, indeed, run through its grounds.

Like most schools of its kind in the South, it has some industrial features, but unlike the other schools, it has now no grade work, that work having been discontinued three years ago. The efforts of the institution are now directed solely towards building up a college proper. The standard is being gradually raised, and it is the laudable ambition of the authorities to have here, in the Central South, a university worthy of the name, that shall supply the educational needs of the people.

For the last few years, however, the school has been much hampered for lack of funds, the $8,000 annual appropriation granted by an act of the Georgia legislature in 1874 having been withdrawn by the Glenn bill,

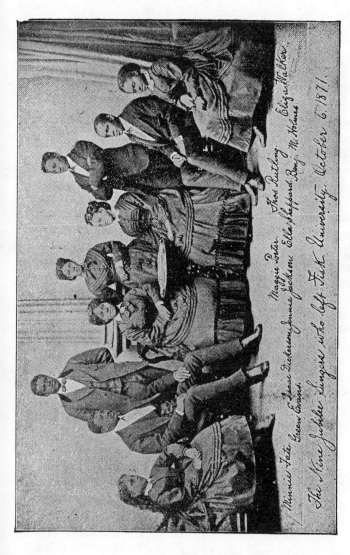

Minnie Tate. Isaac Dickerson, Jennie Jackson, Ella Sheppard, Benj. M. Holmes.

Maggie Porter. Thos. Rutling. Eliza Walker.

Green Evans.

The Nine Jubilee Singers who left Fisk University. October 6, 1871.

FISK JUBILEE SINGERS.

Who for seven years gave concerts in this country and in Europe, and secured funds sufficient to erect
Jubilee Hall.

passed a few years ago by the same legislature. The reason given for the withdrawal was the presence of white pupils in the school. These white pupils, it ought to be said, were children of some of the teachers. The school, nevertheless, lives, has a warm place in the hearts of the people, and a high reputation for the work it has done and is doing.

Tuskegee Normal and Industrial Institute.—In 1881 the Alabama legislature passed a bill appropriating $2,000 yearly for the support of a school at Tuskegee for the education of Negro youth. General Armstrong was asked to suggest a suitable man to establish and direct the work, and he recommended Booker T. Washington. The district in which the school is located is one in which the black people outnumber the whites three to one. Here, on the fourth of June, 1881, he opened the Tuskegee Normal and Industrial Institute in a small church and shanty. Since that time the institution has grown until it has now 80 instructors, about 40 buildings, and over 800 students, all over fourteen years of age, the average age being eighteen and one-half years. Students come from twenty-four states. From the first industrial training has been a prominent feature of this school. This is kept uppermost, to train men and women in head, heart and hand; to meet conditions that exist right about them rather than conditions that existed centuries ago, or that exist a thousand miles away. The institution is Christian, but not denominational. Professor Washington says it is not the type of Christianity that prevails in some places among the colored race, where, as an example, is told the story of the colored man who went to his weekly class meeting and said to his class leader, "I's had a ha'd time since our las' meetin'; I's been sometimes up and sometimes down. 'Spects I's broken eb'ry one ob de ten comman'ments since our las' meetin', but I tanks God I's *not los' my 'ligion yet.*"

In connection with literature and Christian training the students are trained in industrial pursuits. Over twenty-four hundred acres of land are owned by the institute, 650 of which are cultivated. The students receive instruction in various branches of agriculture, horticulture, dairy products, brick masonry, wheel-wrighting, blacksmithing, tinning, carpentering, painting, shoemaking, tailoring, dressmaking, and various branches of industrial training, besides preparing men and women as teachers, preachers, physicians, lawyers, clerks, merchants, machinists, etc. This system enables them to make practical application of the theories which they learn in the class room. The principles of physics are immediately applied in the machine shop, those of chemistry in farming and cooking, those of mathematics in carpentering, etc. There are no idlers in Tuskegee. They erect their own buildings, even manufacturing every brick; they also do the carpenter and other work. Thus the institute secures buildings for permanent use with a minimum of expense, and the students have the industrial training. This also helps the young men and women to get rid of any old idea they may have had that labor is disgraceful; that it is beneath one to use his hands if he has any education. The Tuskegee property is now valued at $300,000, on which there is no mortgage. One great difficulty in endeavoring to better the condition of the Southern Negro is the "mortgage system," which makes them virtually the property of well-to-do planters, taking away all their independence, ambition and self-respect. They live in little cabins, and try to pay sometimes 40 per cent. interest on their property and on their crops, which are often mortgaged before they are raised. The result in poverty and lack of hope for better things can be imagined. Tuskegee Institute is seeking to find and apply a remedy for this state of things. This work they do not consider hopeless or even discouraging. The Negroes acknowledge their ignorance and low condition, but they think that there is no help for it. What they need is intelligent and unselfish leadership in their religious, industrial and intellectual life, and this is what the Tuskegee institution is endeavoring to give them. The trouble is that these people do not know how to utilize the results of their labor. What they earn gets away from them in paying mortgages, and in buying lace, snuff, and cheap jewelry. They have not yet learned the distinctions between cheap and showy imitations of wealth and education, and the culture and refinement which only comes by slow and labored progress. A one-roomed cabin will sometimes have clocks bought on the installment plan for $12, when, in nine cases out of ten, not one in the family can tell when the hands point to six o'clock and when to twelve; or a family will mortgage a year's crop to pay for a funeral or a wedding.

Tuskegee has already succeeded in reforming many districts. At the time of their emancipation practically all of the Negroes lived in one-room cabins; ten years ago nine-tenths of them lived in the same way; whereas today one-third of them have at least doubled their accommodations, and many of them own their farms and homes. The students who come to Tuskegee from wretched, single-roomed hovels, go back to transform them into homes where peace and purity can thrive. Already the graduates of the institution are in great demand all over the South, and other schools are applying the Tuskegee principles and methods of education.

The chief requisites for admission to the institute are a good moral character, attested by recommendations from reliable persons, a good physique and a fair ability to read, write and cipher. No student who cannot read and write will be admitted to the institute. No student is admitted to any department on any terms under fourteen years of age; this rule is rigidly enforced.

Ten years ago a young man born in slavery found his way to the Tuskegee school. By small cash payments and work on the farm he finished the course with a good English education and a practical and theoretical knowledge of farming. Returning to his country home, where five-sixths of the citizens were black, he found them still mortgaging their crops, living on rented land from hand to mouth, and deeply in debt. School had never lasted longer than three months, and was taught in a wreck of a cabin by an inferior teacher. Finding this condition of things, the young man took the three months' public school as a starting point. Soon he organized the older people into a club that came together every week. In these meetings the young man taught them the value of owning a home, the evils of mortgaging, and the importance of educating their children. He taught them how to save money, how to sacrifice—to live on bread and potatoes until they got out of debt, begin buying a home and stop mortgaging. Through the lessons and influence of these meetings during the first year of this young man's work, these people built by their contributions and labor a good frame school house, which replaced the wreck of a log cabin. The next year this work was continued, and those people, by their own gifts, furnished funds for

adding two months to the original school term. Month
by month has been added to the school term, till it now
lasts seven months every year. Already fourteen families within a radius of ten miles have bought and are
buying homes, a large proportion have ceased mortgaging their crops, and are raising their own food supplies.
In the midst of all is the young man educated at Tuskegee in a model cottage and a model farm that serve as
a center of light for the whole community.

A few years ago a young woman was educated and
converted at Tuskegee. After her graduation she went
to one of the plantations where they only had school for
three months in the year in a broken-down log cabin.
She took charge of the school, and went among the
mothers and fathers of the pupils and found out what
their resources were. She taught them how to save
money. The first year many men decided not to mortgage their crops, but to provide suitable homes and a
good schoolhouse. They added to the school term until
now they have a season of eight months. The community is transformed, and the very faces of the people show the revolution that has been wrought in their
lives by that one Christian leader. Every improvement has come through this young woman in their
midst showing them how to direct their efforts, how
to take the money that had hitherto gone for mortgaging, snuff and tobacco, and to use it for their own
uplifting.

The Georgia State Industrial College was established in 1891, beginning its first regular session in
October of that year. In the summer of 1891 a preliminary session was held in Athens, Georgia, while a
permanent location was being selected for its establishment.

Prof. R. R. Wright, A. M., who was a member of the class of 1876 of the Atlanta University, and who had been for eleven years principal of the Ware High School of Augusta, was chosen as its first President.

RICHARD R. WRIGHT, A. M.
President of Georgia State Industrial College
See sketch, page 393.

During the session at Athens, President Wright was assisted by Prof. L. B. Palmer and Mrs. Addrienne McNeal Herndon, both graduates of the Atlanta University.

The Georgia State College was established in pursuance of an act of the state legislature in 1890, when the act of 1874 appropriating to the Atlanta University a sum of $8,000 per annum was repealed, and an enactment made providing for the establishment of a state school for colored youth. This institution is a branch of the State University now at Athens, so is under the general supervision of the Chancellor of the University of Georgia and its Board of Trustees.

The Georgia State College is the only one of its kind in the state for the education of colored youth. A more beautiful as well as healthful situation for a college could not be found in the state.

The main buildings are Boggs Hall, the principal recitation building; Parson Hall, constituting the dormitory and dining hall; and a shop for training in architectural and mechanical drawing, wood and iron working, masonry and decorating. In 1892 three neat cottages were erected as homes for the President and the professors. A magnificent chapel and model school building has just been completed, which stands as a monument to the industrial feature of the College. This building was erected entirely by the students, working under the direction of the principal of the Manual Training department. This department was awarded a medal at the International Exposition held in Atlanta in 1895.

There is a Normal Course of three years besides a regular College department. Industrial Training, which is one of the prominent features, extends throughout the entire course. The last year of this department, however, is elective. There have been eleven graduates from the Normal Course. There is also a Teachers' Training department for the benefit of those who contemplate entering that profession.

Since its first session it has been necessary for the College to almost double the number of instructors, which evidences the steady growth of the institution. Its energetic and persevering President and his assistants have labored untiringly to make of this institution a first-class college for the industrial as well as intellectual training of the colored youth in the state.

The enrollment has increased from forty-two for the first year to more than two hundred. At present there are no scholarships belonging to this institution, though needy students aid themselves by work. In connection with the College there is a farm containing fifty-four acres on which most of the necessary vegetables are cultivated by student labor under the supervision of an experienced agriculturist.

As the result of the generosity of Miss Jennie E. Bill, of Norwich, Connecticut, and other friends, there is for the students an excellent library to which collections are being added from time to time. There are two literary societies, besides a Young Men's Christian Association under whose direction are conducted the prayer meetings and other devotional exercises. The present faculty is composed of some of the best talent afforded by the race.

Central Tennessee College.—Central Tennessee College was chartered in 1866 by the legislature of Tennessee. It is supported by the Methodist Episcopal Church. A large number of the students have engaged in teaching. Many of these teachers have charge of Sunday schools as well as day schools, thus aiding in the religious instruction of the communities where they labor. Many of them are professed Christians. Some are successful preachers, while over three hundred have graduated in the medical department and are now practicing successfully. There are more than five million colored people in the South who are asking for more competent teachers, doctors, dentists, pharmacists and preachers, who can teach the people, better educated farmers and mechanics and more enlightened wives and mothers to lift the home life of the entire people. The aim of this school is to aid in this great work. With a history of nearly a third of a century, the different departments of the College, now fully organized, have accomplished a great work. This gives hope for the future. The College buildings consist of seven brick edifices.

The "Tennesseeans" were a popular troupe who established a national reputation and delighted thousands of intelligent audiences with their popular plantation melodies. With the proceeds obtained by these gifted singers an elegant and commodious four-story brick structure was added to Central Tennessee College.

Meharry Medical College.—The Meharry Medical Department of Central Tennessee College was organized in 1876, for the purpose of furnishing to the colored people of the South an opportunity of obtaining a medical education. At that time there was no medical school in the Southern states that would admit colored students, and in the North the doors of many of the medical colleges were closed against them.

It takes its name from the generous and philanthropic family who so liberally contributed towards its establishment and support. In 1879, through the munificence of the Rev. Samuel Meharry, Shawnee Mound, Ind., and his brothers, Rev. Alexander Meharry, D.D., and Hugh Meharry, Esq., aided by Rev. R. S. Rust, D.D., corresponding secretary of the Freedmen's

MEHARRY MEDICAL COLLEGE,
Nashville, Tennessee.

397

Aid Society of the Methodist Episcopal Church, a lot was purchased, and the beautiful and commodious brick building, now known as the Meharry Medical College, was erected.

This school has conferred the degree of M. D. on 308 students, nearly all of whom are now engaged in the successful practice of their profession. They have been kindly received by the white physicians, whose uniform testimony is that the colored physicians sent out by this school give evidence of very thorough preparation for their work. More than one-half of the educated colored physicians in the Southern states are graduates of this institution. The success of this department is largely due to the untiring zeal and energy of Dr. Hubbard, who has for so many years stood at the head of this department. Dr. Hubbard is probably better informed on the work done by colored physicians of the South than any other man. Meharry Medical college stands today as the most prominent of all the medical schools for colored people. Ninety-six per cent of her graduates are practicing medicine.

Leland University, New Orleans, La.—Leland University was founded, as its name implies, for higher education, a just provision for which is the essential factor in all education, as its source and mainspring. It was founded in New Orleans, a great center of the region of the greatest illiteracy and therefore of greatest need. It was by its founder and its charter opened to all classes of citizens, without distinction of sex or color, and therefore became available, as it was intended to be, to the descendants of the class which was at that time most needy, because of having been shut out from the privilege of education.

At first it was found that this class were unprepared for higher education, not having received the lower, and to accommodate them a temporary provision of primary instruction was made in the university. After thirty years of opportunity and, in view of the progress which the people have made, in both primary and secondary education, a similar necessity no longer exists.

During the first year of the work of the present faculty (session of 1887-88) there were 185 students enrolled, of whom 109 were primary scholars, 76 of the grammar school grade, and only 14 in the normal department, with no college students. For three years about 90 per cent. of our students were below the normal grade, and of these over a hundred were primary, crowding our rooms and our classes with a heterogeneous mass of beginners in the very rudiments of knowledge. By authority of the Board in 1890 was commenced the work of establishing auxiliary schools in the state for primary work. Howe Institute, Alexandria High School and Leland Academy at Donaldsonville, were among the first inaugurated, the object being to bring preparatory work nearer to the people and thus make it available to a larger number. At the same time the terms of admission were, by order of the trustees, raised in the university to prevent competition with country schools, and to improve the work in the higher classes. The planting of these schools has stimulated others, until now ten such institutions exist, where an eight months' course of study like our preparatory department has been given this year to 1,276 pupils, more than ten times as many as could have come to New Orleans if they had desired to do so. Three of these schools are directly auxiliary to Leland. The names of their teachers and pupils appear in its catalogue, and their interests are under the fostering care of its faculty and the thoughtful benevolence of its trustees.

Rev. Edward Cushing Mitchell, D. D.—Since 1887 Dr. Mitchell, a distinguished divine, teacher and author, has been President of Leland University. Through his untiring zeal he has succeeded in raising the standard of the institution and in enlarging and extending its work. The University owes its existence to the late Holbrook Chamberlain, Esq., of Brooklyn, N. Y., who erected the buildings, assisted in its management, and at his death left to it the bulk of his property, about $100,000, as an endowment fund, the interest of which goes to the payment of teachers.

Southland College and Normal and Industrial Institute.—This school was organized by the Indiana Yearly Meeting of the Religious Society of Friends in 1864; the College department was organized in 1872. The first class was graduated in 1876. The leading object of the school is to qualify teachers, and about five hundred have already gone out into the free schools of Arkansas and adjoining states, while some have been employed in schools of higher grade.

The primary object of the school is the preparation of teachers, but other lines of work have been taken up. An Industrial department has been added where is given a practical knowledge of the use of tools in such lines of work as will make students self-sustaining and will fit them for the duties of useful citizenship.

The school is at present in charge of Prof. Wm. Russell and wife. During the past few years the amount of land owned by the College has been more than doubled. A printing press has been put in, a kindergarten department established, and other valuable improvements made. The expenses for tuition, board and washing range from eight to ten dollars per month, and many of the students pay nearly all by work.

The funds to carry on the institution are obtained from the income of an endowment fund of $35,000, from annual appropriations of the Indiana Religious Meetings and from voluntary donations of friends of the school. Of course, the products of the farm and the tuition fees paid, help to increase the income. The school is located at the foot of Crowley's Ridge, nine miles northwest of Helena, Arkansas, in a remarkably healthy climate. A high moral tone and deep religious convictions are characteristics of the students who remain long enough in the school. Southland College has been a factor of peace, true to the teachers who founded it. Leading citizens of Helena attribute much to the Institution in promoting peace and harmony in the county in which it is located. No mob violences have occurred here, and county offices are frequently filled by colored men of the different political parties.

Morris Brown College.—Morris Brown College, the principal school of the African Methodist Episcopal Church, was founded in 1881. The site overlooking the city of Atlanta was purchased at a cost of $3,500. During the first year 107 students were enrolled; about $25,000 has been spent in erecting two large buildings. The present corps of teachers numbers 16; the number of students 430. The course of instruction embraces English, Academic, Normal and Industrial departments. All the members of the faculty are Negroes. Every dollar of the funds which are used in supporting this college comes from Negroes. We run no risk in saying that the work of these Negro minds and hearts suffers nothing in comparison with the best of any race.

A number have graduated from the lower classes. It will have its first classical graduates in '98. This institution bids fair to become the leading institution entirely manned by Negroes. All that it needs is to be properly encouraged and fostered. It has the advantage of Wilburforce in that it is situated in the very heart of the South, where so many of the colored race are anxious to obtain an education.

It needs funds to complete the central building, as well as to carry on the work in general. This institution is indeed an honor to the race. Theory sometimes fails of conviction, but the most obdurate mind will be convinced of such a practical proof of the Negroes' ability.

Prof. James Henderson is president since 1888.

Livingstone College.—Livingstone College is the principal college of the A. M. E. Zion Church. It was organized in 1882, in Salisbury, N. C. Its existence is largely due to the energy of that prince of orators, Rev. J. C. Price, who afterwards became its president. He collected funds both in this country and in Europe. The valuation of the buildings and grounds, now about 50 acres, is estimated at $100,000. Although young in years its graduates have already passed the hundred mark. President Price, its efficient and popular president, devoted his life to the work of this institution. There have been enrolled more than three hundred students. The death of President Price, in 1893, was a blow to Livingstone. The work is being carried on by his successor, Dr. H. Goler.

A humble colored man recently loaned the Baptists of Virginia $13,000, with which to build a seminary at Lynchburg.

Howard University.—Howard University was established by the government primarily through the instrumentality of General O. Howard, the distinguished soldier whose name it bears, and whose spirit its teachers seek to emulate. It has always welcomed all nationalities alike. The work of this university is now well known to the country. It is confessedly the leader in the education of the Afro-American race. Every year the trustees seek to enlarge its scope and fit it for greater usefulness. With its departments of theology, medicine, dentistry, pharmacy, law, industry, music and nurse training, it is accomplishing much in elevating the Negro.

Knoxville College, Knoxville, Tennessee.—This college is under the care of the United Presbyterian Church of North America. It is sustained mostly by contributions from the various congregations to the Board of Missions of the Freedmen. It is the result of benevolent effort to benefit the colored people. Its design is to train teachers for colored schools and preachers for the churches; also to encourage a thorough education of those who wish to advance beyond the studies ordinarily taught in common schools.

Medical Department: The Medical Department was opened in 1895. A four years' course has been provided for and a number of students have already entered this department. Arrangement has been made with the University of Tennessee by making provision for its colored students in Knoxville College. According to agreement with the university, all colored students over fifteen years of age have free tuition. Its location in the chief city of Tennessee gives advantages that are not found elsewhere. As a denominational school, students are received from all parts of the South where the church is represented.

Selma University.—A convention of colored Baptists at Tuscaloosa in 1873, decided to establish a school for preachers and asked the white brethren for money and advice. Receiving no encouragement they went to work among themselves and succeeded in opening the school at Selma in 1878. In that year property was bought at a cost of $3,000, and paid for wholly by the colored people. Improvements have since been going on so that the property today is worth about $20,000. In 1881 Rev. W. H. McAlpine, who was a slave until 1865, and who had done more for the school than any other man, was chosen President. The prospects for the great work are flattering.

Shaw University, Raleigh.—This school was established by Rev. H. M. Tupper, of Massachusetts, in 1865, under the auspices of the American Baptist Home Missionary Society. The work of construction was slow in the beginning but by liberal contributions from Mr. Shaw, J. Estey & Co., George M. Moore and other New England men, enough was raised to erect the Shaw building. In 1875 the school was incorporated as Shaw University. The medical department was begun in the summer of 1881, a fine building having been furnished by the Leonard family of Hampden, Massachusetts. President Tupper opened his first Sunday school in Raleigh in 1865 under an oak tree; in 1892 he presided over an institution having five large brick buildings and in all parts unequaled by any other educational institution in the state. To him is largely due the success of the project, for he, by persistent effort even to the manufacture of brick on the farm and the construction of the building, devoted his whole strength to the work. The school has six departments and is doing a great work in pre-

paring teachers and ministers for the South as well as
for Africa.

Roger Williams University.—The beginning of the
work of the Baptist Home Missionary Society in Nashville dates back to the close of the war. Rev. H. L.
Wayland was the first missionary teacher in that place.
Rev. D. W. Phillips succeeded him, and in 1875 a
large building was erected at a cost of nearly fifty
thousand dollars. The school, from the beginning,
has maintained a high reputation for thorough work.
The institution was incorporated in 1883. With a
number of buildings and a small endowment Roger
Williams University is doing a great work at Nashville,
although from the beginning it has had powerful competitors. The number of students is gradually increasing. The graduates are widely scattered throughout
the South occupying positions of influence and usefulness.

Tougaloo University, Tougaloo, Mississippi.—This
is emphatically the "Black Belt" plantation school of
the American Missionary Society, located in the midst
of America's "Darkest Africa," touching by far the
most numerous and important class on which the future
of the Negro rests, the plantation Negro. The school
was established in 1869. Five hundred acres were
purchased and with them a fine mansion. The work
of chief importance is that of the normal department,
for the future of the race depends largely upon the
teachers trained for the common schools. Stieby Hall,
erected in 1882, is the boys' dormitory, accommodating
from seventy to eighty boys. The Theological department was established about seven years ago and is
doing a great work in that direction. Senator Beard
says it would quite repay those who would study the

problem of saving Negro children of the rural districts of the "Black Belt," to go far out of their way to visit Tougaloo. Tougaloo is a great school where efficiency and economy are found pulling quietly in the same harness as in few institutions.

Biddle University, Charlotte, North Carolina, was opened at the close of the war between the states. The first teachers were Rev. S. C. Alexander and Rev. W. G. Miller. The liberality of Mrs. Mary D. Biddle, of Philadelphia, gave to the institution its first generous contribution. Her husband had yielded his life in the cause of the Union, and Mrs. Biddle requested the privilege of perpetuating his memory in connection with the school. Generous gifts from friends in the North have not been wanting, and the school is on a good financial basis.

The property is vested in a board of trustees, and a clause in the charter makes it the perpetual heritage of the colored people in connection with the Presbyterian Church. There are thirteen buildings. The main building, devoted to recitation rooms, library, chapel, etc., was built at a cost of $40,000. The grounds include sixty acres situated one mile west of Charlotte. The total valuation of grounds and buildings is $125,000. There are four departments, the School of Theology, School of Arts and Sciences, Normal and Preparatory School, and School of Industry, in which are taught the various trades.

Self Support.—The students are being educated to rely upon themselves and become self-supporting. The total earnings of the students for the year ending October, 1895, amounted to $11,291.

Graduates.—The graduates are distributed as follows: Theology, 73; School of Art and Sciences, 118;

BIDDLE UNIVERSITY (MAIN BUILDING), CHARLOTTE, NORTH CAROLINA.

Normal and Preparatory School, 183; 62 are active ministers of the colored Presbyterian Church; 6 are serving at Biddle as professors; 1 is a foreign missionary in Africa and professor of Latin and Greek in Liberia College; 1 is a bishop in the A. M. E. Zion Church. A number are lawyers and physicians, and many are teachers in normal, high and public schools. Since 1891 Rev. D. J. Sanders, D. D., is president. The faculty and not a few of the students are aware of the important part played by the spiritual tone of the university life. Earnest efforts are made to induce new students to enter upon a spiritual life. The college classes contain very few unconverted persons, and the close of each year sees seven-eighths of the entire body of students professed followers of Jesus Christ.

Tuskegee Conference.—One of the helpful features in industrial training in the South is the annual Negro Conference, held at Tuskegee, Alabama. In this conference are found men of all classes, ministers and teachers, as well as farmers and laborers, and these, too, have had an education. The reports from different parts of the South are encouraging. We append extracts from a few of them.

Willis Ligon said: "The first crop I made I was harnessed like a mule to a plow, and my little boy held the handles. Many colored men are getting cotton-gins, grist mills and saw mills, as well as land. I am going to start a new town at my settlement and call it Nazarene." Mr. Ligon has never missed a conference. He owns several large farms and is a stockholder in both the banks of Tuskegee.

Father Mitchell, a gray-haired farmer, said: "I tank God I is living yet. My people has been eating too much. Don't laugh, now. Mr. President, you preached a mighty good text last night. I liked yer prayer 'bout gettin' all de obstacles out ob de way first. I am a hard-working man, I've got sons and daughters. De Nigger race can make the best people in de world. Jest allow me to call you Niggers, case you'se all black. We can get land if any people can. We knows how to work and make a happy home and a good school. I has learned more in de last five years since dese conferences started, dan I ever knowed before in all my sixty years. We wants good leaders as will take de difficulties out of our way. * * * De people don't count as much on religion as dey ought. Religion is a mighty nice thing if you use it right. It takes a pious man to live religion. De longer de worl' stands de wiser it grows. Some of our people is getting too wise. Many likes to dance too much. De jail-house is full and we is running excursions. If you see a man crooked, straighten him by the grace of de Lord. We hollers and shouts too much, and jumps like we was crazy. It is a sad thing to preach de Gospel, de saddest thing dis side ob de grave. Our churches is plumbfull of hypocrites. If a man preaches de pure Gospel dey don't want to hear it. If we had de truth, white folks could live and Niggers could live. Dey tinks more of a bad person than dey does ob a good one. You let a man preach de true Gospel and he won't git many nickels in his pocket; but if he hollers and jumps he gits all the nickels he can hold and chickens besides. I has been in de cause forty-five years, and I knows what preachin' is, and I tell you, if our young race don' do better in ten years we're gone. Now, Mr. President, I fotch you a hog yesterday to help feed this conference, I hoped to see eight or nine in de pen, but mine is de only one. I'll bring you a hog or a cow next year. Father Washington, I'se a-gwine to stick to you as long as I live."

One report for a county in Alabama said: "We have one hundred families owning 4,000 acres of land, and not more than ten live in one-roomed houses." Another reported fifteen persons owning nearly 2,000 acres, and living in good houses. Many similar reports were given from other states. It is not always an easy matter for colored people to purchase land. Many land owners do not like to sell in small tracts; others will not sell to Negroes. The mortgage system has no friends in this conference, not one word being raised in its favor. The tide is turning. Many are still, however, sadly in its clutches but struggling hard to free themselves from its power. In one community the wives have an organization by which to reduce home expenses; instead of buying on credit at greatly increased prices, they bring together their butter, eggs, chickens and the like, till enough is collected to purchase one hundred pounds of meat for cash at half the price they formerly paid. This meat they divide among themselves and save money; 1,300 pounds have thus been bought. The one-roomed cabin was thoroughly discussed and the reports show that its days are numbered. Houses with two, three, four or five rooms are to be seen where formerly the cabin was thought to be sufficient. Tenants are demanding better houses, and land owners are forced to give them or lose good farm hands.

Mr. R. L. Smith, of Oakland, Texas, a young man with only one arm, a school teacher, practical farmer, and a member of the state legislature, said: "About five years ago I began to look into the condition of my people. I found them making good crops, from one and a half to two bales of cotton per acre, but their homes were small and the influences surrounding them bad. In 1892 I started a society called the 'Village Improvement Society.' We have fifty-six members in a village of two hundred people. In five years fifteen families have spent $10,000 in improvements. The surrounding country has been helped by our work. Our smallest house now has four rooms in it and some have eight rooms. Last year we extended the order and called it 'The Farmers' Improvement Society,' with about seven hundred members. We have five purposes: to get out of debt, and keep out, to adopt improved methods of farming, to co-operate in buying and selling, to get homes and to improve them. * * * One result of our efforts has been a marked change in the treatment we have received from the white people. Texas is more liberal than most of the Southern states. I was more or less guided in my work by what I had heard or read of the Tuskegee conferences." Mr. Smith showed many pictures of homes and families in Oakland. He said he had carried on this work in connection with his school and farm, and that the legislature of Texas was so much interested in his coming to Tuskegee that it gave him a leave of absence and promised to defer action on a bill in which he was interested until his return home.

A young teacher and farmer from Choctaw county said: "When we heard what Tuskegee was doing I said to our people, 'We can do it, too.' So we organized a conference in our county. We are under the mortgage system. Our labor is unskilled. Last year of twenty-five families with mortgages on their crops only twelve were able to pay them. Forty-four families lived on rented lands in one 'beat,' six of them in houses with only one room; some raised nothing but cotton. Twenty-four families have recently bought land, ten are building better homes, nine report that they lived for the year without a mortgage. The average length of our school term is three months. We have no school houses but use the churches, which are not fit for service in winter. Sixty per cent. of the teachers hold third-grade certificates, 30 per cent. second grade, and 4 per cent. first grade. Morals are better than they used to be; women are treated better on the whole; less whisky is used, and, as we have no railroads in our county, we are not troubled with excursions. We propose to organize conferences throughout the whole county and gradually bring the people up. Our people get money enough but don't use it right."

Roscoe C. Bruce.—Roscoe C. Bruce, the son of Ex-Senator Bruce from Mississippi, who went from the colored high schools of Washington to Phillips Exeter Academy, New Hampshire, was honored in 1897 by an election as assistant editor for the magazine published by the students of that institution. The color line was not drawn here. Young Bruce is a remarkably bright and handsome fellow and has made many friends at Phillips Exeter. He has distinguished himself for scholarship and oratory. He will graduate in 1898 and will probably enter Harvard University. The catalogue of Harvard University now contains the names of six colored men, three of them in the senior class. In the "Life and Letters of Roscoe Conkling," the circumstances under which young Bruce was named are given, and there appears a letter from Senator Bruce in which he asks permission to christen his son in honor of Mr. Conkling, because when he first

entered the senate chamber to take the oath of office
Mr. Conkling was the first man to offer him welcome.
"The effect upon some members of the senate," wrote
Mr. Bruce, " was so marked that when I was called to
be sworn in, my colleague, Mr. Alcorn, a man who
owed his seat in the senate largely to my efforts, took
refuge behind a newspaper to avoid extending the
courtesy usual upon such occasions. It was at this
point that the grasp of your hand—the first token of
friendship that I had received—and your warm welcome, made me feel and know that in that august body
I had a friend. No one who has not undergone a
similar ordeal can understand and appreciate my feelings on that occasion."

Alabama appropriates $2,000 annually for the sup-
port of a Normal School for the training of colored
teachers. Nearly all the Southern States make annual
contributions for the education of their colored
citizens.

Freedman's Savings Bank.—Still another agency
in the education of the colored people was the Freedman's Savings Bank. While it existed it was one of
the most powerful agencies in the education of the
colored people. The Freedman's Savings Bank was
organized March 3, 1866. It had thirty-three branches,
four of which were located in Georgia, at Atlanta,
Macon, Augusta and Savannah. During the nine
years of its existence the total deposits amounted to
$56,000,000 for the entire South.

When it failed it owed the colored people of Georgia
$57,149.38. While its loss entailed great misery on
many, it taught the colored people that they could
save, and thus laid the basis of the material prosperity
which has attended the efforts of the colored people of

Georgia. The colored people of Georgia pay taxes now on about $16,000,000 worth of real and personal property, and have, perhaps, not less than $2,000,000 on deposit in the banks of the state and in bonds.

Such were some of the various agencies which were at work during that early formative stage of Negro education. And such and so great was the work of preparing the colored people for the public school system which was inaugurated in 1871.

The Colored Press.—Considering the time since the Negro was freed there has been a remarkable advancement in providing literature for the colored people. There have been not a few authors of note of the race, but in the colored press we find a repetition of the press in general. There are in the United States between three hundred and three hundred and fifty colored newspapers, the number varying with the campaigns, etc. There are at least twenty colored papers of large circulation and influence and standing; among these may be mentioned: *The Christian Record, The Star of Zion, The American Baptist, The Christian Index* and *The Afro-American Presbyterian.* The best secular papers are *The New York Age, The Indianapolis Freeman, The Colored American,* of Washington, D. C., *The Richmond Planet,* and *The Philadelphia Tribune.*

Character.—Of many of the papers for colored people it might be said, as of many other papers, that it would be better that they had no existence. The hope of the race lies in education. The colored man must read, and, as has been said before, it would be better for him not to read at all than to read the trashy literature of today. While the colored press in a general way is doing much for the elevation of the Negro, yet the number of papers published and the large circulation of some of them is not a criterion of good work done. The press, pulpit and the platform have been great liberators of the nations, but, in order that this should be the case with the Afro-American press, like that of any race, there must be an ennobling and elevated tone. Without this the daily and weekly paper becomes a curse instead of a blessing. Records of riots, mobs, murders, and every-day misdoings do not elevate the morals of the reading public. Too often it is forgotten that the editorial chair requires more culture than is gotten by reading the newspapers, and to the detriment of the race there are those who are editing some of these race journals that ought to be relegated to the rear.

Able Editors.—The editor who is sending out week by week into the families of his patrons, a paper that is to benefit its readers, ought to be able to grapple with the problems of the day, the problems upon which depend the elevation and the continued advancement of the race. With Dr. Crummell we believe that it would be better that many of these race journals were not to exist, because of the incompetency in the editorial management. Ministers, physicians, lawyers and leaders in general, can do much toward suppressing objectionable literature of today by advocating the patronizing only of such papers as are ennobling and are building up the race. Select your paper, not for its value in dollars and cents, but rather for the contents of its columns.

Religious Papers.—Every family should have at least one religious paper. Even in religious papers some might be greatly improved, but when it comes to the secular paper it were much better not to take a paper at all than to allow the trashy and objectionable newspaper, that has no definite aim, to enter the home. Here is a field that ought not to be overlooked. The colored youth of today will read.

Good Literature.—Let parents and leaders in society everywhere see to it that the literature placed in the hands of the youth of the race is ennobling, elevating and instructive, and a great forward movement will have been made in advancing the interests of the race in general. Banish the low, trashy and sensational literature from your homes. Avoid it as you would a pestilence, and your sons and daughters will in the future rise up and in improved manhood and womanhood pronounce blessings upon your heads.

The First Daily Newspaper published by the colored people was the Cairo Gazette, owned, edited and published by Hon. W. S. Scott, of Cairo, Illinois. The first issue came from the press April 23, 1882.

First Newspaper in the South.—The first race newspaper published in the South for the colored men was the Colored American. It was published in Augusta, Georgia, and was edited by J. T. Shuften in 1865. We find the following description of this paper in the Afro-American Press: "It is designed to be a vehicle for the diffusion of religious, political and general intelligence. It will be devoted to the promotion of harmony and good will between the whites and colored people of the South, and uniting in its advocacy of industry and education among all classes; but particularly the class most in need of our agency. It will steadfastly oppose all forms of vice that prey upon society, and give that counsel that tends to virtue, peace and prosperity and happiness."

Rev. Thos. H. B. Walker was born in Tallahassee, Florida, in 1873. Like most colored boys of the South, he began life at the very bottom; but by his intelligence and perseverance, he has placed himself among the leaders of his race in the "black belt" of the South. Without money or special friends he worked his way through Cookman Institute, Jacksonville, Florida.

REV. THOS. H. B. WALKER.

He was pastor of a church at the age of nineteen. In 1897 he was elected editor of *The Sabbath School Banner.* The same year he organized the St. Joseph Aid Society, whose membership is now found in all parts of the South.

DINING HALL AND DORMITORY.

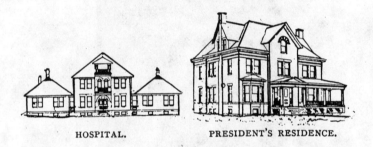

HOSPITAL.

PRESIDENT'S RESIDENCE.

THE NEW DORMITORY

THE NEW BUILDINGS
SPELMAN SEMINARY, ATLANTA, GA.

416b

CHAPTER XIII.

A Religious Nature.—Whatever else the Negro may or may not possess, it is generally conceded that he has an intensely religious nature. His religion, it is true, does not always manifest itself according to the precise rules and requirements of cultured and refined society. He is sometimes boisterous, very demonstrative, and altogether emotional. By the superficial observer, these characteristics are regarded as extremely ludicrous, if not disgusting, and are usually catalogued, with great self-complacency, among the "idiosyncrasies of the Negro." The thoughtful mind, however, recognizes beneath all these crudities a buoyant spirituality —a spirituality which even the malign influences of slavery could not suppress. It was Burke who said, "Religion, to have any force upon men's understandings,—indeed, to exist at all,—must be supposed paramount to law, and independent for its subsistence upon any human institution." This glorious truth, arrived at through reasoning and reflection by England's great political philosopher, seems to have been grasped intuitively by the ignorant Negro in the days of his bondage. Above the law that fixed his hard condition and held him therein, above the sophistry of ecclesiasticism that perverted truth to justify unrighteous legislation, his faith rose sublimely and took hold upon the unseen "Power that maketh for righteousness."

Sustained by Faith.—It was this faith that sustained

417

BISHOP BENJAMIN TUCKER TANNER, KANSAS CITY, KANSAS.
See sketch in Chapter XIV.

him in his darkest hours, that caused melody to well up in his soul, and gush forth in his voice. It was this faith that enabled him to endure patiently, without cherishing feelings of vengeance against those whom he might justly have regarded as oppressors. Finally, it was this faith that formed the substratum of his preliminary training, however inadequate, for the larger life that was to be realized under freedom. "By that mysterious influence," says Dr. Blyden, "which is imparted to man independently of outward circumstances, to not a few of them the preaching of the Gospel, defective as was its practical exemplification, opened a new world of truth and goodness. There streamed into the darkness of their surroundings a light from the Cross of Christ, and they saw that, through suffering and affliction, there is a path to perfect rest above this world; and in the hours of the most degrading and exhausting toil, they sang of the eternal and the unseen; so that while the scrupulous among their masters often, with Jefferson, "trembled for their country," the slaves who had gained a new language and new faculties were enjoying themselves in rapturous music—often laboring and suffering all day, and singing all night sacred songs which, in rude but impressive language, set forth their sad fortunes and their hopes for the future.

Cheerful Music.—No traveler in the South, who passed by the plantations thronged with dusky laborers, and listened to their cheerful music, could ever dream that they beheld in that suffering but joyous race the destroyers of the Southern whites. The captive Jews could not sing by the waters of Babylon, but the Negroes, in the dark dungeons of American slavery, made themselves harps and swept them to some of the most thrilling melodies."

Noticeable Fact.—It is a noticeable fact, and indicative of the susceptibility of the Negro's nature to religious influences, that, with such limited insight into divine truth, there should have sprung up all over the South among them so many effective preachers and exhorters—some of them men of extraordinary natural endowments. Stevens, in his history of the Methodist Episcopal Church, has the following interesting statement:

"Harry Hosier, better known as 'Black Harry,' was the traveling servant of Bishop Asbury, and had a popularity as a preacher which excelled that of the bishop himself. Dr. Rush, whose predilections for Methodist preaching are well known, did not disdain to hear him, and making allowance for his illiteracy (for he could not read), pronounced him the greatest orator in America."

Genuineness.—As to the genuineness of the Negro's religion, the late Bishop Haygood has said: "I know that the religious life of the colored people in the days of slavery was not what it ought to have been, yet among them were the holiest of men and women."

Strangest Characteristic.— The same author has elsewhere expressed an opinion which those endeavoring to educate the race might do well to consider. He says: "As to my opinion—with as good opportunity as most men to know what the religious life of the colored people really is—I say unhesitatingly that his religion is his strongest and best characteristic. All there is of hope for him in this country will rise or fall with the healthy development or the decay of his religion."

Progress Phenomenal.—Under freedom the religious progress of the race has been phenomenal. It would be difficult to find its parallel in the whole history of missions. Over a million of these people are today within the communion of the Baptist churches. Considerably over a million more are within the Methodist fold, while they are to be found also in the Congregational, Presbyterian, and other evangelical denominations. As before the war, even so now, a goodly number of them are adherents of the Romish Church. They are intensely loyal to their denomination, and possess in a larger degree than many other people what is commonly called "church pride."

Organizations. — The most remarkable, however, and at once the most promising feature in their religious development, is the organizations, which, independently of outside patronage, they have created and sustained. The African Methodist Episcopal Church, The Zion African Methodist Episcopal Church, and the Colored Methodist Episcopal Church, in America, are large and influential bodies, containing eight hundred thousand members or more. These bodies, officered and managed throughout by colored men, are ocular demonstrations of the capability of the race, and are inspiring in the people self-respect and self-reliance. Many of their general officers are men of great power and personal magnetism, while some have a national reputation.

Liberality. — In the August (1897) number of "The Gospel in All Lands," appears the following with reference to the religious growth of the colored people since emancipation:

"They have shown a remarkable degree of liberality in contributing toward religious purposes. Notwithstanding their poverty and the discouraging circumstances surrounding them, they have, in addition to the ordinary expenses of maintaining religious worship, including pastors' salaries, contributed probably not less than ten million dollars for the erection of meeting houses. Some of these buildings are large, comparatively costly, convenient and attractive.

Noble Achievements.—"They have done remarkably well, considering all the circumstances, in the matter of educational, missionary, charitable, and philanthropic work; many of their religious institutions of learning being managed by Negro boards of trustees, taught by Negro teachers, and supported largely or entirely by themselves. They are also represented on the boards and in the faculties of the schools maintained for them by Northern benevolence. The aggregate amount which they pay annually toward the education of their children in Christian institutions is a very considerable sum. They have their local, state, and national educational and missionary organizations, and are year by year making progress in the art of organization and administration. While they have very much yet to learn in the matter of systematizing their beneficence, of keeping and rendering accurate accounts of money received and disbursed, they are apt learners, and are making good progress. They edit and publish numerous religious periodicals, some of them evincing vigor, independence, and no little ability."

The Future.—With such a showing, made under the most discouraging circumstances, what may not be expected of the race under improved and constantly improving conditions?

Churches Important.—There are at present between nine and ten millions of Negroes in this country. This includes all who have any computable fraction of

A. M. E. BIG BETHEL CHURCH, ATLANTA, GA.

Negro blood in their veins. All of these, with the exception of about five hundred thousand, are in the Southern states where the emancipation proclamation reached them and made them forever free from involuntary bondage. The Negro churches of the South are, therefore, a large and important factor in the Christianity of that section. In point of church membership the Negro is quite as devoted as are his white brethren. The proportion of colored people who are connected with the churches in the United States is larger than that which obtains among the white people.

Denominations.—As to denomination, the Negro is predominantly Baptist. More than one-half of all Negro communicants are of this faith; next come the Methodists and other branches of the church. The increase in the number of colored communicants since the emancipation proclamation has been marvelous. There were at the outbreak of the war about 275,000 Methodists of color, while at the present there are over a million. Colored Baptists in 1860 did not exceed 250,000, while today they number 1,500,000.

Helping Himself.—The Negro, considering the little wealth he had at command when slavery ceased, has achieved wonders in the accumulation of church property. The value of the churches he owns is $26,626,-000, the number of edifices being 23,770. Making due allowance for the generous help which the whites have given, it still appears that the Negro has not been unwilling to make large sacrifices for the sake of religion, and that his industry, thrift and business capacity have been made to contribute to his successful endeavors to provide himself with suitable accommodations for public worship.

Sums Spent.—In education and evangelization among the Negroes, the various religious bodies have been specially active. Among these bodies the Congregationalists claim to have spent $11,000,000 for the Negro, and spend now nearly $400,000 a year. The Methodists have spent since emancipation $6,000,000, and are now spending annually through the Freedman's Aid and Southern Education Society $350,000; the Presbyterian Board of Missions for Freedmen in twenty years have spent $2,400,000, and in addition to this contribution founded Lincoln University, Pennsylvania, in 1859. The Baptists since 1865, $3,000,000; the Southern Presbyterian Church, $55,000, between 1878 and 1894; the Christian Church, $100,000. This vast outlay has produced a result known and read of all men. No man has attempted to deny the statement that the Negro has improved intellectually. Not even the bitterest of his enemies have denied this statement, and it may be said modestly that there are men and women among the Negroes who can compare favorably with some of the best of the other race.

Christian Ministry.—Professor Bowen says: "A vital question in this consideration is, has the character of the Negro Christian Ministry improved? The bald statement of truth is that the distance between the ministry of today and that of slavery days, or the days immediately following freedom, cannot be measured in words. Then, we had no regularly constituted Negro ministry. A few of our fathers in whose heart the 'woe is me if I preach not' burned with an unquenchable fire, were permitted to speak occasionally to the slaves, and that under the freezing gaze of an overseer's eye, and to this day it is a miracle unsolved how God preserved a knowledge of the truth through the broken vessels of thought amid the dervish worship of the ignorant slaves.

Educated and Consecrated.—Since that day there has been a constant stream of educated and consecrated ministers flowing into the ranks of the Negro population. These have been trained in the great universities of the North. Besides these, there have gone forth from the institutions established in the South for colored people large numbers of genuinely consecrated ministers of every denomination. Whether it be accepted or reflected, the fact is that there are in Negro pulpits all over the land and in the South some Negro preachers who, in intellectual ability, in moral power and purity, and in spiritual insight and breadth of wisdom, are the equal of some of the best of the Anglo-Saxon race."

CHURCHES.

Regular Baptists (Colored).—The colored Baptists of the South constitute the most numerous of regular Baptists. Not all colored Baptists are embraced in this division; only those who have separate churches, associations, and state conventions. There are many colored Baptists in Northern states, who are mostly counted as members of churches belonging to white associations. None of them are included in the following estimates and figures.

The first convention of colored Baptists was organized in North Carolina in 1866, the second in Alabama, and the third in Virginia in 1867, the fourth in Arkansas in 1868, and the fifth in Kentucky in 1869. There are colored conventions in fifteen states and the District of Columbia.

In addition to these organizations the colored Baptists of the United States have others more general in

THANKFUL BAPTIST CHURCH, AUGUSTA. GEORGIA.

character: The American National Convention, the purpose of which is "to consider the moral, intellectual and religious growth of the denomination," to deliberate upon questions of general concern, and to devise methods of bringing the churches and members of the race together; the Consolidated American Missionary Convention, the General Association of the Western States and Territories, the Foreign Mission Convention of the United States, and the New England Missionary Convention. All except the first are missionary in their purpose.

The Regular Baptists (colored) are represented in fifteen states, all in the South, or on the border, and the District of Columbia. In Virginia and Georgia they are very numerous, having in the latter 200,516, and in the former 199,871 communicants. In Alabama they have 142,437; in North Carolina, 134,445; in Mississippi, 136,647; in South Carolina, 125,572, and in Texas, 111,138 members. The aggregate is 1,348,-989 members, who are embraced in 12,533 organizations, with 11,987 church edifices, and church property valued at $9,038,549. There are 414 associations, of which 66 are in Alabama, 63 in Georgia, 49 in Mississippi, and 39 in North Carolina.

African Methodist Episcopal. — This branch of American Methodism was organized in Philadelphia in 1816 by a number of colored members of Methodist Episcopal Church. They withdrew from the parent body in order that they might have larger privileges and more freedom of action among themselves than they believed they could secured in continued association with their white brethren. The Rev. Richard Allen was elected the first bishop of the new church by the same convention that organized it. In the year 1787 Mr. Allen had been made the leader of a class of forty persons of his own color. A few years later he purchased a lot at the corner of Sixth and Lombard streets, Philadelphia, where the first church erected in this country for colored Methodists was occupied in 1794. This site is now covered by an edifice dedicated in 1890, valued at $50,000.

In doctrine, government and usage, the church does not essentially differ from the body from which it sprang. It has an itinerant and a local or non-itinerant ministry, and its territory is divided into annual conferences. It has a general conference, meeting once every four years; bishops or itinerant general superintendents, elected for life, who visit the annual conferences in the episcopal districts to which they are assigned, and presiding elders, who exercise subepiscopal oversight in the districts into which the annual conferences are divided, and it has the probationary system for new members, with exhorters, class leaders, stewards, stewardesses, etc.

There are in the United States, 2,481 organizations; 4,124 edifices, with church property valued at $6,468,-280, and 452,725 communicants or members.

The church is widely distributed, having congregations in forty-one states and territories. The states in which it is not represented are the two Dakotas, Idaho, Maine, Nevada, New Hampshire and Vermont, the territories being Alaska, Oklahoma, and Arizona. Its members are most numerous in South Carolina, where there are 88,172. Georgia comes second with 73,248; Alabama third, with 30,781; Arkansas fourth, with 27,956; Mississippi fifth, with 25,439; Tennessee has 23,718; Texas 23,392, and Florida 22,463. In no other state does the number reach 17,000. The eight

Southern states above given report 315,169 members, or considerably more than two-thirds of the entire membership of the church.

African Union Methodist Protestant.—This body, which has a few congregations divided among eight states, came into existence at about the same time the African Methodist Episcopal Church was organized (1816), differing from the latter chiefly in objections to the itinerancy, to a paid ministry, and to the episcopacy. It has two annual conferences, with 40 organizations, 27 church edifices, church property valued at $55,440, and 3,415 communicants.

African Methodist Episcopal Zion.—A congregation of colored people, organized in New York city, in 1796, was the nucleus of the African Methodist Episcopal Zion Church. This congregation originated in a desire of colored members of the Methodist Episcopal Church to hold separate meetings, in which they "might have an opportunity to exercise their spiritual gifts among themselves, and thereby be more useful to one another." They built a church, which was dedicated in 1800, the full name of the denomination subsequently organized being given to it. The church entered into an agreement in 1801, by which it was to receive certain pastoral supervision from the Methodist Episcopal Church. It had preachers of its own who supplied its pulpits in part. In 1820 this arrangement terminated, and in the same year a union of colored churches in New York, New Haven, Long Island, and Philadelphia was formed and rules of government adopted. Thus was the African Methodist Episcopal Zion Church formally organized.

The first annual conference was held in 1821. It was attended by nineteen preachers, representing six churches and 1,426 members. Next year, James Varick was chosen superintendent of the denomination, which was extended over the states of the North, chiefly, until the close of the civil war, when it entered the South to organize many churches.

In its policy, lay representation has long been a prominent feature. Laymen are in its annual conferences as well as in its general conferences, and there is no bar to the ordination of women. Until 1880 its superintendents, or bishops, were elected for a term of four years. In that year the term of the office was made for life or during a good behavior. Its system is almost identical with that of the Methodist Episcopal Church, except the presence of laymen in the annual conference, the election of presiding elders on the nomination of the presiding bishop, instead of their appointment by the bishop alone, and other small divergences.

Its general conference meets quadrennially. Its territory is divided into seven Episcopal districts, to each of which a bishop is assigned by the general conference.

The church is represented in twenty-eight states and the District of Columbia. It is strongest in North Carolina, where it has 111,949 communicants. Alabama comes next with 79,231 communicants; South Carolina third, with 45,880, and Florida fourth, with 14,791. There are in all 1,704 organizations; 1,587 church edifices; church property valued at $2,714,128, and 349,788 communicants.

Colored Methodist Episcopal.—The Colored Methodist Episcopal Church was organized in 1870, of colored members and ministers of the M. E. Church, South. Before the war this church did a large evan-

FIRST CONGREGATIONAL CHURCH, ATLANTA, GEORGIA.

gelistic work among the Negroes. Many of the Negro slaves received the gospel from the same preachers and in the same churches as their masters, the galleries or a portion of the house being assigned to them. For those who were not privileged to attend organized churches, special missions were begun as early as 1829. In 1845 there were 124,000 members of the slave population, and in 1860 207,000 members. In 1866, after the opening of the South to Northern churches had given the Negro members opportunity to join the A. M. E. Church, the A. M. E. Zion and other Methodist bodies, it was found that there were only 78,000 members left. The General Conference of 1866 authorized these colored members to be organized into separate conferences, and in 1870 two bishops were appointed to organize the colored conferences into a separate and independent church. This church has the same articles of religion, the same form of government, and the same discipline as its parent body. Its bishops are elected for life.

Bishop Holsey declares that the great aim of the church is to evangelize the Negro, and to educate and elevate him. There are 23 annual conferences, 129,383 members. There are 1,750 organizations, with 1,653 church edifices. Valuation of property, $1,713,366. This church is strongest in Georgia, where it has more than 22,000 members, Mississippi comes next with 20,000, Tennessee third, with 18,968, and Alabama fourth, with 18,940.

Congregational Methodists (Colored).—This body consists of congregations of colored members organized into conferences by presidents of the Congregational Methodist Church, to which it corresponds in all particulars of doctrine, polity and usage. The only difference in the churches of the two bodies is that they are composed of white and colored persons, respectively.   There are in all nine organizations and 319 communicants.

Cumberland Presbyterian (Colored).—This body was organized in May, 1869, at Murfreesboro, Tennessee, under the direction of the General Assembly of the Cumberland Presbyterian Church.   It was constituted of colored ministers and members who had been connected with that church.   Its first synod, the Tennessee, was organized in 1871, and its general assembly in 1874.   It has the same doctrinal symbol as the parent body, and the same system of government and discipline, differing only in race.   It has twenty-three presbyteries, and is represented in nine states and one territory.   It has 224 organizations, 183 church edifices, 12,956 communicants and church property valued at $195,826.

It has 81 organizations, 72 church edifices, with an approximate seating capacity of 24,125; 7 halls with a seating capacity of 825; its church property is valued at $88,660, with 2,202 communicants or members.

Sunday School Union of the A. M. E. Church.—Of all the public institutions owned and controlled by Afro-Americans, the Sunday School Union of the African Methodist Episcopal Church deserves special mention.   From a purely business standpoint, it has been a decided success.

Organized August 11, 1882, it has just completed the first fifteen years of its existence.   What as to results?   It is the first colored religious denomination to adopt "Children's Day" as an anniversary of annual observance, and to apply the collections received therefrom to the extension of Sunday school work.   It is the first colored religious organization in the world to purchase and possess real estate paid for by moneys raised exclusively by Sunday school children. It is the first colored religious denomination to issue a series of graded Sunday school helps, such as quarterlies, and lesson papers. It is the first colored religious denomination to print and publish with the aid of its own machinery and material Sunday school literature and requisites.

From the returns of Children's Day, it has received $56,969.57, while the receipts to business aggregate $158,658.

It has donated to needy Sunday schools, in the way of books and periodicals, $5,057.98.

It owns a solid stone front, brick building, situated on the public square, in Nashville, Tennessee, which is of inestimable value to the A. M. E. Church, and would not be parted with for any sum less than $25,000. It is five stories high, including the basement.

Its periodicals have a circulation in almost every state and territory in the West Indies and West and South Africa.

Its property and business is easily worth $40,000, and is free and unencumbered, except a current debt of $1,500, which is partially offset by a cash balance.

It has never assumed the attitude of a public beggar, nor asked a white person for a single penny. Its support from, all sources has come absolutely and exclusively from colored people.

Its founder, Charles Spencer Smith, has been its secretary and treasurer from its organization to the present.

Items.—Hon. Frederick Douglass, in his early life, was a local preacher in the A. M. E. Zion Church.

The first A. M. E. Zion church established south of the Mason and Dixon line, was St. Peter's at Newberne, North Carolina, in 1862.

The American Baptist Home Missionary Society has expended in Georgia for educational work among the 200,000 Negroes there, more than $500,000. Two of the most important schools—Spelman Seminary and the Baptist College—are located at Atlanta.

The colored Baptists of the United States report a membership of 1,348,000, with 11,000 ordained ministers; 13,000 church buildings, valued at $10,000,000, and 9,000 Sunday schools, with more than 500,000 scholars.

Rev. Lott Carey was born in Virginia in 1780, and died November 10, 1828, in Liberia. He was the first colored American missionary to Africa.

Fully nine-tenths of the colored church members are Methodists and Baptists, and between these two they are pretty equally divided.

The oldest colored church in the South is Evans Chapel, Fayetteville, North Carolina (A. M. E. Zion).

Remember, Christian Negroes black as Cain may be refined and join the angelic train.—*Phillis Wheatley*.

Negroes are more religious than white folks. They are more emotional. Emotion is not a virtue, for some emotionalists are sadly wanting in all the virtues.

The amount of knowledge a man has does not secure his usefulness if he has so taken it in that he is lop-sided.—*Blyden*.

If a man wants to know his own strength, he need not measure himself. He needs only to size up the fellows who are pulling against him to find out how strong he is.—*Bishop Grant*.

Rev. E. C. Morris, D. D., born May 7, 1855, was a native of Murray county, Georgia. He and his parents were slaves until liberated by the Emancipation Proclamation of "Father Abraham."

His early educational advantages were limited to the common school, but as he was a careful student and a close observer, his knowledge of men and current events made him a practical business man and a wise adviser.

In 1879 he took the pastorate of the Centennial Baptist church of Helena, Arkansas, which position he has held continuously to the present time. His ability is also recognized as an organizer in educational, missionary and literary interests. He established, and for two years edited the first religious paper published by his race in the state of Arkansas. In 1884, he organized the Arkansas Baptist College, and for sixteen years has been chairman of its board of trustees. For nineteen years he has been president of the Baptist state convention. Since 1894 he has been president of

REV. E. C. MORRIS, D. D.

the National Baptist convention, the largest deliberative body of negroes in the world. It was his active brain that conceived the idea of the National Baptist

Young People's Union Board. In addition to his other duties, that of editor-in-chief of the "Convention Teacher" was undertaken by his energetic hand.

REV. M. W. D. NORMAN, D. D.

Rev. M. W. D. Norman, D. D.—Rev. Moses W. D. Norman of North Carolina was educated at Plymouth Normal School and Shaw University. In the fall of 1893 he was appointed Professor of Theology in Shaw

University. This position he resigned in 1896 to accept the presidency of Roanoke Institute.

MRS. HENRIETTA M. ARCHER,
Principal of the Department of Latin and Music in
A. & M. College, Normal, Ala., and Associate with
the National Colored Woman's Association.

Provident Hospital.—This institution, located at Chicago, was founded in 1891, and incorporated through the united efforts of a few earnest men. With the exception of Freedman's Hospital at Washington, it is the only institution engaged in special work in behalf of the colored people. It is unique in its character, and those for whom its benefits are more specially intended are grateful for and appreciative of its advantages.

Training School for Nurses.—In it is established a school in which young colored women are fitted for nurses, and thus a new field for their independence has been developed. A course of two years has been laid out, and already three classes have graduated. In addition to the regular hospital duties, visiting nurses are sent out among the poor and sick colored people, with most gratifying results.

Receipts.—The fifth annual report of the board of trustees gives as the total receipts nearly $30,000, of which more than $11,000 were voluntarily contributed by patients themselves, and the remainder by friends of the institution.

Patients.—The number of colored patients in the hospital for the first five years was 655.

Gratitude.—Words cannot express the gratitude of the colored people in the establishment of this home which has brought new and liberal facilities to the needy of the colored race.

Hale Infirmary.—In Montgomery, Alabama, in the eastern part of the city, near Hall street, is a large eighteen-room building with this inscription on the corner-stone: "Infirmary, given by James Hale, for the benefit of his race, and erected by his wife, as a memorial to their deceased daughter and son, Sarah and James."

It was the desire of James Hale to do something to help the poor and aged of his people, but before he was able to carry out his plans, he was called away to "that home over there," in the heavenly city of rest. He told his wife, however, to carry out his wishes;

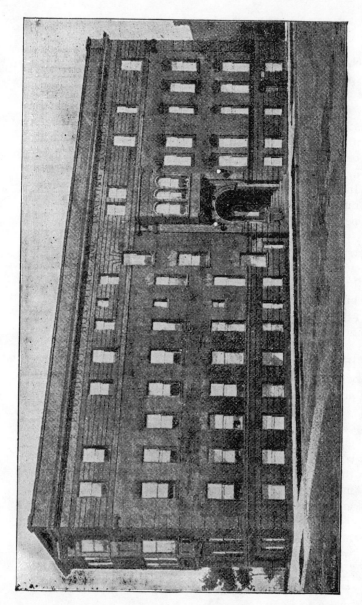

PROVIDENT HOSPITAL, CHICAGO, ILLINOIS.

and, faithful to her promise to her dying husband, this good woman did not cease work until the desires of her husband were fulfilled. And indeed, although the infirmary is in full operation today, she has not stopped work, but is going about among the poor, the aged and the homeless, doing all she can to lighten their burdens of life. Those who are sick, those who are alone, those who have no homes, and those who have fallen among thieves, she is lifting them up, building up their wounds and taking them to her inn, the Hale Infirmary. "The property as it stands today is worth $7,000, and, knowing the needs of my people as I do, I can say for a truth, James Hale could not have left his money to a better cause. Our people have been buying church property and building churches and preparing to live in heaven, for more than a generation. To this I have no objection, but I think the time is near at hand when we should begin to mix a little business with our religion, and while building our churches, let us also build homes for ourselves, homes for the orphans, the poor and the aged of our race, and also infirmaries and hospitals where the lame, sick and the injured can be cared for."

Mrs. Watts' Orphanage.—At Covington, Georgia, is located an institution which is doing much good for the state and for our people. There, in that quiet little city, is an orphanage and industrial school under the management of Mrs. D. Pace Watts. That good woman is toiling on with her work, spending her earnings and her life, all for the good she may do for the poor and parentless of her race, and is building up the kingdom of God among them, and, in her way, as best she can, is teaching them how to make honest and honorable citizens.

How sweet must be the lives of those who pass beyond the whirlpool of society and lose themselves in the midst of spiritual work among the poor, the friendless, the motherless and the fatherless of the communities in which they live. There they work and pray to make the world better, often without pay, without thanks, and without encouragement, but they labor on with the belief that some day, and somewhere, they will be rewarded.

Such has been the life work of Mrs. Diana Pace Watts. She has toiled with her work at Covington almost single-handed, and has overcome many obstacles. The extent of her work cannot be told in such a short article; suffice it to say, however, she is doing much good for her race and the state, and deserves the co-operation and support of all who are interested in Christian work among the lowly.

To Rescue Colored People.—The Rev. George W. Dickey, pastor of the Burning Bush Mission, Chicago, Illinois, recently purchased the three-story brick building at 2838 Dearborn street, for the purpose of converting it into a home for homeless and unfortunate women. It will be called a Rescue and Industrial institute. The plan has been under consideration for some time, and recently a few wealthy Baptists took hold of the matter, with the Rev. Mr. Dickey, and the result is that the home will be opened as soon as the alterations can be made in the two upper floors.

The property cost $10,500, and is a three-story brick building, 25x98 feet, on a lot 110 feet deep. There will be sleeping apartments on the top floor, and on the second floor the women will be taught sewing, housekeeping, cooking, stenography, and typewriting, and whatever else will enable them to be self-supporting. The plan of Rev. Dickey is one of several to give practical aid to the unemployed among the colored people. The Rev. Dickey, in speaking of his work, says:

"We need to do something for our young women.

AMANDA SMITH.

They come to Chicago in large numbers from the South every year, and drift about in this great city without any guidance or friends. In a short while they go to the dogs. It is the one reason why one can go into the various stations of the city and see such a large percentage of colored criminals. I think it is about time for the Christian people to bestir themselves and do something practical in the way of giving protection and kindly assistance to unemployed colored men and women. Our home is established for this purpose. And, while we are colored people, I can assure you that we will not close our doors against the needy of any race or color.''

Amanda Smith Industrial Orphan Home for Colored Children.—Amanda Smith, who has labored much for the elevation of her people, was greatly impressed with the need of an orphan home for colored children, and in 1895 secured possession of a property in North Harvey, Chicago, Illinois, worth $6,000. Through the sale of her book, evangelistic work and donations, she has already secured considerable toward the payment for the building. She is putting all her time and strength into collecting funds so that the Home may be free of debt. While she is spending her time in the evangelistic field, and in collecting for the orphanage, her permanent address is 2940 South Park avenue, Chicago, Illinois.

There is no doubt that this institution will be a great blessing to the colored people of Chicago and the North when it is once fully established.

Other Institutions.—The presence of the orphanage at Covington, the Carrie Steele Orphans' Home, and the Carter Home for old people and boys, in Atlanta, the Old Folks' Home at Norfolk, Virginia, the Old Folks' Home at Philadelphia, the Orphans' Home at St. Louis, and the Home for Working Girls at Washington, D. C., are only some of the evidences which show to what extent and with what earnestness the women of our race have entered upon the work.

CHAPTER XIV.

Frederick Douglass, the most remarkable man of Negro blood yet produced in the United States was born in Talbot county, Maryland, in February, 1817, and had just completed his seventy-eighth year, at the time of his death. He was the mulatto son of a slave mother, and consequently himself born a slave. At a very early age he went to Baltimore to live, where he acquired a rudimentary education. His owner allowed him to employ his own time at three dollars per week, and he obtained work in a shipyard. When just twenty-one years old he ran away to New York, and from there went to New Bedford, Massachusetts, where he supported himself as a laborer. He came, by some means, under the observation of William Lloyd Garrison, who assisted his efforts at self-education, and under Garrison's auspices he was brought out as an orator at abolition meetings in New England. In 1841 he attended an anti-slavery meeting at Nantucket, and made a speech that brought him into national notice. After this, as agent of the Massachusetts Anti-Slavery Society, he traveled through the Northern states making abolition speeches. Anti-slavery agitation was a sensitive and exciting theme at that period of the country's history, and the bold utterances of the colored orator, the first person of his race to display such capability, made him a very much discussed person. He afterward edited *The North Star*, an abolition paper, at Rochester, New York, and published one or two books giving his

HON. FREDRICK DOUGLASS.

experience as a slave, and intended to promote the then fast growing abolition sentiment.

The Maryland family to whom Douglass had always belonged as a slave were named Lloyds, but after going North he adopted for himself the name he has since borne.   When he had become distinguished his friends in England raised a purse of $750 with which his freedom was legally purchased.

He visited England in 1845, and made many speeches there that were well received.   He was charged with conspiracy in the John Brown raids into Virginia in 1859, and Governor Wise made a requisition for his arrest on the governor of Michigan.   Legal complications were avoided by a second visit to England.   Of this visit Douglass later beautifully said: "I fled from the talons of the American eagle to nestle in the mane of the British lion."   When the Civil War broke out he urged emancipation and the employment of the Negro troops.   Later he was active in organizing Negro regiments in the North.   After the war he held various offices under Republican administration.   Mr. Cleveland removed him from his office of Recorder of Deeds of the District of Columbia in 1886, and three years later Mr. Harrison made him minister to Hayti, the last official position that he filled.   The Haytian government made him one of the commissioners for its exhibit at the Columbian Exposition at Chicago.

In early life, while residing at New Bedford, Massachusetts, Douglass was married to a woman of his own color, by whom he had two sons and a daughter, who survive him.   A few years ago he was married to Helen Pitts, a white woman from New England, who was employed as clerk in the office when he was Recorder of Deeds.   In appearance, Douglass' Caucasian blood was very manifest. He was of bright complexion, with prominent, clearly defined features, and hair only slightly curly. In old age he wore his hair and beard long, which gave him an air at once striking and venerable. His oratorical gift was of no ordinary quality, and no man in American public life was a greater factor in that agitation which led up to the events of 1860-65, and created such a revolution in the country's condition. He leaves a fortune, the accumulation of savings during a long life, estimated by some as high as $200,000.

William Lloyd Garrison relates the following story of Douglass and Sojourner Truth, a character as remarkable in her way as Douglass was in his. She was a thorough African of unmixed blood, gaunt and black. She was born a slave in New York, and emancipated when slavery was abolished in that state. She could neither read nor write, whereas Douglass had educated himself and was the peer of any so-called self-educated white man. At an anti-slavery meeting, when the aspect of affairs was particularly dark, Douglass was speaking and indulging in gloomy views of the situation. Sojourner, who was a listener, and was possessed with an intense religious faith, was disturbed at the tone of his despondency, and in a moment relieved her feelings and those of the meeting as well, by saying in her deep voice: "Is God dead, Frederick?" Nobody could appreciate the hit better than himself, and the closing remarks were in a more hopeful strain.

Hon. Josiah T. Settle, of Memphis, says: "On one occasion, some time before emancipation, he attended the Fourth of July celebration, I think, at Rochester; he was then a man of international fame, and was called upon to speak   I have not seen the speech in print for more than thirty years, but as I read it then and remember it now, taken in connection with the times and circumstances under which it was made, the man and the occasion, nothing could have been more truly eloquent.   When he arose and looked over his audience, among other things he said: 'Why am I called upon to speak on an occasion such as this? Why should I celebrate your Fourth of July?   What freedom have I and my people to celebrate?   Above your shouts and the roar of your cannon I can hear the crack of the slave whip, the clanking of the chains, and the groans of my oppressed brethren in the South. Your rejoicings do but fill to overflowing my cup of bitterness.   You were willing to bare your breasts to cannon to evade a tax on tea, but you turn a deaf ear to three millions of human beings, made in the image of God, who are vainly pleading to you in chains that they may own their own bodies, and that they may be protected in the commonest ties of husband and wife, parent and child.   While you celebrate the anniversary of your independence, you have coiled up in the youthful bosom of your republic the serpent of slavery, sucking her life's blood, and sending its poison into every member of her body.   Your Declaration of Independence is a lie!   And your flag contaminates the very air of God.   Every stripe upon it represents the blood and bondage of my people, and every star glitters to your country's shame.' "

From a memorial address in "Talks for the Times," we take the following; "If I were asked to sum up in a word what made Frederick Douglass great, I should say a noble purpose, fixed and unchangeable, a purpose to render to mankind the largest possible service.

Verily, he has served us well, faithfully, unselfishly, and now, full of years, and full of honors, loaded with such distinctions as this poor world has to give, he dies, dies as he lived, a brave, strong, good man. No more shall we behold that manly form. No more shall we listen to those eloquent lips upon which, for over fifty years, so many thousands have hung with rapture, those eloquent lips that made his name famous in two hemispheres, and will surely keep it so as long as freedom has a history. God grant that the mantle of this old hero may fall upon a worthy successor! God grant that our young men, contemplating his life and emulating his example, may be lifted up to a higher conception of life, of duty, of responsibility, of usefulness!"

William Still.—We abridge the following from the "Life of William Still," as it is given in the revised edition of the "Underground Railroad":

His parents, Levin and Sidney, were both slaves on the eastern shore of Maryland. "Massa, I'd sooner die than stay a slave!" was the declaration of his father to his young master before either was twenty-one years of age. The master saw that it would be impossible to change this determination of the slave, and felt that it would be policy under the circumstances to drive the best bargain he could. He decided to sell him to himself, or in other words, give him the chance of buying his freedom. The price was named and accepted by the slave. His former diligence was now doubly taxed to complete the hard task of working out his freedom. At last, by dint of perseverance and economy, he succeeded. Being free, he could not breathe the air tainted by slavery, hence, severing the sacred ties of family, bidding good-bye to his wife and four children (two boys and two girls), and trusting God for the future, he started northward and located near Greenwich, New Jersey.   The wife felt more keenly than ever the yoke of bondage; she, too, resolved to break it, but not in the tedious way her husband had done.   For the sake of liberty and of being reunited to her husband, she resolved to accept the trials and dangers of escape, and if not successful, the death which such an attempt often involved. Under the influence of a mighty resolution, hoping for such indirect aid as her husband could furnish, she set out with her four children on her toilsome fugitive journey.   Then came days of watching, waiting and fear of detection, nights perilous with forced travel, times of despair as swamps and forests interposed, rivers intervened or starvation threatened.   Success crowned her perils and sacrifices.   The father's heart and hand had been diligent in her movements, as she had anticipated.   The family was joyfully reunited, and a home was provided near Greenwich.   The old name of Steele became Still.   Every precaution was taken to preserve the secret of their past existence. But the scent of the slave hunter was not to be baffled by these precautions.   In a few months, a capturing gang, terrible as an army with banners, suddenly pounced upon the peaceful household, and the wife and four children were dragged back to their old slave quarters in Maryland.   Liberty's draught once tasted, the lips of the slave mother longed for it again.   Plans for a second attempt were laid.   None seemed feasible that included her four children.   Agonizing as was the thought of severing herself from her children, she could not overcome the dreadful alternative by any ingenuity of her own.   At last, the plan was laid out;

she would leave her two boys under the care of her dear mother, who was also in bondage. What tears watered the sad conclusion! She would save the girls, the youngest and weakest. The sorrowful night came. Nerved for the hour and the painful occasion, she rushed to the little straw bed on which her four children were sleeping, kissed her boys farewell without waking them, clasped her two little girls in her strong, true arms, bade her mother good-bye, and trusting in God, began again the perilous march to freedom. Not recounting the trials and hardships and dangers overcome, she reached the free soil of New Jersey, and rejoined her husband with her two little girls. And now greater precaution was necessary, hence a home in the depths of the Jersey pines, seven miles east of Medford, was chosen. Guarding their family history, working peaceably and industriously, dealing honestly, walking reverently, Levin Still was permitted to escape the pursuit of the slave hunter, and to enjoy the blessings of home. His acres became his own; thrift brought this reward to him. His family increased until it numbered eighteen children in all, the youngest of whom was William Still, the subject of our sketch. Suffice it to say of the two sons in slavery, that they were sold and taken South. One of them died in slavery, and the other, Peter Still, returned to the family forty years later. When old enough, William began to work on the farm, the stock of which consisted of a horse and a yoke of oxen. The cranberry meadows near by furnished employment for him and his brothers. In the winter, the Still family were occupied in putting up cordwood. In the rich agricultural district west of Medford, he succeeded in obtaining work during harvest, always receiving kind treatment and good wages. Whisky was served, according to custom, to the harvest hands. One day, William, exhausted by the heat, and his efforts to do a full hand's work, was induced to take a drink. It sickened him so that he was forced to return home, and report a quarter of a day's work lost labor. This humiliated him so that he resolved never to touch the accursed stuff again. If there is anything in his life of which he is proud, it is the faithful keeping of the vow then registered.

William received no schooling until he was seventeen years of age, when a teacher was secured who was favorably inclined to the colored race. He then dropped all work and attended school. He subscribed for *The Colored American*, but the postmaster did not consider it proper to dispense that kind of literature through the mails, and so withheld the paper for a number of weeks. At last he was informed that he could have his papers if he paid what was due on them. He paid thirty cents postage, and was given a bundle of papers which, when he got home and unfolded, were undelivered numbers of other papers not his own. He, however, applied at once to the postmaster, and carried his point. In 1844, when he was twenty-three years old, he went to Philadelphia with only $3 in his pocket. Here he was obliged to confront the question of color. He was not able to secure steady work, discouragement and failure met him on every hand. After being engaged in work for some time, he found that he was not making enough to pay his modest board bill. During the next summer, he worked in a brick yard. Determined to provide for the coming winter better than he did for the first winter spent in Philadelphia, he resolved to start a business of his own. He engaged in the oyster business, but a very brief experience proved to him that he was not capable of carrying it on. Through the pious representations of a rogue the money he had on hand was temporarily loaned, and the prospective profit became a real loss. He then became a second-hand clothing dealer, but this plunged him into bankruptcy. He then got a position as a waiter in a Broad street house, but the surroundings were so disgusting and the work so hard that in three weeks, hearing of a vacancy in the family of an aged widow of great wealth, he ventured to try for the place. Here he was engaged after a searching examination at $14 per month. By faithfulness, he soon won the esteem of the lady, and found that, although she was exacting in requiring her rules to be obeyed, yet she was kind and always ready to aid him. His duties were light, and as the good lady discovered his taste for books, she extended all encouragement to him that she could. She permitted him to keep up his connection with the Sunday school at the Moral Reform Retreat, and assisted him in acquiring knowledge of books. After spending eighteen months very profitably and pleasantly in the home of this old lady, she left the city to reside with her daughter in New York. This ended William's engagement, and he was sorry enough to part with one who was so kind to him. With the references from the good old lady, he soon secured a place with the family of a retired merchant until he heard that a clerk was needed in the office of the Pennsylvania Anti-Slavery Society. He made application for the position, and was informed that the committee would employ him provided the salary suited, $3.75 per week. In the meantime, having won a lady and made her his wife, he looked around for further employment in order that he might eke out a comfortable subsistence for himself and wife. This he procured as janitor of the library building, at a salary of $6 per month. His wife, in the meantime, carried on dressmaking. His faithfulness and ability in office work soon induced the committee in charge of the Anti-Slavery office to increase his salary. He had become an earnest, confidential worker in the underground railroad matters, and his house had been known as a safe and convenient station on the line of northward march. He was ever on the alert to aid slaves to escape. Many of the successful attempts that he made to liberate Negroes are recorded in his volume, "The Underground Railroad." He resigned as chairman of the committee in 1861, and immediately began business as a dealer in stoves, also the sale of coal on a small scale, and this business increased until he has become one of the noted coal dealers of the city. He was unanimously elected a member of the Philadelphia Board of Trade, and has for years been reaping the reward of energy and integrity in the shape of a daily enlarging confidence. In 1872 he published his work, "The Underground Railroad." The manuscript had been very carefully secreted during the war, as no other of the underground railroad managers had dared to make any note of the work. At the Centennial Exposition in 1876 his book attracted much attention. Mr. Still, although past seventy-five years of age, is still vigorous and active. He is still engaged in philanthropic work. He is actively engaged as president, etc., on the board of "The Home for Aged and Infirm Colored People," for more than thirty years. His life has been a busy and useful one. He was connected with a society for improving the condition of the Negro race, of which Benjamin Franklin was first president, and which was organized one year before the United States government.

The reader will, no doubt, desire to know something concerning the two boys who were sold in slavery into the South. We take the following from the life of William Still, giving an account of his meeting with his brother:

"One summer day, in 1850, as I was busily engaged in mailing the weekly issue of the *Pennsylvania Freeman*, two colored men entered the office. One of them was a resident of Philadelphia, and well known to me; the other I never had seen. My acquaintance introduced the stranger as coming from the South, and with the added remark 'He will tell you his own story.' I paused, and the stranger began in a very deliberate manner, saying: 'I am from Alabama. I have come in search of my people. I and my little brother were kidnapped about forty years ago, and I thought by coming to Philadelphia and having notices written and read in the colored churches old people would remember about it, and I could find my mother and people.'

"After going on with his story for a few mintues in this way, I became fully satisfied that, if his story were as he had given it thus far, I could save valuable time by asking a few questions. I therefore asked:

" 'Where were you kidnapped from?'

"A.—'I don't know.'

"Q.—'Don't you know the name of the place?'

"A.—'No.'

"Q.—Don't you know the name of any town, river, neighborhood or state?'

"A.—'No.'

"Q.—'What was your name?'

"A.—'Peter.'

"Q.—'What was your little brother's name?'

"A.—'Levin.'

"Q.—'What were the names of your father and mother?'

"A.—'Mother's name was Sidney and father's name was Levin?'

"Q.—'Do you remember the name of any other person?'

"A.—'I know the name of one white man.' (Here he named him.)

"By this time I was simply thunderstruck, so to speak. I had to summon all my powers of control in the presence of the stranger, so fully was I convinced by this time that he was one of my long-lost brothers. I scarcely knew what to do for a little time, but by and by I dismissed the pilot, saying I would look further into the case after I got through with my mailing and take care of the stranger over night. This was satisfactory to the pilot, but hardly so to the stranger, till he was advised by his friend that it would be all right.

"Before intimating to my brother the discovery I had made, I allowed a full hour to pass, meanwhile plying him with a thousand questions touching his entire life. Then, seating myself by his side, I said: 'I think I can tell you all about your kinfolk—mother, father, etc.,' and went on to say, 'You are an own brother of mine.'

"As anxious as he had been all his life to find his lost parents and relatives, this news was at the moment too good for him to fully credit. He was as one dumb-founded. I went on to assure him of the truth of all I had said, by relating our family history in detail, and dwelling particularly on mother's escapes, and how, in her second attempt, she was obliged to leave her two little boys, Levin and Peter, behind, in the care of their grandmother.

"Having explained the matter to Peter thus fully, his doubts vanished and he went home with me. Our two sisters living in Philadelphia, who were acquainted with all the secrets of the family history, were soon called in, and became joyful witnesses of the marvel·ous restoration. Outside of myself and sisters, I felt sure he might have enquired the city over without having obtained the slightest cue to his lost relations.

"The next day he was taken to our mother's home in New Jersey, and fully recognized by her, not a shadow of doubt appearing as to his identity, as he was her very image.

"Allow me to remark just here that it was this heartrending history connected with my own family that first prompted me to keep the records of the underground railroad. Thousands of escapes, harrowing separations, dreadful longings, dark gropings after lost parents, brothers, sisters, and identities, seemed ever to be pressing on my mind. While I knew the danger of keeping strict records, and while I did not dream that in my day slavery would be blotted out, or that the time would come when I could publish these records, it used to afford me great satisfaction to take them down fresh from the lips of fugitives on the way to freedom, and to preserve them as they had given them. But, thank God! the end of slavery came ere we looked for it, and the records are no longer preserved in secret, nor is their presence a source of danger."

Francis Ellen Watkins Harper was born in Baltimore

in 1825, not of slave parentage, and yet subjected to the oppression which bond and free alike endured under the slave laws. Since reaching her majority, in looking back, the following sentences from her own pen express the loneliness of her childhood days: "Have I yearned for a mother's love? The grave was my robber. Before three years had scattered their blight around my path, death had won my mother from me. Would a strong arm of a brother have been welcome? I was my mother's only child." An aunt cared for her during her early years. She was sent to school until she was about thirteen years of age, and then put to work to earn her living. It was her fortune to work for a lady willing to let her have any book in her library to read at her leisure, except a novel.

She had an ardent thirst for knowledge, and a remarkable talent for composition. She was noted for her industry, rarely trifling away time, as many girls are wont to do. In early life she acquired a taste for reading and poetry, and soon found, as she says, "she could string verses together and make them jingle." Scarcely had she reached her majority before she had written a book, "Forest Leaves," consisting of prose and poetry. The following is one of the poems of the volume. At the time it was also printed in an English paper. Not having either the volume or the paper at hand, Mrs. Harper has kindly sent us a copy which she has quoted from memory, although she is seventy-two years of age:

ETHIOPIA.

Yes, Ethiopia yet shall stretch
　　Her bleeding hands abroad;
Her cry of agony shall reach
　　The burning throne of God.

The tyrant's yoke from off her neck,
　His fetters from her soul,
The mighty hand of God shall break
　And spurn the base control.

Redeemed from dust, and freed from chains.
　Her sons shall lift their eyes;
From lofty hills and verdant plains
　Shall shouts of triumph rise.

Upon the dark, despairing brow
　Shall play a smile of peace;
For God shall bend unto her woe,
　And bid her sorrows cease.

'Neath sheltering vines and stately palms
　Shall laughing children play;
And aged sires, with joyous psalms,
　Shall gladden every day.

Secure by night and blest by day,
　Shall pass her happy hours;
No human tigers hunt for prey
　Within her peaceful bowers.

Then, Ethiopia, stretch, O, stretch
　Thy bleeding hands abroad;
Thy cry of agony shall reach
　And find the throne of God.

Her taste for poetry was nurtured and fed in her
uncle's school, which she attended for a number of
years. Among the early recollections of her life are
some reminiscences of Whittier and Garrison. Of
her uncle, she says: "Our teacher, in instructing his
pupils, did more than simply carry us through the
routine of lessons, and nearly sixty years have not
affected what I learned in that little school room,
which was only a few yards from a slave-pen."

All her writings have a highly moral and elevated
tone. In 1851 she left Baltimore to seek a home in a
free state, and for a short time resided in Ohio, where

she was engaged in teaching.   She soon left that state, and engaged in teaching in Little York, Pennsylvania. While in York she had frequent opportunities of seeing passengers of the underground railroad.   In one of her letters, she alluded to a traveler, thus: "I saw a passenger per the underground yesterday.   Notwithstanding the abomination of the nineteenth century, the fugitive slave law men still determine to be free.   Notwithstanding all the darkness in which they keep the slaves, it seems that somehow light is dawning upon their minds.   These poor fugitives are a property that can walk.   Just to think that from the rain-bow crowned Niagara to the swollen waters of the Mexican Gulf, from the restless murmur of the Atlantic to the ceaseless roar of the Pacific, the poor, half-starved, flying fugitive has no resting place for the sole of his foot."   In 1853 Maryland, her native state, enacted a law forbidding free people of color from the North from going into the state, on pain of being imprisoned and sold into slavery.   A free man, who had unwittingly violated this infamous statute, had recently been sold in Georgia, but had escaped thence by hiding behind the wheel-house of a boat bound northward.   Before he reached the desired haven, he was discovered and remanded to slavery, and soon after died from the effects of exposure and suffering.   In a letter to a friend referring to this outrage, Mrs. Harper wrote: "Upon that grave I pledged myself to the Anti-Slavery cause."   She soon went to Philadelphia, making her home at the station of the underground railroad.   Although anxious to enter the anti-slavery field as a worker, her modesty prevented her from pressing her claims, and, being but little known, no especial encouragement was ten-dered her. From Philadelphia she went to Boston, and soon was found lecturing in New Bedford Her first effort made such an impression that she was at once engaged by the State Anti-Slavery Society of Maine. Her ability and labors were everywhere appreciated, and her meetings were largely attended. Open doors, hospitable homes, and helping hands were proof that she had found her field of labor in pleading for the cause of her people in bondage.

For a year and one-half, she continued in the Eastern states, and then visited the fugitives in Canada. Her newly acquired reputation as a lecturer opened wide for her the door in Pennsylvania and Ohio. Her constant traveling required her absence from what she might call home, and she often expressed the desire that she might be able to enjoy the blessings of a home, "and yet," says she, "I do not regret that I have espoused this cause. Perhaps I have been of some service to the cause of human rights, and I hope the consciousness that I have not lived in vain will be a halo of peace around my dying bed, a heavenly sunshine lighting up the dark valley and shadow of death." She was far from desiring at her death a burial in a slave state, as expressed in the following language:

"Make me a grave wher'er you will,
In a lowly plain or a lofty hill;
Make it among earth's humblest graves,
But not in a land where men are slaves."

In the fall of 1860, Mrs. Harper was married to Fenton Harper, a widower and a resident of Ohio. The means she had saved from the sale of her books and from lectures she invested in a small farm near Columbus. Notwithstanding her family cares, she only ceased from her literary and anti-slavery labors when compelled to do so by other duties. In 1864 death deprived her of her husband. After the war, she spent much of her time in laboring for her people in the South. Mrs. Harper traveled extensively, going on the plantations among the lowly as well as to the cities and towns, addressing schools, churches, meetings in court houses, etc., influenced wholly by the noble impulses of her own heart, working her way along unsustained by any society. The work among the freedmen of today may sometimes have difficulties and trials to encounter, but for Mrs. Harper, in the days of reconstruction, when the Negro had no rights that a white man might respect, to go alone into these waste places of the South and bring comfort and encouragement to the down-trodded of her race, often endangering her life, was more than the average individual of today would consent to do. After many years of hard labor in the South, Mrs. Harper returned to Philadelphia, where she has since had her home. She is, however, not idle, but is always looking to the necessities of those around her, whom she may lift up by her encouraging and helpful advice. Mrs. Harper is a woman of high moral tone, with superior native powers, highly cultivated, and a captivating eloquence that hold her audience in rapt attention from the beginning to the close. She always speaks well, but particularly so when the subject relates to the condition of her people, in whose welfare, before and since the war, she has taken the deepest interest.

The following lines were written by Mrs. Francis E. Harper on the return from Cleveland, Ohio, of a poor, ill-fated girl, under the Fugitive Slave law:

TO THE UNION SAVERS OF CLEVELAND.

"Men of Cleveland, had a vulture
  Sought a timid dove for prey,
Would you not, with human pity,
  Drive the gory bird away?

Had you seen a feeble lambkin
  Shrinking from a wolf so bold,
Would ye not, to shield the trembler,
  In your arms have made its fold?

But when she, a hunted sister,
  Stretched her hands that ye might save,
Colder far than Zembla's regions
  Was the answer that ye gave.

On the Union's bloody altar
  Was the hapless victim laid;
Mercy, truth, and justice shuddered,
  But your hands would give no aid.

And ye sent her back to torture,
  Robbed of freedom and of right,
Thus the wretched captive stranger
  Back to slavery's gloomy night.

Back where brutal men may trample
  On her honor and her fame;
And unto her lips so dusky,
  Press the cup of woe and shame.

There is blood upon your city,
  Dark and dismal is the stain;
And your hands would fail to cleanse it
  Though Lake Erie ye should drain.

There's a curse upon your Union,
  Fearful sounds are in the air;
As if thunderbolts were framing
  Answers to the bondsman's prayer.

Ye may offer human victims
  Like the heathen priests of old;
And may barter manly honor
  For the Union and for gold.

But ye cannot stay the whirlwind
   When the storm begins to break;
And our God doth rise in judgment
   For the poor and needy's sake.

And your sin-cursed, guilty Union,
   Shall be shaken to its base,
Till ye learn that simple justice
   Is the right of every race."

Since freedom she has also been engaged in the temperance field, and for many years has held the position of superintendent of colored work in the Woman's Christian Temperance Union.   She has contributed freely to the columns of the *Union Signal*, the weekly paper of that organization.   She has been a member from the beginning of the "Woman's Congress," holding for a time the position of director.   She has spoken at and attended the "National Council of Women."   Although seventy-two years old, she is still in the lecture field, and is actively engaged in different lines of literary work.   Her home is 1006 Bainbridge street, Philadelphia, Pennsylvania.   There is probably no woman, white or colored, who has come so intimately in contact with the colored people in the South, for she has labored in every Southern state except Arkansas and Texas.   She has never lacked for evidences of hearty appreciation and gratitude.

EDUCATORS.

The items of the following biographical sketch have been gleaned from different sources but principally from an article by Dr. Parks, of Gammon Theological Seminary.

(H. F. Kletzing.)

Prof. W. H. Crogman, A. M., who occupies the chair of Greek and Latin in Clark University, Atlanta, Georgia, in Christian character, scholarship in his department, literary ability, general culture, and distinguished services, stands, it is safe to say, at the very head of the colored race. In all the particulars mentioned, he would honor a professorship in any college in the land.

The subject of this sketch was born on the Island of St. Martin's, May 5, 1841. In 1855 he went to sea on a vessel on which Mr. B. L. Boomer was mate. Mr. Boomer took a deep interest in him, and afterwards took him to his home in Massachusetts. Mr. Boomer's brothers were sea captains. The boy, Willie Crogman, followed the sea with this family for eleven years. He visited many lands, and, observant and thoughtful, obtained a wide knowledge of various nationalities and parts of the world. His visits included especially England, various points of the continent of Europe, Calcutta and Bombay in Asia, and various places in South America. Mr. Boomer says:

"It has been my good fortune to know our good friend all the way since he was fifteen years old, and it would afford me the greatest satisfaction if I could feel that his great success in all these years had in any manner been furthered by me. On the contrary, his untiring perseverance, diligent, wise and studious use of his time and money, made him from the first independent of all save our love, respect and never-ceasing interest."

In 1866, at the suggestion of Mr. Boomer, he began to earn means to attend an academy, and in 1868 entered Pierce Academy, in Massachusetts. Of his work during the two years in this school, Prof. J. W. P. Jenks, of Brown University, who was then the principal of the academy, says:

"Beginning with me in the elementary English

branches, I may safely say, in them all, he accomplished in one quarter as much as the average student did in two, mastering almost intuitively, and with equal facility, both mathematical and linguistical principles.   I formed him into a class of one, lest he should be hindered by the dullness of others.   In the third quarter he commenced French, and, as I have often said, surpassed every one of the hundreds of students, in both rapidity of advancement and accuracy of scholarship.   I need say no more, except that his record since leaving the academy, taking all the extenuating circumstances into the account, has reflected greater honor upon me as its principal, and his almost sole instructor while connected with it, than any other alumnus.''

After completing this academic course, Prof. Crogman started South to give his life to the Christian education of his race.   He spent three years as instructor in English branches at Claflin University, Orangeburg, South Carolina.   The experience of these years impressed upon him the need of a knowledge of Greek and Latin, and at the age of twenty-nine he began the study of Latin by himself.   In the fall of 1873, he entered Atlanta University, completing the full classical course in 1876.   Through industry, thorough scholarship and rapid advancement, he completed the four years course in three, then carrying off as his bride one of the noblest and most gifted and cultured young ladies, Miss Lavinia C. Mott, of Charlotte, North Carolina, Professor Crogman entered upon the work to which he has given all these years.   Called at once to the position in the faculty of Clark University, he has occupied his present chair since 1880.   For more than twenty long years, Professor Crogman has been an incessant laborer, and continuous in self sacrificing, in order that he might break the fetters of ignorance and superstition, and give liberty to the captives. His earnestness and faithfulness in the class-room, where he is so much at home, produces an eloquence more effective than a thousand orators upon the stage. Learned and yet modest, humble and yet dignified, he carries with him a personality that is his own. As the result of his labor, let the voices from a thousand hamlets in this and adjoining states speak out; let the young men and women from a thousand homes, who have imbibed knowledge and manhood at his feet come forward and tell the story.

Pages might be written containing tributes from his students through all these years. His is a life whose influence is not bounded by any section of country. To him more than to any other instructor are many of the educated colored people of the South indebted for the success with which they are meeting.

At his fiftieth anniversary, letters from students expressive of their highest appreciation of him were read, the excellent qualities that characterize him as a man and as a teacher were vividly set forth, as well as his thorough work in class-room, system and method in instructing, manly and helpful talks that often were a source of inspiration and led many to noble resolves.

Professor Crogman's library is large, choice and costly, and every book in it shows that it has been used. He is a close and thorough student.

He was a lay delegate to the General Conference of the M. E. Church of 1880, 1884 and 1888, and one of the secretaries of the last two of these, being the first colored man placed on the staff of secretaries of a general conference of that church.

At his fiftieth anniversary, already referred to, his friends presented him with an elegant gold watch, a beautiful set of Carlsbad china, nine handsomely bound volumes of ancient classics, and a large ornamental inkstand, from which rolled out one hundred dollars in gold.

Mrs. Crogman, a graduate of Atlanta University, in her character and services as his helpmeet, and as queen of one of the most refined and cultured homes, and as mother of eight most promising children, is worthy of no less honor than the professor himself.

Some years ago a university of good standing conferred upon Professor Crogman the degree of LL.D., but in his modesty he insists on declining the honor, and most of his friends defer to his wishes in not using the title, though they regard him as worthy of the honor it implies. Professor Crogman, though closely confined to his class-room for most of the year, has addressed with great acceptability not only his own people, on various occasions, but some of the most prominent audiences in this country, notably at Ocean Grove, in Beecher's church, and at the National Teachers' Association. His address, a few years ago, at the meeting of the last named in Madison, Wisconsin, was generally regarded as one of the ablest and most eloquent.

His life is a busy one. Besides attending to the many duties devolving upon him, he is author of a volume, "Talks for the Times," which cannot but be a blessing to all who read it. This volume is receiving the highest encomiums from both press and educators in all parts of the land. These addresses are rhetorically beautiful, intellectually brilliant, and show the author to be perfectly familiar with history, philosophy and current literature.

Bishop Mallalieu says of him: "He is a man in whom I have the greatest confidence. He is an honor to the human race. I wish the world was full of such men."

As chief Exposition Commissioner for the colored people of the state of Georgia, it was he who made the exhibit of the cotton states and international exposition of Atlanta, in 1895, such a remarkable success. His race feels proud of him. Well may they wish that he were many times multiplied.

Professor Crogman has been presiding in the school room for more than twenty years, and has occupied the chair of languages at Clark University for nearly that length of time, and during these years he has been secretary of the trustee boards of both Clark University and Gammon Theological Seminary. Besides these heavy duties, he has taken an active part in all movements that had for their object the betterment of the state, the city, the United States and his people.

The story of his life shows something of the adverse circumstances under which he has labored, the manhood, scholarship, usefulness to his race and humanity, and the honor his indefatigable industry, perseverance, hard work, and Christian faith have achieved, and points the way to every aspiring youth, however lowly and unfavorable his circumstances. Few men have rendered more faithful and useful services in educational work than Professor Crogman. Few men have steadily and unwaveringly maintained a more straightforward and manly course, or acted more wisely under all circumstances, than has he. He is every inch a Christian gentleman, a living teacher in no mere technical nor narrow sense. His platform utterances show thorough preparation and are received with delight by whites and blacks alike.

Well does Professor Parks say: "In a true estimate, not only of many enlarged and ennobled individual lives, but also of the great movement since emancipation in the elevation of the colored people, he must be given an important place."

PROF. W. SCARBOROUGH, LL. D.
For twenty years Professor in Wilberforce University.

Prof. W. S. Scarborough, LL. D.—The subject of this sketch was born in Macon, Georgia, February 16, 1852. He inherited a passionate love for knowledge, besides an aptness to overcome all obstacles in obtaining it. The Georgia law required that any Negro caught with a spelling book in his hand should receive severe punishment, and the white man who taught the Negro should pay a heavy penalty or go to the penitentiary. Yet, young Scarborough was so keen that with his book concealed he spent part of the time in a private school ostensibly to play. He continued in this clandestine way to attend undisturbed one of the few private schools up to the close of the war, and was then placed under the instructions of a Miss Kidd, from the North. Later he entered the Atlanta University, where he spent two years in preparation for a Northern college. In 1871 he graduated from the preparatory department of the Atlanta University, and in the fall entered Oberlin College, where he spent four years. He was a hard working student, which made him popular with his classmates; his genial disposition and gentlemanly bearing won for him many friends. Immediately after graduation in 1875, he taught Latin, Greek and mathematics in the Lewis High School, but in 1876 he returned to Oberlin, and spent some months in studying Hebrew and Hellenistic Greek. He then became Principal of Payne Institute, Cokesville, South Carolina, and in 1877 was called to the chair of ancient languages in Wilberforce University, near Xenia, Ohio, which position he has held for many years with marked ability. His experience is large and varied. Clear in explanation, polished in language and bearing, profound in scholarship, a perfect gentleman, he has been able to impress himself upon many young minds as few young men have been able to do. With unflinching steadfastness of purpose, unwavering uprightness and straightforward devotion to principle, he has been enabled to attain the heights and win the fame so undeniably his.

In 1880 he prepared his "First Lessons in Greek," which was published by Barnes & Co. This book has received the highest encomiums from the press, and what is still better, received practical recognition, that of adoption by schools and colleges, both white and colored. He has been a frequent contributor to the press, and has been quite active in political life, being elected to state conventions, and quite frequently an active worker in the campaigns as speaker.

Professor Scarborough has, however, won his laurels as a scholar. As a teacher and philologist his ability is unquestioned. He has paid especial attention to Sanscrit and other old languages, and has not neglected the modern. He is author of a number of works, notably "Latin Moods and Tenses," "Questions on Latin Grammar, with Appendix." As a member of the American Philological Association, he has contributed valuable papers at different times. Prof Scarborough stands out as one of the ripest scholars and prominent educators of his race.

Principal Booker T. Washington, A. M.—"I was born a slave on a plantation in Virginia, in 1857 or 1858, I think. My first memory of life is that of a one-room log cabin with a dirt floor and a hole in the center that served as a winter home for sweet potatoes, and, wrapped in a few rags on this dirt floor, I spent my nights, and, clad in a single garment about the plantation, I often spent my days. The morning of freedom came, and, though a child, I recall vividly my appearance with that of forty or fifty slaves before the veranda of the 'big house,' to hear read the documents that made us men instead of property. With the long-prayed-for freedom in actual possession, each started out into the world to find new friends and new homes. My mother decided to locate in West Virginia, and after many days and nights of weary travel, we found ourselves among the salt furnaces and coal mines of West Virginia. Soon after reaching West Virginia I began to work in the coal mines for the support of my mother.

"While doing this, I heard, in some way, I do not now remember how, of General Armstrong's school at Hampton, Virginia. I heard at the same time, which impressed me most, that it was a school where a poor boy could work for his education, so far as his board was concerned. As soon as I heard of Hampton, I made up my mind that in some way I was going to find my way to that institution. I began at once to save every nickel I could get hold of. At length, with my own savings and a little help from my brother and mother, I started for Hampton, although at the time I hardly knew where Hampton was, or how much it would cost to reach the school. After walking a portion of the distance, traveling in a stage coach and cars the remainder of the journey, I at length found myself in the city of Richmond, Virginia. I also found myself without money, friends or a place to stay all night. The last cent of my money had been expended. After walking about the city till midnight, growing almost discouraged and quite exhausted, I crept under a sidewalk and slept all that night. The next morning, as good luck would have it, I found myself near a ship that was unloading pig-iron. I applied to the captain for work, and he gave it, and I worked on this ship by day and slept under the sidewalk by night, till I had earned money enough to continue my way to Hampton, where I soon arrived, with 50 cents in my pocket.

"I at once found General Armstrong, and told him what I had come for, and what my condition was. In his great hearty way, he said that if I was worth anything he would give me a chance to work for my education. While at Hampton, I resolved, if God permitted me to finish the course of study, I would enter the far South, the black belt of the Gulf states, and give my life in providing as best I could the same kind of chance for self-help for the youth of my race that I found ready for me when I went to Hampton, and so, in 1881, I left Hampton and went to Tuskegee and started the Normal and Industrial Institute in a small church and shanty, with one teacher and thirty students.

"Since then the institution of Tuskegee has grown till we have connected with the institution eighty-one instructors and 850 young men and women, representing nineteen states; and, if I add the families of our instructors, we have on our grounds constantly a population of about 1,000 souls. The students are about equally divided between the sexes, and their average is 18½ years. In planning the course of training at Tuskegee we have steadily tried to keep in view our condition and our needs rather than to pattern our course of study directly after that of a people whose opportunities of civilization have been far different and far superior to ours. From the first, industrial or hand training has been made a special feature of our work."

Pres. Richard Robert Wright, A. M.—The parents of Richard Robert Wright were South Carolinians. Coming to Georgia in 1853, they first settled in Dalton, where Richard was born. In his boyhood he worked on the farm. Immediately after the war, he attended school in Cuthbert. Subsequently, on the removal of his parents to Atlanta, he enjoyed the privileges of the city schools, and in course of time was graduated from the college course of Atlanta University.

Immediately upon graduation he returned to Cuthbert, and was made principal of the Howard Normal School, which position he held for four years. In 1878 he called the first convention of Negro teachers ever assembled in Georgia, and was for three years president of that body. When, in 1880, it assumed the name of the Georgia State Teachers' Association he was again elected president. In the same year he was called to the principalship of the Ware High School, in Augusta, the first high school ever established in the state, and supported by city funds. For ten years Mr. Wright remained at the head of this school, or until he was called by the state to organize the Georgia State Industrial College, over which he now presides. He is also vice-president of the Board of Trustees of Atlanta University. By request, he represented, in 1881, the work of the American Missionary Association, at its annual meeting in Worcester, Massachusetts.

Besides his services to education, President Wright has mingled some in politics, both state and national. He was a member of the National Republican Convention that nominated Garfield; also a member of the one that nominated and of the one that renominated Harrison. In one of the national conventions he served on the platform committee with Governor, now President, McKinley.

For ten years President Wright was editor of an influential newspaper, and wrote for others, being once a regular correspondent of a Democratic daily.

Recently the following tribute to President Wright appeared in a reputable newspaper. Coming from Prof. Thomas N. Chase, one of President Wright's old teachers, the tribute has the more force:

"Pres. R. R. Wright became my pupil in 1869. I have had an intimate acquaintance with him ever since. He was one of the brightest students Atlanta University has had, and is its most prominent graduate. Col. A. E. Buck has said to me more than once that President Wright was the ablest colored man in Georgia, and I concur with him in his estimate. As principal of the Howard Normal School at Cuthbert, and then as principal of the Ware High School in Augusta, and later as president of the State College at Savannah, as editor of a paper for many years, as trustee of Atlanta University, as the institution's commencement orator, by his public addresses in all the large cities of his state, by conducting of teachers' institutes, by his printed speeches and essays, and in other ways, President Wright has come to be the best known and most influential colored man in the state of Georgia, and best of all, he has maintained an untarnished reputation, and his example and teachings have always been on the side of morality and virtue."

Such, in brief, has been the life and career of the little black, barefooted boy who, shortly after the war, when General Howard, addressing a school in the city of Atlanta, asked the question, "What shall I tell your friends in the North?" instantly replied: "Tell them we are rising." The poet Whittier, hearing of this, immortalized it in verses, of which the following is a stanza:

' Oh, black boy of Atlanta, but half was spoken;
The slave's chains and the master's are broken,
The one curse of the races held both in tether,
They are rising, all are rising, the black and white together."

PROF. WM. E. HOLMES,
President Central City College, Macon, Ga.

Prof. Wm. E. Holmes, A. M.—Prof. William E. Holmes, President of Central City College, is another worthy representative of his race. Like many others born in obscurity, he has, by honesty, diligence, and studious habits, lifted himself to a position of respectability and great usefulness among his fellow men. Born of slave parents, he has, at least, shown that he deserved to be free.

His taste for books developed early, and in the last years of the war we find him attending school. Immediately after the war, he had the privilege of sitting as pupil under the "Yankee school marm." To him, as to so many others, the quickening of the heart was also the quickening of the brain. Converted at eighteen, he became the more desirous to enlarge his mental vision, and fit himself for service to his race in the large field opened up by emancipation. Consequently, he entered, in his native city, the Augusta Institute, where he spent several years. Subsequently, on the removal of that institution to Atlanta, under the changed name of the Atlanta Baptist Seminary, Mr. Holmes followed it, and in a few years was graduated from it. The best proof, perhaps, of his worthiness is seen in the fact that on graduation he was given a position in the seminary, which he has held up to 1899 with efficiency and honor. His degree of Master of Arts is from the University of Chicago.

Personally, Professor Holmes is a royal man. Courteous, kind, obliging, free from the ambition that is always "o'erleaping itself," ever ready to contribute to the happiness of others, he becomes an object of love and esteem wherever known. In his home life he has been blessed with the companionship of a devoted and sympathetic partner, formerly Miss Elizabeth Easley, a graduate of Atlanta University, but now the proud mother of several intelligent children.

Prof. John Wesley Gilbert, A. M.—The subject of this sketch was born July 6, 1864, in Hephzibah, Richmond county, Georgia. His mother, herself a slave, brought the young Gilbert, when six months old, to Augusta, the city which, with little interruption, has been his home as well as the scene of his early struggles for a livelihood and an education. The only son of a widow, he was nursed in the arms of

32 Progress

poverty. "Six months of the year," to use his own words, "I ploughed, hoed, picked cotton, split rails, and spent the other six months in the public schools of Augusta." In this and other honorable ways he supported himself and helped his mother.

Having completed the work of the public schools, he attended for some months the Baptist Seminary, in his own city, but for lack of means was obliged to withdraw from the school for three years. At this period in his life he began to despair of securing a liberal education. Nevertheless, he kept up his studies, working by day and perusing books by night. In the year 1883, the "Paine Institute," under the patronage of the Methodist Church, South, opened in Augusta. This Mr. Gilbert attended for three years, or rather for six months in each of three years. About this time Rev. George Williams Walker became president of the Institute—a noble-hearted Christian man, and as sincere a friend as the Negro ever had. This gentleman became interested in Mr. Gilbert, and after his graduation from the institute loaned him, money enough to enter Brown University, Providence, Rhode Island. This money was supplemented by such as he could earn while a student. He shoveled snow in the winter, taught pupils at night, availed himself of every opportunity to gain "an honest dollar." To his very great credit, it should be said that, notwithstanding this extra demand upon his time and strength, he maintained a uniformly high standing in his classes, and, upon his graduation from the classical course, was awarded the scholarship for "excellence" in Greek in the American School at Athens, Greece. He was the first and only Negro admitted to that school. He traveled all over Greece, took part in the excavations in Eretria, carried on by the school during the session of 1890-91, contributed accounts of that year's excavations to the *New York Independent*, found and traced the ancient walls of Eretria, locating the towers of that structure, made, in collaboration with Professor Pickard, a map of ancient Eretria, and wrote a thesis on the Demes of Attica. Before returning to his native land, Professor Gilbert visited all the largest and most important cities of Europe, getting thus a comprehensive view of the customs, manners and political systems of that ancient land—the nursery of arms, the prolific mother of arts and sciences. In recognition of his work in Greece, Brown University conferred on him, in 1891, the degree of Master of Arts.

With the exception of the time spent in Europe, Professor Gilbert has taught in Paine Institute since 1888. Affable, kind-hearted, sympathetic, he wins admiration and respect among all classes. To the responsible duties of teacher he has now added those of preacher, being at present a minister in the Colored Methodist Episcopal Church in America. Few young men have achieved as much, and few have a brighter future.

To close this sketch, however, without referring to the gentle partner of his life would be like leaving Hamlet out of Hamlet. In the spring of 1889 he was happily and pleasantly married to Miss Osceola K. Pleasant, a young lady of one of the best families in Augusta. Educated at Fisk University, she also holds a diploma from Paine Institute. To this true and affectionate helpmeet, the fond mother of his children, he is indebted for no small degree of his success, for every true wife is an inspiration to her husband.

In conclusion, we are happy to say that, while penning this sketch, the announcement is made that Professor John Wesley Gilbert has recently been elected a member of the American Philological Association.

President J. C. Price, D. D., Livingstone College.— We take the following extracts from the memorial address given by President Goler, the successor of President Price:

President Price was born in North Carolina, in the dark days when the outlook for Negro development was exceedingly discouraging. Emancipation and the opening of the schools to all classes found him a lad of nine years in the eager pursuit of the rudiments of knowledge, under the care and keeping of a self-denying Christian mother, who early instilled in his mind those principles which subsequently developed into that manly deportment, that uprightness of character, that geniality and pliability of disposition which captivated his companions and made him everywhere a favorite. It was while still a youth, studying law in Shaw University at Raleigh, that it pleased God to reveal Himself to him. He sought and found salvation in the crucified Redeemer, was saved by the working of the mighty power, and experienced the joy that comes from believing. Soon after his conversion, he felt that necessity was laid upon him to preach the gospel, to lift up Jesus by his voice as well as in his exemplary life, and so for better preparation he entered Lincoln University in Pennsylvania in 1875. It was there I first met to admire and afterward to love him. Lincoln is a Presbyterian institution, but opens wide her doors to all creeds and all colors. He was a Methodist, and brought with him to the university some of the distinguishing characteristics of that denomination. He invariably absented himself from the dining hall on Fridays, and spent the time in fasting and prayer. As a student, he was docile, obedient to his instructors, courteous to his companions, true to his books, honest in the class-room, industrious in his studies and punctual at the prayer meeting. He exerted a healthy influence in the institution. He was one of those whom we find occasionally, yet rarely, in all schools, a model young man. It was while finishing up his course in theology that Bishop Hood, quick to see what is in a young man, and recognizing his rare qualities of head and heart, ordained him to the order of deacon, and finally of elder in the A. M. E. Zion Church. He was subsequently elected to the general conference of 1880. There, coming in contact with the superior minds of the general church, his gifts and graces were recognized and readily appreciated and here won for himself the distinguished honor of representing, with others, the A. M. E. Church at the ecumenical conference in England in 1881. His efforts there laid the foundation of Livingstone College. This work was near his heart and in its interest, as one of the means of race elevation, he spent the energies of his short but eventful life. He was no self-seeker. He did not labor for the notice of society or the prizes of the world, but the one controlling idea of his life was to lift his race out of the ignorance and moral degradation into which the misfortune of a cruel past had sunk them, and to lead them to higher planes of intelligence and social refinement. He was forcible in his appeals for justice and fair dealing; honest in his statements, and true to his convictions, yet he carried no gall in his nature. No

bitterness escaped his lips. There was no rancor in
his bosom. He had faith in the power of Christ to
eradicate the evils of society. He believed in the ultimate triumph of truth and righteousness and was
satisfied that the evils of society will be rooted out,
when men receive the power of Christ in their hearts
rather than the knowledge of Jesus in their heads.

As president of this institution he governed by love.
He held his teachers about him in hearty co-operation
with all his plans. They stood by him, not because
they received their pay—for there was not and is not
much pay here—but because they loved the president.
I remember a letter he wrote to a friend to teach here
with him at the beginning of this work, and here is
the inducement he offered: "We are just starting the
work. I cannot promise you any pay the first year,
but after that some provision will be made." With
this not over-bright prospect, two teachers, who are
still in the institution, came to him.

It pained him to send a needy student away, and so
large was his heart and so sympathetic withal, that
none appealed to him in vain, even to the denying
himself of home necessities.

He was devoted to his work, he apprehended that
God had called him to it, and no inducement could
draw him away. Men, recognizing the great powers
of oratory and the logical acumen with which God
endowed him, urged him to seek for himself honors in
the paths of politics, and pave his way to the legislative halls of the nation. The President of the republic, appreciating his ability and his moral worth,
appointed him to a post of honor in a foreign country.
There was money in it, and he needed money, there
was honor in it, and men love honor, but he refused

the honor and the emolument, preferring to labor for his little school in North Carolina, simply remarking, "I think I can do more good in Salisbury." The honors that have come to him, both at home and abroad, would have had an inflating effect upon the self-seeker and the egotist. But who ever saw Price inflated? Who ever charged Price with egotism? If there was one thing that particularly character-ized him, it was modesty; he was as unassuming as a little child. As we stand off and hold up his qualities, oh, how they loom! He envied no man his gifts or his prosperity, but unostentatiously endeav-ored to do his own work faithfully and well. An undisputed leader of his people, he came to them always in the character of a helper, and appeared un-conscious of his leadership. Where is there a greater Negro than Price? Great, not in the sense that men ordinarily estimate greatness, but great in *goodness*, great in *devotion to duty*, great in his faith in the possi-bilities of the future for the race, great in his concep-tion of individual responsibilities, great in his humility and unshaken faith in the living God. Frederick Douglass calls him "the ablest advocate of the race." And Price is dead. How befitting the words of David, "Know ye not that there is a prince and a great man fallen this day in Israel?"

Miss Lucy Laney.—There is probably no one of all the educators of the colored race who stands higher, or who has done more work in pushing forward the education of the Negro woman, than the subject of our sketch. Miss Laney is a graduate of Atlanta Uni-versity, and, after graduation, she taught school in a number of places in Georgia. Relinquishing a salary of $400 a year in 1886, she went to Augusta for the purpose of establishing an industrial boarding school. No aid was promised her, but she went forward and became responsible for the support of the teachers and the expense of the institution. The first year her school enrolled 140 pupils. It has steadily increased in power and influence, as well as numbers, from the first. It is, at present, under the auspices of the Presbyterian Church, and through the benevolence of a Northern lady, a five-story brick building has been erected. Miss Laney's assistants, Miss Jackson, Miss Smallwood and Mrs. Mary R. Phelps, are competent teachers, and together they are doing a great work in that part of the state. Dr. George C. Rowe puts it in this way:

> "Among the women of our race
>   We know of few, if any,
> Who fill a nobler, worthier place—
>   Than earnest Lucy Laney."

Miss Laney, who conceived the idea of founding this school for the uplifting of the Negro woman, and who began it on her own responsibility, has succeeded in a remarkable manner. Haines Normal and Industrial Institute has two departments, a normal and a college preparatory. The normal department prepares the students for teachers. This department is ably presided over by Miss M. C. Jackson, who in her training class succeeds admirably in making practical teachers. The college department fits young men and women so that they are able to pass entrance examinations in our best colleges.

Haines Normal Institute and its noble workers, Miss Laney and Miss Jackson, are doing a great and good work in Augusta. This is the only Presbyterian school for the colored in Georgia. It deserves what it is receiving—the liberal support of the church.

Margaret Murry Washington was born in Macon, Mississippi, March 9, 1865, being one of ten children. Here she received her early English education. After spending nine years at Fisk University, in 1889 she graduated from the classical course in that institution, one other girl and herself being the only girls in a large class of boys. While in school Margaret Murry had very poor health, and the same ambitious spirit and iron will that now master her physical weakness pulled her through the long years of study during her college course.

When she graduated from Fisk University she was employed as teacher of English literature at the Tuskegee Normal and Industrial Institute. Recognizing exceptional strength of mind and disciplinary power, the trustees of the above mentioned institution the next year appointed her Lady Principal, which position she so well filled that now many matters naturally falling to the duties of the lady principal are carried to Mrs. Washington both by teachers and students. She not only in position, as the wife of the principal of the institution, but in reality, stands next to him in power and influence.

In the fall of 1892 Margaret Murry became the wife of Booker T. Washington, and is a power in the home as well as in the public. Her boys, the youngest of which was three years old when she went into their home, are as fond of her as any boys are of their own mother.

As to personal appearance, Mrs. Washington is a mulatto, with reddish-brown hair, gray hazel eyes, strong features, and a large, commanding figure.

Mrs. Washington is the leader of the movement to work directly for and among the less fortunate class of the Negro race, and has promoted social settlement, organizations and various other clubs and movements looking to the elevation mentally, and especially morally, of the women of her race.

There are few women who have so strong a personality as Mrs. Washington, which power directs while others execute her commands.

Mrs. Booker T. Washington has the honor of being the first president of the National Federation of Colored Women's Clubs, now the National Association of Colored Women.

Prof. W. E. Burghardt Dubois was born in Great Barrington, Massachusetts, February 23, 1868. He was educated in the public schools, and at Fisk University, Harvard University and the university at Berlin. He was two years a fellow of Harvard, and holds her degree of Ph. D. He taught at Wilberforce, Ohio, two years, and was assistant in sociology in the University of Pennsylvania in 1896, for the purpose of studying the Negro in Philadelphia. He is at present professor of economics and history in Atlanta University. Professor Dubois is the author of "Suppression of the African Slave Trade," also "Harvard Historical Students, No. 1." He was married in 1896 to Nina Gomer, of Cedar Rapids, Iowa. Of his appointment as professor in Atlanta University the Independent says: "We are very glad that this institution, devoted to the education of colored people, has elected to so important a professorship a thoroughly competent colored man."

Prof. C. W. Luckie graduated from the college department of Atlanta University in the class of 1883. He went directly to Texas, spending four years as principal of the colored schools of Huntsville. Then he was elected to the professorship of English in Prairie View State Normal School, which position he has since held to the satisfaction of all. With such a grand field as Texas in which to labor, Professor Luckie may look for laurels yet unearned.

Prof. Wm. Lewis Bulkley.—The subject of this sketch was born of free parents in Greenville, South Carolina, on the 23d day of March, 1861.

His father, Vincent Henry, and his mother, Madora, being also of free parentage, had enjoyed educational advantages before the war. Vincent Henry Bulkley became, shortly after the war, a Methodist Episcopal clergyman, and remained in the service of this church as one of its most faithful ministers till the day of his death. He was sent as a delegate to the Ecumenical Conference of Methodism, which met in London, England, in 1881.

The parents of William Lewis, having "tasted of the Pierian spring," had a consuming desire that at least their eldest son should "drink deep," and began by sending him to school at a very early age.

His earliest recollections of school life are a poor frame building, with an old, gray-haired Negro schoolmaster, who had picked up a little "larnin' 'fo' de wah." The curriculum in this institution was a Webster's blue-back speller (a species fast becoming extinct). The magic wand that made the pupils look studious and "wondrous wise" was a well-grown hickory switch, an article that was neither an ornament or a mere scarecrow, as the back of more than one dullard can testify. In fact, that period of life was to William "the reign of terror."

From this school he passed into one taught by some Northern missionaries, whose great-heartedness had brought them into that dark section of South Carolina. Prominent among these early teachers were Rev. L. M. Dunton and wife, of New York state, two of the most faithful workers that ever came to help degraded mankind. By a strange ordering of fate, he is associated at present with these last two persons in Claflin University.

At sixteen he began to teach in the public schools of his state, when scholars were legion, books were few and salaries were mere promissory notes.

In 1878 he entered Claflin University, where, through the assistance of self-sacrificing parents, and whatever work he could get to do at the school, he continued in study four years, finishing in 1882 as the first college graduate.

He taught two years in his Alma Mater, and then went, in 1884, to Wesleyan University, Middletown, Connecticut. At this, the best institution of learning in the Methodist Church, he paid his expenses by different jobs, and by what money he could raise during vacations in a hard canvass for nursery goods, pictures, or steam cookers.

It often affords amusement to him to tell of how he cooked his own meals, consisting largely of oatmeal or pancakes, at an outlay of 10 cents a day, and how he used to wash such of his clothes as did not need starch and hang them by the stove to dry. He saved many a nickel by folding his rough-dried handkerchiefs in a book and then sitting upon it, while he "ground" trigonometry or tackled the mysteries of logic.

The death of a devoted father precipitated his return to South Carolina. He resumed work at Claflin, and has taught there ever since, save a year and a half which he spent with his wife and child in study at Strassburg, Germany, and Paris.

In 1893 he completed his "in absentia" study of the Latin language and literature at Syracuse University, Syracuse, New York, and received the degree of Ph. D. Professor Smalley, of the Latin department, says: "I have been well pleased with Professor Bulkley's work. He has the spirit of an investigator, and of an independent thinker, that refuses to accept the conclusions of editors without a careful examination of the reasons for himself. He has done much work on the literature, and toward mastering the principles of the languages, and shows excellent ability in grasping the thought of an author, and has unusual facility in rendering into idiomatic English."

Professor Bulkley's forte is in the field of languages. In addition to the Latin and Greek, he has spent some time in the study of French, German and Spanish.

In reviewing a new French book for English students, he detected an error which was subtle and misleading. He called the attention of the author to the fact, and received a long reply, from which the following is clipped: "I shall certainly introduce this exception in subsequent editions of the French book, and wish to thank you for bringing this omission, singularly committed by so many of the highest authorities, and most complete books and dictionaries, to my attention."

Professor Bulkley was elected to the World's Sunday School Convention which met in London, England, in 1889, and was also a delegate to the General Conference of the Methodist Episcopal Church at Cleveland, Ohio, in 1896. In 1888, he married Mary Fisher Carroll, of Columbia, South Carolina, an honor graduate of Claflin. Three promising little girls now bless their happy home.

He is a member of the American Philological Association. His present position is the professorship of Latin and Greek and the vice-presidency in Claflin University, Orangeburg, South Carolina.

BISHOP L. H. HOLSEY, D. D.

MINISTERS.

L. H. Holsey, D. D., Bishop C. M. E. Church, was born in the state of Georgia, July 3, 1842, near the city of Columbus. His mother was the slave of James Holsey, who was also his father. His mother was of African descent, and of pure blood of that race, with fine form and features. When he was about seven years of age, his father and first master died.

He was then taken away from his mother, and never lived with her again, except about three or four years, during which time she lived on the same place in Hancock county that he did with his second owner. In 1857, Mr. T. L. Wynn, his second owner, died, and he became the servant of Col. R. M. Johnstone, who resided in the same place. He lived with him until emancipation. The first three years after emancipation, he conducted a farm in Hancock county, near Sparta. He felt that he was called to preach from his youth, and the brightest place in his memory is vivid with the aspirations and longings that then glowed upon his heart, and framed and flashed through his soul. He was licensed to preach in 1868, and served nearly two years on the Hancock circuit. On January 9, 1869, he was sent by Bishop Pierce to Savannah, Georgia, to serve there that year. In 1871 he was sent to Augusta, Georgia, as pastor of Trinity Church, which at that time was one of the largest and most prominent churches belonging to the colored members of the Methodist Episcopal Church, South. At this church he remained two years and three months, at the end of which time (March, 1873) he was elected to the Episcopal office, and was ordained by Bishop W. H. Miles, one of the first bishops of the Colored Methodist Episcopal Church in America. He was a delegate to the first General Conference of his church, which convened in Jackson, Tennessee, 1870, at which time and place the church was organized as a separate and distinct organization from that of the

Methodist Episcopal Church, South, of which it had formed a part. He was delegate to the first Ecumenical Conference, which met in London in 1881, and also a delegate to the one that was held in Washington in 1891. He was a delegate, and the first delegate of his church, to the Conference of the Methodist Episcopal Church, South, held in Nashville, in 1882.

He founded the Paine Institute, located in Augusta, and made the initiatory steps for the beginning of the Lane College, at Jackson, Tennessee. For twenty years he has been secretary of the College of Bishops, and the general corresponding secretary of the connection, and perhaps has been most prominent in all the leading movements of the church.

He also compiled the Hymnal and Manual of the Discipline of his church, and is editor-in-chief of *The Gospel Trumpet*, a paper that is published in the interest of the church and race. This paper is published in Atlanta, Georgia, where he lives at present (1897). In this year (1897) he has been appointed as Commissioner of Education for his church. He has been prominent in all the movements connected with his church and race, and has traveled and labored successfully throughout all parts of the Southern states, and has done much to educate and Christianize his people.

Alexander Crummell, D. D., was born in New York city, March 3, 1819; educated with Henry Highland Garnet at Canaan, New Hampshire (1835); he remained at Canaan till the school was broken up by a mob, when he went, in 1836, to Oneida Institute, New York.

Under the direction of Rev. Peter Williams, rector of St. Phillip's Church, New York, he became a candidate for orders in the Protestant Episcopal Church in 1839, but, on account of color, was refused admission in the General Theological Seminary.

Having been ordained deacon by Bishop Griswold, and having studied with Rev. Dr. A. H. Vinton, he was ordained priest in Philadelphia by Bishop Lee of Delaware.   This was in 1844.

Doctor Crummell graduated from the University of Cambridge, England, in 1852.   Thereafter removed to Liberia, West Africa, where he was a professor and minister of the gospel for twenty years.   From 1873 till 1894, Doctor Crummell was rector of St. Luke's Church in Washington, D. C.   Having retired from the ministry, Doctor Crummell is giving himself up to work for the Negro race, in which he is intensely interested.

In March, 1897, at the formation of the American Negro Academy, "an organization of authors, scholars, graduates and writers, men of African descent, for the promotion of letters, art, literature and science," Doctor Crummell was chosen president unanimously.

Doctor Crummell recently celebrated the fiftieth anniversary of his ordination.   Referring to his early days he says: "The pro-slavery and caste spirit dominated the country, and it was as strong in the church as in the state.   Three other colored candidates had been admitted to seminaries, but with limitations and indignities to which it was impossible for me to submit."   Concerning his reception in England, he says: "I was received in England with a generosity which almost bewildered me after such sufferings in my native land.   I preached in London, Liverpool, Birmingham and other cities of England.   This was a period of grand opportunities and richest experiences, almost unlimited privileges and cherished remembrances. I was introduced into the best society of England, and made friends with the Froudes, Thackerays, Thorntons and other distinguished gentlemen." He is a fluent speaker and writer; scholarly, instructive and entertaining in all that he says and does. Doctor Crummell stands among the first of those who have labored for the elevation of the African race. He is at present in England.

Rev. Edward W. Blyden, A.M., D.D., LL.D.—Rev. Edward Blyden was born in the West Indies, he is of Negro parentage. Early in youth he was impressed with the love for his fatherland. He came to the United States in his seventeenth year and sought admission to an institution of learning, but the prejudice against his race was so great that he was not admitted. He went to Liberia and there entered the Presbyterian school, and after some years was elected to professorship in the newly founded college of Liberia. In 1864 he was appointed Secretary of State by the President of Liberia. In 1877 he was appointed Minister Plenipotentiary of the Republic of Liberia at the Court of St. James. In 1880 he was elected Fellow of the American Philological Association. The honorary degrees he holds were conferred upon him by American colleges.

He is a strong man and careful instructor, a diligent student, and is constantly seeking new plans and methods by which he may be able to elevate his people. Dr. Blyden has written many articles and is the author of several books. He has in his labors come in contact with some of the literary men of his day.

Bishop Henry M. Turner, of the A. M. E. Church,

BISHOP HENRY McNEAL TURNER, D. D., LL. D.

Asabiski Hall.

ROANOKE INSTITUTE, ELIZABETH CITY.

Established in 1896 by Roanoke Missionary Baptist Association.
Now 200 Students in Attendance.

NEW ELECTRIC LIGHT PLANT AND
POWER HOUSE, SPELMAN SEMI-
NARY, ATLANTA, GA.

was born in Newberry, South Carolina, in 1834. His parents were free, but he was bound out to a slave owner and was required to work side by side with slaves until he was fifteen years old, when he ran away from his master and entered the service of a firm of attorneys in Aberville. Here he learned to read and write, often spending much time at night after his employers had gone home.

He was licensed as a minister at twenty years of age; he then entered Trinity college, Baltimore, where he spent four years, intending to go to Africa after completing his education. He was made chaplain of the first regiment of colored troops. He was then under the Freedman's Bureau service for a time, but the necessity of religious and educational work among his people caused him to resign and enter the ministry of the A. M. E. Church. He was once appointed postmaster at Macon, Ga., but resigned on account of the opposition of the white people. In 1880 he was elected bishop of the A. M. E. Church.

Bishop Turner has written much on the Negro question. He has visited Africa five times and organized conferences in Sierre Leone and Liberia. The bishop is a firm believer in deportation, and insists his race will ultimately return to Africa, and that it is the duty of our government to help them to return. He thinks the black man will have greater opportunities, and will improve faster if he is placed in a republic by himself, and that this alone will bring peace and quiet to our country as far as the race question is concerned. He insists upon it that two races of people under the same government, the same institutions, and subject to the same laws with no social contact is an impossibility and will only produce evil results.

Bishop B. W. Arnett.—Bishop B. W. Arnett's boy-hood days were spent on a farm in Pennsyivania, where he had figured as a cow boy; afterward he took to

steamboat life until 1856. In 1864 he commenced the study of the ministry, and in 1865 he was licensed to preach, and received as his first appointment Walnut Hills' Church, Cincinnati, Ohio. He was a delegate to the International Convention of the Young Men's Christian Association in Washington in 1871, where he delivered an address upon "The

BISHOP B. W. ARNETT.

Stand the W. M. C. A. Takes in Relation to Colored Young Men."

He served in the lower house of the Ohio Legislature in 1876 two years; in 1876 he was elected secretary of the General Conference of the A. M. E. Church, at Atlanta, Georgia.

Bishop Arnett is an entertaining speaker and stands high in the estimation of his people.

Bishop Benjamin Tucker Tanner was born in Pittsburg, December 25, 1835. Studied at Avery College and Western University, Allegheny, Pennsylvania; entered ministry in 1860; editor of *Christian Recorder* from 1868 to 1884; then elected editor of A. M. E. Church *Review* till his election to the Bishopric, in

1888, of the African Methodist Episcopal Church.   He is author of "Apology for African Methodism," "Outline of History," "Negro Origin," "Theological Lectures," "The Color of Solomon," "Is the Negro Cursed?" etc.   He is a contributor to numerous jour-

REV. HENRY HUGH PROCTOR.

nals, among them the *Independent.*   He now presides over the district including Kansas, Missouri, Colorado, Nebraska, Wyoming, Montana and New Mexico.

Henry Hugh Proctor, B.A., B.D.—In a one-room log cabin, ante-bellum in type, near Fayetteville, Tennessee, the subject of our sketch was born, December 8, 1868. Ten years were spent on the farm. To get better school advantages, the family moved to town. After going through the public schools, he began to teach. Later he became principal of the school of his native town.

In the fall of 1884 he entered Fisk University, Nashville, Tennessee. By digging, type-setting, teaching and preaching, he helped pay his way. During his course he was, among other things, society president, college paper editor, and intercollegiate oratorical contestant. At Fisk he experienced a call to preach, and began to exercise his talents in the vicinity of the university. On the completion of his literary course in 1891, he entered the Divinity School of Yale University, New Haven, Connecticut. He spoke and sung his way through Yale, and during his three years of study in the East he was heard in many of the leading churches of New England. His classmates chose him among the eight out of a class of thirty to deliver commencement addresses, and to him the faculty assigned the coveted post of honor, that of delivering the final oration of the day. He was the first Negro to speak at a Yale commencement, and his address on the African's forthcoming contribution of love to Christianity was widely published.

Called to the pastorate of the First Congregational Church of Atlanta, Georgia, he entered the practical work of the ministry immediately after his graduation. After three years of hard and tactful labor the church, which had been somewhat disintegrated, secured a firm financial footing, and doubled its membership, thus becoming the largest Congregational church in the South. The pastor is broad but aggressive liberal but positive in his views on social and religious questions. In his preaching he deals with questions of practical Christianity with simplicity. He is frequently called upon to make addresses on popular occasions throughout the state. He is correspondent for a number of first-class Northern periodicals. In connection with the publication of an article from his pen, the *Boston Congregationalist* says of him: "He is one of the best equipped and trained of the Afro-American clergymen in the South, and is an orator of much promise."

Rev. Francis J. Grimke was born in Charleston, S. C , in 1850; came North in 1865, and entered Lincoln University in 1866, from which he graduated in 1870; studied law three years, and then decided to enter the ministry; entered Princeton Theological Seminary in the fall of 1875, and graduated in 1878. He immediately afterwards became pastor of the Fifteenth Street Presbyterian Church in Washington, D. C., where he continued until the fall of 1885. Owing to failing health, he resigned his charge, and accepted a call to the Laura Street Presbyterian Church of Jacksonville, Florida, where he continued to labor until the winter of 1889. His health having improved, he accepted a call to return to the church in Washington, where he has been ever since.

Bishop James Walker Hood, D.D., LL.D.— Doctor Hood is the oldest Negro bishop in the world. He was elected bishop by the American Methodist Episcopal Zion Church at Charlotte, North Carolina, in 1872. The church has ordered a celebration of the bishop's episcopal labors. An extended programme has been prepared by a committee of which R. S. Rives is chairman. This anniversary was celebrated September 18, 1897.

Bishop C. R. Harris was born in Fayetteville, North Carolina. His father died when he was three years old, and left his widow with ten children. The mother, at once finding that the discussion of slavery was detrimental to free colored people in the South, sold out her little property, and went to Ohio, where Harris was educated in good schools, and when the war closed Robert and Cicero Harris were among the first to enter the field in the South. They went to Fayetteville, and established a colored school under the auspices of the American Missionary Association. Through their efforts an appropriation was secured from the Freedman's Bureau, and a two-story school building was erected. Afterwards Governor Vance visited the school, and at his suggestion the legislature established this, the first colored state normal school. Rev. J. W. Smith, the able editor of the *Star of Zion*, Charlotte, North Carolina, was a pupil in this school when Governor Vance visited it, and he gave several figures on the blackboard in multiplication, division and fractions for Mr. Smith to solve, and encouraged him by saying he would make a good bookkeeper. Professor C. R. Harris taught at Fayetteville until 1872, when he took charge of a public school at Charlotte. Later he was connected with what is now Livingstone College, and assisted much in building up that institution in its early days. In 1880 he was elected Bishop of the A. M. E. Zion Church. He has been a member of every general conference since 1876, and as an educator he stands high. His success in Episcopal work has been as pronounced as in other fields of labor in which he has worked.

Howard University conferred upon him the degree of Doctor of Divinity in 1881. A person must merit what he gets from this institution, for it bestows its honors with great caution. The life of Bishop Harris has been spent in the unselfish service of his fellow men, and is an illustration of fair opportunities in youth worthily followed up, and of energies devoted to the service of humanity receiving their due recognition and reward.

Rev. W. G. Alexander, D. D., was born December 25, 1856, in Orange county, Virginia. Early in life he was employed by Rev. Thomas E. Green, of Washington, D. C. Rev. Mr. Green, being a man of large means, took a great interest in young Alexander, and educated him as if he were his own son. After finishing his course in preparatory work, he was admitted to Howard University. At the age of twenty-two he entered the African Methodist Episcopal ministry His early years in the ministry were spent in hard circuit work. He has successfully filled pastorates at many prominent places in the South, and at present is pastor of Big Bethel, Atlanta, Georgia. While pastor in Virginia, he was appointed by Governor Lee Curator of the Hampton Normal and Agricultural Institute. In 1889 he was elected Fraternal Messenger to the General Conference of the Colored Methodist Episcopal Church at Little Rock, Arkansas. In 1892 he was elected to the Presidency of Payne University, Selma, Alabama, but declined, preferring to remain in the ranks of the traveling ministry. He was one of the principal colored speakers at the Congress of Religions at the Columbian Exposition in Chicago in 1893. He is at present dean of the theological department of the Morris Brown College, Atlanta, and acceptably fills the professorship of theology and sacred literature.

As the pastor of Big Bethel, he has succeeded
admirably in canceling the debt by means of a debt

REV. W. G. ALEXANDER.

chart which he has invented. This chart consists of a
number of squares, and as soon as any one has contributed ten dollars the name of the contributor is placed

in a square.   The church is valued at nearly $100,000.
Reverend Alexander is very popular among his people.
He has a large and choice library of books.

Wilberforce University, Xenia, Ohio, conferred
upon him the honorary degree of D. D.

He is the author of "Living Words," "The Negro in
Commerce and Finance," and " The Efficient Sunday
School." Many of his friends think that he would
grace a bishop's chair. His experience and ability
make him one of the most popular and ablest ministers
of his denomination.

Rev. James. A. Davis, D.D., is one of the prominent
ministers of the Methodist Episcopal Church, and for
the past ten years has filled some of the best and most
influential churches. Doctor Davis is a native of Kentucky. He was taken to Ohio by his mother in his infancy, who, in company with others, was set free, and
located in Mercer county. His father, who belonged to
a different master, in the meantime escaped to Canada,
and in 1862 his mother joined him in Windsor,
Canada, where they remained until after the war.
He was licensed to preach in 1879. In 1887 he was
sent to Greencastle, Indiana, where, in connection with
his pastorate, he completed a course of theology in De
Pauw University. He is at present stationed in Nashville. For him the years are full of promise.

Rev. W. D. Balay is the organizer of the Afro-
American Industrial Union of America; the object of
the organization is to elevate and uplift the race.
Besides spending his time on the work of the union,
he is pastor of the Baptist Church of Oak Cliff,
Texas. Mr. Balay has labored hard to make himself
useful to his race, and has succeeded in a remarkable
way.

Rev. Joseph Albert Booker, A. M., was born at Portland, Arkansas. His mother died when he was but one year old. His father, having been found guilty of a knowledge of books, and of communicating the same, was charged with spoiling the "good Niggers." For this he was whipped to death when the son was three years of age. With such adverse circumstances to begin with, young Booker was sent to school by his grandmother. He soon acquired sufficient education to teach at the age of seventeen. He first taught a subscription school. He afterward entered Roger Williams Academy, graduating therefrom in 1886. Soon thereafter he was elected President of Arkansas Baptist College. President Booker is one of the youngest of our Negro college presidents, and with a long life before him, and great opportunities about him, he bids fair to become a useful and influential man in the great work of elevating the race.

Rev. E. R. Carter was born in Clark county, Georgia, in 1856, and was a slave until the overthrow of the Confederacy in 1865. Soon thereafter he entered school, and in 1874 began teaching. He entered Atlanta Baptist Seminary in 1879. Poverty compelled him to subsist upon the scantiest meals, but undaunted, the youth held to his purpose through all his experiences of hardship, self-denial and sacrifice. In 1882 he was called to the First Baptist Church of Atlanta, which position he has most acceptably filled since. In 1884 he graduated from the the theological department of the Atlanta Baptist Seminary. Mr. Carter enjoys the esteem and confidence of all classes and denominations. He is the author of several books: "Our Pulpit Illustrated," "The Black Side." Rev. Mr. Carter has traveled extensively. His is a busy life. To serve others and to do his part in the great work of elevating the race is the supreme aim of his life.

REV. E. R. CARTER, ATLANTA, GEORGIA.

Rev. Z. T. Pardee, who was born a slave at Sparta,

Georgia, is one of the pioneer preachers of the Baptist Church in Texas.

Rev. James Robinson Carnes, pastor of the A. M. E. Bethel Church of Dallas, Texas, was born in Tennessee. His parents were slaves, his grandmother a pure African woman and his grandfather a Guinea Negro. Before the breaking out of the civil war, Texas was supposed to be the best place to send slaves for safe keeping. In 1860 he and his mother were sent to Columbus, Texas. Without having the privilege of an education as many others have had, he nevertheless has worked his way to the front, and has served many prominent churches in Texas. He is a ready speaker, and takes high grounds on all moral and religious subjects He is a progressive and successful worker for the elevation of his people along all lines.

Rev. W. B. West studied at Gammon Theological Seminary, Atlanta, and is now presiding elder of the Dallas District of the C. M. E. Church, and editor of the *Western Index*, published at Dallas. He was born a slave and was raised on a farm, but like many others has pushed his way to the front, and is now one of the leaders of the race.

Bishop Daniel Payne is sometimes called "The Apostle of Education." He was a carpenter by trade He taught school until his school was closed by slave-holders. He then left his native city, Charleston, South Carolina, with the determination never to return until slavery was abolished. In 1840 he joined the Philadelphia Conference of the A. M. E. Church as a local preacher. After serving churches at Washington, Baltimore and other cities, he was elected bishop. In 1863 he purchased for the A. M. E. Church Wilberforce University, Ohio, and the success

that this school has met with is altogether due to the
energy and earnest zeal of this devoted man.   In 1881
he presided over the Ecumenical Conference in London
of the M. E. Church, and in 1893 was one of those

REV. W. B. WEST.

who presided over the World's Parliament of Religions
in Chicago. He died in Wilberforce, Ohio, in 1893,
being at the time President of the Payne Theological
Seminary at Wilberforce.

Rev. M. C. D. Mason was born of slave parents on a
sugar farm near Houma, Louisiana, in 1859.   In 1875

he entered the State Agricultural College at New Orleans. From 1877 to 1880 he taught a town school and then entered New Orleans University. In 1883 he joined the Louisiana Conference of the M. E. Church. He won great popularity as a preacher and a pastor while serving Lloyd Street Church, Atlanta. He completed a course of theology in Gammon Theological Seminary while in Atlanta, and immediately thereafter was appointed field agent of the Southern Educational Society of the M. E. Church. He still holds this position, and is doing a good work for the race. He is a man of fine scholarly ability, discriminating minutely in choice of books and the subjects of which he treats. His life is an inspiration to all who come under his influence.

Rev. Paul H. Kennedy was born in Elizabethtown, Kentucky. He had an earnest desire to acquire an education, but was hindered by that institution, slavery. During the early part of the Rebellion the Union soldiers appeared near his home, and he expressed the desire to be free. The soldiers concealed him in a wagon, but he was afterward returned to his master. Soon after he set out on foot, and walked to Louisville, and enlisted in the 109th Regiment of Colored Troops. He declares that the walk from slavery to freedom, although a long one, was a pleasant trip. In 1876 he was appointed pastor of the First Baptist Church of Clarkesville, Tennessee. Afterward he entered Roger Williams University, where he prepared himself for his life work. He has served as pastor of some of the largest Baptist Churches of the colored race in the country. He is author of several books, and also designed the Afro-American chart, which was exhibited at the World's Fair, Chicago.

Rev. G. V. Clark was brought by his slave mother to Atlanta when about three years old. In 1862 he was put by his master in the service of the Confederate hospital, where he remained until the close of the war. He began going to school in his seventeenth year, and soon after entered Atlanta University, and then Howard University, Washington. After teaching for a time, he graduated in Howard University in 1881. He was pastor of the First Congregational Church in Atlanta for seven years. Since then he has served some of the largest Congregational churches of the South. He is a popular lecturer and speaker.

Rev. Wm. Howard Day, A.M., D.D.— Dr. Wm. Howard Day, General Secretary of the A. M. E. Zion Church, and Chief Secretary of the Philadelphia Conference, was born in New York city, and is the only man living who when a babe was baptized by Bishop Varick, the founder of the Zion Church. He prepared for college at New York city and Northampton, Massachusetts, but on account of color prejudice he was obliged to go to Oberlin College, Ohio, as the only institution with a curriculum equal to that of Yale, admitting men of color. Graduated in 1847, and taking the degree A.B., he received the degree of A.M. in 1859 from Oberlin, his alma mater, and later on D.D., from Livingstone College. He was elected professor of languages and mathematics by two colleges, 1857; offered Latin tutorship, Lincoln, England, 1862. He visited Great Britain 1859, and was received by the Rt. Hon. the Earl Spencer at Spencer house, England; and by her grace the Duchess of Sutherland, the first lady in the kingdom next to her majesty, the Queen, at Stafford house, London. Subsequently by the lord provost of Edin-

burg, Scotland; main speaker at a meeting of 3,000
persons, in Music Hall, Dublin, Ireland, presided over
by the Lord Mayor, clad in his official robe and jewel
of office; addressed other thousands in England,
Ireland and Scotland; in 1866 was ordained Deacon
and Elder at Petersburg, Virginia, by Rt. Rev. J. J.
Clinton; elected General Secretary by the General
Conference in 1876, 1888, 1892 and 1896, for four years;
pastor, presiding elder, general missionary, supervisor
of missions, intellectual instructor, etc., during the
past fifteen years in the Philadelphia and Baltimore
Conference; unanimously elected President of the
Board of School Control, Harrisburg, 1891-92, the
only instance on record in the United States where a
man of color, and the only colored member, has been
successfully elected president of twenty-five men,
fifteen Republicans and ten Democrats. Elected
President of the Dauphin county (Pennsylvania)
Directors' Association (comprising all the educational
boards in the county), for five successive years, he the
only colored member in the county, 1891-96, the only
instance in the United States where such a fact appears.
The fact carries its own comment, and in every respect
is doubly creditable to the Board and to Doctor Day.

Rev. Emperor Williams was born a slave in Nashville, Tennessee. He was sold into Louisiana in 1841
to a builder. The builder had a difficult piece of
cornice, and none of his white men could put it up. Williams told his master that he could do it, and his master
replied that if he could put it up he should have his
freedom. Williams studied over the plan all night,
and the next day took a gang of men and accomplished
the difficult task. He was given his freedom. Afterward he attempted to buy his wife, offering $2,000 for

her, but her master would not sell her.   Soon afterward General Butler took New Orleans, and Williams got his wife for nothing and took his money and bought a home.   While a slave Williams frequently wrote passes for himself.   His master once asked him where he learned to write the passes.   He said: "While I was collecting your rents for you."   Thus frequently did the Negro succeed in getting the rudiments of an education.

LAWYERS.

The following is taken from an address by the Hon. J. T. Settle, delivered at Greenville, Mississippi:

Gentlemen of the Colored Bar Association of Mississippi: I have listened with pleasure and profit to your excellent addresses on different legal topics, and I can pay you no higher compliment than to say you are an honor to the profession. I look upon this meeting as the dawn of a new era in the history of our race. It is no new thing for us to meet and participate in the public assemblages of men; in fact, one of the misfortunes of our people has been a too great love for meetings and conventions of every kind, out of which little if any permanent good has ever accrued to us. The emotional side of our nature has ever been so easily reached that we have been too often used as instruments in the hands of others.

First Annual Meeting.—This organization, of which this is the first annual meeting, marks the advent of the colored citizen into a new field of labor. It evidences the existence of a sufficient number of colored lawyers in Mississippi engaged in active practice of the law to form a state organization to promote their interests individually and collectively, and in doing this they cannot fail to promote the interests of the entire race and to contribute to the general welfare of our common country, for we are as much a part of our composite nationality as any element it contains. It is no new thing for the residents of this beautiful delta to see gatherings of colored men.

Politics and Religion have given us conventions and conferences at short intervals until some have come to believe that we take to them as naturally as birds to the air and fishes to the sea. But whoever thought that here in this beautiful city, queen of the valley, beside this great inland sea, would meet the first colored bar association ever organized in the United States? And I think I may safely say that never in the history of the race has there been a meeting fraught with more significance. It shows that the various and trying ordeals through which we have passed during the last fifteen or twenty years in this beautiful Southland, have evolved a class of men, educated, thoughtful and conservative—indeed, men who are alive to the present and prepared to meet the demands of the future.

No Hope of Success.—Many of our friends and all of our enemies discourage us by saying that this was the one profession in which we could not hope to succeed. We have been compelled to realize that we are the representatives of that race which has labored in mental and physical servitude and suffered from political and social degradation since the planting of civilization on this continent. We realize in the beginning that the undertaking to become practical lawyers, and to acquire such a mastery of the law as to enter favorably upon its practice, was a serious one, and doubly so to us.

Prejudice.—We have met unreasoning prejudice

which denied us excellence of any kind, which declared that we were without intellectual vigor and inventive power, and destitute of strength to grasp and persistency to retain and master any complex and profound proposition. In many instances we have commenced our trial before a jury whose pre-formed judgment would disqualify them from sitting in any other case. We have often found, not our clients, but ourselves on trial, and not ourselves alone, but the whole race with us—a race which is condemned for the failure of its individuals, while the success of every member of it is pronounced exceptional and due to incidental conditions.

Equal to Struggles.—We have made good soldiers and successful teachers, we have produced some great preachers and distinguished speakers, and this meeting demonstrated the fact that we are equal to the hard, tough and long continued struggles of the bar, in some respects the severest test that can be applied to a man; and yet the world may be slow to admit our success until, perhaps, we have produced an attorney-general or a justice of the supreme court.

Not All Succeed.—I do not mean to say that every young man of color who has begun the practice of law has succeeded; no, not by any means. Nor is this true of the young men of any race, for along life's highway, in all of the professions, are many wrecks which mark the weakness and frailty of human character; and here I think I may safely say that one of the principal causes of failure in the legal profession is the want of sufficient preparation.

An Oily Tongue.—Some persons unwisely think that all that is necessary to constitute a successful lawyer is an oily tongue, a vivid imagination and a great capacity to lie; in fact, some people profess to think that lawyer and liar are synonymous terms. Such persons, it is needless for me to say, know but little of the law and still less of the lawyer. They forget or do not think, that the contests of lawyers are not "ex-parte." They confront each other before learned and astute courts and in the presence of the world, where lies and frauds have the least possible chance of success, and where exposure would usually prove fatal to a cause.

A Good Education.—No lawyer can build a splendid professional career upon an insufficient education any more than he can build a monument of stone upon a foundation of sand. I do not mean to say a collegiate education is absolutely necessary to a successful career, but it is a great help. Few men ever reached distinction in the law who were not thorough scholars. Many also fail who are well equipped intellectually because they depend upon the oily tongue and vivid imagination rather than real earnest work.

Courage.—Courage, moral and physical, are both necessary elements of character. There is probably no element of character that inspires so much admiration and creates so quick and enthusiastic a following as this. A man who is afraid of nothing in the discharge of his duty, afraid of no consequence personal to himself, has his battle half won before he strikes a blow. So great is the popular admiration of courage that it has always been surrounded by a halo of romance.

Earnestness and Enthusiasm are also so essential that I cannot refrain from mentioning them in this connection. I name them together because they are so nearly akin; indeed, enthusiasm is only earnestness carried to white heat; they are the only qualities that can take the place of personal magnetism in compelling sympathy. Earnestness comes from strong conviction and strong feeling; enthusiasm rising out of it is the fusion and sublimation of all the elements of power within a man, and is strong in proportion as it is rational; the moment it becomes mere passion it becomes weakness. The world refuses to be moved by men who are not in earnest. Human nature is very much like iron—if you would bend it or shape it you must heat it. Earnestness is the furnace; enthusiasm the fire whose flames need only to envelop other minds to make plastic or ductile.

Citizens.—We are citizens of this country by nativity, not by choice or adoption, and here, under God's providence, we mean to stay, and strike glad hands with all lovers of justice, work out our own destinies and vie with every other nationality in developing the material resources and contributing to the greatness of our beloved Southland. Agitators may discuss the so-called race problem, but in the busy, active duties of life we have no time for theories. We should prepare ourselves by every energy of mind and soul to solve the problem put to us by those by whom we are surrounded, and with whom we live, viz.: "The survival of the fittest." Citizens by nativity, we have no other land to love. To this we have given our labor for more than one hundred years; in defense of her flag we have given our lives; to sustain her integrity we have contributed whatever was demanded of us. At all times have we been faithful and reliable.

We have never been numbered among our country's enemies. We have never been found in the ranks of the Socialists and Anarchists in their attack upon

social order and our free institutions.   Yet we have
lived under a condition of things at times unequaled
in the history of civilized government.

True to Our Native Land.—Erin's sons were never
truer to the Emerald Isle, nor the Highlander to Scot-

HON. J. T. SETTLE.

land's cliffs and crags than we to the land of our birth.
What member of any race ever gave expression to
loftier sentiments of patriotism in the American Congress than the distinguished lawyer and scholar, Hon.

John M. Langston, of Virginia, when from his seat in that august body he said: "Ah, my white fellow citizens on the other side of the house, and on every side, black as we are, no man shall go ahead of us in devotion to this country, in devotion to its free institutions, for we hold our lives, our property and our sacred honor in pledge to the welfare of our country and of all our fellow citizens. Do you want us to fight for our flag? Call on us and we will come. Do you want men to tarry at home and take care of your wives and children, to take care of your homes and protect your interests? Call on us, and we will sacredly keep and perform every trust and obligation."

History and Patriotism.—Every member of the race echoes these sentiments, and in the years to come, when man's passions and prejudices have subsided, impartial history will give to no race a prouder place in their country's history than we shall possess, and no race or condition of people will be prompted by a purer or loftier patriotism than we, in our efforts to make our beloved South the home of a happy, prosperous and contented people.

Hon. J. T. Settle.—The subject of this sketch was born upon the mountains of East Tennessee, September 30, 1850, while his parents were "in transit" from North Carolina to Mississippi. In 1856 he was carried to Ohio and located at Hamilton, where he attended the public school until 1866, when he was sent to Oberlin, where he prepared and entered college in 1868. He was one of the three or four colored boys in a class numbering forty-five or fifty. Yet he was chosen as one of the eight orators to represent his class when they entered college, an honor much coveted by all students.

Mr. Settle completed his Freshman year and entered the Sophomore class at Oberlin. In 1869, having lost his father, who had indeed been a father in the broadest sense of the word, he left Oberlin, went to Washington City, and entered the Sophomore class of Howard University, where he pursued his college studies and taught in the preparatory department.

He graduated from the college department of Howard University in 1872. In the latter portion of his senior year he was elected "Reading Clerk" of the House of Delegates (the District of Columbia then being under a territorial form of government) and at the time of his graduation was performing his duties as reading clerk of the legislature, teaching a class in Latin and one in mathematics daily at the university and pursuing his own studies at the same time.

Immediately upon his graduation from college he entered the law department of the same institution.

Upon his graduation from the law department he was selected as one of the orators to represent his class. He was admitted to the bar of the Supreme Court of the District of Columbia, but having determined to make his chosen profession his life's work, he left the District of Columbia in the spring of 1875 and located in North Mississippi, where he at once engaged in the practice of law. He returned the same year and was married to Miss Therese T. Voglesong, of Annapolis, Maryland, and again made his home in Mississippi. In 1876 he was a delegate to the National Republican convention. He was the only delegate from Mississippi who voted for the nomination of Roscoe Conkling for President, and continued to vote for him as long as his name was before the convention.

Mr. Settle was elector for the state at large on the

Hayes and Wheeler ticket. In 1880 he was Presidential elector on the Garfield and Arthur ticket.

In 1883 Mr. Settle was nominated and elected to the legislature upon an independent ticket, being strongly opposed to the fusion his party made with the Democracy. It was during this canvass that he made the most brilliant efforts of his life. He was met by the ablest speakers on both sides; but before the people he was irresistible, and was triumphantly elected by more than 1,200 majority.

Upon his return from the legislature he determined to abandon active participation in politics and devote his time and energy to the practice of law: he left Mississippi and located in Memphis, where he is now living. About two months after his location in Memphis, he was appointed assistant attorney-general of the criminal court of Shelby county; which position he held over two years. The manner in which he discharged the responsible duties of prosecuting are thus put by the Hon. A. H. Douglass, who was upon the bench at that time: "His uniform attention to official business, his manly courtesy and amiability, won him the esteem and respect of the bench, the bar and litigants, and went very far to break down the existing prejudices against his color in the profession. His talent is fully recognized and his integrity has in no instance been in the least questioned from any source. He prosecuted without acerbity and with fairness, but neglected no legitimate resources to fix the conviction on the really guilty. He is such a master of elocution, and displays such fluency, and indeed brilliancy, that he invariably captivated those who listened to him. He is remarkably simple in his manners, and utterly without ostentation, and is an honor to his profession."

He is now comfortably situated in a handsome two-story residence in a beautiful part of the city, where he enjoys the esteem and confidence of a large circle of friends.

Hon. Samuel McElwee, Lawyer, Legislator, Orator. —It is wonderful how easily some men rise in the world, and how hard others struggle to accomplish the same things. Every step with some seems marked with severe toils, bitter hardships, and apparently insurmountable difficulties. But when at last the goal has been attained, the prize seems ever so sweet, aye, sweeter that it could possibly be without the conflicts and discouragements. Samuel Allen McElwee is a brave soul, who can wear on the forehead, "Through difficulties to the stars." The chains of slavery bound his body not half so tightly as ignorance his mind. When the war ended he could not write. He was a farmer's boy, for many years going to school but three months in the year. Yet he studied until midnight, burning patiently the light which would give him an opportunity to read, which in future years gave him a brighter light whereby he might see the condition of his race, and find a remedy for their many ills. Though worn with the daily toil, he never neglected his studies, and on examination day entered with his class and passed the tests from the year 1868 to 1874. He then taught school. He often tells how, at that time, he was influenced by *The National Era*, Fred Douglass' paper, and how he longed for more education. He matriculated at Oberlin, and waited on the table, picked currants, and washed dishes for his board. At the end of the year he went to Mississippi, where he taught school for five years. Then he taught a year in Alabama. He once walked thirty miles to secure a school in Tennessee. He was often without money, and even a place to sleep. Anxious to obtain means to return to college, he commenced selling Lyman's Historical Charts, Bibles and Medicines. Failing to make enough money to return to college, he determined to study under a private teacher. After teaching a large school in the day, he would walk ten miles two nights in the week to recite in Latin, Greek, German and Algebra to a white student at Vanderbilt University. Mark that, young man; victory awaits the daring, and reward always follows the persevering. The student teacher was so impressed with the story of this Negro's perseverance in seeking an education that he told the president of Fisk University of the ambitious boy. The president invited him to enter the University. After a year in the senior preparatory class, he entered college and graduated in 1883. In the campaign of 1882, he traveled over the eighth and ninth districts of Tennessee for the Republican party, advocating a just settlement of the state debt. While he was yet a student in January, 1883, he took his seat in the Tennessee legislature, and served three terms as a statesman and orator. He studied law in Central Tennessee College, and was graduated in 1885. He was a delegate to the Chicago convention which nominated Hon. J. G. Blaine, and with six others voted for him on every ballot. Mr. McElwee takes a deep interest in the moral, social and industrial future of his people. He is a magnetic speaker, forcible debater, and an indefatigable worker, a manly man and a truly honest citizen. His speech on "Mobs," in the Tennessee legislature, was widely circulated. Mr. McElwee's popularity with the people of his race is unbounded. He lives honestly and soberly, thus

challenging their admiration and winning their friendship. Mr. McElwee was married in 1888 to Miss
Georgia Shelton, the daughter of one of Nashville's
most prominent and refined families. In a beautiful

HON. J. C. NAPIER.

residence, opposite Central Tennessee College, Mr.
and Mrs. McElwee, with their two children, reside.
Their hospitality is widely known. The past few
years have been devoted solely to the practice of law,
in which he ranks with the best white legal lights

before the national bar.   He has a lucrative practice.
His impassioned and forcible eloquence appeals to
judge and jury in defense of right and condemnation
of wrong.   Mr. McElwee declares that his color is no
barrier to his practice, and that he receives due recognition from the judges and the legal fraternity in
general.   He is still a hard student, and finds pleasant
society with his books, and in keeping abreast with the
latest legal news of the day.   He is a brilliant conver-
sationalist, of pleasing address, and a ready speaker.
He is a devout member of St. Paul's Methodist Episcopal Church, and perhaps the fact that he is a true
Christian gentleman speaks the best for the man.

Among the Older Members of the Legal Profession
are D. Augustus Straker, of Detroit; J. C. Napier and
S. A. McElwee, of Nashville; Hale G. Parker, of Chi-
cago; J. Madison Vance, of New Orleans, O. F. Gar-
rett, of Greenville, Mississippi; H. F. Bowles, of
Natchez; J. E. Burgee, Chattanooga, Tennessee; W.
M. Gibbs and S. A. Jones, of Little Rock, Arkansas;
J. T. Little and B. F. Booth, of Memphis, Tennessee.

James Carrol Napier.—The subject of this sketch
was born near Nashville, Tennessee, June 9, 1848.
He received his primary education in such schools as
were permitted for colored people in Nashville before
the war, and in 1859 was sent to Wilberforce University, near Xenia, Ohio.   From thence he went to
Oberlin, where he remained until near the completion
of his junior college year, when he left school to accept
a position in the government service in the War department at Washington, D. C.   In 1873 he was graduated
from the law department of Howard University, and
was admitted to the bar by the Supreme Court of the
District of Columbia.   Passing a civil service examina-

tion, he was appointed to a first-class clerkship in the bureau of the Sixth Auditor, the first of his race in that branch of the government service. His services in that position were so satisfactory that he was in a short time promoted to a clerkship in the bookkeeping division, which position he resigned, after three years' service, to take the responsible position of Revenue Agent for the Internal Revenue District embracing the states of Kentucky, Tennessee, Alabama and Louisiana, in which position he was repeatedly complimented by the department for the efficiency with which he performed his duties. Desiring to return to his home at Nashville, he resigned the position of Internal Revenue Agent to become a Gauger in the Fifth Internal Revenue District of Tennessee, and after a long and honorable service in such capacity, was promoted to be a Deputy Collector, which position he filled with great credit to himself and the entire satisfaction of the government until the advent of Cleveland's first administration, when he was relieved to give place to a Democrat.

In 1878 Mr. Napier revisited Washington to marry the only daughter of Hon. John M. Langston, then Minister to Hayti, a woman of broad culture, high education and superior intellect, a step which has never been regretted by either.

Immediately after his retirement from the government service, Mr. Napier entered upon the practice of law at Nashville, and has been engaged therein continuously to the present time. Beginning as an inexperienced practitioner, he has, by dint of industry and close application, advanced step by step to the enviable position which he now occupies as a citizen and a member of the Nashville bar. As was natural, he has associated politics with law, and in this field he has been eminently successful also.   Never descending to the plane of the ward politician, his political life has been so straightforward, clean and fearless as to give confidence and inspiration to his party associates and demand the respect of men of all parties. He was four times elected a member of the City Council of Nashville, and as the representative of the colored population of that city, with the assistance of his fellow citizens, secured the appointment of colored teachers in the public schools, the erection of new and additional school buildings, and did much to better their educational and financial condition.   He is the representative of the colored Republicans in the State of Tennessee, and has been a member of the Republican State Executive Committee for sixteen consecutive years, during which time he has served a considerable period as its acting chairman, and six years as its secretary.   He has been four times elected a delegate to the National Republican Convention, once as the representative of his Congressional District, and three times from the state-at-large, one of the highest honors within the gift of the Republicans of a state.   He is at present a member of the National Executive Committee of the Republican League.

Mr. Napier has not only been successful as a lawyer and politician, but financially as well.   Fortune has followed honor, and he is regarded as one of the most substantial citizens of Nashville.   May we not hope that such an exhibition of tact, industry and intelligence will be an inspiration to the youth of the country wherever this sketch is read.

Colored Attorneys of Nashville, Tenn.:

Abbot, G. T.

Anderson, G. F.

Cheairs, H. B.

Cameron, H. A.

Crosthwait, W. A.

Ewing, P. A.

Ewing, T. G., Sr.

Grant, J. W.

Hodgkins, W. H.

Kizer, J. W.

Menefee, A.

Napier, J. C.

McElwee, S. A.

Robinson, G. T.

Smith, N. B.

Woods, Z. T.

The Colored Bar of Chicago.—Over thirty colored men and one colored woman have been regularly admitted to the Illinois bar, and are now practicing law in Chicago. Considering the fact that less than forty years ago a large majority of the race in this country to which these colored lawyers belong, and that several of the lawyers themselves, were slaves, the race prejudice that they had to overcome, and the difficulties they had to encounter, with no rich and influential friends to give them a helping hand, the record they have made at the bar is an honor to the race, and well may their example be held up to the colored men and women of other cities as worthy of imitation. It is stated on good authority that no other city has had as large a number of colored lawyers. They are not only graduates of law colleges, but of universities as well. Some of them have been teachers for years.

Names.—The names of the colored lawyers of Chicago in the order in which they were admitted to the bar are: Lloyd G. Wheeler, Richard A. Dawson, Ferdinand L. Barnett, Louis Washington, Edward H. Morris, J. W. E. Thomas, Maurice Bauman, John G. Jones, R. O. Lee, George W. W. Lytle, S. Laing Williams, Franklin A. Dennison, Charles P. Walker,

Edward G. Alexander, Lewis W. Cummings, W. W. Johnson, S. A. T. Watkins, William H. Ward, M. A. Mardis, Albert G. Hubbard, James H. Lewis, J. Gray Lucas, Hale Giddings Parker, Jas. E. White, W. B. Akers, Charles W. Scrutchin, R. M. Mitchell, William G. Anderson, Thomas L. Johnson, Miss Ida Platt, John L. Turner, Beauregard F. Mosely, E. H. Wright.

Lloyd G. Wheeler was the first colored man ever admitted to the Chicago bar. Mr. Wheeler is an intelligent and worthy gentleman, an honor to his race, and no disgrace to the bar of Illinois. He married the niece of John Jones, now deceased, one of the most worthy and respectable of Chicago colored citizens, who had been a slave, and who, by working over hours at tailoring, purchased his freedom. It was at Mr. Jones' house that John Brown was secreted when a reward was offered for his delivery. Mr. Jones died in 1879, wealthy, and at the time of his

LLOYD G. WHEELER.

death was carrying on a profitable business. To this business Mr. Williams has given his undivided attention since that time.

Louis Washington was born in Alabama. His complexion is no counterfeit, it is plain, genuine black. He was a slave until 1863, when, inspired by the love of freedom, not having heard of President Lincoln's proclamation freeing the slaves, and having been told there was a large army at Vicksburg which liberated all the slaves who came into its lines, he left his master's service unbidden, walked barefooted from Enon to Vicksburg, and there entered the service. After the war, by dint of hard work and strict economy, he succeeded in acquiring money enough to attend school. While at Wheaton College, Illinois, the bank in which he deposited his money failed, and he lost nearly three hundred dollars, which compelled him to forego the pleasure of completing his course. He afterward took a course in the Union College of Law, and was admitted to the Illinois bar in 1879.

E. H. Morris, the leader of the colored bar in Chicago, was born a slave in Kentucky in 1859. He has lived in Chicago twenty-six years. When he was admitted to the bar, in 1879, he was unable to purchase a suit of clothes to make himself presentable, and so kept on his long overcoat, and during the examination had it buttoned up so as not to show the fractures which time and wear had made in his antiquated pants. Contrast the situation of this poor lawyer with that of the Mr. Morris of today! He now receives in cash for his professional services over ten thousand dollars a year, not including his services as south town attorney. He is worth more than $50,000 in Chicago real estate.

J. W. E. Thomas served a year in the Illinois House of Representatives, and is among the wealthiest colored men in the city of Chicago.

S. Laing Williams entered the University of Michigan and graduated with the class of 1881, receiving the A. B. degree.
After teaching for some time in Alabama, he was appointed to a position in the Pension office at Washington. In 1885 he resigned and came to Chicago to practice law. While in Washington he entered the law department of the Columbian University, and after finishing his course took postgraduate work in the same school. Mr. Williams is a fine student, and in scholarly ability has no superior among the colored lawyers of Chicago. He is the husband of Mrs. Fannie Barrier Williams, who is the first and only colored woman ever admitted to membership in the Chicago Woman's Club.

S. LAING WILLIAMS.

Franklin A. Dennison was born in San Antonio, Texas, and educated at Lincoln University, Pennsylvania, and was admitted to the Illinois bar in 1879. For a number of years he was chief assisting prosecuting attorney.

Miss Ida Platt was born in Chicago of colored parents, September, 1863. She was educated in the public schools of Chicago, and graduated from the High School with honor at the age of sixteen. She is the only colored woman admitted to the Illinois bar. For nearly nine years she was private secretary in

an insurance office, then, while stenographer in a law office, commenced the study of law. She graduated from the Chicago College of Law in 1894, and received her license to practice in June of that year. One of the judges of the court, in signing his name to her license, said: "We have done today what we never did before; admitted a colored woman to the bar; and it may now be truly said that persons are now admitted to the Illinois bar without re-

MISS IDA PLATT, OF CHICAGO.
First colored lady admitted to the bar in Illinois.

gard to race, sex or color." Miss Platt is a woman of very decided ability, and entered upon her professional career with talents possessed by few.

Taylor G. Ewing was born of slave parents near Nashville in 1849. He experienced all the horrors of slavery until 1861, when he ran off, going to Nashville, where he managed to get work at Fort Negley.

After the close of the war, he began work as a barber. During the evening he attended school with the determination to obtain an education. He then went to teaching, and taught school for four years, and then received an appointment in the revenue service, which he held until 1885. During this time, he began the study of law, and in 1886 he was admitted to the bar, and since then has engaged in the practice of law, and has succeeded in building up a large and lucrative practice. By thrift and economy he has accumulated considerable property, and is estimated to be worth about $10,000.

Alfred Menefee.—Probably the oldest colored man practicing law is Alfred Menefee. He is seventy years of age, and is a successful lawyer in Nashville, although he has never had the advantages of a scholastic training.

J. W. Grant.—In the fourth year of the war, J. W. Grant was taken from his home near Sparta, Tennessee, by the 14th U. S. colored troops. After experiencing the hardships of soldier life, he returned to his mother, and then, besides attempting to support his mother and sisters, he attended school as best he could until he was sufficiently educated to teach. He entered Fisk University in 1871. The close of the first year found him without a dollar or any opening to make a cent. Not being able to secure means to return to school, he taught for twelve successive years. In 1887 he entered Central Tennessee College, graduating in 1890, and immediately entered the law department of that institution. In 1894 he was chosen a member of the faculty of the law department of Central Tennessee College, and in 1895 he was elected Dean of the college, which position he now holds. He is worth $10,000, and has a beautiful residence in Nashville. His only daughter will graduate from Fisk University in 1899.

William Richard Morris was born February 22, 1859, near Flemingsburg, Kentucky. He entered Fisk University at Nashville, Tennessee, when seventeen years of age, and graduated with high honors from the classical department in the class of 1884. As a student he was apt, studious, strictly first grade in all his studies, and was known as a bright scholar, a fine essayist, a logical debater, a correct thinker, and an eloquent, forcible speaker. For five years he taught in Fisk University, giving entire satisfaction in teaching mathematics, languages and the sciences. He was at the time the only colored teacher of the institution.

In 1885, he represented the colored people of the South at the annual meeting of the A. M. A., at Madison, Wisconsin, and delivered an address entitled, "The Negro at Present," that won for him a broad reputation. In 1886, the State Superintendent of Education of Tennessee employed him to hold institutes for colored teachers of that state.

He received the degree of Master of Arts from his Alma Mater in 1887, and the same year was admitted to the bar by the Supreme Court of Illinois in a class of twenty-four, he being the only colored man. In the examination he and two others received the same and highest mark. He has also been admitted to the bar by the Supreme Court of Tennessee, and practiced some at Chicago and Nashville.

In June, 1889, he resigned his position at Fisk University, came to Minneapolis, and, having been admitted to the bar by the Supreme Court, opened a law office, and was the first colored lawyer to appear before the courts of Hennepin county, Minnesota.

HON. JOHN M. LANGSTON.

Hon. John M. Langston, A. M., LL. D., was born a slave in Virginia. He takes the name of his mother. His father was his owner, and upon his death John was set free. Thereupon he was sent to Ohio, and educated at Oberlin, graduating in 1853. In 1867 he was appointed inspector of the colored schools, and made a trip through the South, and the same year was admitted to practice in the United States Supreme Court. For some years he was dean of the law department of Howard University. In 1877 he was appointed Minister to Hayti by President Hayes. Upon his return in 1885, he was elected president of the Virginia Normal and Collegiate Institute, which position he filled for two years, and was then elected a member of the LIst Congress to represent the state of Virginia. Mr. Langston has exerted a wide influence for good on the race in the many positions he has held. He has for years been at the head of the legal profession among men of his color in Washington. He is a man of wealth, and lives in his beautiful "Hillsdale Cottage" in Washington. Mr. Langston is one of the ablest lawyers of his race. He is author of "Freedom and Citizenship" and "From the Virginia Plantation to the National Capitol."

Isaac F. Bradley.—This gentleman is a rising young lawyer of Kansas City, Wyandotte county, Kansas. He is studious, honorable and upright in his dealings, and is highly respected by both bench and bar of Wyandotte county, and well deserves the success he is now enjoying.

Mr. Bradley was born at Hazelwood Hall, near Cambridge, Saline county, Missouri, September 8, 1862.

As a result of the criminal practice of that cruel institution which flourised at that time, he never saw his father; hence, from the beginning his way was not smooth, thus he received very little schooling in his youth. Being anxious, however, to obtain a good education, he saved his earnings, and in 1881, entered Lincoln Institute at Jefferson City, Missouri, from which he graduated with the full course in June, 1885. In the fall of the same year he entered the law school of the Kansas State University; took the degree LL. B., June 1887, and was admitted to the practice of law; opened an office in Kansas City, Kansas, and now enjoys a good practice. In April, 1889, he was elected justice of the peace for two years, and discharged the duties with credit. He is active in politics, ready and willing at all times to espouse the cause of his race. He is now first assistant prosecuting attorney of Wyandotte county, Kansas, the most populous and wealthy county in the state.

B. S. Smith, the subject of this sketch, is one of the most widely, as well as favorably, known negro attorneys west of the Mississippi river. He was born in Arkansas, August 6, 1862, of slave parentage. Left an orphan at an early age, he wandered to central Illinois, where in 1876 he took up his residence in Springfield, and entered the public schools of that city, working for his board and lodging, and in 1883 graduated with honor from the High School (one of the finest in the state). Thereupon he immediately secured employment on a stock farm in Logan county, where he worked until October, 1884, when, having earned sufficient money to attend college, he entered the law department of the University of Michigan, and graduated from that institution in 1886.

Mr. Smith immediately entered upon the practice of his profession, locating in Kansas City, Kansas, in 1887, where he now has a lucrative and growing practice, stands high in the community, having served four years as an alderman in his adopted home, and was elected on the Republican ticket, presidential elector in 1892. He has now abandoned politics altogether, and devotes his entire time to his practice.

HON. S. J. JENKINS, AUSTIN, TEXAS.

S. J. Jenkins is a prominent lawyer of Austin, Texas. He has been prominent in politics, and is at present President of the Deaf, Dumb and Blind Asylum at Austin.

Daniel M. Mason is one of the prominent lawyers of Dallas, Texas. Mr. Mason entered Howard University in 1886, graduating in 1890. He then entered tne law department of this institution, and graduated with honors two years later. Since then he has practiced law in Dallas, Texas, and as a young man of his profession is meeting with success.

THE COLORED MAN IN MEDICINE.

Voodoos.—When the civil war was over, and the smoke of battle had cleared away, the field in the South was occupied by the red-eyed "voodoo," who styled himself a "doctor." There were, at that time, possibly two or three exceptions to this rule, but only two or three.

Should you ask these voodoos, better known among the illiterate as "root-workers," what might be their business, the answer would quickly be given something like this: "My trade, dat am a doctor." "Is that so?" "Yes, sar, I is a root doctor from 'way back; and when I gets done standing at de forks ob de road at midnight, pullin' up roots twixt de hollowing ob de owels, and gittin' a little fresh dirt from de grave yard, honey, der am suffin 'agwinter drop."

This being, with his weird stories, went forth among a people who were rocked, as it were, in the cradle of superstition, and early became monarch of all he surveyed. He was known and feared throughout the country. He claimed to be able to cure anything from consumption to an unruly wife or husband, and furnishing charms to make love matches, and to keep the wife or husband at home, was one of his specialties.

Every patient they called on they diagnosed the trouble thus: He or she was tricked; if pneumonia, they were tricked; if a fever, they were tricked; or if a case of consumption, they were tricked.

Their stock of medicine, if such we must call it.

generally consisted of such things as these: small bags of graveyard soil, rabbits' feet, rusty nails, needles, pins, goose grease, snake skins, and many other such things.

I say, a little more than a generation ago, this was the class of so-called "colored doctors" that predominated in the South, and which for many years was a great stumbling block to the educated physicians of our race, because it seemed to be understood that all "colored doctors" were and must be "root doctors."

But thank Him who holds the destinies of races in His hands that in the flight of years, and in this electric age of progress, this "voodoo doctor" has almost—not entirely, but almost—passed away, while his territory is being occupied by colored physicians whose qualifications in education, character and honor are equal to similar qualifications in the physicians of any other race.

The Contrast.—Thirty years ago, there were few, if any, Negro physicians to be found, says Dr. L. T. Burbridge, while today there is scarcely a Southern town and a large proportion of the Northern towns and cities that cannot boast of one or more colored physicians, regular graduates of authorized medical colleges. While this is true, we are compelled to admit that there is a field for many more. It is estimated that there is one white physician to every 300 of his people, while there is only one colored doctor to every 9,000 of his people. This furnishes an idea of our need, for we feel assured that when the colored physician become more numerous, so as not to be a rare object, then he will be more respected by all classes of people. Then, too, we feel proud to state that the practice of the colored doctor is by no means confined solely to his own race.   The Negro physician enjoys in many instances a small but growing white patronage.   This, in itself, is a confession of a recognition of skill and ability, wrung, as it were, from the lips of the oppressor.

Patronage.—The colored physician does not ask patronage on the score of color, and on the other hand he does not want to be denied work on that account. He does not ask that allowances be made for his deficiencies because he is a Negro, and on the other hand, he does not want to be denied the privileges that skill and ability should demand for any medical man, whether white or black.   A recognition of skill and competency is all that he asks, regardless of color.   In other words, he wants to be treated as a man—one who has fully prepared himself to do the work as thoroughly and skillfully as any other man, of whatever nationality.   The Negro physician realizes the fact that this is his only hope for successfully overcoming the many discouraging features of his work, and with this fact in view, he has ever bent diligently to the accomplishment of the task set before him.

Advantages.—The advantages offered to the colored man for a medical education are good.   Meharry, New Orleans and Shaw Medical Colleges, in the South, are doing good work, and in the North but few, if any, doors are closed against the colored aspirant; while England, France and Germany all extend to him a welcoming hand.   And, if yet we have not a Treve, we have a Newman, if we have not a Koch, we have a Stewart, and if we have not a Sims, we have a Boyd. These are among the pioneers of the Negro medical profession, and where they leave off their posterity will take up and carry on the work so well begun.

Influence.—While the farmer, the mechanic, the teacher, the newspaper man, and the lawyers of our race are laboring in their spheres, the physicians of the race are spending their talents, their little means, and their life for the elevation of their people, physically, morally and spiritually, and too often without remuneration. These men are doing much good for their people and the communities in which they live.

Physicians of Today.—The colored physicians in the South today are men and women fully equipped in education, morals and integrity for the high calling they have elected, as their noble work will show.

In the United States today there are about one thousand colored physicians, men and women, and more than seven hundred of them are located in the Southern states. While they represent the homeopathic and eclectic schools, yet the regulars are largely in the majority.

Women.—The colored women have gone into the profession very rapidly. They are scattered throughout the South, and are doing a good practice. While most of the medical schools are open to them, they come largely from Ann Arbor, Howard, Meharry and the school in Kentucky, and also the Woman's Medical College of Philadelphia. Dr. Alice McCain, of Savannah, Georgia, is the only lady physician in that state. Her husband is a fine physician also. She is a graduate of the Woman's Medical College of Philadelphia, and he of the University of Vermont.

There is one thing commendable about our female physicians, as well as our male physicians, and that is they come from good schools, and are fully prepared for their work. They, too, should be encouraged as they go forth to their labors.

Reception by White Profession.—The white physicians of the South, especially the better class of them, give the colored members of the profession a hearty welcome into the field. They always have a kind word for them; they encourage the people to employ their own physicians; they lend them their instruments, and come in consultation whenever called. This is not local, but is reported to us from all parts of the South.

Their Wealth.—The colored physicians in the South, most of them, are in better circumstances than their brethren in the North and East. Most of them have beautiful homes, fine horses, city and town lots; while some have plantations and others large bank accounts. One of the wealthiest colored physicians with whom we are acquainted is Dr. H. T. Noel, of Tennessee, whose wealth is estimated to be about $85,000.

The American Medical Association of Colored Physicians and Surgeons was organized in November, 1895, at Atlanta, Georgia. Its necessity grew out of the fact that colored physicians of the South are not admitted to the old organization. The second bi-ennial meeting will be held in Nashville, Tennessee, October 15 and 16, 1897. A large attendance is expected.

Dr. R. F. Boyd, of Nashville, Tennessee, is president; Dr. D. L. Martin is secretary. The programme of the coming session includes many of the most prominent colored physicians of the country.

The Southern Empire State Medical Association of Georgia held its fourth annual meeting in Macon, July 1 and 2, 1897. This association is composed of the colored physicians and surgeons of the state. It is in a flourishing condition. It was organized by Dr. H. R. Butler, A. M., M. D., who was elected the first president and served one year.

The colored physicians are organized in six states: North Carolina, South Carolina, Georgia, Tennessee, Florida, and Texas.

Dr. Robert Fulton Boyd was born in Giles county,

DR. R. F. BOYD,
Professor in Meharry Medical College, Nashville, Tenn.

Tennessee, where he spent his early boyhood days. At the age of eight years, he was taken to Nashville to live with Dr. Paul Eve, a noted surgeon of his day. It was here that he first conceived the idea of making a physician of himself.   He attended night school at the old Fisk School, and learned to spell and to read from McGuffey's First Reader; from 1868 to 1870 he worked on a farm, then returned to Nashville to learn the brick trade.   He had not yet learned to write, and· was anxious for an education, and in 1872 hired himself to Gen. James Hickman to work half a day and go to school the other half.   He earned enough for clothing by teaching old colored people their letters, so that they might read the Bible.   In 1875 he began teaching school and rapidly rose in that profession.   He became principal of the Pulaski schools, and was employed by the State Superintendent to hold state institutes for colored teachers in middle Tennessee.   In 1880 he entered Meharry Medical College, and graduated in 1882.   In the same year he was appointed adjunct professor of chemistry in Meharry Medical College, and at the same time entered the college department of Central Tennessee College, graduating in 1886.   He then entered the dental department of Meharry Medical College, and graduated in 1887.   He paid his expenses all this time by teaching in the various departments of the Central Tennessee College.   In 1887 he entered the practice of his profession in Nashville, where he has since done a work second in importance and magnitude to no other physician.

Mr. Boyd is a hard worker, and uses all his powers to elevate and educate his race.   He is a typical example of what young men can do in spite of the greatest opposition.   He has built for himself a practice that is an honor to any man.   His office, instruments, horses and buggies compare favorably with those of any other physician. He has instituted a society for the study of sociology and ethics among colored people. In this respect alone he has done much for the betterment of the colored people in Nashville. In 1890 he took a post-graduate course, and in 1892 he took a second post-graduate course in a Chicago medical college. He is at present a member of the faculty of Meharry Medical College, being professor of gynecology and clinical medicine. He owns the valuable property, 417 and 419 Cedar street, Nashville, worth $20,000. It is a building used for offices, and contains forty rooms. He was once nominated candidate for mayor of Nashville, and the legislature of Tennessee. Connected with his office is an infirmary for the care of the sick and surgical cases. Trained nurses are always on hand. He gives two hours three times a week to the sick and indigent poor during the college year. Many now attend his free clinic and are helped. Dr. Boyd is a polite and affable gentleman, respected both by whites and blacks, and an honor to the race which he so ably represents. He is president of the American Medical Association of Colored Physicians and Surgeons, and in every respect leads his race in everything that is elevating and ennobling. His friends are urging him for surgeon-in-chief of the Freedman's Hospital at Washington, D. C. He is well endorsed, and has numerous letters of recommendation and petitions to President McKinley to appoint him. While the people of Nashville are glad to see Dr. Boyd honored and have his ambitions and aspirations gratified, they do not want him to leave them.

Daniel H. Williams, Chicago, Ill., son of Daniel and Sarah (Price) Williams, grandson of Daniel Williams,

was born January 18, 1858, at Hollidaysburg, Pa.
He attended the Janesville, Wis., high school, and was
graduated from the Janesville Classical Academy in
1878. Commenced the study of medicine at Janesville in
1880, under Surgeon-General Henry Palmer; attended
three courses of lectures at Chicago Medical College,
from which he was graduated March 28, 1883, his
education having been obtained through his own exertions, his parents being unable to render financial
assistance. In May, 1883, he located permanently in
the practice of medicine in Chicago.

Dr. Williams is a member of the American Medical
Association, Illinois State Medical Society, Chicago
Medical Society, and Ninth International Medical Congress. He was surgeon to South Side Dispensary,
Chicago, 1884-'92; Surgeon to Provident Hospital,
1890-'93; physician to Protestant Orphan Asylum,
1884-'93; member of Illinois State Board of Health,
1889; reappointed, 1891. He is also a member of the
Hamilton Club, of Chicago. Was appointed surgeon
in charge of the Freedmen's Hospital, Washington,
D. C., February 15, 1894.

Dr. Williams stands at the head of the list of the
great surgeons of our country. He came into prominence when a very young man a few years ago by performing one of the most difficult of surgical operations
on the heart and pericardium, which properly consisted
in operating upon and saving the life of a man who
had been stabbed in the heart. Since his advent to
Freedmen's Hospital he has continued to perform very
difficult operations, and has directed more attention to
Freedmen's and the work being done there than many
institutions of the kind in the country. He recently
performed an operation which is regarded by the med-

ical profession as not only one of the rarest, but also one of the most hazardous—the Cæsarian section. The race has reason to be proud of him for the great service he is rendering it.

J. W. E. BOWEN, D. D., PH. D.
Professor of Historical Theology in Gammon Theological Seminary.

J. W. E. Bowen, D. D., Ph. D.—Doctor Bowen was born in New Orleans in 1855. His father, Edward

Bowen, was a free man, his mother a slave. At the age of five the boy and his mother were bought out of slavery by the father. At the age of seventeen young Bowen entered the New Orleans University, a school established by the Methodist Episcopal church at the close of the Rebellion.

Soon after his graduation from the university, Doctor Bowen became professor of Latin and Greek in the Central Tennessee College at Nashville, Tennessee.

In 1882, having resigned his professorship, he entered Boston University, where he studied for four years. In 1887 this University conferred upon him the degree of Ph.D. In 1892 he received the degree of D.D. from Gammon Theological Seminary.

After graduating from Boston University he entered the New England conference of the Methodist Episcopal church.

His pastorates included leading churches in Boston, Newark, Baltimore, and Washington, and covered a period of eleven years. While pastor of the church in Washington, he pursued the study of the Semitic languages.

Doctor Bowen's next promotion was his election as professor of Historical Theology in Gammon Theological Seminary at Atlanta, Georgia, which position he holds at this writing.

At the general conference of his church, held at Chicago in May, 1900, he came within a few votes of being elected one of the bishops of that great church.

Amid all the cares of the pastorate and teacher he found time to do much writing. Some of his works are: "Plain Talks to the Colored People of America,"

"Appeal to the King," "The Comparative Status of the Negro at the Close of the War and To-day," "The Struggle for Supremacy between Church and State in the Middle Ages," "The American and the African Negro," "University Addresses," and "Discussions in Philosophy and Theology."

David Lee Johnstone enrolled as a student at the State Normal School at Tuskegee, September 14, 1885, completing the course in 1889. His vacations were spent at Pratt City, Alabama, working there as a miner to earn money enough to return to school in the fall and to support an invalid father.

After completing his course he returned to Pratt City, and found employment as a teacher in the public schools, which position he held for four years. Having a desire to complete a course in pharmacy and not being able to accumulate a sufficient amount at teaching, he resigned and accepted a contract in the mines at Milldale, Alabama. This employment, although very hard, was more lucrative, and the 1st of September, 1894, he entered the pharmaceutical department of Meharry Medical College, Nashville. During vacation he continued working in the mines. At graduation he was elected by the members of his class to represent them in the commencement exercises. He soon found employment with the Peoples' Drug Company, of Birmingham, Alabama.

In April, 1896, he opened the Union Drug Store, at Birmingham, Alabama, and continued in it until December of that year, when it was swept out by fire. His purpose, however, was not to be defeated by losses, and in April, 1897, he again opened the doors of the Union Drug Company, and is doing a prosperous business.

Dr. W. A. Hadley was born of slave parents in 1850. He attended Fisk University, and was one of the first normal teachers sent out from that institution. In 1878 he entered Meharry Medical College, from which he graduated in 1880. After practicing medicine four years, he returned to teaching, and is at present principal of one of the Nashville schools. His house is modern in every respect, and is a perfect, ideal home. One remarkable feature in Dr. Hadley's home is a collection of pictures, all of which were painted by his daughter, who is the principal of music in the Tuskegee Normal School, and enjoys the distinction of being the first graduate in music from Fisk University. Dr. Hadley's real estate and other property are valued at $14,000.

B. E. Scruggs, M. D., was born of Christian parents in Huntsville, Alabama. He received his education at Central Alabama College and Central Tennessee College, at Nashville. He graduated from Meharry Medical College in 1897, and in July of the same year he passed the state medical examination, standing highest of any of those who were examined at that time. He has had a successful practice ever since. In 1892 he was elected alderman of the city of Huntsville, and re-

B. E. SCRUGGS, M. D.,
Huntsville, Alabama.

elected in 1897 by the largest vote of any aspirant. He is the first Afro-American of Alabama to graduate from a school of medicine. Dr. Scruggs was married to Miss Sophia J. Davidson in 1881. He owns some property, and is in good circumstances.

Dr. Ferdinand A. Stewart was born in Mobile, Alabama, in 1862. He completed the classical course in Fisk University in 1885, and three years later graduated in the medical department of Harvard University with the first honors of his class of over one hundred, all of whom were white excepting himself. Since 1888 he has been practicing medicine in Nashville, and has succeeded admirably, both professionally and financially. He has no other ambition than to serve his people in his professional capacity.

Dr. Henry Fitzbutler, of Louisville, was born December 22, 1842. He graduated in the Michigan University in 1872. He was granted a charter by the legislature of Kentucky in 1888 to practice medicine, having graduated at the Louisville National Medical College. He was the first regular physician of the Negro race to enter upon the practice of medicine in the state of Kentucky.

T. T. Wendell.—The subject of this sketch, Mr. T. T. Wendell, was born July 24, 1871, at Nashville, Tennessee. At an early age he evinced great aptitude for study, and very often led his classes in the public schools of his native city. After completing the prescribed course in the city schools, and possessing a strong desire to become proficient in medicine, he entered Meharry College, where he pursued his studies with diligence and vigor, graduating from the pharmaceutical department in the class of 1894, with marked distinction, being the valedictorian of the largest class graduating from that famous institution.

Mr. Wendell, now realizing that it was time for him to repay his widowed mother for the care and many sacrifices she made for his advancement, secured a position at Henderson, Kentucky, as manager of The Citizens' Drug Company, which position he held until a more remunerative one was offered by Dr. W. H. Ballard at Lexington. He is now filling this position to the satisfaction of his employer and his many friends, who are numerous, which is testified to by the fact that although in the *Leader* (a daily paper) contest for the most popular clerk in the city, he was opposed by ten others, all white, yet when the votes were counted Mr. Wendell had over five hundred votes more than his next highest competitor.

F. B. Coffin, Ph. G., Pharmacist and Poet.—F. B. Coffin was born in 1869, in Holly Springs, Mississippi. His father being poor and having a large family, Frank had very meagre educational advantages. At the age of ten, he lost his best earthly friend, his mother. His older brothers and sisters scattered over the South as teachers, and morally and intellectually he was left to his own guidance. He was raised in the sturdy mold of tireless industry. Against his will, but to please his father, he stayed on the farm until seventeen years of age, receiving three months' schooling annually. He read all kinds of literature that came to his hand, good and bad, but through the influence of his brothers, he cast away the trashy novel and more than ever desired an education. His elder brothers having left home, he was his father's only stay, and the remark was often made, "What would I do without Frank." Through correspondece with his brothers, the desire to attend school was constantly increasing, and in 1886, by the aid and consent of his father and brothers, he entered Fisk University, where both his brothers had graduated. He spent his vacations on the farm, and in 1889, with his father's consent, he remained in Nashville, where he was able to earn more money. At the beginning of his senior year, he was called home by the sickness of his father. This was a severe trial to him, as he was thus cut off from his classmates, and not permitted to graduate with them. In writing to one of his classmates, he says: "If misfortune prevents my graduating with you you will hear from me somewhere, for Fisk has kindled a fire of determination and it cannot be extinguished." After his father's death, he taught school for a time, but was disgusted with it through the fact that in gaining and holding a position merit was drowned by political wire-pulling. In 1891 he entered Meharry Medical College and graduated in 1893. He is now conducting a drug store at Little Rock, Arkansas, and is thoroughly awake to the necessity of competing if he would excel. He takes as his motto, "No step backward," and is working with all the energy of his soul to range among the successful ones of our closing century. Mr. Coffin has just published a volume of poems of about two hundred pages, forty of which relate to the crime of lynching. He is preparing another book of poems, which he hopes to publish in the near future. He is a lover of children, and is actively engaged in Christian work. He stands fearlessly for right, without regard to what the effect may be upon his business.

Dr. Sarah Helen Fitzbutler graduated in medicine and surgery in the Louisville National Medical College with the class of 1892. Doctor Butler is the first woman to receive the regular degree to practice medicine in Kentucky.

The Louisville National Medical College is doing much, by its thorough work, to disarm the public mind of race prejudice. The race may justly feel proud of what its representatives are achieving. Its attainments are worthy of schools that boast of much higher standing.

J. B. Banks, M. D., taught school for a short time,

DR. J. B. BANKS, NATCHEZ, MISSISSIPPI.

then entered Leland University, New Orleans, in 1877, working evenings and mornings for his board and lodging. The yellow fever compelled him to leave. He then went to the country where he obtained a private school of ten or fifteen pupils. After paying his board of $5 a month, he had one dollar left for his work. He afterward succeeded in finding better paying employment and managed, besides supporting his aged grandparents through the next winter, to save $30. He then taught for a number of years, and entered Meharry Medical College in 1885. After graduating he at once returned to Mississippi, and passed his examination before the State Medical Board. He, with seven white applicants, was successful, while the same number of whites were unsuccessful. He at once began practicing medicine, and in 1889 moved to Natchez, Mississippi, where he has a fair practice. In 1890 he was appointed a member of the Board of Surgeons of the United States at Natchez. Doctor Banks enjoys the esteem of his own race and of the white citizens of Natchez and the surrounding country. He owns a comfortable home, valued at $3,000; is married and has two children. He is a prominent member and officer of the African M. E. Church of Natchez.

Thomas A. Curtis was born in Alabama. His parents were slaves, but by earnest effort his father educated himself and became state senator from Alabama. The son, after graduating from the State Normal School, taught for some years in Texas, and then entered Meharry Dental School, from which he graduated in 1889. His success as the first colored dentist of Alabama is assured. During the first year he earned more than $2,000. With such an energetic spirit as he possesses it is needless to say that he has each year improved in proficiency in his profession and in the increase of his practice.

Prof. Geo. W. Carver is director of the agricultural department of the famous industrial school at Tuskegee, Alabama. He is a graduate of the State Agricultural College at Ames, Iowa, from which he received his Master's degree.

PROF. GEO. W. CARVER, M. AG.

From childhood he seems to have had a passion for music, painting, flowers, stones, minerals, and like objects of beauty and interest. The study of the character and productive ability of soils seem to have been in him an instinct. As a boy he was known as the "Plant Doctor."

His painting, the "Yucca and Cactus," was exhibited at the World's Fair in Chicago.

It is, perhaps, safe to say that he has the largest private collection of botanical and geological specimens in the state of Alabama.

But in order to reach his present position of ability and usefulness he had a long and weary road to travel. He was born a slave in Missouri during the period of the Civil war. Prof. Carver expresses the deepest gratitude to Mr. and Mrs. Carver to whom his mother belonged until set free by the war. For some years his foster-parents (Mr. and Mrs. Carver) cared for him, and during this time he acquired the rudiments of an education.

When ten years of age he began his wanderings through Kansas, Missouri, and Iowa, in his struggles for intellectual and bodily food. He had to meet not only the difficulties of an ordinary poor boy in his efforts to gain a position in the world, but he must overcome natural race-prejudice among his white associates. But he has won an exalted position worthy the best minds.

While working his way at school Carver exhibited a remarkably versatile mind. At one time he was a successful laundryman, at another a skilled cook, and again an ingenious milliner. He also knit his own mittens and stockings. He shows, with commendable pride, three hundred samples of knitting, crocheting, and embroidering.

AUTHORS AND LITERARY WORKERS.

Paul Laurence Dunbar.—The first poet of his race in the English language was Paul Laurence Dunbar,

PAUL LAURENCE DUNBAR,
The Famous Colored Poet.

whose parents were full blood Negroes. His father escaped from slavery in Kentucky to freedom in Canada, and at a time when there was no hope of freedom otherwise. His mother was liberated by the Emancipation Proclamation, and came North to Ohio. Paul was born at Dayton, Ohio, and grew up with such opportunities for mental training as befalls the children of the poor. His father was a plasterer, and after learning to read, he loved chiefly to read history. His mother had a passion for literature, with a special delight for poetry.

After his father died, mother and son struggled on in still deeper poverty. His writings attracted many, and it was not long before his friends recognized that in him was found the first instance of an American Negro who had evinced an innate distinction in literature, although many of his race had proven themselves proficient in music, oratory, and some of the other arts. It is said that Paul Dunbar was the only man of pure African blood and of American civilization to feel the Negro life æsthetically and to express it lyrically. While all of his poems are beautiful in sentiment, yet those pieces where he studied the modes and traits of his race we find the most charming. His refined and delicate art is shown most clearly where he describes the range between appetite and emotion. He reveals in these an ironical perception of the Negro's limitation with a tenderness that is quite new.

If Mr. Dunbar does nothing more than he has done, he may rightfully be said to have made the strongest claim for the Negro in English literature that the Negro has ever made. Although we may not agree in all he says, we can hardly refuse to enjoy it.

Well may it be said of many of his productions that they are works of art. Let us notice a few of the many beautiful and practical sentiments expressed. The following is from "Accountability":

"But we all fits into places dat no othah ones could fill,
And we does the things we has to, big er little, poor er ill.
John cain't take the place o' Henry, Su an' Sally ain't alike;
Bass aint nuthin' like a sucker, shad ain't nuthin' like a pike.

When you come to think about it, how it's all planned out, it's
  splendid.
Nuthin's done ere evah has been 'dout hit's somefin' dat's intended;
Don't keer what you does, you has to, an' hit sholy beats de
  dickens.
Viney, go put on de kettle, I got one o' mastah's chickens."

Then again, notice the sentiment expressed in the
following stanza on the grand old man, Frederick
Douglass, in all respects the representative of his
race:

"Through good and ill report, he cleaved his way right, with his
  face set towards the heights,
Nor feared to face the foeman's dread array—
The lash of scorn, the sting of petty spites.
He dared the lightning in the lightning's track,
And answered thunder with his thunder back."

What poet has more graphically and in fewer words
expressed the realities of life than Mr. Dunbar in the
following stanza:

"A crust of bread and a corner to sleep in,
A minute to smile, and an hour to weep in;
A pint of joy to a peck of trouble,
And never a laugh but the moans come double;
And that is life!"

"Rising of the Storm" is beautifully expressed,
while "An Ante-bellum Sermon" gives us an insight
into the real life of the Negro of those days. The
"Banjo Song" carries back many a gray-haired freedman to the time when the banjo, taken from the wall,
brought cheer and comfort to the weary slave.

Who has more really pictured the lawyer's ways

than he when he describes the effort of the contending sides to paint either in blackest crime the condition of the persons on one hand, and to gild with virtuous graces the fair name as seen from the other side? Pertinently does he ask:

> "How an angel an' a devil
> Can persess the self-same soul!"

Our sympathies are aroused in "Deacon Jones' Grievance," when he so pathetically pleads with the parson to modify the "hifaluting style" of modern song in the churches, and the objection to being made an object of ridicule, when a solo was being sung and he struck in to help the poor fellow out, and the whole church scowled at him. "The Spelling Bee" brings to mind the days of yore so vividly that we wish we were there. "Keep Pluggin' Away," although a quaint motto, carries with it many a noble and worthy truth.

All the gallant sons of Ham that have fought for freedom are anew fired with the spirit of patriotism and loyalty to Uncle Sam in reading "The Colored Soldiers," in which the bravery of the Negro at Fort Wagner and Fort Pillow are so graphically set forth. Well does it close with this stanza:

> "So all honor and all glory to these noble sons of Ham,
> The gallant colored soldiers who fought for Uncle Sam."

A sigh escapes many a longing heart as we read the "Ol' Tunes," as the new-fashioned anthems prevent the 'joining of the uncultured and untrained voices. Every Negro rejoices in freedom, and yet what ex-slave who was blessed with a humane and kind master does not sigh when he reads "The Deserted Plantation," which brings to the mind the days of long ago?

We have space for but one more selection from this gifted author of the colored race:

MORTALITY.

"Ashes to ashes! dust to dust!
What of his loving?   What of his lust?
What of his passion?   What of his pain?
What of his poverty?   What his pride?
Earth, the great mother, has called him again;
Deeply he sleeps, the world's verdict defied.
Shall he be tried again?   Shall he go free?
Who shall the court convene?   Where shall it be?
No answer on the land, none from the sea!
Only we know that as he died, we must—
You with your theory, you with your trust—
Ashes to ashes, dust to dust!"

A London correspondent says: "Paul Dunbar, the American Negro Poet, has captured London.   He has been received with marked attention by good society, and he is in big demand in the most fashionable drawing-rooms.   No color line is drawn in England, and the talented American is much sought after.   He reads his verses at receptions, garden parties and other entertainments, and he has received the most favorable criticisms from the press.   Mr. Dunbar came to London well recommended by W. D. Howells and other American literary lights well known to the British public.   His humble origin and the story of his self-culture, struggles and final triumph have won him a peculiar regard here, where the Negro slave and the prejudices against him and his descendants have never existed.   Mr. Dunbar expects to spend several months in London, and he will have no lack of occupation, judging by his early successes.   His mission promises to be all that he hopes it to be."

Frances E. W. Harper.—We have already noticed

Mrs. Harper as one of the forerunners of liberty. It is, however, due Mrs. Harper that we also mention her as an author, for, since the emancipation she has written a number of works besides spending much of the time in the lecture field. Some of her writings are the following: "Moses, a story of the Nile;" "Sketches of Southern Life," in which she portrays the life of the Negro; "Shalmanezer." Her book of poems contains some excellent and practical thoughts. "The Dying Bondman" is so touching that we reproduce it here:

THE DYING BONDMAN.

Life was trembling, faintly trembling,
  On the bondman's latest breath,
And he felt the chilling pressure
  Of the cold, hard hand of Death.

He had been an Afric chieftain,
  Worn his manhood as a crown;
But upon the field of battle
  Had been fiercely stricken down.

He had longed to gain his freedom,
  Waited, watched and hoped in vain,
Till his life was slowly ebbing—
  Almost broken was his chain.

By his bedside stood the master,
  Gazing on the dying one,
Knowing by the dull-grey shadows
  That life's sands were almost run.

"Master," said the dying bondman,
  "Home and friends I soon shall see;
But before I reach my country,
  Master, write that I am free.

"For the spirits of my fathers
  Would shrink back from me in pride,
If I told them at our greeting
  I a slave had lived and died.

"Give to me the precious token,
    That my kindred dead may see—
Master! write it, write it quickly!
    Master! write that I am free!"

At his earnest plea the master
    Wrote for him the glad release,
O'er his wan and wasted features
    Flitted one sweet smile of peace.

Eagerly he grasped the writing;
    "I am free at last!" he said.
Backward fell upon the pillow,
    He was free among the dead.

Among other interesting poems are found, "Saving the Boys;" "Nothing and Something;" "My Mother's Kiss;" "Home, Sweet Home." Probably the volume which has received the most favorable reception is her "Iola Leroy," presenting a vivid view of scenes at the South before, during and after the war. It is written in a vigorous and graphic manner, and is effective in appealing to the finer sensibilities of the American public and, at the same time, addresses itself to those logical sequences of mind that follow out of that fundamental principle of Christianity, the fatherhood of God and the brotherhood of man.

Mrs. Harper introduces into her work many thrilling war scenes and succeeds in making her romance one of the most interesting. It pleads the cause of the race whose destinies were never more closely involved with those of the nation than at the present time. Mrs. Harper is one of the ablest writers among the women of the colored race.

Phillis Wheatley.—This girl was brought on a slave ship from Africa to Boston in 1761, and bought by Mrs. John Wheatley, an intelligent and cultured lady. When bought her clothing consisted of a piece of dirty

carpet around her loins. Mrs. Wheatley was impressed by her intelligent countenance, and selected her
from a large number of slaves. Through kind treatment and encouragement she learned easily, and developed a talent for poetry. She wrote a book of poems
of about forty pieces, and the literary merit of these
poems disposed some to question their origin. At one
time she addressed a poem to George Washington,
and received a kind and courteous reply.

Mrs. Mary R. Phelps.—In Union county, South Carolina, on the first day of May, 1867, was born to
Adeline and Hilliard Rice the subject of this sketch.
Many names of the rising young women of her race
have, doubtless, received more public eulogy, but few
names deserve a more worthy mention than that of
Mrs. Mary R. Phelps. There were many qualities
noticeable about her when quite young, all significant
of her future usefulness. But the one especially interesting to her parents and friends was the voluntary
devotion to books and other reading matter. Her
perusing picture books, papers, etc., awakened an
interest in her to enquire about the words which often
accompanied such pictures. In this way she learned
to read simple readings by the time she was four years
old. At the age of five years she entered the public
schools of Union county, the annual terms of which
were of but two or three months' duration. So remarkable was her progress as a student and scholar under adverse circumstances, that at the age of thirteen she accepted, with consent of her parents, the charge of a large
school in a rural district of Spartanburg county, South
Carolina, was examined, received a certificate of qualification, and taught the term with such remarkable credit
as to win the approval of both her patrons and trustees.

Her parents, being thus encouraged, determined with renewed efforts to have her educated, notwithstanding their limited advantages.   They sent her to Benedict Institute (now Benedict College), Columbia, South Carolina, and afterward to Scotia Seminary, at Concord, North Carolina, from which institution she graduated.   Since completing her course in school, she has contributed to various journals, etc., and has been offered a liberal salary for her services.   But, in consideration of the need of well-prepared educators among the race, that it may become what it can be, she chose to use her talent in assisting that grand purpose.   Aside from her accomplishment in the literary line, Mrs. Phelps has acquired a practical knowledge in the arts of music, painting, dressmaking, etc., to any of which she can creditably apply herself. Her career as a teacher has been one of usefulness and success.   She spent each vacation of her school life in teaching, which experience greatly increased her devotion to that work.   Hence, when she was no longer a school girl she entered into the teachers' field as a profession.   She was principal of a public school at Glenn Springs, South Carolina, for three years.   In 1890 she resigned that school to accept a position in the graded school at Rome, Georgia, where she taught for some time.   She then taught in Milledgeville, after which she was married to Mr. J. L. Phelps in 1891.   The demand for well trained teachers was so great that in 1893 she again consented to act as assistant principal in Cleveland Academy, Helena, South Carolina, and more recently has held a position in Haines ˌInstitute, Augusta, Georgia.   Mrs. Phelps is an earnest Sabbath school worker, and her labors for God and the church have been greatly blessed.

Mrs. Fanny Barrier Williams came into prominence during the World's Columbian Exposition. Her address at the Woman's Congress on the "Intellectual Progress of the Colored Woman" created a profound impression. Since the close of the Exposition, Mrs. Williams has received invitations from all parts of the country to deliver addresses. She was born in Brockport, New York, and received a collegiate education. Her complexion is a clear, light brown, and her voice is singularly soft and sympathetic in tone. She is a woman of more than usual intelligence, and as a lecturer is in great demand. Her most popular lectures are: "What Will You Do with Our Women;" "Christianity and the American Negro;" "Prudence Crandall, or, a Modern Canterbury Tale;" "Opportunities of Western Women;" "The Opportunities and Responsibilities of American Colored Women."

Mrs. M. A. McCurdy was born in Carthage, Indiana, in 1852. She acquired the rudiments of an education in the mixed schools of that place, but, being deprived of attending any other school by the death of her father, she labored diligently, and before she was nineteen years of age had prepared herself for teaching, and secured a school near her home. After teaching for some time, she was married to J. A. Mason, and for more than eight years filled with profit and precision the worthy position of wife and mother. The hand of death removed from her four precious jewels and her husband, leaving her alone to battle life's conflicts. She then entered the temperance work, and became a noted worker in Richmond, Indiana. For a time she edited a temperance paper in that city. A desire to go South and labor among her people seemed to impress itself more and more upon her mind until 1886, when she was led to Atlanta, where sne became editor of the *Southern Recorder*. Here, besides her work in temperance and as editor, she built up a fine mission during her four years' stay, St. James' M. E. Church, of that city. In 1890 she was married to Rev. C. McCurdy, of Rome, Georgia. Her labors in Rome since that time have been varied and greatly appreciated by the people. She is engaged in industrial work among the women of her race; is corresponding secretary for the W. C. T. U. for the state of Georgia; president of the missionary work in the Presbyterian Church, and editor of *The Woman's World*, a paper devoted to the intellectual, moral and spiritual progress of the people. In all these departments of work she has made herself known and felt not only in the city of Rome, but throughout the state. Her work will outlive empires and the stars.

Mrs. Ida B. Wells Barnett.—The subject of this sketch became noted for her crusades against the lynching evil. Shocked by the awful barbarity of that species of outlawry, brought home to her by the lynching of three highly respectable colored men of Memphis, because of a neighborhood quarrel, Miss Wells started out to call the attention of the American people to the dangerous growth of this evil. Denied a hearing in America she went to England and there from pulpit, platform and in the public press her appeal was effectively made. In 1895 she married Ferdinand L. Barnett, Jr., of the Chicago bar.

Edward E. Cooper.—Among the strange happenings in Washington is to see many new men, unknown quantities in the politics and history of our people, pushing themselves to the front, clamorously calling upon the President to give them an office for their great services to the party in power. On the other hand, you see the real leaders, men of thought and action, quietly and modestly moving on in the even tenor of their way, working out their own destinies and the destinies of the people, asking no political favors. To one of these latter men we wish to refer, a quiet, modest, resolute man, who, by his indefatigable will and tenacity

E. E. COOPER,
Editor "Colored American,"
Washington, D. C.

of purpose, is making a name which will be honored when many of our so-called great men will be forgotten, E. E. Cooper, editor and manager of the *Colored American*. Mr. Cooper was born in Tennessee about thirty-five years ago. He early went to Indianapolis, where he was educated. After graduation he entered upon his journalistic career, which has been a unique one. He established in Indianapolis the first colored illustrated paper published in the United States, *The Freeman*, a new order in colored journalism. Everybody knows of its phenomenal success. After seeing *The Freeman* established on a firm financial basis, Mr. Cooper sold his interest and turned his travels toward the National Capitol, where he founded the *Colored American*, a paper which has lifted colored journalism in the Capitol to a plane it never reached before. Here his best work is being done; bravely does he champion the Negro's cause. His influence is widespread, it is national. His acquaintanceship with political leaders has given him an influence not possessed by any other young man of his race. His success with the *American* has been gratifying, some weeks during the last campaign it having reached a circulation of 100,000 copies.

Henry O. Tanner.—Henry O. Tanner, son of Bishop Benjamin Tucker Tanner, of the African Methodist Episcopal Church, was born and reared in the city of Philadelphia. As a boy he enjoyed the privileges of the city schools. Early in life the natural bent of his genius began to manifest itself. Consequently, he entered the Pennsylvania Academy of Fine Arts, and became a pupil of Professor Eakins. Under this efficient and faithful instructor, Mr. Tanner secured that foundation upon which he has since so magnificently built.

Like many others, however, Mr. Tanner has had to struggle with the gaunt wolf, poverty. Shortly after leaving the academy he, among other ventures, started a photograph gallery in Atlanta, Georgia. This was not a success. He then spent a year at Clark University, where he taught freehand drawing and gave instruction in painting to private classes, colored and white, at the institution and in the city. One summer vacation he spent at Highlands, North Carolina, a health resort, where he also instructed classes of white people, some of them Southern.

For a long time it was the topmost desire of Mr. Tanner's heart to go to Paris, and study under the great masters of art in that brilliant metropolis. It was by the severest economy, together with assistance

from friends, that he was enabled to gratify his desire.
Nor was he altogether relieved from embarrassment
after reaching Paris, for, within a short time after his
arrival, he fell sick, and lay in the hospital for two
months with typhoid fever. On his recovery he again
resumed with a hopeful heart, but under discouraging
circumstances, the pursuit of his studies. For two
years he was a pupil of Benjamin Constant. "Becoming stranded again," as he quaintly states it, he returned to America for about eighteen months. Within
this time he sold several pictures. Of these "The
Banjo Lesson," his first picture exhibited at the Salon,
was sold to Mr. Robert C. Ogden, a tried friend and
patron of Mr. Tanner, and to whom, as Mr. Tanner
acknowledges, he "is much indebted for whatever
of success he has had." Another picture, entitled,
"Thankful Poor," he sold to Mr. John T. Morris.
Here, too, it may be said that at the Columbian Exposition were exhibited one hundred pictures from
American art students, at home and abroad. Of this
hundred was one of Mr. Tanner's, "The First Lesson
on the Bagpipe," painted from a scene in Brittany.
At the close of the exposition a committee of art critics
was appointed to select from the hundred the forty
best, and catalogue them, inserting cuts of each. Mr.
Tanner's picture was one of the forty. This picture
was afterwards exhibited at the "Cotton States and
International Exposition," Atlanta, Georgia, and attracted the attention of many.

With moneys realized from his sales while in America
he returned to Paris in 1894, and resumed his studies
under Jean Paul Laurens and Benjamin Constant. His
first picture to receive any official recognition was the
one entitled, "Daniel in the Lion's Den"—mention

honorable, 1896. Then came the picture of the year, "Lazarus Rising from the Dead," which received "third medal," and was purchased by the French government. These, now, are the achievements of a young man. What may the race expect of him?

But, outside his art, much might be said of the man. He belongs to that class whom to know is to admire and to love. Genial, simple in manner, generous, with an intense desire to serve and uplift his race, he moves among his fellows with the appearance of a man who has found his life-work and is in love with it. To such men the people must look for loftiest inspiration and safest guidance.

Mr. Tanner is spending his summer vacation (1897) with his parents at Kansas City, Kansas. He likes Paris because of the companionship of artists, and he will probably spend the rest of his life-time there; still, he glories in the fact that he is an American citizen, and he will retain that title as long as he lives. During his stay at home he has been painting portraits of his parents. When he returns to Paris he will begin work on another Biblical painting, "The Annunciation," which he hopes will surpass his "Raising of Lazarus," which made him famous as an artist.

Clark Hampton.—Young Clark Hampton, whose painting of "Napoleon at Waterloo" is receiving such widespread attention, is really a genius. He is only eighteen years old, and the sole support of a widowed mother. In his modest studio is to be found a charming original sketch, "Waiting in the Wildwood." The boy is ambitious, and, although finding it difficult to support his mother and to continue his work, he is determined to press forward. "If I live, the race shall yet be proud of me," says this youth.

Edmonia Lewis probably surpasses every other person of her race as a sculptor. She is of lowly birth, and was left an orphan when quite young, but her determination has enabled her to overcome difficulties. When visiting Boston the first time, she saw a statue of Benjamin Franklin. She was so touched by the sight that the latent talent within her broke forth in, "I, too, can make a stone man!" She was introduced by William Lloyd Garrison to one of Boston's famous sculptors, and as she triumphed in her work she has won a position as an artist on two continents. Some of the masterpieces of her hands are: "Hagar in the Wilderness," "Hiawatha's Wooing," busts of Longfellow, John Brown and Wendell Phillips. Her studio in Rome has become an object of interest to travelers from all countries.

MISCELLANEOUS.

We have mentioned in these pages a number of colored men representing the different classes. There are many others as able as these who may imagine that we have neglected to mention them. This is not a biography, but our object in mentioning a number of these different classes is to show the progress made since freedom. Many colored women might be named. It should be remembered that they have had fewer privileges of education before the war and since than the men of their race, yet there are a number of them who have shown themselves capable and useful.

Hon. H. C. Smith, who has represented one of the districts of Ohio in the legislature for a number of years, and is editor and proprietor of the *Cleveland Gazette*, is one of the young men of whom the race may feel proud. It is but fitting to say that his election to the Ohio legislature in 1893 has made him even more popular than before among the people. He has made a record that has amply vindicated the choice and judgment of his constituents.

John Mitchell, Jr., who was born of slave parents, has for a number of years been editor of the *Richmond Planet*, a weekly paper.

Amanda Smith, born in slavery, has, through poverty and adversity, pushed her way upward until she is one of the most spiritual and eloquent exhorters and lecturers of her race in the world. She is a member of the Methodist Episcopal Church, and has traveled extensively in America, Europe and Africa. She has written her biography, which has a wide sale. She is now engaged in raising funds for a home for colored orphan children in Chicago. Her visits to the churches throughout the North and West are an inspiration and a blessing, and she has succeeded in a remarkable manner in the work for which she has so long been laboring.

Mrs. Charlotte Fortune Grimke is a native of Pennsylvania. She was educated in Massachusetts, and proved to be a student of more than ordinary ability and application. Mrs. Grimke has been a contributor to the columns of the *Atlantic Monthly* and other representative magazines of the East.

Rev. W. A. Lewis, of West Tennessee, was compelled to work at home by his stepfather, who thought it a crime for a stepson to attend school. He worked hard on the farm in the day, and walked a mile at night to take lessons of a white lady, paying a dollar a month for instruction. He picked berries and sold melons at odd times to pay his tuition. Such qualities might worthily be emulated today.

John William McKinney is a successful lawyer in

Sherman, Texas.   He was admitted to the bar in 1891, and was elected delegate from the state at large by the Union Republican convention in 1892.   In 1894 he was nominated by the Republicans for Congress.

Richard T. Greener, one of the most cultured Afro-Americans, was for many years dean of the law department of Howard University.

REV. CYRUS MYERS.

Rev. Cyrus Myers, of Simpson county, Mississippi, who has become prominent in his efforts to have Congress pass a bill pensioning ex-slaves, is a remarkable Negro of the old slave class.   Rev. Myers brought with him over 6,000 signatures of Mississippi ex-slaves. He is seventy-nine years old, and was a slave forty-seven years.   He is black, tall, eloquent and full of reminiscences.   He was a novelty at Washington in that he is not an office-seeker, but is working for his race.

Charles L. Remond was the first Negro to take the

platform as a regular lecturer in the anti-slavery cause, and was the ablest representative that the race had till the appearance of Frederick Douglass in 1842.

W. E. King is one of the rising young men of Dallas, Texas. Improving the opportunities given him in his youth, he has succeeded in making himself useful. He is at present editor of the *Weekly Express*, and is yielding an influence for true worth and progress with his race. Among the young men of the state who are devoting their lives to the welfare of the race Mr. King stands prominent.

B. K. Bruce. On the 23d day of May, 1881, President Garfield appointed ex-Senator B. K. Bruce, of Mississippi, Registrar of the United States Treasury. This was the first colored man whose signature made money of worthless paper.

Professor M. A. Hopkins, of Franklintown, North Carolina, a colored teacher of marked ability, was appointed by President Cleveland, first term, as Minister to Liberia.

Miss L. Vina Givens, of Dallas, Texas, has, by her natural ability, become prominent in the musical world of Texas. Through adverse circumstances she has risen, and is today one of the sweetest singers of Dallas.

COLORED AUTHORS AND NAMES OF PUBLICATIONS.

Albert, A. E. P., D. D.—The Negro Evangelist.
 Plantation Melodies.
 Universal Reign of Jesus.
Alexander, William T.—History of the Colored Race in America.
Alexander, Rev. W. G.—Living Words.
 The Negro in Commerce and Finance.
 The Efficient Sunday School.

Anderson, Rev. J. Harvey—Directory of the A. M. E. Zion Church.

Arnett, Bishop.—Negro Literature.

The Centennial Budget.

Bannecker, Benjamin.—Science.

Bates, R. C.—Architecture and Building.

Benjamin, R. C. O., D. D.—Africa, the Hope of the Negro.

Future of the American Negro.

History of the British West Indies.

Life of Toussiant L'Ouverture.

Origin of the Negro Race.

The Southland.

The Boy Doctor.

Don't.

Blackwell, G. L.—The Model Homestead.

Blyden, E. W., LL.D.—Christianity, Islam and the Negro Race.

From West Africa to Palestine.

Liberia's Offering.

Booth, Rev. C. O.—Plain Theology for Plain People.

Bowen, J. W. E., D. D.—Plain Talks.

Africa and the American Negro.

Brawley, Rev. E. M.—The Negro Baptist Pulpit.

Brown, Rev. R. T.—Doctrines of Christ and the Church.

Pastor's Annual and Financial Report.

Brown, William Wells.—The Black Man.

The Negro in the Rebellion.

The Rising Sun.

Carter, Rev. E. R.—Our Pulpit Illustrated.

The Black Side.

The Holy Land.

Clark, P. H.—Black Brigade.

Coleman, Mrs. L. N. C.—Poor Ben.

Cooper, Mrs. A. J.—A Voice from the South.

Crogman, W.H., A. M.—Talks for the Times.

Crummell, Rev. Alex., D. D.—Africa and America.
> The Future of Africa.

Davis, D. W.—Poems.

Douglass, Frederick.—Life and Times of Frederick
> Douglass.
> My Bondage and My Freedom.
> Narrative of My Experience in Slavery.

DuBois, W. E. Burghardt, Ph. D.—The Suppression of
> the African Slave Trade to the United States of
> America, 1838-1870.

Dunbar, Paul L.—Oak and Ivy.
> Poems.
> Negro Love Song.

Dyson, J. F., B. D.—Are We Africans or Americans?
> Origin of Color.
> Political X Roads—Which Way?
> Richard Allen's Place in History.

Earl, Victoria.—Aunt Linda.

Early, Sarah.—Life and Labors of Rev. J. W. Early.

Embry, J. C., D. D.—Digest of Christian Theology.
> Our Father's House.

Fortune, T. T.—Black and White.

Gordon, J. E.—Political Works.

Gregory, J. M.—Hon. Frederick Douglass.

Green, Dr. A. R.—History of Independent Methodism.

Hagood, Rev. L. M., M. D.—The Colored Man in the
> M. E. Church.

Harper, Mrs. F. E. W.—Iola Leroy; or, Shadows
> Uplifted.
> Forest Leaves.

Sketches of Southern Life.

Moses: A Story of the Nile.

Miscellaneous Poems.

Shalmanezer.

Hood, Bishop J. W., D. D.—Book of Sermons.

History of the A. M. E. Z. Church.

Johnson, Mrs. A. E.—Clarence and Corinne.

The Hazely Family.

Johnson, E. A.—School History of the Negro Race in America.

Jones, S. T., D. D.—Book of Sermons.

Langston, Hon. John M.—Freedom and Citizenship.

From the Virginia Plantation to the National Capitol.

Lectures and Addresses.

Majors, M. A.—Noted Negro Women.

Matthews, Mrs W. E.—Aunt Linda.

Moore, Bishop J. J.—History of the A. M. E. Church

Mossell, Mrs. N. F.—The Work of Afro-American Women.

Payne, Bishop Daniel.—Domestic Education.

History of the A. M. E. Church.

Recollections of Seventy Years.

Official Sermons of the A. M. E. Church.

The Semi-Centenary of the A. M. E. Church.

Pegues, Rev. A. W., Ph. D.—Our Baptist Ministers and Schools.

Pendleton, Lewis.—The Sons of Ham.

Penn, I. Garland.—The Afro-American Press and Its Editors.

Ransom, R. C.—School Days at Wilberforce.

Rowe, Rev. George C.—Patriotic Poems.

The Aim of Life.

Thoughts in Verse.

Rush, Bishop.—Rise and Progress of Zion Church.

Scarborough, W. S.. A. M., Ph. D., LL. D.—First Lessons in Greek.

Latih Moods and Tenses.

Questions on Latin Grammar.

Scruggs, L. A.—Afro-American Women of Distinction.

Grammar Land.

Simmons, William, D. D.—Men of Mark.

Smith, Rev. C. S.—Glimpses of Africa.

Smith, Rev. S. E.—Anti-Separate Coach History of Kentucky.

Smith, W. H.—Earnest Pleas.

Smith, Amanda.—A Story of My Life.

Stevenson, Rev. J. W., M. D.—Church Financiering.

Stewart, T. McCants.—Liberia.

Still, William.—The Underground Railroad.

The Kidnapped and Ransomed.

Straker, D. A.—The New South Investigated.

Tanner, Benjamin Tucker.—Apology for American Methodism.

Is the Negro Cursed?

Outline of History.

The Negro's Origin.

The Negro (African and American).

Theological Lectures.

Taylor, M. W.—Plantation Melodies.

Trotter, J. M.—Music and Some Highly Musical People.

Troy, Rev. William.—Hairbreadth Escapes from Slavery to Freedom.

Turner, Bishop—African Letters.

Methodist Polity.

Negro in All Ages.

Wayman, Bishop A. W.—Cyclopedia of the A. M. E. Church.

Wheatley, Phillis.—Memoirs of Poems.

Wheeler, B. F., A. M.—Sacred Heart.

Whitman, A. A.—Not a Man, and Yet a Man.
   The Rape of Florida.
   Poems.

Wells, Ida B.—A Red Record.

Williams, Prof. D. B.—Science and Art of Elocution.
   Freedom and Progress.

Williams, George W., LL. D.—A History of the Negro Troops in the Rebellion.
   History of the Negro Race in America.

Wilson, J. T.—Black Phalanx (History of Negro Soldiers).
   Emancipation.
   Twenty-two Years of Freedom.
   Voice of a New Race.

Wright, Prof. R. R.—A Brief Historical Sketch of Negro Education in Georgia.

Rev. Charles T. Walker, D. D., pastor of the Mount Olivet Baptist church, New York City, was born a slave in Richmond county, Georgia, January 11, 1859. He was the youngest of eleven children. His father was buried the day before his son's birth.

When about eight years old his mother also passed away, leaving him to battle for himself.

In 1873, while working in a cotton field, he suddenly decided to be at peace with God. He went into the woods where for three days he wrestled, without food or drink, when the struggle ended and he was happily converted.

After spending several years in public school, he felt

that he was called to the ministry. Accordingly he entered the Theological Institute, at Augusta, Georgia. For five years he studied showing much energy and ability.

REV. CHARLES T. WALKER, D. D.
Pastor Mount Olivet Baptist Church, New York City.

He was licensed to preach in 1876, and ordained to the ministry when but eighteen years old. He was immediately elected pastor of his mother-church, which had been organized in 1848. The house had been built by slaves after they had worked all day for their masters.

After successful pastorates at Waynesboro, La Grange, and Augusta, Georgia, his friends at Augusta sent him to Europe and the Holy Land. On his return he wrote a book on "A Colored Man Abroad."

He has given much time to evangelistic work, and counts 10,000 conversions under his preaching. He has been called the "Black Spurgeon," and is sometimes known as the "Colored John the Baptist."

In addition to his pastoral and evangelistic work, he has done much to encourage education among his own people. He was one of the founders of the Walker Baptist Institute at Augusta, Georgia. He is still its financial secretary.

He is trustee of the Atlanta Baptist College, vice-president of the National Baptist Convention of the United States, and one of the vice-presidents of the International and Interdenominational Sunday School Convention of America and Canada.

While doing heavy pastoral work in New York, he was instrumental in organizing a colored Y. M. C. A. of 500 members. They are now engaged in raising money for permanent quarters of their own.

Doctor Walker is still a student, and is at present engaged in the study of the Hebrew and the Spanish languages.

As a speaker he is eloquent and convincing. His "Appeal to Cæsar," in which he replies to Rev. Henry Frank upon his criticism of the negro race, and his review of the Montgomery conference, are perhaps his most noted efforts.

During the Spanish-American war, Dr. Walker was chaplain of the 9th Immune regiment, and served in Santiago and San Luis, Cuba.

CHAPTER XV.

PLANTATION MELODIES.

INCIDENTS, EXPERIENCES AND PLEASANTRIES.

Hampton and Its Students.—For many years the Hampton school has been making an effort to preserve and collect the spiritual songs of the Negroes in America, and to give to its students so great a love for these beautiful utterances of the emotions of an enslaved and deeply religious race that they would strive as they went out to gather up and preserve a form of emotional expression only too likely to pass away in the transition period through which the colored people are now passing. So impossible is it to reproduce this music under changed conditions that there is danger lest even where both words and music are preserved, the spirit which gives it its peculiar charm may be lost forever. The educated Negro cannot sing the old songs as his father sang them. He may yet evolve a higher and nobler music of his own, but the old spirituals, squeezed as it were out of the human heart by the pressure of slavery, are a part of his history that he cannot afford to lose—a breaking forth from bondage of that thing which could never be enslaved, the genius of a race.

Hampton and its students have done more to preserve Negro melodies than any other agency.

The following are a few of the many songs that might be given. Most of them are taken from the Hampton collection.

THE ANGELS DONE CHANGED MY NAME.

" I went to the hillside, I went to pray;
    I know the angels done changed my name—
Done changed my name for the coming day;
    I knew the angels done changed my name.

" I looked at my hands, my hands was new, .
    I knew the angels done changed my name;
I looked at my feet, and my feet was, too—
    Thank God the angels done changed my name."

While the Negro brought out from bondage no literature and no theology, yet he did bring with him the plantation songs which show in Christian song that the doctrines of Christianity were held by these people in the days of slavery. We cannot expect to find the same modes of expression now that prevailed among them while in slavery, but that they held to the fundamental truths of religion must be recognized by all who study these songs. That they believed in Christ as a Savior from sin and in the Atonement is beautifully illustrated in the refrain—

" I've been redeemed! I've been redeemed!
    Been washed in de blood ob de lamb."

The Divinity of Christ is shown in—

" Jus' stan' right still and steady yo'self:
    I know that my Redeemer lives.
Oh, jus' let me tell yo' about God hisself:
    I know that my Redeemer lives."

At Tougaloo, Mississippi, they sing a hymn which especially emphasizes the personality of Satan, which, it seems, they never doubted—

" Ole Satan he wears de hypocrite shoe;
    If yo' don' min' he slip it on yo'."

Frederick Douglass says that—

" Run to Jesus, shun the danger,
    I don't expect to stay much longer here."

sung on the plantation where he was a slave, first suggested to him the thought of escaping from slavery, or,
as he put it, " Praying with his feet."

While their lives were full of misery on account of
the oppressions of their masters, their songs do not
show anywhere a revengeful spirit.   They looked forward with confidence, expecting to be relieved in the
land of the redeemed.

> " Shine, shine, I'll meet you in that morning.
>   Oh, my soul's goin' to shine, to shine:
>   I'm goin' to sit down to a welcome table—
>   Shine, shine, my soul's goin' to shine."

SWING LOW, SWEET CHARIOT.

> Oh, de good ole chariot swing so low,
> Good ole chariot swing so low,
> Oh, de good ole chariot swing so low,
> I don't want to leave me behind.
> Chorus.—Oh, swing low, sweet chariot.
>   Swing low, sweet chariot,
>   Swing low, sweet chariot,
>   I don't want to leave me behind.
>
> Oh, de good ole chariot will take us all home,
> I don't want to leave me behind.
> Cho.—Oh, swing low, sweet, etc.

THE DANVILLE CHARIOT.

> Chorus.—Oh, swing low, sweet chariot;
>   Pray let me enter in,
>   I don't want to stay here no longer.
>
> I done been to heaven, an' I done been tired,
> I been to the water, an' I been baptized—
>   I don't want to stay no longer.
> O, down to the water I was led,
> My soul got fed with heav'nly bread—
>   I don't want to stay here no longer.
> Cho.—Oh, swing low, sweet chariot, etc.

RUST UNIVERSITY, HOLLY SPRINGS, MISS.

I had a little book, an' I read it through,
I got my Jesus as well as you;
   Oh, I got a mother in the promised land.
I hope my mother will feed dem lambs—
   I don't want to stay here no longer.
Cho.—Oh, swing low, sweet chariot, etc.

Oh, some go to church for to holler an' shout,
Before six months they're all turned out—
   I don't want to stay here no longer.
Oh, some go to church for to laugh an' talk,
But dey knows nothin' 'bout dat Christian walk—
   I don't want to stay here no longer.
Cho.—Oh, swing low, sweet chariot, etc.

Oh, shout, shout, de deb'l is about;
Oh, shut your do' an' keep him out—
   I don't want to stay here no longer.
For he is so much-a like-a snaky in de grass,
Ef you don' mind he will get you at las'—
   I don't want to stay here no longer.
Cho.—Oh, swing low, sweet chariot, etc.

VIEW DE LAND.

I'm born of God, I know I am—View de land, view de land!
And you deny it if you can—Go view de heav'nly land.
I want to go to heaven when I die—View de land, view de land!
To shout salvation as I fly—Go view de heav'nly land.

  Chorus.—
    Oh, 'way over Jordan—View de land, view de land!
    'Way over Jordan—Go view de heavenly land.

What kind of shoes is dem-a you wear? View de land, etc.
Dat you can walk upon the air? Go view, etc.
Dem shoes I wear are de Gospel shoes—View the land, etc.
An' you can wear dem ef-a you choose—Go view, etc.—Cho.

Der' is a tree in paradise—View the land, etc.
De Christian he call it de tree ob life—Go view, etc.
I spects to eat de fruit right off o' dat tree—View de land, etc.
Ef busy old Satan will let-a me be—Go view, etc.—Cho.

You say yer Jesus set-a you free—View de land, etc.
Why don't you let-a your neighbor be? Go view, etc.

You say you're aiming for de skies—View de land, etc.
Why don't you stop-a your telling lies?   Go view, etc.—Cho.

OH, YES.

Ef eber I land on de oder sho'—Oh, yes!
I'll neber come here for to sing no more—Oh, yes!
A golden band all round my waist,
An' de palms of victory in my hand,
An' de golden slippers on to my feet—
Gwine to walk up an' down o' dem golden street.

> Chorus.—Oh, wait till I put on my robe—
>> Wait till I put on my robe. Oh, yes! Oh, yes⸵

An', my lobely bretherin, dat ain't all—Oh, yes
I'm not done a-talkin' about my Lord.
An' a golden crown a-placed on-a my head,
An' my long white robe a-come a-dazzlin' down;
Now wait till I get on my Gospel shoes,
Gwine to walk about de heaven an' a-carry de news.—Cho.

I'm anchored in Christ, Christ anchored in me—Oh, yes!
All de debils in hell can't a-pluck me out;
An' I wonder what Satan's grumbling about.
He's bound into hell, an' he can't git out,
But he shall be loose and hab his sway—
Yea, at de great resurrection day.—Cho.

I went down de hillside to make a-one prayer—Oh, yes!
An' when I got dere Ole Satan was dere—Oh, yes!
An' what do you t'ink he said to me? Oh, yes!
Said, "Off from here you'd better be."   Oh, yes!
And what for to do I did not know—Oh, yes!
But I fell on my knees and I cried 'Oh, Lord!'—Oh, yes!
Now, my Jesus bein' so good an' kind,
Yea, to the with-er-ed, halt, and blind—
My Jesus lowered His mercy down,
An' snatch-a me from a-dem doors ob hell.
He a-snatch-a me from dem doors ob hell,
An' took-a me in a-wid him to dwell.—Cho.

I was in de church an' prayin' loud,
An' on my knees to Jesus bowed;
Ole Satan tole me to my face

"I'll git you when-a you leave dis place."
Oh, brother, dat scare me to my heart,
I was 'fraid to walk-a when it was dark.—Cho.

I started home, but I did pray,
An' I met ole Satan on de way;
Ole Satan made a-one grab at me,
But he missed my soul an' I went free.
My sins went a-lumberin' down to hell,
An' my soul went a-leaping up Zion's hill.
I tell ye what, bretherin, you'd better not laugh,
Ole Satan'll run you down his path;
If he runs you as he run me
You'll be glad to fall upon your knee.

    Chorus.—Oh, wait till I put on my robe.
          Wait till I put on my robe—Oh, yes! Oh, yes!

MY LORD DELIVERED DANIEL.

    I met a pilgrim on de way,
    An' I ask him whar he's a gwine.
    I'm bound for Canaan's happy land,
    An' dis is de shouting band.   Go on!

Chorus.—My Lord delibered Daniel,
         My Lord delibered Daniel,
         My Lord delibered Daniel—
         Why can't he deliber me?

    Some say dat John de Baptist
    Was nothing but a Jew;
    But de Bible doth inform us
    Dat he was a preacher, too.—Yes, he was!
Chorus.—My Lord delibered Daniel, etc.

    Oh, Daniel cast in the lions' den,
    He pray both night and day;
    De angel came from Galilee,
    And lock de lions' jaw.   Dat's so.
Chorus.—My Lord delibered Daniel, etc.

    He delibered Daniel from de lions' den,
    Jonah from de belly ob de whale,
    An' de Hebrew children from de fiery furnace—
    An' why not ebery man?   Oh, yes!
Chorus.—My Lord delibered Daniel, etc.

De richest man dat eber I saw
Was de one dat beg de most;
His soul was filled wid Jesus,
An' wid de Holy Ghost.   Yes, it was.
Chorus.—My Lord delibered Daniel, etc.

NOBODY KNOWS THE TROUBLE I'VE SEEN.

Sometimes I'm up, sometimes I'm down—Oh, yes, Lord.
Sometimes I'm almost to de groun'—Oh, yes, Lord.
Although you see me goin' long so—Oh, yes, Lord.
I have my trials here below.—Oh, yes, Lord.
Chorus.—Oh, nobody knows de trouble I've seen,
      Nobody knows but Jesus;
      Nobody knows de trouble I've seen—
      Glory Hallelujah!

One day when I was walkin' along—Oh, yes, Lord.
De element opened, an' de love came down—Oh, yes, Lord.
I never shall forget dat day—Oh, yes, Lord.
When Jesus washed my sins away.—Oh, yes, Lord.
Chorus.—Oh, nobody knows the trouble, etc.

HAIL ! HAIL ! HAIL !

Oh, look up yander, what I see—
  I'm on my journey home;
Bright angels comin' arter me—
  I'm on my journey home.
Chorus.—Children, hail! hail! hail!
    I'm gwine jine saints above;
    Hail! hail! hail!
    I'm on my journey home.

If you git dere before I do—
  I'm on my journey home;
Look out for me, I'm comin' too—
  I'm on my journey home.
Chorus.—Children, hail! etc.

Oh, hallelujah to de Lamb!
  I'm on my journey home;
King Jesus died for ebery man—
  I'm on my journey home.
Chorus.—Children, hail! etc.

SCRIPTURAL REMINISCENCES.

Aunt Patty: "Bress me, Uncle Abum, ef yer doesn't call to mind Baalam gwine down ter J'rusalem."

Uncle Abram (with a weakness for Aunt Patty): "Yaas, and does yer 'member dar stood an angel in de way?"

WISE SAYINGS—"MULTUM IN PARVO."

"Long ha'r don't hide de brand on de horse."

"Muddy roads call de mile-post a liar."

"'Tis hard to make clo'es fit a miserbul man."

"De stopper gits de longes' res' in de empty jug."

"De church bells sometimes do better wuk dan de sermon."

"Some o' de wus lookin' animals at de county fa'r got to pay to get in."

"De price ob your hat ain't de medjer ob your brain."

"Ef your coat-tail cotch a-fire, don't wait till you kin see de blaze 'fo' you put it out."

"De graveyard is de cheapes' boardin'-house."

"Dar's a fam'ly coolness 'twix' de mule an' de single-tree."

"It pesters a man dreadful when he git mad an' don' know who to cuss."

"Buyin' on credit is robbin' next 'ear's crop."

"Chris'mas without holiday is like a candle without a wick."

" De crawfish in a hurry look like he tryin' to git dar yistiddy."

" Lean houn' lead de pack when de rabbit in sight."

" Little flakes make de deepes' snow."

" Knot in de plank will show froo de whitewash."

" A short yardstick is a po' thing to fight de debbul wid."

" Dirt show de quickes' on de cleanes' cotton."

" De candy-pullin' kin call louder dan de log-rollin'."

" De bes' apple float on de top o' de peck medjer."

" De right sort o' 'ligion heaps de half-bushel."

" De steel hoe dat laughs at de iron one is like de man dat is 'shamed o' his grand-daddy."

" A mule kin tote so much goodness in his face dat he don't hab none lef' for his hind legs."

" Some grabble walks may lead to de jail."

" De cow-bell can't keep a secret."

" Ripe apples make de tree look taller."

" De red rose don't brag in de dark."

" Blind horse knows when de trough empty."

" De noise of de wheels don't medjer de load in de wagon."

" Las' 'ear's hot spell cools off mighty fast."

" Little hole in your pocket is wusser'n a big one at de knee."

" Appetite don't reggerlate de time o' day."

" De quagmire don't hang out no sign."

" One pusson kin th'ead a needle better than two."

" De pint o' de pin is de easiest en' to find."

" De green top don't medjer de price o' de turnup."

" Muzzle on de yard dog unlocks de smokehouse."

" 'Tis hard for de bes' an' smartes' folks in de wul' to git 'long widout a little tech o' good luck."

" De billy-goat gits in his hardes' licks when he looks like he gwine to back out o' de fight."

Miss Anita Hemming, tall, brunette, and graceful, was one of the graduates at Vassar in 1897, and, although the world did not know it, there was then enacted a great scene, showing the advance of woman into the life-giving but long-forgotten precept that all men are born free and equal. This young woman, who stood side by side with her classmates, keeping pace with them in studies and accomplishments, for four years

EQUAL TO THE EMERGENCY.

Hebe: "Unc Isrul, mammy says, huccome de milk so watery on top in de mornn'?"
Patriarch: "Tell you' mammy dat's de bes' sort o' milk, dat's de dew on it—de cows been layin' in de dew."
Hebe: "An' she tell me to ax you what meck it so blue."
Patriarch: "You ax your mammy what meck she so black!"

kept the secret of her birth from her associates—the secret that blood that marks a race of slaves flowed through her veins. It was just before examination when the faculty, to their utter astonishment, learned that into that stately and exclusive institution an alien race had gained admission. To this school for young ladies of the highest circle of society this modest, studious, refined young lady had gained admission without making known the secret of her birth. The question for the faculty to decide was a hard one. The girl, in deportment, scholarship, and in every way, was worthy, but yet would the public receive the innovation. After due consideration the young woman, whose only fault lay in the accident of her birth, was informed that she would be allowed to graduate with her class.

Then the girls of the finishing class heard the story. Some of them were from the proudest old families of the South, but they took her hands with right good comradeship, and the real ordeal for her had passed.

Miss Hemming stood among her associates at commencement in her simple white gown, a mark for many eyes. Her dark hair, with its burnished waves, was brushed back from her low, broad brow; a deep flush burned in her cheeks, and she was fairer than many of the blue-blooded girls around her. Then she went out into the world. But the attitude taken by Vassar's august faculty could not be ignored, and the young alumnus of 1897 gained the position of assistant in the Boston public library.

Fred Douglass.—In the course of an address made to a colored school in Talbot county, Maryland, where he was born a slave, Frederick Douglass said: "I once knew a little colored boy, whose father and mother died when he was six years old. He was a slave, and had no one to care for him. He slept on a dirt floor in a hovel, and in cold weather would crawl into a meal bag, headforemost, and leave his feet in the ashes to keep them warm. Often he would roast an ear of corn and eat it to satisfy his hunger, and many times has he crawled under the barn or stable and secured eggs, which he would roast in the fire and eat.

This boy did not wear pants, like you do, but a tow linen shirt. Schools were unknown to him, and he learned to spell from an old Webster's spelling book, and to read and write from posters on cellars and barn doors, while boys and men would help him. He would then preach and speak, and soon became well known. He became presidential elector, United states marshal, United States recorder, United States diplomat, and accumulated some wealth. He wore broadcloth, and didn't have to divide crumbs with the dogs under the table. That boy was Frederick Douglass.

What was possible for me is possible for you. Don't think because you are colored you can't accomplish anything. Strive earnestly to add to your knowledge. So long as you remain in ignorance, so long will you fail to command the respect of your fellow men.''

Fred Douglass.—Fred Douglass has said that President Lincoln was the only white man with whom he ever associated in this country who did not make him feel that he was colored and a supposed inferior, and that only in England and on the continent among the Caucasians had he been permitted to realize that he was a man and an equal.

Everything Must Go.—In a lecture by Rev. William

Johnson, illustrating the law that "everything must go," he gives the following: "A minister told me that he fell in love with his wife at first sight, and married after six months' acquaintance. 'But,' said he, 'during that whole time I went to see her every day. At four o'clock I was always there.' Some young men do not choose that delightful hour to visit, but go later. One young man lingered at the gate after a long visit, and the girl began to cry. He said, 'Dear, don't cry; I will come to see you again.' But she cried on. 'O, darling, don't cry so; I will be sure to come again.' Still she cried. At last he said: 'Love, did I not tell you that I would soon come again to see you?' And through her tears she replied: 'Yes, but I am afraid you never will go; that is what is the matter with me.' We must all go."

In the same lecture on the subject of practical philosophy, he gives the following:

"Uncle Jim was once asked a great question. It was: 'If you had to be blown up which would you choose, to be blown up on the railroad or the steamboat?' 'Well,' said Uncle Jim, 'I don't want to be blowed up no way; but if I had to be blowed up I would rather be blowed up on de railroad, because, you see, if you is blowed up on de railroad, dar you is, but if you is blowed up oh de steamboat, whar is you?' He was practical in his philosophy."

Faithful Service Rewarded.—On July 10, 1897, Alexander B. Williamson, colored, of Memphis, Tennessee, didn't have a cent that he could call his own. July 11 he went to the probate judge, J. S. Galloway, and qualified to take possession of a fortune valued at $45,000, that had been left him under the will of the late Mrs. Clara Mariani. This is the reward the Negro gets for a lifetime of devotion to duty in the service of the family of the woman who has just died. He has for years been in charge of the affairs of Mrs. Mariani, and has always been found honest, diligent and peculiarly trustworthy. She gave him credit for having done much to make the fortune she left behind, and as she had no relatives living to whom she could leave her property, she thought it was only just that it should go to this faithful servant.

Mr. Moody.—When Mr. Moody was preaching in Washington, he asserted that if Jesus Christ should return to this world in person and appear in that city the people would not consent to be governed by him. He asked the audience if they would receive him, and to emphasize the assertion, he appealed to an aged Negro man sitting near the pulpit. "Would you vote for him?" The reply came promptly, "It would do no good; they wouldn't count my vote."

A Negro Huckster was driving his wagon through the streets of Richmond, yelling at the top of his voice, "'Tatoes, 'tatoes!" A black woman standing at a gate said to him: "Hush yo' mouf, nigger, an' stop makin' such a fuss!" "Yo' he'rd me then?" he said. "He'rd yo'! I could hear yo' a mile!" "That is why I am yelling," said he. 'Tatoes! 'tatoes!"

THE FUNERAL.

I was walking in Savannah, past a church decayed and dim,
When there slowly through the window came a plaintive funeral
    hymn;
And a sympathy awakened and a wonder quickly grew
Till I found myself environed in a little Negro pew.

Out in front a colored couple sat in sorrow, nearly wild,
On the altar was a coffin, in the coffin was a child.
I could picture him when living—curly hair, protruding lip—
And had seen perhaps a thousand in my hurried Southern trip.

But no baby ever rested in the soothing arms of death
That had fanned more flames of sorrow with his fluttering breath;
And no funeral ever glistened with more sympathy profound
Than was in the chain of tear drops that enclasped those mourn-
ers round.

Rose a sad old colored preacher at the little wooden desk.
With a manner grandly awkward, with a countenance grotesque;
With simplicity and shrewdness on his Ethiopian face,
With the ignorance and wisdom of a crushed, undying race.

And he said, " Now don' be weepin' for dis pretty bit o' clay—
For de little boy who lived there he done gone an' run away!
He was doin' very finely, an' he 'preciate your love,
But his sure 'nuff Father want him in de large house up above.

" Now He didn't give you dat baby, by a hundred thousand mile!
He just think you need some sunshine, an' He lend it for a while!
An' He let you keep 'an' love him till your heart was bigger
grown;
An' dese silver tears you're sheddin's just de interest on de loan.

" Here yer oder pretty chillun!—Don't be makin' it appear
Dat your love got sort o' 'nopolized by this little fellow here.
Don't pile up too much sorrows on deir little mental shelves,
So's to kind o' set 'em wonderin' if dey're no account demselves!

" Just you think, you poor deah mounahs, creepin' 'long o'er
sorrow's way,
What a blessed little picnic dis yere baby's got to-day!
Your good faders and good moders crowd de little fellow round
In de angel-tended garden in de Big Plantation Ground!

" An' dey ask him, ' Was your feet sore?' an' take off his little
shoes.
An' dey wash him, an' dey kiss him, an' dey say, ' Now, what's
de news?'
An de Lord done cut his tongue loose, den de little fellow say,
' All our folks down in de valley tries to keep de hebbenly way.'

" An' his eyes dey brightly sparkle at de pretty tings he view;
Den a tear come, an' he whisper, ' But I want my parents, too!'
But de angel Chief Musician teach dat boy a little song—
Says, ' If only dey be faithful, dey will soon be comin' 'long.'

"An' he'll get an education dat will probably be worth
Seberal times as much as any you cou_d buy for him on earth;
He'll be in de Lawd's big schoolhouse, widout no contempt or fear,
While dere's no end to de bad things might have happened to
    him here.

"So, my poor, dejected, mounahs, let your hearts wid Jesus rest,
An' don't go to criticisin' dat ar One wot knows de best!
But have sent us many comforts He have right to take away—
Te de Lawd be praise an' glory, now an' ever!   Let us pray."
                    —Will M. Carleton.

A LULLABY.

Bedtime's come fu' little boys,
    Po' little lamb.
Too tiahed out to make a noise,
    Po' little lamb.
You gwine t' have to-morrer sho'?
Yes, you tole me dat befo',
Don't you fool me, chile, no mo',
    Po' little lamb.

You been bad de livelong day,
    Po' little lamb.
Th'owin' stones an' runnin' 'way,
    Po little lamb.
My, but you's a-runnin' wild!
Look jes' lak some po' folks' chile;
Mam gwine whup you atter while,
    Po' little lamb.

Come hyeah! you mos' tiahed to def,
    Po' little lamb.
Played yo'sel' clean out o' bref,
    Po little lamb.
See dem han's now—sich a sight!
Would you evah b'lieve dey's white?
Stan' still 'twell I wash dem right,
    Po' little lamb.

Jes' cain't hol' yo' haid up straight,
    Po' little lamb.
Hadn't oughter played so late
    'Po' little lamb.

"A stitch in time saves nine"
Copyright 1895 by Russell Bros—

Mammy do' know whut she'd do,
Ef de chillun's all lak you;
You's a caution now, fu' true,
    Po' little lamb.

Lay yo' haid down in my lap,
    Po' little lamb.
Y'ought to have a right good slap,
    Po' little lamb.
You been runnin' roun' a heap.
Shet dem eyes an' don't you peep—
Dah now, dah now, go to sleep—
    Po' little lamb.

            —Paul Lawrence Dunbar.

WHEN THE WARM DAYS COME.

When the warm days come, an' the green is all around,
An' the bushes are noddin' to their shadders on the ground;
When the meader lark is singin' 'round its nest hid in the grass,
An' the brown thrush is a-swingin' 'mongst the thorn an' sassa-
    fras.

When the Juneberry's in blossom, tho' the oak tree still is bare;
When the blows are all a-fallin' from the cherry an' the pear;
When the orchard is in blossom, an' the roads are gittin' dry
An' the lilacs are a-flirtin' with the lazy butterfly.

When the world is full of sunshine, an' workin' seems a sin,
An' you don't want to do nothin' but jest sit an' soak it in;
When the very fields look sleepy from the wild bee's drowsy hum,
An' the birds all go to matin', when the warm days come.

THANKSGIVING IN DIXIE.

Now de fros' am in de meader,
    An' we's habin' chilly weader,
An' de owel air a hootin' ter de moon,
    An 'de cotton 'pears to thickin,
    Atter ebery curful pickin',
An' de bossman call de niggers good an' soon.

    Fur de lighted knot air burnin',
    An' de cider mill air turnin',
An' de taters air all ready futter roas'.

An' de possum he's er feelin'
Of de 'simmon's juicy peelin',
Whattle make him fat and fitten futter roas'.

An de sunshine's pale an' saller,
An' de leaves air turnin yaller'
An' de turkey gobbler gobbleth in de lan';
An' de pound cake air a bakin',
An de fat'nin' pigs er quakin',
For Thanksgivin' Day air mighty close at han'.

Hit's de day 'at saint an' sinner
Has good eatin's fur his dinner,
An' thanks de Lord 'at's kep' him safe an' soun'.
An' I hopes de sin confessin's
An' de Heabenly Father's blessin's
Will be plentiful enough to go er roun'.

—Ellen Frizell Wycoft.

DAT THANKSGIVIN' TURKEY.

Turkey gobbler, proud and fat,
Scratchin' grabble like a cat—
Now he don't know where he's at—
    Oh, dat wishbone!
Scratchin' grabble wid his feet,
Dat's what makes such tender meat.
Golly! ain't he plump and sweet—
    Sweet wishbone!

Now's de snowflakes in de sky,
Co'n pones costin' mighty high,
I must make dese feathers fly—
    Oh, dat wishbone!
Lightwood fire de cabin cheer—
Turkey, now we're glad you's here,
Thanksgivin' come but once a year—
    Sweet wishbone!

A colored philosopher is reported to have said: "Life, my bredden, am mos'ly made up of prayin' for rain an' then wishin' it would cl'ar off."

A Figurative Prayer.—A white minister was conducting revival services in a colored church in North

Carolina.   After exhorting a bit he asked an old colored deacon to lead in prayer.   According to the
Roanoke *News*, this is the appeal which the brother in
black offered for his brother in white:

"O Lord, gib him de eye ob de eagle, det he spy out
sin afar off.   Wav his hands to de gospel plow.   Tie
his tongue to de line ob truth.   Nail his ear to de
gospel pole.   Bow his head 'way down between his
knees, and his knees way down in some lonesome, dark
and narrer valley where prayer is much wanted to be
made.   'Noint him wid de kerosene ile of salvation,
and sot him on fire."

The above is matched by the white clergyman in a
northern town, who warned his hearers lately "not to
walk in a slippery path lest they be sucked, maelstrom-
like, into its meshes!"   This metaphor suggests that
of another clergyman who prayed "that the word
might be as a nail driven in a sure place, sending its
roots downward and its branches upward."

WHEN DE CO'N PONE'S HOT.

Dey is times in life when Nature
  Seems to slip a cog an' go,
Jes' a-rattlin' down creation,
  Lak an ocean's overflow;
When de worl' jes' stahts' a-spinnin'
  Lak a picaninny's top,
An' yo' cup o' joy is brimmin'
  'Twell it seems about to slop,
An' you feel jes' lak a racah
  Dat is trainin' fu' to trot—
When yo' mammy ses de blessin'
  An' de co'n pone's hot.

When you set down at de table,
  Kin' o' weary lak an' sad,
An' you'se jes' a little tiahed,
  An' purhaps a little mad;

How yo' gloom tu'ns into gladness,
    How yo' joy drives out de doubt,
When de oven do' is opened
    An' de smell comes po'in' out!
Why, de 'lectric light o' Heaven
    Seems to settle on de spot,
When yo' mammy ses de blessin'
    An de co'n pone's hot.

When de cabbage pot is steamin
    An' de bacon's good an' fat,
When de chittlin's is a-sputter'n'
    So's to show yo' whah dey's at;
Take away yo' sody biscuit,
    Take away yo' cake and pie,
Fu' de glory time is comin',
    An' it's 'proachin' very nigh,
An' yo' want to jump an' hollah,
    Do' you know you'd bettah not,
When yo' mammy ses de blessin'
    An' de co'n pone's hot.

I have heerd o' lots o' sermons,
    An' I've heerd o' lots o' prayers;
An' I've listened to some singin'
    Dat has tuk me up de stairs
Of de Glory Lan', an' sent me
    Jes' below de Mahster's th'one,
An' have lef' my haht a-singin'
    In a happy aftah tone;
But dem wu's so sweetly murmured
    Seem to tech de softes' spot,
When my mammy ses de blessin'
    An' de co'n pone's hot.

                    —*Paul Lawrence Dunbar.*

CHAPTER XVI.

Just Judgment.—It is frequently the case that we judge by our immediate surroundings. Upon these surroundings will depend our decisions, whether pessimistic or optimistic in sentiment. It were better for us as individuals, as well as a people, if more frequently we were to permit ourselves to take a wider range, both as to extent and as to time.

Compare, if you will, the condition of the Negro race half a century ago with that of today, and the most despondent must dismiss his fears and acknowledge the progress so marked.

Then and Now.—Then the Negro was a piece of property; now he is an American citizen.

Then chains and the lash and hounds were sending a constant terror to the heart of the poor slave; now the most humble of the race may claim the ballot and protection from wrongs under the law of the state.

Then the Negro had no rights that the white man need respect; now the Negro and the white man are equal before the law.

Education.—Then it was thought that the Negro could not learn; now he has demonstrated that such thoughts were born of ignorance and prejudice.

Then there were laws against Negro education; now laws adorn our statute books that require the education of the black man.

Then there was not a school for the Negro; now there are more than twenty-five thousand schools.

Then a Negro teacher was an impossibility; now twenty-five thousand Negro teachers are instructing the youth of the race.

Then the number of Negroes that could read were easily counted; now it requires a census-taker to inform us that four millions have learned to read and write.

Then there were no Negroes in our public schools; now there are over a million being instructed in them.

Then there was gross darkness of ignorance throughout all the realms of the race; now the light of intelligence has pierced these clouds and illumined the minds of thousands, who find a black skin no impediment to broad scholarship and astute and clear-sighted comprehension.

Then the conception of a college or professional school for Negroes would have been regarded the product of a demented brain; now colleges and universities, medical schools and schools of law for the colored race are freely dotted on the map of our Southland.

Then the charming Negro melodies were unknown; now the Fisk Jubilee Singers, the Tennesseeans and the Hamptons have sung the fame of the Negro around the world.

Religion.—Then the colored man, naturally inclined to religion, had neither churches nor preachers; now there are thousands of colored churches, owning nearly twenty millions of property, with a membership of nearly four millions, besides publishing houses and a number of religious educational institutions wholly controlled by colored men.

Home.—Then the Negro had no place that to him would express one of the most endearing words in the language; now a great multitude can truly say, "There is no place like home."

Social and Family Ties.—Then these sacred ties were ruthlessly broken by the auction block; now no power, aside from the individuals themselves can sunder these ties while life remains.

Financial.—Then the Negro owned no foot of land, nor property of any kind; now his accumulations are rated at three hundred millions.

Unanswerable.—Behold this array of contrasted facts, undisputed and unsurpassed. Who will deny that they furnish an unanswerable argument of progression in all lines. Mark the long column of America's dark sons moving steadily and surely up the hill of progress, removing one by one the obstacles impeding the onward step and spirit of advancement of the age.

Then, although with the unthinking and unreflecting multitude you may say, "It does not move," your better judgment and nobler self asserting its rights with the Galileo of old, must exclaim, "Nevertheless, it moves."

True Condition.—We are not blind to the true condition of the race. When we assert that great progress has been made by the race, we would not have it understood that the race as a whole has caught this spirit of progress. This is not the case; there are thousands today who are removed but a step above slavery. The means at hand and the short period of time that has elapsed since emancipation have not permitted the work to be as general as might be wished.

Our Position.—We must emphatically assert that, considering circumstances, the Negro has made remarkable progress. The work still remaining to be done is great and large, but, noting advantages, the Negro compares favorably with any race. Just judgment demands that in considering the lower, ignorant, immoral class among the blacks, we must not overlook the same condition among the whites who have had the benefit of centuries of civilization. Point one hand to the awful condition of the lower classes of the Negro and with the other you may single out similar conditions among the slums of our large cities and other places where the refuse of Europe's depraved classes are dumped in masses upon our shores. Mark, also, the fact that alleged immorality among Negro women is largely due to the immorality of white men. Then will the Christ spirit labor for elevation of man as man, without regard to the color of his skin.

The Present Status.—The present status of the Negro is such as is highly commendable. Paying taxes upon $300,000,000 worth of property throughout this country, occupying offices of high trust and honor as national gifts, educating his children, accumulating wealth, and advancing in every line of industry, the Negro has need to congratulate himself and praise his Maker for such full and free benedictions so copiously showered upon him the past dark and stormy thirty years.

Leaders.—"Talks for the Times" says: "At the close of the war, the Negro found himself in the condition of a man who wakes up out of sleep in the midst of a dream in which all things seemed strange and confused. It took him some time to adjust himself to the new state of affairs. He was restless; he could hardly realize that he was free. As the impotent man, sitting at the gate of the temple, when healed by Peter, not only praised God, but walked and leaped to satisfy himself of the genuineness of his cure, so the Negro, to test his freedom, began to move about. His movements, at first, were individual, then general, as leaders sprang into existence; and it is really remarkable how many are the leaders when the masses are ignorant. For the first ten or twelve years after the war, nothing was more common in the South than leaders. Every little politician, every crank, constituted himself a Moses to lead the Negro somewhere; and various were their cries. One cried, 'On to Arkansas!' and another 'On to Texas!' and another 'On to Africa!' and each one had a following more or less. One man told me that he had succeeded in leading away from South Carolina and Georgia to Arkansas and Texas 25,000 persons.''

Levers That Move the World.—Professor Harris says: "The most powerful men of the world are not those who control the markets, but they who control the hearts and direct the thoughts of their fellow men. Jesus Christ, in His life and teachings, has left us a much richer legacy than if He had turned every stone of Judea into a nugget of gold; than if He had forecast all the inventions of all the ages and had made the streams of Palestine resonant with the hum of factory wheels, had lighted up the streets of Jerusalem with the electric light, and had enabled Herod to talk with Augustus Cæsar by means of the telephone. Homer, singing his Iliad, while begging his bread; poor blind Milton, in his Paradise Lost; the thinker, Bunyan, in his Pilgrim's Progress; Carlyle, writing his Heroes and Hero Worship, with only a silver spoon between him and the wolf at the door, have made the world far richer and happier and better than they ever could have done had they devoted their lives to the amassing of wealth. These are the men who hold the levers that move the world. Their influence is far deeper and longer lasting than that of any Wall street broker or railroad king. These are the men who fashion the lives and determine the character of generations to come. These are the men to whom the world looks for hope in time of despair, and light in time of darkness. They are the very salt of our civilization, and without the impulse, the hope and the inspiration which we gather from them and their lives, we should relapse into barbarism. Let us imitate them.

Warfare Against Wrong.—As Hannibal, almost as soon as he was born into the world, was made to swear eternal warfare against Rome, so should the educated, Christian young men of our race, as soon as they are born into the Kingdom of God, dedicate themselves to a life-long warfare against the degradation and wrongs of our people. As Cato was so possessed by the sense of danger that threatened Rome from Carthage that he ended all of his speeches with "Carthage must be destroyed," so should the educated young men of our race be so possessed with a sense of the dangers that are not only coming to us from without, but are also existing within, that the remedy for these evils should be the keynote of every song, the burden of every prayer, and the theme of every address.

A Hundred Men.—Dr. Josiah Strong is authority for the statement that at one time Napoleon Bonaparte wanted one hundred men to do a piece of strategic work. In calling for a hundred volunteers, he explained to his regiment that although ultimate victory would be secured, every one of those one hundred men would be instantly killed. Notwithstanding this warning of certain death, not only one hundred soldiers, but the whole regiment, down to a man, stepped forward and offered themselves to the Emperor's service.

Arouse to Action.—If one man, like Napoleon Bonaparte, could waken such enthusiasm among his soldiers that they were willing to die for him, how much more should the condition and needs of our people awaken a similar enthusiasm among us? How much more should we be aroused to action by the pitiable condition of our race—by their moral degradation, by their intellectual poverty, and by their wrongs which cry day and night unto the God of heaven for vengeance. How much more should we be moved by that large army of rag-clad, husk-fed, unwashed, disease-breeding colored people, so ignorant that, like the Ninevites, they do not know their right hand from their left, and by that nearly two hundred who are lynched every year, men who are "butchered" by midnight revelers, "to make for them a Roman holiday?"

Just Tribute.—Dr. Haygood says: "With all his faults and imperfections, many of them cruelly exaggerated by caricaturists and sensational writers, I bear this testimony to the Negro preacher in the South: Life would be much harder there without him. With rare exceptions, they have been found on the side of law and order, and in our days of distress and storm they were, as a class, conservators of the peace. There are some shocking exceptions. They have urged their people to send their children to school, and have been useful in a thousand ways. The tens who fall into disgrace and sin are widely advertised; the hundreds who simply do their duty are unknown to the newspaper world. I have seen them in their many religious moods; in their most death-like trances, and in their wildest outbreaks of excitement. I have preached to them in town and country and on the plan-

tations.   I have been their pastor, have led their classes
and prayer meetings, conducted their love feasts and
taught them the catechism.   I have married them,
baptized their children and buried their dead.   In the
reality of religion among them I have the most entire
confidence, nor can I ever doubt it while it is a reality
to me.   In many things their motions may be crude,
their conceptions of truth realistic, sometimes to a
painful, sometimes to a grotesque, degree.   They are
more emotional than ethical.

"Strongest Characteristic.—The average of their
morals is not high; they do many things they ought
not; nevertheless, their religion is their most striking
and important, their strongest and their most formative characteristic.   They are more remarkable here
than anywhere else; their religion has had more to do
in shaping their better character in this country than
all other influences combined; it will most determine
what they are to become in their future development.
It is wrong to condemn them harshly when judged by
the standard white people hardly dare apply to
themselves with their two thousand years the start of
them.   The just God did not judge half-barbarous
Israel, wandering in the twilight about the wilderness
of Sinai, as he judges us on whom the sun of righteousness has risen with the full light of the Gospel
day.''

Unparalled.—The history of the Negro on this continent is full of pathetic and tragic romance, and of
startling, unparalleled incident.   The seizure in Africa,
the forcible abduction and cruel exportation, the coer-
cive enslavement, the subjection to environments which
emasculate a race of all noble aspirations and doom
inevitably to hopeless ignorance and inferiority, living

in the midst of enlightenments and noblest civilization, and yet forbidden to enjoy the benefits of which others were partakers, for four years amid battle, and yet, for the most part, having no personal share in the conflict, by statute and organic law of nations held in fetters and inequality, and then, in the twinkling of an eye, lifted from bondage to freedom, from slavery to citizenship, from dependence on others and guardianship to suffrage and eligibility to office, can be predicated of no other race. Other peoples, after long and weary years of discipline and struggle against heaviest odds, have won liberty and free government. This race, almost without lifting a hand, unappreciative of the boon except in the lowest aspects of it, and unprepared for privileges and responsibilities, has been lifted to a plane of citizenship and freedom such as is enjoyed, in an equal degree, by no people in the world outside of the United States.

Thought.—Professor H. T. Kealing, A. M., editor of the A. M. E. Church *Review* recently said: "One does not begin to be a man till he rises above physical sensation into thought realms. Man should feel the mind and soul as well as the body. What a pitiable sight to see a 300-pound body inhabited by a two-ounce mind. The Negro can look for honorable connection with the progress, invention and civilization of the age only by his thought relation to it. It is not sufficient that when a telegraph system is begun we should dig the postholes. It will not give us a place among the great American forces that are threading this country with railroads for us to cut the ties. Muscle is not manhood. Physical size is not greatness. If it were, the elephant is a greater man than man. Thought, power, character, and integrity are the elements we need.

Age of Progress.—"It is not enough to congratulate ourselves on living in an age of progress. If a train is passing through this city, and a passenger in the rear coach hopes to sit still and overtake a passenger in the front coach, his hope will be vain. He must put forth personal locomotion. Now the train of progress is passing through the land. There is a man on the front coach, we call him the white man. There is a man on the rear coach, we call him the black man. We must do something ourselves for ourselves before we enter among the producing forces.

Companionship.—"Give us men who can retrospect the past and project intelligent glances into the future. Make your companionship with Homer, Dante, Darwin, Emerson, and Carlyle.

Confusion.—"Some assert that the Negro is retrograding, and they cite the confusion and unclassified state of our society in proof. But this confusion is to me a strong sign of advancement.

"Suppose two men are asleep in the dirt and mud. There is no confusion there. All is peace—the peace of common filth and lethargy. But suppose one of them attempts to get up. The other insists that he lie still; now arises a struggle; now comes confusion. There was once no confusion among us. We were all down and asleep. Now some of us are getting up, and the struggle is on; but who would not rather have confusion of getting up than the peace of slumber? Rise above adverse circumstances. Be masters of circumstances."

Marvel of Ages.—"Talks for the Times" says: "But it may be well for us now to take a retrospective view of the path we have traveled as freedmen. It is thirty-two years since Abraham Lincoln gave to the world his immortal proclamation.   For thirty-two years we have enjoyed freedom, however imperfect it may have been.   Have we shown ourselves worthy of it?   Thanks be to God, we are not our own judges!   The world has sat in judgment upon us.   Our friends and our enemies have united in the confession that the progress of the American Negro under freedom is one of the marvels of the age.   It has no parallel in the world's history.   National statistics, statistics of states, reports of benevolent organizations, all prove this beyond the shadow of a doubt.   We have written the last thirty-two years of our history in acts.   We have done a great many things which the philosophers prophesied we could not do.   First, it was predicted that we should all die out under freedom, and many simple-minded people slept soundly on that theory until the census of 1880 revealed the startling fact that, instead of dying out, we are increasing fearfully and wonderfully.   It became evident then that, although we are a race of idiots and fools, we are not such fools as to live through American slavery and die out under American freedom—live, forsooth, when we ought to die, and die when we ought to live!   No, no, no, we are not so demented as all that, whatever may be the shape and thickness of our skulls.

The Future.—George Williams aptly says: "But what of the future?   Can the Negro endure the sharp competition of American civilization?   Can he keep his position against the tendencies to amalgamation?   Since it has been proven that the Negro is not dying out, but, on the contrary, possesses the powers of reproduction to a remarkable degree, a new source of danger has been discovered.   It is said that the Negro will perish, will be absorbed by the dominant race ere long; that where races are crossed the inferior race suffers; and that mixed races lack the power to reproduce species, and that hence the disappearance of the Negro is but a question of time.

Perished.—Whatever merit this view possessed before the war of the Rebellion, it is obsolete under the present organization of society. The environment of the Negro, the downward tendencies of his social life, and the exposed state in which slave laws left him, have all perished. In addition to his aptitude for study and capacity for improvement, he is now under the protecting and restraining influence of congenial climate; and pure sociological laws will impart to his offspring the power of reproduction and the ability to maintain an excellent social footing with the other races of the world.

Race Prejudice.—Race prejudice is bound to give way before the potent influences of character, education and wealth. Without wealth there can be no leisure, without leisure there can be no thought, and without thought there can be no progress.

Twofold.—The future work of the Negro is twofold; subjective and objective. Years will be devoted to his own education and improvement here in America He will sound the depths of education, accumulate wealth, and then turn his attention to the civilization of Africa. The United States will yet establish a line of steamships between this country and the Dark Continent. Touching at the grain coast, the ivory coast, and the gold coast, America will carry the African missionaries, Bibles, papers, improved machinery, instead of rum and chains. And Africa, in return, will send America indigo, palm-oil, ivory, gold, diamonds, costly wood, and her richest treasures, instead of slaves. Tribes will be converted to Christianity; cities will rise; states will be founded; geography and science will enrich and enlarge their discoveries; and a telegraph cable binding the heart of Africa to the ear of the civilized world, every throb of joy or sorrow will pulsate again in millions of souls. In the interpretation of History, the plans of God must be discerned, "For a thousand years in Thy sight are but as yesterday when it is passed, and as a watch in the night."

Advancement.—Doctor Carroll says: "What he has done for himself under great difficulties and discouragements in the last third of the nineteenth century is a splendid prophecy of what he will be in the twentieth century. He has quickly learned that superior position is open to him in just the same terms as to any other citizen, and that if he would have his superiority recognized he must demonstrate it. Prejudice cannot withstand demonstration. It must yield, however, slowly; and colored statesmen, merchants, bankers, lawyers, doctors, ministers, educators, will win their way by forces which are not an accident of race or color, but are developed by culture.

Difficulties.—The strong, senseless, but galling prejudices which confront the Negro are by no means his greatest obstacles to success. There are ignorance, vice and thriftlessness, which, like their opposite virtues, are not confined to a particular race, but beset humanity in general. He has shown that he has the power to rise above the condition of a slave, and I look confidently forward to a brilliant future for him. I have no idea that he will leave this country. His greatest achievements will be here on the soil that is as much his as ours. Here are found the conditions which are needed for his development, and here he will stay to contribute his share to the prosperity and glory of our great nation. I should expect to see a larger immigration from Africa in the twentieth century than emigration to Africa."

Evangelization.—It is not his duty to evangelize Africa. The responsibility for that great work rests on Christians in every nation. He will simply take his part in it. We may expect it will be a large part. His zeal will be great, his qualifications unquestionable, and we may hope that the redemption of his own race in the Dark Continent will stimulate his heartiest endeavors and his largest sacrifices.

Possibilities.—We see in him as a free man excellencies and possibilities to which slavery made us blind. He has struggled against our doubts and fears, and has fairly conquered our long-lived, pertinacious prejudices. Many, even of those who wanted him to be free and gave him their sympathy, had grave misgivings as to his capacity for the highest duties of citizenship. He has had to prove, since the war, that schools and educational processes are of use to him. The first teachers who came South to instruct him were eagerly questioned as to his ability to learn. When this doubt was satisfied, another was expressed: Was not his ability to learn exceptional? Was the higher education possible to any of his race? We feel a sense of shame in simply recounting the historical fact; but it is a fact, and the greatest achievement of the Negro of the nineteenth century is in forcing from us the acknowledgment of his large capacity.

Ability Must Be Recognized.—Professor Booker T. Washington says: "The race problem will work itself out in proportion as the black man, by reason of his skill, intelligence and character, can produce something that the white man wants or respects. One race respects another in proportion as it contributes to the markets of the world, hence the value of industrial training. The black man that has mortgages on a dozen white men's homes will have no trouble in voting. The black man that spends $10,000 a year in freight charges can select his own seat in a railroad car, else a Pullman palace car will be put on for him. When the black man, by reason of his knowledge of the chemistry of the soil and improved methods of agriculture, can produce forty bushels of corn on any acre of land, while his white brother produces only twenty bushels, the white man will come to the black man to learn, and they will be good friends. The black man that has $50,000 to lend will never want for friends and customers among his white neighbors. It is right and important that all the privileges of the Constitution should be ours; but it is vastly more important to us that we be prepared for the exercise of these privileges. Those who died and suffered on the battle field performed their duty heroically and well, but a duty remains to you and me. The mere fiat of law could not make a dependent man an independent man; could not make an ignorant man an intelligent voter; could not make one man respect another; these results come to the Negro as to all races, by beginning at the bottom and gradually working toward the highest civilization and accomplishments.

Our Passport.—"Tell them that by the way of the shop, the field, the skilled hand, habits of thrift and economy, by way of industrial school and college, we are coming. We are crawling up, working up, yea, bursting up. Often through oppression, unjust discrimination and prejudice, but through them all we are coming up, and with proper habits, intelligence and property, there is no power on earth that can permanently stay our progress. During the next half century and more, my race must continue passing through the severe American crucible. We are to be tested in our patience, our forbearance, our perseverance, our power to endure wrong, to withstand temptations, to economize, to acquire and use skill; our ability to compete, to succeed in commerce, to disregard the superficial for the real, the appearance for the substance, to be great and yet small, learned and yet simple, high and yet the servant of all. This—this is the passport to all that is best in the life of our republic, and the Negro must possess it or be debarred.

Hopeful and Cheerful Spirit.—"I am exceedingly anxious that every colored man and woman should keep a hopeful and cheerful spirit as to the future. Despite all of our disadvantages and hardships, ever since our forefathers set foot upon American soil as slaves, our pathway has been marked by progress. Think of it! We went into slavery a piece of property; we came out American citizens. We went into slavery without a language; we came out speaking the proud Anglo-Saxon tongue. We went into slavery with slave chains about our wrists; we came out with the American ballot in our hands."

Be Charitable to the South.—Some of our Northern people are very impatient with the manner in which the Southerner treats the Negro.

Let it be known to such that as late as 1831 Miss Prudence Crandall, who first admitted a colored girl into her school and afterwards established a school for colored girls, was subjected to all kinds of inhumani-

ties.   Dealers in all sorts of wares and produce agreed
to sell nothing to Miss Crandall, the stage driver
declined to carry her pupils, neighbors refused a pail
of fresh water, even though they knew that their own
sons had filled her well with stable refuse.   Boys and
rowdies were allowed unchecked liberty, and were
even encouraged to exercise their utmost ingenuity in
mischievous annoyances.   Stones and bad eggs were
thrown against her windows.   Her parents were threatened with heavy fines for visiting her.   She was
arrested and put into jail.   Town meetings were held.
The legislature, upon petition, passed laws against her
action, the crime being nothing more than teaching a
dozen Negro girls.   Religious services were disturbed,
efforts were made to set fire to her house, and finally,
in the darkness of the night, a body of men beat in
the windows of her house with iron bars.   This brave
woman was then compelled to break up her school,
and send her pupils home.

Do you say this was in the Sunny South?   No; this
happened two generations ago in the sober state of
Connecticut.

Have Courage.—Let those who think that the Negro
has no rights that the white man need respect look at
that picture and then compare it with the unbounded
enthusiasm and the royal welcome given Booker T.
Washington at the unveiling of the Shaw monument
in Boston in 1897.

Two Generations.—If two generations have made
such a change in sentiment, the most despondent and
disheartened may take courage, for prejudice against
color is certainly dying out.

Bishop Duncan once said: "I was born among you.
Don't think yourselves as 'colored people,' but think

about yourselves as those whom God has called to be men. I never put in my definition of 'man' the idea of color. Be men, and I assure you that lines of longitude will not measure the respect given you. Determine that you will solve your own problem by being true to the estate to which you are called in these latter days.''

Not in Congress.—The future of the race is not so much in Congress and the legislature, as in man himself. While, on the one hand, the white man must learn in many cases to treat the colored man as a man, on the other hand, nothing will so soon bring about the harmony and pleasant feeling desired as the upright conduct of the Negro himself. His progress in the past generation has surprised the most sanguine and hopeful ones. The solution of the Negro problem lies in the same direction.

Not Imaginary, but Real.—There is a future before the race. In the face of many opposing forces, in defiance of the predictions of despondent ones, a great and useful future lies just beyond. Home life, for no people rises higher than its home life, must be pure, happy and intelligent. Then will the future waft upon its breezes sweet and noble influences and results that will touch every phase of the world's life, and bring men into sweeter harmony with one another and with God.

CHAPTER XVII.

STATISTICS OF THE RACE.

AREA AND POPULATION OF THE WORLD.

	Area of the World in Square Miles.	No. of Inhabitants.
Asia	14,710,000	855,000,000
Africa	11,514,000	130,000,000
North America	6,446,000	89,250,000
South America	6,837,000	36,420,000
Australia	3,288,000	4,730,000

NUMBER OF INHABITANTS OF THE WORLD BY RACES.

Caucasian	545,000,000
Mongolian	630,000,000
Negro	225,000,000
Malay	35,000,000
Indian	15,000,000

POPULATION OF THE UNITED STATES.

(Census of 1890.)

Total population	62,622,350
White population	54,983,250
African population	7,470,040
Pure Africans	6,337,980
Mulattoes (one-half pure)	956,989
Quadroons (one-quarter pure)	105,135
Octaroons (one-eighth pure)	69,936

Mississippi contains the largest number of pure Negroes—657,393; Virginia the next largest number —621,781. Virginia contains the largest number of Mulattoes, Quadroons and Octaroons—122,441; Louisiana the next largest number—90,953.

MALE AND FEMALE CHILDREN OF SCHOOL AGE IN THE UNITED STATES.

Total number of white males from 5 to 20 years of age inclusive	9,655,372
Colored	1,587,328
Total number white females from 5 to 20 years of age inclusive	9,595,193
Colored	1,609,499

POPULATION OF EACH STATE AND TERRITORY IN THE UNITED STATES ARRANGED IN ALPHABETICAL ORDER.
CENSUS OF 1890.

	Persons of Negro Descent.			White.	*Total Popula-tion.
	Males.	Females.	Total.		
1 Alabama	336,997	341,492	679,489	833,718	1,513,017
2 Arkansas...............	159,014	150,103	309,117	818,752	1,128,179
3 Arizona................	1,173	184	1,357	55,580	59,620
4 Connecticut	5,930	6,372	12,302	733,438	746,258
5 Colorado..............	3,602	2,613	6,215	404,468	412,198
6 California	6,347	4,975	11,322	1,111,672	1,208,130
7 Delaware..............	14,455	13,931	28,386	140,066	168,493
8 District of Columbia..	33,721	41,851	75,572	154,695	230,392
9 Florida...............	83,967	82,213	166,180	224,949	391,422
10 Georgia...............	430,072	428,743	858,815	978.357	1,837,353
11 Idaho.................	118	83	201	82,018	84,385
12 Illinois..............	30,148	26,880	57,028	3,768,472	3,826,351
13 Indiana...............	23,523	21,692	45,215	2,146,736	2,192,404
14 Iowa..................	5,712	4,973	10,685	1,901,086	1,911,896
15 Louisiana.............	277,134	282,059	559,193	558,395	1,118,587
16 Kansas................	25,248	24,462	49,710	1,376,553	1,427,096
17 Kentucky.............	133,547	134,524	268,071	1,590.462	1,858,635
18 Maine.................	614	576	1,190	659,263	661,086
19 Massachusetts........	10,879	11,265	22,144	2,215,373	2,238,943
20 Maryland.............	105,684	109,972	215,657	826,493	1,042,390
21 Michigan.............	7,986	7,237	15,223	2,072,884	2,093,889
22 Minnesota............	2,167	1,516	3,683	1,296,159	1,301,826
23 Missouri.............	75,336	74,848	150,184	2,528,458	2,679,184
24 Mississippi..........	372,278	370,281	742,559	544,851	1,289,600
25 Montana..............	1,053	437	1,490	127,271	132,159
26 Nebraska.............	5,243	3,670	8,913	1,046,888	1,059,910
27 Nevada	162	80	242	39,084	45,761
28 New Hampshire.......	323	291	614	375,840	376,530
29 New Jersey...........	23,410	24,228	47,638	1,396,581	1,444,933
30 New Mexico...........	1,220	736	1,956	142,719	153,593
31 New York.............	33,503	36,589	70,092	5,923,952	5,997,853
32 North Carolina.......	275,230	285,788	561,018	1,055,382	1,617,947
33 North Dakota.........	219	154	373	182,123	182,719
34 Ohio.................	45,076	42,037	87,113	3,584,805	3,672,316
35 Oklahoma.............	1,613	1,360	2,973	58,826	61,834
36 Oregon...............	743	443	1,186	301,758	313,767
37 Pennsylvania.........	54,731	52,865	107,596	5,148,257	5,258,014
38 Rhode Island.........	3,394	3,999	7,393	337,859	345,506
39 South Carolina.......	341,821	347,113	688,934	462,008	1,151,149
40 South Dakota.........	363	178	541	327,290	328,808
41 Tennessee	213,521	217,157	430,678	1,336,637	1,767,518
42 Texas.................	245,461	242,710	488,171	1,745,935	2,235,523
43 Utah	392	196	588	205,899	207,905
44 Vermont..............	493	444	937	331,418	332,422
45 Virginia.............	310,828	324,610	635,438	1,020,122	1,655,980
46 West Virginia........	17,991	14,699	32,690	730,077	762,794
47 Washington	1,104	498	1,602	340,513	349,390
48 Wisconsin	1,363	1,081	2,444	1,680,473	1,686,880
49 Wyoming..............	652	270	922	59,275	60,705
The United States.......	3,725,561	3,744,479	7,470,040	54,983,890	62,622,350

*This includes 168,320, Chinese, Japanese, and civilized Indians.

POPULATION OF THE UNITED STATES. VOTING AGES—MALES, 21 YEARS AND OVER.

	STATE OR TERRITORY.	White.	Colored.	Total.
1	Alabama..................	184,059	140,763	324,822
2	Arizona..................	21,160	2,536	23,696
3	Arkansas.................	188,296	69,572	257,868
4	California	390,228	72,061	462,289
5	Colorado	161,015	3,905	164,920
6	Connecticut..............	220,115	3,976	224,092
7	Delaware	40,007	7,552	47,559
8	District of Columbia........	46,159	18,346	64,505
9	Florida..................	58,068	38,145	96,213
10	Georgia..................	219,094	179,028	398,122
11	Idaho...................	29,525	1,965	31,490
12	Illinois	1,054,469	18,200	1,072,663
13	Indiana..................	581,987	13,070	595,066
14	Iowa....................	517,006	3,326	520,332
15	Kansas..................	370,688	12,543	383,231
16	Kentucky................	387,371	63,421	450,792
17	Louisiana................	130,748	119,815	250,563
18	Maine...................	200,609	632	201,241
19	Maryland	218,843	51,835	270,738
20	Massachusetts.............	657,042	7,967	665,009
21	Michigan................	611,008	6,437	617,445
22	Minnesota...............	374,027	2,009	376,036
23	Mississippi..............	120,611	150,469	271,080
24	Missouri.................	667,451	38,267	705,718
25	Montana.................	61,984	3,467	65,415
26	Nebraska................	297,281	4,219	301,500
27	Nevada..................	17,002	3,949	20,951
28	New Hampshire...........	117,889	246	118,135
29	New Jersey..............	398,966	14,564	413,530
30	New Mexico..............	41,478	3,473	44,951
31	New York................	1,745,418	24,231	1,769,649
32	North Carolina...........	233,307	109,346	342,653
33	North Dakota.............	55,769	190	55,959
34	Ohio	990,542	25,922	1,016,464
35	Oklahoma	18,238	923	19,161
36	Oregon..................	102,113	9,631	111,744
37	Pennsylvania.............	1,426,996	34,873	1,461,869
38	Rhode Island.............	97,756	2,261	100,017
39	South Carolina	102,657	132,949	235,606
40	South Dakota	96,177	588	96,765
41	Tennessee................	310,014	92,462	402,476
42	Texas...................	434,010	101,932	535,942
43	Utah	53,235	1,236	51,471

POPULATION OF THE UNITED STATES—Continued.

STATE OR TERRITORY.	White.	Colored.	Total.
44 Vermont......................	101,369	328	101,697
45 Virginia......................	248,035	130,747	378,782
46 Washington	141,934	4,984	146,918
47 West Virginia...............	172,198	9,202	181,400
48 Wisconsin...................	459,893	1,829	461,722
49 Wyoming	26,050	994	27,044

POPULATION OF THE UNITED STATES FOR THE
CENSUS YEARS.

Census Year.	White.	Negro.	Aggregate Population.
1790......................	3,172,002	757,202	3,929,214
1800......................	4,306,446	1,002,037	5,308,483
1810......................	5,862,166	1,377,808	7,239,881
1820.............	7,862,073	1,771,656	9,633,822
1830......................10,537,378		2,328,642	12,866,020
1840......................14,195,805		2,873,648	17,069,453
1850......................19,553,068		3,638,808	23,191,876
1860......................26,922,537		4,441,836	31,443,321
1870......................33,589,377		4,880,009	38,558,371
1880......................43,402,970		6,580,793	50,155,783
1890...................... 54,983,890		7,470,040	62,622,250

CONJUGAL CONDITION OF PERSONS OF NEGRO
DESCENT IN THE UNITED STATES.

(Census of 1890.)

Single...4,669,513
Married 2,363,231
Widowed... 411,888
Divorced 15,907
Unknown 9,501
                                                      _____
Total 7,470,040

CONJUGAL CONDITION OF PERSONS OF NEGRO
DESCENT TWENTY YEARS OF AGE AND OVER.

	Males.	Females.	Total.
Single	424,552	271,224	695,776
Married 1,171,671		1,122,619	2,294,290
Widowed	91,633	317,893	409,526
Divorced	5,199	10,391	15,590
Unknown....................	4,408	4,563	8,971

ILLITERATE POPULATION OF NEGRO DESCENT TEN
YEARS OF AGE AND OVER.

Males...1,438,923
Females...1,603,745
                                                      ─────────
   Total 3,042,668
Total Negro population of the United States ten years
   of age and over...................................5,328,972

SKETCH OF THE NEGRO IN THE UNITED STATES.

Occupations.—In 1890 out of a total population of 62,-
000,000, 34 per cent. were engaged in gainful occupations; of the Negroes, numbering 7,500,000, 3,000,000,
or 41 per cent., were engaged in gainful occupations.
The proportion was much greater than with the total
population. According to the statistics of 1890, the male
Negroes were slightly more occupied than were the
native whites, while among the female Negroes, the
proportion of wage earners was much greater. Out
of every 100 native whites, all pursuing gainful occupations, 85 were males and 15 were females; out of
every 100 Negroes, 69 were males and 31 females. A
larger proportion of women pursued gainful occupations among the Negroes than among the whites. Of
the male Negro wage earners, more than three-fifths
were farmers, and a little less than one-fourth were
servants; of the females, less than one-half were
farmers, and more than one-half were servants. This
large proportion of female Negro farmers was doubtless made up principally of women and female children
employed in the cotton fields.

Ownership of Farms and Homes.—The statistics of
farm and home ownership and mortgaged indebtedness
throw some light upon the pecuniary condition of the
Negro. The total number of farms and homes in the
country in 1890 was a little more than twelve millions.

of which the Negroes occupied nearly one and a half millions. The proportion of Negroes of the total population at that time was about 12 per cent., showing a deficiency in the proportion occupying farms and homes. The number of farms in the country was 4,767,179; of these 549,642 were occupied by Negroes. The number of homes in the country was 7,922,973, of which 861,137 were occupied by Negroes.

Tenants.—Of the farms occupied by Negroes, 120,-738 were owned by the occupants; more than three-fourths of the farms occupied by Negroes were rented. In other words, more than three-fourths of the Negro farmers were tenants, while less than one-fourth of the white farmers were tenants. Of farms owned by Negroes, more were without indebtedness than those owned by whites; of houses owned by Negroes, 126,264 were free from incumbrance, showing a greater proportion of homes without indebtedness than among the whites.

Summary.—In summing up the principal points, it is seen that in the matter of occupation the Negro is engaged in agriculture or personal service; he has made little progress in a generation in manufacture, transportation or trade. This could certainly not be expected of the first generation out of slavery. The Negro has, during this generation, however, made good prospects toward acquiring property, especially in farms and homes, and in just so far as they have acquired possession of real estate it is safe to say they have become more valuable citizens. The outlook for them is very favorable as agriculturists, but it will require considerable time for them to become an important factor in manufacture, transportation or commerce.

Distribution of the Negro Race.—Negroes are distributed very unequally all over the country; while they are found in every state and territory, and in almost every county in the land, the vast body of them are found in the Southern states, in those states lying south of the Mason and Dixon line and the Ohio River, to the north boundary of Missouri, and westward as far as Texas. They are most plentiful in Maryland, Virginia, South Carolina and Mississippi, and secondary in North Carolina, Tennessee, Georgia, Alabama and Louisiana. In the Northern and Western states they are very sparsely distributed, with scarcely an exception, being less than four of them to a square mile, while in many places there is less than one to a square mile.

The Negroes in Cities.—The tendency, as a population of a country increases, is that the increase constantly raises the proportion of the population in the cities. The proportion of the Negroes in the cities has, however, been less than that of the whites, but they have gained upon the whites in this regard.

NEGROES IN THE SLAVE STATES.

Delaware.—In Delaware, the proportion of Negroes in 1790 was about 22 per cent. This proportion increased greatly until 1840; since then it has diminished, and in 1890 was about 17 per cent.

In Maryland over one-third of the population were Negroes in 1790, and in 1810 it had increased to 38 per cent.; in 1890 it was but 21 per cent.

District of Columbia.—Here the proportion of Negroes in 1800 was about 29 per cent.; in 1860 the proportion was 19 per cent. During the war many Negroes took refuge within the capital, since which time it is about one-third of the total population.

In Kentucky one-sixth of the population were Negroes in 1790; in 1830 it was about one-fourth; at present it is about 14 per cent., less than one-sixth.

In Tennessee one-tenth of the population were Negroes in 1790; in 1880 it was a little more than one-fourth, since which time it has diminished a trifle.

Missouri had about one-sixth of its inhabitants Negroes when the first record was given. It has diminished rapidly, and in 1890 it was less than one-sixteenth of the population.

Virginia.—In 1790 the Negroes constituted not less than two-fifths of the inhabitants. The proportion increased until 1810, and in 1890 it was little more than one-fourth.

All of the above are border states, and show a similar history, excepting Tennessee and the District of Columbia; the remaining show a different history.

North Carolina started in 1790 with 27 per cent., and has increased slowly until it reached 38 per cent.

South Carolina started with 44 per cent., and in 1880 more than three-fifths of the population were Negroes; since then there has been a trifling decrease.

Georgia started with 36 per cent., and continued to increase until 1880, since when there has been a slight reduction.

Florida began with 47 per cent. of the population Negroes, but in the last decade has been diminishing rapidly.

Alabama commenced with one-third of her people Negroes, and increased until 1870; since then there has been a decrease.

Mississippi began with 41 per cent. of her people Negroes, and has increased up to the present time.

Louisiana began with 55 per cent., but on the whole

diminished, and in 1890 one-half of the people were Negroes.

Texas began in 1850, when 28 per cent. of her people were Negroes, and increased to 31 per cent., and then decreased rapidly, largely due to immigration to the central part of the state.

Arkansas began when a little less than one-eighth of its people were Negroes. In 1890 the Negroes formed more than one-fourth of the total population.

Conclusions.—This indicates in a general way the southward migration of the race to the cotton states, and an increase until in the recent past.

Conjugal Condition.—Comparing the conjugal condition of the Negroes with those of the whites there are two points of difference: First, the Negroes marry younger than the whites, and second, the proportion of widows at most ages is greater than among the whites. The first is in accord with a shorter life period of the race, and the second is a result of a greater death rate in the race.

Statistics of divorce show more frequent divorces among the Negroes than among the whites.

Mortality.—The rate of mortality among the Negro population is considerably greater than among the whites; it is, however, difficult to obtain an accurate record of the relative death rates of the two races. In some of the larger cities the death rate is very nearly if not quite double that of the native white. The rural districts seem to show that the disproportion among the death rates is not so great. as it is in the larger cities.

Criminality.— The proportion of criminals among the Negroes is much greater than among the whites. The last census shows that the proportion of Negroes was only four times as great as the whites. It should, however, be kept in mind that the statistics include among its criminal class the commitments of Negroes for petty offenses, which with that race is a greater offense in proportion than among the whites.

Paupers.—No investigations have been made among these persons receiving out door relief either permanently or temporarily. The census reports are of those who receive aid from alms houses. As these are not found in large numbers in the South the Negro paupers, compared with the whites, cannot be accurately stated.

Illiteracy and Education.—There has been a remarkable increase of the race in the elements of education. During the prevalence of slavery this race was kept in ignorance; indeed, generally throughout the South, it was held as a crime to teach the Negro to read and write, and naturally, when they became freedmen, only a trifling proportion of them were acquainted with the elements of education. Five years after they became free, the census shows that only two-tenths of all Negroes over ten years could write. Ten years later the proportion had increased to three-tenths, and in 1890, only a generation after they were emancipated, not less than forty-three out of every one hundred were able to read and write. These figures show a rapidly increasing progress in elementary education. In 1860 the number of Negroes who were enrolled in the schools of the South was trifling. Since the abolition of slavery the number has increased with great rapidity.

Summary.—The following conclusions may be stated from the preceding investigations. The Negroes, without increasing rapidly in this country, are diminishing in numbers relative to the whites.   They are moving southward from the border states into those of the South Atlantic and Gulf states.   They prefer the country rather than the city life.   The proportion of criminals is much greater than among the whites, and the paupers at least as great, and the indications are the number of attendants at school is far behind the number of whites, but is rapidly gaining upon the race.   To raise a people from slavery to civilization is a matter, not of years, but of many generations.   Their industry, morality and education is a source of highest gratification to all friends of the race excepting those who expected a miraculous conversion.

Colored Physicians.—It is difficult to give the exact number of colored physicians in our country.   Of course, in the term "colored physicians" we include only those who have received diplomas from reputable medical schools.   The first attempt ever made to compile a list of these was made by Dr. Hubbard, Dean of Meharry Medical College, through whose kindness we are enabled to give the following table. This table was first compiled at the close of 1895, and there is probably no one who would be able to give more accurate statistics concerning colored physicians than Dr. Hubbard.   We have added one column, bringing the list up to 1897, and have made it as complete as possible.   The numbers in the last column are given by officers of the different institutions, and include all the graduates in medicine, dentistry and pharmacy, while the remaining table gives only the graduates in medicine who practice in the Southern states:

	Alabama.	Arkansas.	Florida.	Georgia.	Kentucky.	Louisiana.	Mississippi.	Missouri.	North Carolina.	South Carolina.	Tennessee.	Texas.	Virginia.	West Virginia.	Total, Dec., 1895.	Total No. Graduates Oct. 1, 1897.
Meharry Medical College	5	17	7	19	16	8	8	17	2	5	51	55	..	..	210	379
Howard University	3	..	1	9	9	2	..	2	2	11	1	2	12	..	54	500
Leonard Medical School	1	2	2	7	..	..	..	..	19	9	..	..	9	2	51	102
New Orleans University	..	..	..	..	13	..	..	..	..	..	..	6	..	..	19	27
Louisville National	..	..	..	20	..	1	..	..	..	2	1	..	..	..	24	49
Other Colleges	4	3	1	4	8	2	..	..	1	1	1	2	..	..	27	....
Total	13	22	11	39	53	25	9	19	23	26	55	65	23	2	385	....

The following institutions have been established for the education of colored physicians:

The Medical Department of Howard University, Washington, D. C., was established in 1868, and has, we are informed by the secretary, graduated about 500 colored and 200 white students. This includes the medical, dental and pharmaceutical departments.

Meharry Medical College is the medical department of Central Tennessee College, Nashville. It was opened in 1876, and has had 308 graduates in medicine, 40 in pharmacy, and 31 in dentistry. The medical department has been in operation 21 years, the dental department 11, and the pharmaceutical 8. Over one-half of the colored physicians of the South are graduates of Meharry Medical College. Ninety-two per cent. of the graduates of this medical college are practicing medicine. Meharry is under the care of the Freedman's Aid and Southern Educational Society of the M. E. Church.

Leonard Medical College, of Shaw University, Raleigh, North Carolina, has had 80 graduates in medicine, and 22 in pharmacy. Leonard Medical College is supported by the Baptist Home Missionary Society.

The Louisville National Medical College was opened in 1888, and in 1897 had 49 graduates.

The Medical Department of New Orleans University was organized in 1889. Twenty-seven Negroes have received diplomas from this department. It is under the care of the same society as Meharry Medical College.

The Medical Department of Knoxville College was opened in November, 1895.

There are about one thousand colored physicians in the United States, of which number Nashville has twenty-three.

The first female student in the world who received a diploma in law was Miss C. B. Ray, a colored lady of New York city. She graduated at Howard University, Washington, D. C.

Doctor Hubbard bears testimony to the fact that the colored physicians are kindly received by all the best Southern white physicians. The white physicians find the colored practice is not desirable, and since such institutions as Meharry are able to come up to the standard, they are welcomed by the profession. The colored physicians undergo the same examinations as the whites.

Three counties in Tennessee — Fayette, Haywood and Shelby—have more colored persons than white.

The colored scholastic population of Tennessee is 176,614, while the daily attendance will average 105,458.

According to the latest census report, there are 3,115 deaf and dumb and 7,060 blind Afro-Americans in this country.

The Bureau of Education furnishes the following suggestive table:

SIXTEEN FORMER SLAVE STATES AND THE DISTRICT OF COLUMBIA.

Year.	Com.School. White.	Enrollment. Colored.	Expenditures. (Both Races.)
1876-77	1,827,139	571,506	$11,231,073
1877-78	2,034,946	675,150	12,093,091
1878-79	2,013,684	685,942	12,174,141
1879-80	2,215,674	784,709	12,678,685
1880-81	2,234,877	802,374	13,656,814
1881-82	2,249,263	802,982	15,241,740
1882-83	2,370,110	817,240	16,363,471
1883-84	2,546,448	1,002,313	17,884,558
1884-85	2,676,911	1,030,463	19,253,874
1885-86	2,773,145	1,048,659	20,208,113
1886-87	2,975,773	1,118,556	20,821,969
1887-88	3,110,606	1,140,405	21,810,158
1888-89	3,197,830	1,213,092	23,171,878
1889-90	3,402,420	1,296,959	24,880,107
1890-91	3,570,624	1,329,549	26,690,310
1891-92	3,607,549	1,354,316	27,691,488
1892-93	3,697,899	1,367,515	28,535,738
1893-94	3,835,593	1,424,995	29,170,351

Total amount expended in 18 years............$353,557,559

CRIME, PAUPERISM, AND BENEVOLENCE.

The following is taken from the census report of 1890. It is interesting to compare the numbers of the different races:

	Prisoners.	Juvenile Offenders.	Paupers.	Inmates of Benevolent Institutions.	Insane Paupers.	Total.
White	57,310	12,903	66,578	106,836	55,053	298,680
Negroes	24,277	1,930	6,418	4,102	3,601	40,328
Indians	322	12	36	923	28	1,321
Chinese	407	1	13	41	184	646
Japanese	13	....	....	8	....	21
Total	82,329	14,846	73,045	111,910	58,866	340,996

COMMON SCHOOL STATISTICS CLASSIFIED BY RACE—1894-95.

Enrolled in the Public Schools of sixteen Southern States and District of Columbia.

	White.	Colored.	No. of Teachers. White.	Colored
Alabama	190,305	115,709	4,412	2,196
Arkansas	216,863	82,429	5,124	1,796
Delaware	28,316	4,857	734	106
Dist. of Columbia	26,903	14,654	660	331
Florida	59,503	37,272	2,151	772
Georgia	262,530	174,152	5,827	3,206
Kentucky	394,508	73,463	8,578	1,373
Louisiana	92,613	63,313	2,506	915
Maryland	161,252	43,492	3,797	716
Mississippi	162,830	187,785	4,591	3,264
Missouri	612,378	32,199	13,750	737
North Carolina	242,572	128,318	5,285	3,075
South Carolina	103,729	119,292	2,696	1,869
Tennessee	381,632	101,524	6,928	1,909
Texas	463,888	134,720	9,960	2,502
Virginia	235,533	120,453	6,211	2,081
West Virginia	210,059	7,649	6,066	233
Total	3,845,414	1,441,282	89,276	27,081

There are 1,441,282 Afro-American children in the public schools of the sixteen Southern states. This is an encouraging showing. A generation ago it was a penitentiary offense in all the South to educate an Afro-American.

SCHOOLS FOR THE EDUCATION OF THE COLORED RACE.

The following are the latest statistics of schools for the education of the colored·race taken from the report of the Commissioner of Education for the year 1895. Since many of them are controlled by churches we give them under the heads of the different churches supporting and controlling them.

We give the institution, its location, and the number of students in each.

BAPTISTS.

	Students.
Selma University, Selma, Alabama........................	218
Arkansas Baptist College, Little Rock, Ark................	390
Arkadelphia Academy, Arkadelphia, Ark...................	90
Wayland Seminary, Washington, D. C....................	161
Florida Institute, Live Oak, Fla...........................	136
Jerual Academy, Athens, Ga............................	250
Atlanta Baptist Seminary, Atlanta, Ga...................	141
Spelman Ladies' Seminary, Atlanta, Ga..................	630
Walker Baptist Institute, Augusta, Ga...................	190
La Grange Academy, La Grange, Ga.....................	425
Leland University, New Orleans, La......................	157
Jackson College, Jackson, Miss.........................	150
Shaw University, Raleigh, N. C..........................	362
Shiloh University, Warrenton, N. C......................	60
Water's Normal Institute, Winston, N. C.................	215
Benedict College, Columbia, S. C........................	135
Roger Williams University, Nashville, Tenn...............	224
Hearne Academy and Normal and Industrial School, Hearne, Tex..	76
Bishop College, Marshall, Tex...........................	360
Richmond Theological Seminary, Richmond, Va...........	185
Curry College, Longfield, Va............................	95
Hartshorn Memorial College, Richmond, Va..............	111
Storer's College, Harpers Ferry, W. Va..................	143

Total number of students in Baptist Schools............ **4556**

METHODIST EPISCOPAL.

Central Alabama Academy, Huntsville, Ala..............	130
Philander Smith College, Little Rock, Ark...............	312
Shorter University, Arkadelphia, Ark....................	82
Cookman Institute, Jacksonville, Fla....................	269
Emerson Home for Ladies, Oklahoma, Fla...............	50
Payne Institute, Augusta, Ga...........................	250
Gammon School of Theology, Atlanta, Ga...............	86
Clark University, So. Atlanta, Ga.......................	341
Gilbert Academy, and Industrial College, Baldwin, La.....	170
New Orleans University, New Orleans, La...............	603
Morgan College, Baltimore, Md.........................	93
Rush University, Holly Springs, Miss....................	230

Students.

Meridian Academy, Meridian, Miss........................ 169
G. R. Smith College, Sedalia, Mo........................ 200
Bennett College, Greensboro, N. C........................ 203
Browning Industrial Home, Camden, S. C................. 150
Allen University, Columbia, S. C........................ 375
Morristown Normal Academy, Morristown, Tenn.......... 312
Central Tennessee College, Nashville, Tenn., Including Me-
harry Medical College, the number in attendance at this
school for 1900 and 1901................................ 775
Wiley University, Marshall, Tex........................ 284

Total number of students in Methodist Episcopal Schools, 5084

UNITED PRESBYTERIAN.

Knoxville College, Knoxville, Tenn...................... 312
Norfolk Mission College, Norfolk, Va.................... 600

Total number of students enrolled in United Presbyterian Schools.. 912

EPISCOPAL.

St. Paul Normal and Industrial School, Lawrenceville, Va.. 256
Bishop Payne's Divinity and Industrial School, Petersburg,
Va.. 8

Total number of students in Episcopal Schools........ 264

AFRICAN METHODIST EPISCOPAL.

Edward Walter's College, Jackson, Miss................. 159
Morris Brown College, Atlanta, Ga...................... 484
Wilberforce University, Wilberforce, O 305
Paul Quinn College, Waco, Tex.......................... 125

Total number of students in A. M. E. Schools..........1073

CHRISTIAN.

Christian Bible School, Louisville, Ky.................. 26
Southern Christian Institute, Edwards, Miss............ 95
Franklinton Christian College, Franklinton, N. C........ 140

Total number of students in Christian Schools......... 261

A. M. E. ZION.

Livingston College, Salisbury, N. C.................... 340

PRESBYTERIAN. Students.

Stillman Institute, Tuscaloosa, Ala........................	30
Hayne's Normal and Industrial School, Augusta, Ga.......	495
Biddle University, Charlotte, N. C.........................	260
Scolia Seminary for Ladies, Concord, N.C.................	284
Albion Academy, and Normal School, Franklinton, N. C...	311
Lincoln University, Pennsylvania.........................	196
Harbison University, Beaufort, S. C......................	105
Brainard Institute, Chester, S. C.........................	151
Ingleside Ladies' Seminary, Burkeville, Va...............	110

Total number of students in Presbyterian Schools...... 1942

FRIENDS.

Southland College, Southland, Ark........................	179
Freedman's Normal Institute, Maryville, Tenn............	201

Total number of students in Friends' Schools.......... 380

ROMAN CATHOLIC.

St. Augustin Ladies' Academy, Lebanon, Ky..............	76
Mt. Carmel Convent, New Liberia.............(no report.)	

CONGREGATIONALISTS.

Trinity Normal Schools, Athena, Ala......................	268
Lincoln Normal Schools, Marion, Ala......................	230
Burrell College, Selma, Ala...............................	276
Talladega College, Talladega, Ala.........................	581
Orange Park Normal and Manual Training School, Orange Park, Fla..	101
Knox Institute, Athens, Ga...............................	244
Storr's College, Atlanta, Ga...............................	272
Dorchester Academy, McIntosh, Ga........................	393
Ballard Normal School, Macon, Ga........................	443
Allen Normal and Industrial School, Thomasville, Ga......	185
Chandler Ladies' Normal School, Lexington, Ky...........	245
Straight University, New Orleans, La.....................	569
Tougaloo University, Tougaloo, Miss......................	377
Lincoln Academy, King's Mountain, N. C.................	198
Gregory Normal Institute, Wilmington, N.C..............	360
Avery Normal Institute, Charleston, S. C.................	410
Brewer Normal School, Greenwood, S. C.................	231
Warren Institute, Jonesboro, Tenn.......................	113

Students.

Fisk University, Nashville, Tenn......................... 459
Tillotson College, Austin, Tex........................... 193

Total number of students in Congregationalist Schools.. 6148

NON-SECTARIAN.

Calhoun Colored School, Calhoun, Ala.................... 251
State Normal School, Montgomery, Ala.................. 975
State Normal and Industrial School, Normal, Ala......... 476
Tuskegee Normal and Industrial Institute, Tuskegee, Ala.. 1231
Arkansas Normal College, Pine Bluff, Ark............... 255
State College for Colored Students, Dover, Del........... 61
Howard University, Washington, D. C.................... 587
Normal School, Washington, D. C....................... 26
High School, Washington, D. C.......................... 737
State Normal and Industrial School, Tallahassee, Fla...... 58
Georgia State Industrial College, College, Ga............ 500
Beech Institute, Savannah, Ga.................(no record)
Atlanta University, Atlanta, Ga......................... 300
Haven Normal Academy, Waynesboro, Ga............... 272
Roswell Public School, Roswell, Ga...................... 289
West Broad Street School, Athens, Ga................... 457
Sumner High School, Cairo, Ill.......................... 28
Governor High School, Evansville, Ind.................. 65
Scribner High School, New Albany, Ind................. 189
Berea College, Berea, Ky............................... 200
State Normal School, Frankfort, Ky..................... 126
Central High School, Louisville, Ky.................... 996
Paris Colored High School, Paris, Ky................... 336
Southern University, New Orleans, La.................. 308
Alexandria Academy, Alexandria, La...........(no report)
Baltimore City High School, Baltimore, Md.............. 140
Baltimore Normal School, Hebbville, Md................ 17
Industrial Home for Girls, Melvale, Md................. 160
Princess Anne Academy, Princess Anne, Md............. 67
Mount Hermon Female Seminary, Clinton, Miss.......... 192
State Colored Normal School, Holly Springs, Miss........ 190
Alcorn Agricultural School and Medical College, West Side,
    Miss 305
Douglas High School, Hannibal, Mo.................... 45
Lincoln Institute, Jefferson City, Mo.................. 245

Students.

Lincoln High School, Kansas City, Mo.................... 100
Hale's College, Mill Springs, Mo........................... 73
Colored Normal and Industrial Schools, Bordentown, N. J.. 109
Ashboro Normal School, Ashboro, N. C.................... 190
Washburn Seminary, Beaufort, N. C...................... 161
Clinton Normal School, Clinton, N. C...................... 75
State Colored Normal School, Elizabeth City, N. C......... 111
State Colored Normal School, Fayetteville, N. C........... 106
State Colored Norman School, Franklintown, N. C......... 256
State Colored Normal School, Goldsboro, N. C............. 105
Agricultural and Mechanic College, for the colored race,
    Greensboro, N. C.. 187
Whitin Normal School, Lumberton, N. C.................. 81
Barrett Collegiate and Industrial Institute, Pee Dee, N. C.. 180
State Colored Normal School, Plymouth, N. C............. 180
City High School, Reedsville, N.C........................ 811
State Colored Normal School, Salisbury, N. C............. 101
Rankin-Richards Institute, Windsor, N. C................. 110
Scofield Normal and Industrial School, Aikin, S. C......... 223
Wallingford Academy, Charleston, S. C.................... 221
Claflin University, Orangeburg, S. C...................... 570
Beaufort Academy, Beaufort, S. C........................ 388
Penn Industrial and Normal School, Frogmore, S. C....... 276
Austin High School, Knoxville, Tenn...................... 307
Hannibal Medical College, Memphis, Tenn................ 7
LeMoyne Normal Institute, Memphis, Tenn............... 620
Meig's High School, Nashville, Tenn...................... 584
Bradley Academy, Murphysboro, Tenn.................... 342
Mary Allen Seminary, for Ladies, Crockett, Tenn.......... 232
Central High School, Galveston, Tex...................... 250
Prairie View Normal Institute, Prairie View, Tex.......... 207
East End High School, Brenham, Tex..................... 448
Hampton Normal Institute, Hampton, Va................. 1017
Public High School, Manchester, Va...................... 50
Peabody School, Petersburg, Va.......................... 715
Virginia Normal and Collegiate Institute, Petersburg, Va.. 331
Valley Training School, Staunton, Va..................... 41
West Virginia Colored Institute, Farm, Va................ 78
Manasas Industrial School, Manasas, Va.................. 77

The following table, abstracted from the census publications, shows the number of Negroes in all occupations and in each of the five groups of occupations by sex and by states and territories:

STATES OR TERRITORY.	All Occupations.		Agricultural, Fisheries and Mining.		Professional Service.	
	Males.	Females.	Males.	Females.	Males.	Females.
The United States	2,101,233	971,890	1,329,584	427,835	25,171	8,829
Alabama	192,322	101,085	146,361	66,123	1,471	491
Alaska						
Arizona	1,091	71	29		3	
Arkansas	86,861	30,115	68,219	19,069	1,226	238
California	4,301	1,041	1,084	14	86	21
Colorado	2,765	792	180	4	75	13
Connecticut	4,064	1,964	879	1	61	10
Delaware	9,334	3,016	4,157	34	97	32
District of Columbia	21,238	18,770	553	15	390	335
Florida	46,302	19,071	23,690	7,629	776	223
Georgia	246,913	122,352	172,496	54,073	2,122	958
Idaho	83	23	16	1		
Illinois	19,270	4,713	4,328	134	486	116
Indiana	14,648	4,210	3,273	37	330	126
Iowa	3,615	780	973	11	78	11
Kansas	13,889	3,400	4,171	110	357	69
Kentucky	76,411	31,255	38,456	1,013	1,406	420
Louisiana	159,180	88,978	111,820	49,428	1,251	355
Maine	409	145	104	2	8	2
Maryland	63,166	32,642	29,516	743	640	275
Massachusetts	7,593	3,435	601	4	162	57
Michigan	5,065	1,329	1,458	45	115	39
Minnesota	1,719	383	72	2	57	13
Mississippi	198,531	105,306	167,995	77,925	1,970	775
Missouri	43,940	16,715	15,757	324	897	337
Montana	971	140	41		25	4
Nebraska	3,741	959	242	3	63	7
Nevada	130	22	41	1		
New Hampshire	242	107	60		5	
New Jersey	16,143	7,738	4,166	29	287	82
New Mexico	888	156	163	3	10	
New York	23,272	13,664	3,081	25	571	135
North Carolina	148,370	68,220	106,493	33,796	1,619	565
North Dakota	146	23	35		7	
Ohio	28,085	7,791	6,201	108	617	246
Oklahoma	958	125	635	17	22	3
Oregon	536	99	106	2	23	5
Pennsylvania	37,534	15,704	4,602	29	584	197
Rhode Island	2,337	1,362	270	2	38	18
South Carolina	186,714	102,836	149,915	73,588	1,543	506
South Dakota	284	43	33	1	1	2
Tennessee	121,016	44,701	72,316	12,510	1,736	592
Texas	123,395	46,691	85,824	20,758	2,031	563
Utah	298	51	21		1	
Vermont	322	109	112	1	3	
Virginia	169,343	71,752	93,745	10,164	1,654	911
Washington	902	153	250	2	16	2
West Virginia	11,478	2,623	4,790	50	166	63
Wisconsin	855	205	168	4	27	11
Wyoming	563	75	141		58	1

Table showing the number of Negroes in all occupations, etc.—Continued·

STATE OR TERRITORY.	Domestic or Personal Service.		Trade and Transportation.		Manufacturing and Mechanical Industries.	
	Males.	Females.	Males.	Females.	Males.	Females.
The United States........	457,426	505,898	143,350	2,399	146,126	26,929
Alabama	25,426	30,380	9,147	140	9,917	951
Alaska						
Arizona..................	1,034	67	13		12	4
Arkansas................	11,226	10,506	2,787	27	3,403	275
California...............	2,316	897	457	3	358	106
Colorado	1,702	715	406	5	402	55
Connecticut.............	1,925	1,781	634	7	565	165
Delaware................	3,631	2,878	633	21	816	51
District of Columbia.....	12,680	16,734	4,776	195	2,839	1,490
Florida	13,299	10,421	4,106	52	4,501	746
Georgia	39,294	65,025	16,397	372	16,604	1,924
Idaho	57	21	8		2	1
Illinois	10,865	4,061	1,994	41	1,602	361
Indiana.................	7,950	3,849	1,426	23	1,669	175
Iowa	1,966	672	289	1	309	35
Kansas	6,898	3,077	1,148	20	1,315	124
Kentucky................	22,649	28,916	7,381	66	6,519	840
Louisiana...............	31,609	31,292	6,045	129	8,455	2,774
Maine	174	128	68	2	55	11
Maryland...............	21,014	30,406	7,538	144	4,458	1,074
Massachusetts	4,296	2,914	1,402	34	1,132	426
Michigan...............	2,495	1,102	448	6	549	137
Minnesota..............	1,286	315	216	5	88	48
Mississippi.............	17,209	25,729	5,671	74	5,686	803
Missouri................	18,899	15,614	4,862	44	3,525	396
Montana	815	122	45	1	45	13
Nebraska...............	2,743	881	323	4	370	64
Nevada.................	67	18	17	1	5	2
New Hampshire	81	84	24		72	23
New Jersey.............	7,715	7,389	2,111	25	1,864	263
New Mexico.............	651	150	40		24	3
New York...............	13,151	12,445	4,231	54	2,288	1,005
North Carolina..........	20,580	31,393	7,564	106	12,114	2,360
North Dakota...........	90	22	10		4	1
Ohio	14,814	6,955	3,027	40	3,426	442
Oklahoma	231	102	28	1	42	2
Oregon	328	81	42	1	37	10
Pennsylvania............	22,505	14,297	5,213	104	4,630	1,077
Rhode Island...........	1,161	1,169	546	3	322	170
South Carolina..........	18,554	26,213	6,860	188	9,842	2,341
South Dakota...........	115	35	121	1	14	4
Tennessee	25,606	30,333	10,954	125	10,404	1,141
Texas..................	23,360	24,840	6,386	69	5,794	461
Utah	248	48	14	1	14	2
Vermont................	143	102	33		31	6
Virginia................	39,425	55,941	15,655	253	18,864	4,483
Washington	480	134	69		87	15
West Virginia...........	3,515	2,462	2,080	7	927	41
Wisconsin..............	481	161	74	1	105	28
Wyoming...............	313	71	31	3	20	

TOTAL ILLITERATE POPULATION OF PERSONS OF NEGRO DESCENT IN THE UNITED STATES TEN YEARS OF AGE AND OVER ENGAGED IN OCCUPATIONS.

	Male.	Female.	Total.
Agriculture, Fishing and Mining,	915,452	318,331	1,233,783
Professional services	1,559	81	1,640
Domestic and Personal Services,	221,003	303,591	524,594
Trade and Transportation	62,349	1,018	63,367
Manufacturing and Mechanical Industries...................	64,099	7,947	72,048
In all occupations	1,264,462	630,970	1,895,432

POPULATION FOR CITIES HAVING 50,000 INHABITANTS OR MORE—1890.

Cities.	White.	Colored.
New York, N. Y.........................	1,489,627	25,674
Chicago, Ill...........................	1,084,998	14,852
Philadelphia, Pa......................	1,006,590	40,374
Brooklyn, N. Y.......................	795,397	10,946
St. Louis, Mo.........................	424,704	27,066
Boston, Mass..........................	439,887	8,590
Baltimore, Md.........................	367,143	67,296
San Francisco, Cal....................	270,696	28,301
Cincinnati, O.........................	285,224	11,684
Cleveland, O..........................	258,318	3,035
Buffalo, N. Y.........................	254,495	1,169
New Orleans, La.......................	177,376	64,663
Pittsburgh, Pa........................	230,660	7,957
Washington, D. C.....................	154,695	75,697
Detroit, Mich.........................	202,422	3,454
Milwaukee, Wis........................	204,001	467
Newark, N. J..........................	177,559	4,271
Minneapolis, Minn....................	163,384	1,354
Jersey City, N. J.....................	160,766	2,237
Louisville, Ky........................	132,457	28,672
Omaha, Neb............................	135,794	4,658
Rochester, N. Y.......................	133,318	578
St. Paul, Minn........................	131,632	1,524
Kansas City, Mo.......................	118,821	13,895
Providence, R. I......................	128,095	4,051

POPULATION OF CITIES.—Continued.

Cities.	White.	Colored.
Denver, Colo...........................	102,642	4,071
Indianapolis, Ind	96,282	9,154
Allegheny, Pa..........................	102,759	2,528
Albany, N. Y..........................	93,782	1,141
Columbus, O	82,603	5,547
Syracuse, N. Y........................	87,276	867
Worcester, Mass.......................	83,679	976
Toledo, O	80,349	1,085
Richmond, Va..........................	49,034	32,354
New Haven, Conn......................	78,795	2,503
Paterson, N. J.........................	77,644	703
Lowell, Mass..........................	77,390	306
Nashville, Tenn	46,773	29,395
Scranton, Pa..........................	74,934	281
Fall River, Mass.......................	74,189	209
Cambridge, Mass......................	68,001	2,027
Atlanta, Ga...........................	37,416	28,117
Memphis, Tenn.......................	35,766	28,729
Wilmington, Del.......................	53,754	7,677
Dayton, O.............................	59,054	2,166
Troy, N. Y............................	60,441	515
Grand Rapids, Mich	59,657	621
Reading, Pa...........................	58,260	401
Camden, N. J..........................	53,392	4,921
Trenton, N. J..........................	55,726	1,732
Lynn, Mass............................	54,997	730
Lincoln, Neb..........................	53,758	1,396
Charleston, S. C.......................	23,919	31,036
Hartford, Conn........................	51,776	1,454
St. Joseph, Mo........................	48,628	3,696
Evansville, Ind........................	45,186	5,570
Los Angeles, Cal......................	47,205	3,190
Des Moines, Ia	48,944	1,149

The colored people of Massachusetts are taxed for property valued at $9,004,122.

The increase of colored population in the last decade is greater than that of any other state.

WHITE AND COLORED POPULATION BY COUNTIES OF ALL THE SOUTHERN STATES.

ALABAMA.

Counties.	White.	Colored.
1 Autauga	4,796	8,418
2 Baldwin	5,678	3,263
3 Barbour	13,454	21,442
4 Bibb	9,080	14,744
5 Blount	20,155	1,770
6 Bullock	6,055	21,005
7 Butler	11,326	10,315
8 Calhoun	23,947	9,879
9 Chambers	12,460	13,858
10 Cherokee	17,656	2,803
11 Chilton	11,483	3,066
12 Costow	8,209	9,313
13 Clarke	9,685	12,939
14 Clay	14,061	1,704
15 Clerburne	12,427	791
16 Coffee	10,237	1,933
17 Colbert	12,361	7,828
18 Conecuh	7,987	6,606
19 Coosa	10,552	5,354
20 Covington	6,695	841
21 Crenshaw	11,745	3,679
22 Cullman	13,401	38
23 Dale	13,867	3,358
24 Dallas	8,016	41,329
25 DeKalb	19,897	1,204
26 Elmore	11,443	10,288
27 Escambia	5,843	2,650
28 Etowah	18,171	3,755
29 Fayette	11,141	1,682
30 Franklin	9,520	1,160
31 Geneva	9,664	1,026
32 Greene	3,235	18,771
33 Hale	5,180	22,321
34 Henry	16,038	8,8c9
35 Jackson	24,179	3,840
36 Jefferson	56,334	32,142

Counties.	White.	Colored.
37 Lamar	11,439	2,748
38 Lauderdale	16,647	7,091
39 Lawrence	12,553	8,171
40 Lee	12,197	16,497
41 Limestone	12,198	9,002
42 Lowndes	4,563	26,985
43 Macon	4,251	14,188
44 Madison	19,345	18,769
45 Marengo	7,946	25,149
46 Marion	10,769	578
47 Marshall	17,652	1,279
48 Mobile	28,369	22,804
49 Monroe	8,379	10,608
50 Montgomery	14,682	41,485
51 Morgan	18,013	6,073
52 Perry	6,812	22,516
53 Pickens	9,284	13,185
54 Pike	15,349	9,070
55 Randolph	13,914	3,303
56 Russell	5,814	18,279
57 St. Clair	14,303	3,050
58 Shelby	14,289	6,596
59 Sumter	5,943	23,631
60 Talladega	15,399	13,944
61 Tallapoosa	16,951	8,508
62 Tuscaloosa	18,261	12,091
63 Walker	14,422	1,656
64 Washington	4,686	3,249
65 Wilcox	6,794	24,022
66 Winston	6,516	36

ARKANSAS.

Counties.	White.	Colored.
1 Arkansas	7,899	3,533
2 Ashley	6,427	6,868
3 Baxter	8,409	18
4 Benton	27,622	94
5 Boone	15,723	93
6 Bradley	5,108	2,864

Counties.	White.	Colored.
7 Calhoun......	4,547	2,720
8 Carroll.......	17,205	83
9 Chicot	1,392	10,027
10 Clark.........	14,201	6,796
11 Clay	12,156	44
12 Cleburne......	7,832	52
13 Cleveland	8,034	3,328
14 Columbia.....	12,580	7,313
15 Conway	11,788	7,671
16 Craighead....	11,506	517
17 Crawford.....	19,410	2,304
18 Crittenden....	2,050	11,890
19 Cross	3,802	2,891
20 Dallas	6,026	3,267
21 Desha........	2,119	8,205
22 Drew.........	1,487	9,865
23 Faulkner	14,994	3,346
24 Franklin......	19,256	678
25 Fulton	10,898	86
26 Garland......	12,547	2,781
27 Grant........	6,750	1,036
28 Greene	7,747	161
29 Hempstead...	11,819	10,977
30 Hot Spring...	10,358	1,249
31 Howard......	10,734	3,055
32 Independence	20,381	1,580
33 Izard........	12,776	262
34 Jackson	10,849	4,330
35 Jefferson.....	10,941	29,930
36 Johnson	16,125	613
37 Lafayette.....	3,157	4,543
38 Lawrence	12,151	833
39 Lee..........	4,691	13,195
40 Lincoln	3,784	6,461
41 Little River..	4,902	4,001
42 Logan	19,646	1,128
43 Lonoke	11,278	7,985
44 Madison......	17,134	58
45 Marion.......	10,358	39
46 Miller........	8,147	6,566

Counties.	White.	Colored.
47 Mississippi ...	5,735	5,901
48 Monroe	6,124	9,212
49 Montgomery..	7,621	302
50 Nevada.......	10,526	4,306
51 Newton......	9,943	7
52 Ouachita.....	8,076	8,957
53 Perry.........	6,597	941
54 Phillips.......	5,695	19,646
55 Pike..........	8,053	484
56 Poinsett	3,726	546
57 Polk..........	9,237	48
58 Pope	17,837	1,621
59 Prairie.......	7,011	4,363
60 Pulaski	25,329	22,000
61 Randolph	13,890	596
62 St. Francois..	5,141	8,002
63 Saline........	9,827	1,478
64 Scott.........	12,601	34
65 Searcy	9,630	34
66 Sebastian	29,398	3,802
67 Sevier	8,616	1,456
68 Sharp........	10,240	178
69 Stone.........	6,930	113
70 Union	8,605	6,372
71 Van Buren...	8,405	162
72 Washington..	31,004	1,010
73 White........	2,379	2,567
74 Woodruff	6,452	7,557
75 Yell..........	16,652	1,363
DELAWARE.		
1 Kent	24,625	8,036
2 New Castle ..	82,779	14,365
3 Sussex	32,662	5,985
FLORIDA.		
1 Alachua......	9,673	13,260
2 Baker........	2,588	745
3 Bradford.....	5,961	1,555
4 Brevard	2,836	541
5 Calhoun......	1,132	549
6 Citrus ....,...	2,090	304

Counties.	White.	Colored.
7 Clay..........	2,632	1,521
8 Columbia	6,393	6,484
9 Dade.........	640	87
10 DeSoto.......	4,805	139
11 Duval........	11,970	14,802
12 Escambia.....	11,475	8,706
13 Franklin	1,950	1,358
14 Gadsden......	4,446	7,448
15 Hamilton	5,337	3,170
16 Hernando....	1,584	892
17 Hillsboro.....	11,996	2,917
18 Holmes.......	4,152	184
19 Jackson......	6,332	11,211
20 Jefferson.....	3,559	12,199
21 Lafayette	3,447	239
22 Lake	6,190	1,844
23 Lee..........	1,334	80
24 Leon.........	3,121	14,631
25 Levy.........	4,457	2,129
26 Liberty	818	634
27 Madison......	5,556	8,760
28 Manatee	2,714	181
29 Marion	9,310	11,485
30 Monroe	12,815	5,935
31 Nassau.......	3,951	4,338
32 Orange	9,039	3,536
33 Osceola	9,657	476
34 Pasco........	3,872	376
35 Polk..........	7,121	784
36 Putnam......	6,404	4,778
37 St. John......	5,508	3,195
38 Santa Rosa...	5,768	2,192
39 Sumter	3,864	498
40 Suwanee	5,581	4,943
41 Taylor	1,971	151
42 Volusia	6,004	2,462
43 Wakulla	1,738	1,379
44 Walton.......	4,072	743
45 Washington..	5,087	1,339

GEORGIA.

Counties.	White.	Colored.
1 Appling	6,214	2,464
2 Baker........	1,595	4,549
3 Baldwin......	5,262	9,343
4 Banks........	6,999	1,563
5 Bartow.......	14,574	6,041
6 Berrien	8,277	2,417
7 Bibb.........	19,029	23,336
8 Brooks.......	6,342	7,637
9 Bryan	2,833	2,687
10 Bulloch.......	9,023	4,689
11 Burke........	5,817	22,680
12 Butts	5,167	5,398
13 Calhoun......	2,239	6,199
14 Camden......	2,041	4,137
15 Campbell	5,621	3,493
16 Carroll.......	18,450	3,851
17 Catoosa	4,795	636
18 Charlton	2,465	870
19 Chatham.....	22,965	34,757
20 Chattahoochee	1,837	3,065
21 Chattooga....	9,204	1,998
22 Cherokee.....	13,904	1,508
23 Clark	7,072	8,111
24 Clay	3,002	4,815
25 Clayton	5,220	3 075
26 Clinch	4,292	2,360
27 Cobb.........	15,510	6,774
28 Coffee........	6,621	3,858
29 Colquitt......	4,317	477
30 Columbia	3,243	8,038
31 Coweta	9,740	12,612
32 Crawford.....	4,159	5,156
33 Dade.........	4,614	1,093
34 Dawson......	5,353	259
35 Decatur......	9,116	10,811
36 De Kalb......	11,214	5,977
37 Dodge........	6,143	5,309
38 Dooley.......	9,232	8,914
39 Dougherty ...	1,975	10,231

Counties.	White.	Colored.	Counties.	White.	Colored.
40 Douglas......	5,993	1,801	80 McIntosh....	1,258	5,212
41 Early........	3,670	6,122	81 Macon......	4,001	9,181
42 Echols.......	2,059	1,020	82 Madison.....	7,361	3,662
43 Effingham....	3,388	2,210	83 Marion......	3,467	4,261
44 Elbert........	7,492	7,884	84 Meriwether..	9,201	11,538
45 Emanuel.....	9,396	5,306	85 Miller.......	2,701	1,574
46 Fannin	8,612	112	86 Milton	5,536	672
47 Fayette......	5,654	3,074	87 Mitchell	4,800	6,106
48 Floyd........	17,970	10,414	88 Monroe......	6,621	12,516
49 Forsyth......	9,866	1,288	89 Montgomery	5,990	3,658
50 Franklin	11,372	3,298	90 Morgan......	5,043	10,997
51 Fulton........	49,238	35,397	91 Murray	7,977	484
52 Gilmer.......	9,005	69	92 Muscogee ...	12,395	15,362
53 Glascock.....	2,552	1,168	93 Newton	7,145	7,164
54 Glynn........	5,669	7,741	94 Oconee	3,881	3,832
55 Gordon	11,030	1,727	95 Oglethorpe..	5,686	11,264
56 Greene.......	5,332	11,719	96 Paulding....	10,443	1,505
57 Gwinnett.....	16,903	2,996	97 Pickens	7,832	349
58 Habersham...	9,984	1,589	98 Pierce.......	4,396	1,983
59 Hall	15,280	2,767	99 Pike	8,223	8,077
60 Hancock.....	4,739	12,410	100 Polk........	10,289	4,654
61 Haralson.....	10,199	1,117	101 Pulaski	6,558	1,001
62 Harris	5,999	10,797	102 Putnam	3,939	10,903
63 Hart	7,930	2,957	103 Quitman.....	1,421	3,05
64 Heard........	6,215	3,342	104 Rabun......	5,440	166
65 Henry	8,629	7,591	105 Randolph....	5,794	9,473
66 Houston......	5,272	16,341	106 Richmond...	22,346	22,818
67 Irwin	4,241	2,075	107 Rockdale....	4,127	2,686
68 Jackson	13,780	5,396	108 Schley	2,238	3,205
69 Jasper	5,392	8,487	109 Screven.....	6,916	7,507
70 Jefferson.....	6,450	10,763	110 Spalding....	5,835	7,281
71 Johnson......	4,673	1,456	111 Stewart......	4,198	11,484
72 Jones........	3,931	8,778	112 Sumpter	7,008	11,598
73 Laurens......	7,654	6,093	113 Talbot	4,019	9,239
74 Lee..........	1,432	7,242	114 Taliaferro...	2,464	4,227
75 Liberty	4,207	8,673	115 Tattnall	7,138	3,115
76 Lincoln	2,473	3,673	116 Taylor......	4,598	4,068
77 Lowndes.....	7,128	7,974	117 Telfair......	3,142	2,335
78 Lumpkin.....	6,453	414	118 Terrell......	5,334	9,169
79 McDuffie.....	3,267	5,522	119 Thomas.....	11,122	15,029

Counties.	White.	Colored.
120 Towns	3,990	74
121 Troup	7,062	13,661
122 Twiggs	2,748	5,447
123 Union	7,584	165
124 Upson	6,065	6,123
125 Walker	11,350	1,932
126 Walton	10,312	7,155
127 Ware	5,178	3,619
128 Warren	4,201	6,756
129 Washington.	10,312	14,925
130 Wayne	5,290	2,195
131 Webster	2,423	3,272
132 White	5,489	662
133 Whitfield	10,984	1,930
134 Wilcox	4,825	3,155
135 Wilkes	5,616	12,464
136 Wilkinson	5,567	5,214
137 Worth	5,872	4,176

KENTUCKY.

Counties.	White.	Colored.
1 Adair	11,893	1,828
2 Allen	12,650	1,042
3 Anderson	9,547	1,063
4 Ballard	6,978	1,412
5 Barren	17,765	3,724
6 Bath	11,235	1,578
7 Bell	9,570	740
8 Bone	11,134	1,112
9 Bourbon	10,179	6,797
10 Boyd	13,328	705
11 Boyle	8,139	4,809
12 Bracken	11,723	646
13 Breathitt	8,536	169
14 Breckenridge.	16,896	2,080
15 Bullitt	7,243	1,048
16 Butler	13,183	773
17 Caldwell	10,450	2,736
18 Calloway	13,583	1,092
19 Campbell	43,522	686
20 Carlisle	7,213	389
21 Carroll	8,509	757

Counties.	White.	Colored.
22 Carter	17,067	137
23 Casey	11,331	516
24 Christian	18,886	15,231
25 Clark	10,608	4,826
26 Clay	12,034	413
27 Clinton	6,859	188
28 Crittenden	12,188	930
29 Cumberland.	7,456	996
30 Daviess	27,751	5,367
31 Edmonson	7,547	458
32 Elliott	9,187	27
33 Estill	10,255	581
34 Fayette	22,069	13,625
35 Fleming	14,453	1,625
36 Floyd	11,105	136
37 Franklin	16,508	4,757
38 Fulton	7,797	2,208
39 Gallatin	4,114	497
40 Garrard	8,114	3,024
41 Grant	12,188	483
42 Graves	25,378	3,154
43 Grayson	18,199	489
44 Greene	9,572	1,891
45 Greenup	5,573	338
46 Hancock	8,476	758
47 Hardin	18,957	2,347
48 Harlan	6,041	154
49 Harrison	14,447	2,467
50 Hart	14,437	2,002
51 Henderson	21,313	8,219
52 Henry	11,799	2,365
53 Hickman	9,869	1,768
54 Hopkins	20,072	3,433
55 Jackson	8,207	54
56 Jefferson	154,981	33,595
57 Jessamine	17,542	3,706
58 Johnson	10,943	84
59 Kenton	51,491	2,667
60 Knott	5,365	73
61 Knox	12,984	778

Counties.	White.	Colored.
62 Larue	8,642	791
63 Laurel	13,188	555
64 Lawrence	17,526	176
65 Lee	5,746	459
66 Leslie	3,932	32
67 Letcher	6,845	75
68 Lewis	14,626	177
69 Lincoln	12,388	3,574
70 Livingston	8,725	741
71 Logan	17,243	6,560
72 Lyon	6,310	1,317
73 McCracken	15,346	5,703
74 McLean	9,101	786
75 Madison	16,949	7,399
76 Magoffin	9,036	160
77 Marion	12,500	3,148
78 Marshall	10,945	342
79 Martin	4,186	23
80 Mason	16,604	4,168
81 Meade	8,715	769
82 Menifee	4,639	27
83 Mercer	11,959	3,075
84 Metcalfe	8,971	900
85 Monroe	10,449	540
86 Montgomery	8,724	3,643
87 Morgan	11,200	49
88 Muhlenberg	15,596	2,359
89 Nelson	12,596	3,821
90 Nicholas	9,448	1,316
91 Ohio	21,600	1,346
92 Oldham	5,107	1,647
93 Owen	16,249	1,427
94 Owsley	5,891	84
95 Pendleton	15,839	507
96 Perry	6,171	160
97 Pike	17,212	166
98 Powell	4,319	379
99 Pulaski	24,440	1,291
100 Robertson	4,529	155
101 Rockcastle	9,686	155

Counties.	White.	Colored.
102 Rowen	6,023	106
103 Russell	7,870	266
104 Scott	11,482	5,063
105 Shelby	11,744	4,776
106 Simpson	8,504	2,374
107 Spencer	5,510	1,250
108 Taylor	7,879	1,474
109 Todd	10,513	6,301
110 Trigg	10,250	3,652
111 Trimble	6,819	321
112 Union	15,573	2,656
113 Warren	22,229	7,926
114 Washington	11,528	2,094
115 Wayne	12,234	618
116 Webster	15,284	1,912
117 Whitley	15,828	752
118 Wolfe	7,058	122
119 Woodford	7,527	4,853

LOUISIANA.

	White.	Colored.
1 Acadia	11,602	1,629
2 Ascension	8,233	11,270
3 Assumption	10,726	8,890
4 Aroyelles	12,904	12,161
5 Bienville	7,840	6,268
6 Bossier	4,102	16,225
7 Caddo	8,003	23,541
8 Calcasieu	16,834	3,194
9 Caldwell	2,707	8,106
10 Cameron	2,402	426
11 Catahoula	6,992	4,976
12 Claiborne	9,796	13,512
13 Concordia	1,757	13,112
14 DeSota	6,638	13,220
15 East B. Rouge	9,494	16,420
16 East Carroll	997	11,360
17 East Felicana	5,196	12,707
18 Franklin	2,860	4,040
19 Grant	4,844	3,416
20 Iberia	10,519	10,477
21 Iberville	6,696	15,142

Counties.	White.	Colored.
22 Jackson	4,844	2,608
23 Jefferson	6,716	6,484
24 Lafayette	9,080	6,884
25 Laforche	14,270	7,819
26 Lincoln	8,481	6,269
27 Livingston	4,898	871
28 Madison	931	13,204
29 Morehouse	3,519	13,267
30 Natchitoches	10,254	15,551
31 Orleans	177,376	64,491
32 Ouachita	5,641	12,344
33 Plaquemines	5,283	7,258
34 Point Coupee	4,696	14,917
35 Rapids	11,823	15,800
36 Red River	3,557	7,760
37 Richland	3,017	7,213
38 Sabine	7,312	2,067
39 St. Bernard	2,347	1,977
40 St. Charles	1,986	5,751
41 St. Helena	3,473	4,589
42 St. James	5,691	9,997
43 St. John the Baptist	4,680	6,637
44 St. Landry	17,856	22,274
45 St. Martin	7,050	7,821
46 St. Mary	7,976	1,435
47 St. Tammany	6,398	3,702
48 Tangipahoa	7,943	4,698
49 Tensas	1,153	15,492
50 Terrebonne	10,412	9,699
51 Union	9,901	7,403
52 Vermilion	11,335	2,899
53 Vernon	5,363	540
54 Washington	4,635	2,632
55 Webster	5,172	7,289
56 West B. Rouge	2,398	5,964
57 West Carroll	1,438	2,310
58 West Feliciana	2,276	12,785
59 Winn	6,072	1,010

MARYLAND.

Counties.	White.	Colored.
1 Alleghany	40,135	1,431
2 Anne Arundel	19,580	14,509
3 Baltimore	62,676	10,330
4 Balti're City	367,143	67,104
5 Calvert	4,796	5,064
6 Caroline	10,092	3,811
7 Carroll	30,241	2,133
8 Cecil	21,850	3,978
9 Charles	7,054	8,136
10 Dorchester	16,133	8,709
11 Frederick	42,983	6,528
12 Garrett	14,028	185
13 Harford	22,617	6,376
14 Howard	12,159	4,110
15 Kent	10,664	6,807
16 Montgomery	17,500	9,685
17 Prince George	14,867	11,210
18 Queen Anne	11,904	6,567
19 St. Mary	8,153	7,666
20 Somerset	14,650	9,505
21 Talbut	12,248	7,483
22 Washington	37,274	2,507
23 Wicomico	14,731	5,199
24 Worcester	13,012	6,734

MISSISSIPPI.

Counties.	White.	Colored.
1 Adams	6,128	19,895
2 Alcorn	9,605	3,510
3 Amite	7,600	10,597
4 Attala	12,742	9,444
5 Benton	5,665	4,919
6 Bolivar	3,222	26,737
7 Calhoun	11,276	3,412
8 Carroll	8,161	10,611
9 Chickasaw	8,491	11,400
10 Choctaw	8,208	2,638
11 Claiborne	3,533	10,980
12 Clarke	7,716	8,104
13 Clay	5,627	12,982
14 Coahoma	2,245	16,069

Counties.	White.	Colored.
15 Copiah	14,632	15,600
16 Covington	5,319	2,971
17 De Soto	6,955	17,224
18 Franklin	5,484	4,934
19 Greene	2,936	933
20 Grenada	3,896	11,076
21 Hancock	5,770	2,509
22 Harrison	9,163.	3,314
23 Hinds	10,892	28,368
24 Holmes	7,084	23,883
25 Issaquena	736	11,579
26 Itawamba	10,723	985
27 Jackson	7,814	3,436
28 Jasper	7,368	7,238
29 Jefferson	3,589	15,356
30 Jones	7,082	1,246
31 Kemper	7,869	10,058
32 Lafayette	11,700	8,853
33 Landerdale	14,671	14,972
34 Lawrence	6,240	6,078
35 Leake	9,350	5,018
36 Lee	12,510	7,530
37 Leflore	2,597	14,267
38 Lincoln	10,325	7,587
39 Lowndes	6,009	21,036
40 Madison	6,031	21,290
41 Marion	6,530	3,002
42 Marshall	9,731	16,306
43 Monroe	12,109	18,619
44 Montgomery	7,448	7,009
45 Neshoba	8,351	2,172
46 Newton	10,119	6,156
47 Noxuber	4,709	22,629
48 Oktibbeha	5,759	11,934
49 Panola	9,248	11,729
50 Pearl River	2,301	656
51 Perry	4,582	1,874
52 Pike	10,581	10,620
53 Pontotoc	10,583	4,355
54 Prentiss	10,833	2,845

Counties.	White.	Colored.
55 Quitman	894	2,392
56 Rankin	7,507	10,413
57 Scott	7,000	4,616
58 Sharkey	1,223	7,141
59 Simpson	6,229	3,909
60 Smith	8,924	1,711
61 Sunflower	2 530	6,850
62 Tallahatchee	5,154	9,207
63 Tate	8,495	10,756
64 Tippah	10,026	2,925
65 Tishomingo	8,311	991
66 Tunica	1,259	10,895
67 Union	11,608	3,998
68 Warren	8,803	24,356
69 Washington	4,838	35,530
70 Wayne	5,799	4,011
71 Webster	9,080	2,980
72 Wilkinson	3,962	13,626
73 Winstone	6,987	5,061
74 Yalobusha	7,683	8,941
75 Yazoo	8,690	27,701

MISSOURI.

Counties.	White.	Colored.
1 Adair	17,114	309
2 Andrew	15,751	249
3 Atchison	15,485	46
4 Adrain	20,230	1,840
5 Barry	22,846	97
6 Barton	8,457	47
7 Bates	31,817	404
8 Benton	14,807	165
9 Bollinger	13,097	19
10 Boone	21,364	4,677
11 Buchanan	66,116	3,974
12 Butler	9,568	596
13 Caldwell	14,777	374
14 Calloway	20,645	4,484
15 Camden	9,943	97
16 Cape Girard'u	20,022	2,038
17 Carroll	24,365	1,377
18 Carter	4,650	9

Counties.	White.	Colored.	Counties.	White.	Colored.
19 Cass	22,517	784	59 Livingston	19,803	865
20 Cedar	15,493	127	60 McDowell	11,270	3
21 Chariton	22,763	3,490	61 Macon	29,378	1,196
22 Christian	13,929	92	62 Madison	9,027	241
23 Clark	14,956	170	63 Maries	8,597	3
24 Clay	18,503	1,348	64 Marion	22,510	3,721
25 Clinton	16,052	1,086	65 Mercer	14,508	73
26 Cole	15,345	1,935	66 Miller	13,933	228
27 Cooper	19,161	3,539	67 Mississippi	8,025	2,108
28 Crawford	11,883	78	68 Moniteau	14,787	843
29 Dade	17,238	287	69 Monroe	18,740	2,049
30 Dallas	12,592	55	70 Montgomery	15,183	1,667
31 Daviess	20,079	376	71 Morgan	11,897	414
32 De Kalb	14,428	110	72 New Madrid	7,284	2,033
33 Dent	12,108	41	73 Newton	21,417	681
34 Douglas	14,078	33	74 Nodaway	30,777	135
35 Dunklin	14,927	158	75 Oregon	10,445	22
36 Franklin	26,262	1,794	76 Osage	12,709	371
37 Gasconade	11,620	86	77 Ozark	9,783	12
38 Gentry	18,982	36	78 Pemiscot	5,563	412
39 Greene	45,169	3,441	79 Perry	12,745	492
40 Grundy	17,620	254	80 Pettis	28,351	2,799
41 Harrison	20,979	56	81 Phelps	12,355	281
42 Henry	27,076	1,158	82 Pike	21,400	4,919
43 Hickory	9,428	25	83 Platt	15,036	1,210
44 Holt	15,389	80	84 Polk	20,176	163
45 Howard	12,826	4,544	85 Pulaski	9,364	23
46 Howell	18,410	208	86 Putnam	15,331	34
47 Iron	8,799	320	87 Ralls	11,216	1,077
48 Jackson	145,322	14,992	88 Randolph	21,957	2,935
49 Jasper	49,571	913	89 Ray	22,460	1,749
50 Jefferson	21,415	1,067	90 Reynolds	6,784	19
51 Johnson	26,302	1,829	91 Ripley	8,511	1
52 Knox	13,287	214	92 St. Charles	20,656	2,315
53 Laclede	14,229	472	93 St. Clair	16,503	244
54 Lafayette	26,011	4,170	94 St. Genevieve	9,386	496
55 Lawrence	25,861	364	95 St. Francis	16,802	545
56 Lewis	14,885	1,050	96 St. Louis	32,836	3,469
57 Lincoln	16,306	2,039	97 " City	427,704	26,865
58 Linn	23,311	808	98 Saline	28,659	5,101

Counties.	White.	Colored.
99 Schuyler	11,246	3
100 Scotland	12,562	112
101 Scott	10,735	493
102 Shannon	8,894	4
103 Shelby	14,886	755
104 Stoddard	17,192	135
105 Stone	7,080	10
106 Sullivan	18,955	45
107 Taney	7,970	3
108 Texas	19,385	21
109 Vernon	31,273	231
110 Warren	9,188	725
111 Washington	12,381	772
112 Wayne	11,823	104
113 Webster	15,008	167
114 Worth	8,737	1
115 Wright	14,115	364

NORTH CAROLINA.

Counties.	White.	Colored.
1 Alamance	12,688	5,583
2 Alexander	8,588	842
3 Alleghany	6,061	462
4 Anson	10,237	9,790
5 Ash	15,033	595
6 Beaufort	11,869	9,203
7 Bertie	7,885	11,291
8 Baden	8,646	8,117
9 Brunswick	6,139	4,761
10 Buncombe	28,640	6,626
11 Burke	12,378	2,561
12 Cabarrus	12,683	5,459
13 Caldwell	10,737	1,561
14 Camden	3,347	2,320
15 Carteret	8,528	2,297
16 Caswell	6,639	9,389
17 Catawba	16,073	2,616
18 Chatham	17,214	8,199
19 Cherokee	9,655	321
20 Chowan	4,010	5,157
21 Clay	4,055	142
22 Cleveland	17,301	3,093

Counties.	White.	Colored.
23 Columbus	11,804	6,052
24 Craven	7,175	13,358
25 Cumberland	14,952	12,369
26 Currituck	4,731	2,016
27 Dare	3,362	406
28 Davidson	18,174	3,528
29 Davie	8,769	2,852
30 Duplin	11,600	7,090
31 Durham	10,712	7,329
32 Edgecombe	8,513	15,600
33 Forsythe	19,433	9,001
34 Franklin	10,755	10,335
35 Gaston	12,927	4,837
36 Gates	5,539	4,713
37 Graham	3,137	176
38 Granville	12,122	12,362
39 Greene	5,281	4,758
40 Guilford	19,820	8,232
41 Halifax	9,614	19,294
42 Harnett	9,453	4,247
43 Haywood	12,829	517
44 Henderson	11,211	1,378
45 Hertford	5,906	7,945
46 Hyde	4,962	3,941
47 Iredell	19,516	5,946
48 Jackson	8,680	832
49 Johnson	19,917	7,322
50 Jones	3,885	3,518
51 Lenoir	8,517	6,362
52 Lincoln	10,028	2,558
53 McDowell	9,114	1,825
54 Macon	9,436	666
55 Madison	17,095	710
56 Martin	7,838	7,383
57 Mecklenburg	23,141	19,532
58 Mitchell	12,252	555
59 Montgomery	8,982	2,257
60 Moore	13,985	6,494
61 Nash	12,186	8,521
62 New Hanover	10,089	13,937

Counties.	White.	Colored.
63 Northampton.	9,224	12,018
64 Onslow	7,392	2,911
65 Orange	9,705	5,243
66 Pamlico	4,767	2,379
67 Pasquotank	5,201	5,547
68 Pender	5,967	6,547
69 Perquimans	4,719	5,574
70 Person	8,251	6,900
71 Pitt	13,192	12,327
72 Polk	4,807	1,095
73 Randolph	21,848	3,347
74 Richmond	10,989	12,959
75 Robeson	16,629	14,854
76 Rockingham	15,197	10,166
77 Rowan	17,142	6,981
78 Rutherford	15,073	3,697
79 Samson	15,960	9,136
80 Stanley	10,629	1,507
81 Stokes	14,386	2,813
82 Surry	16,926	2,355
83 Swaim	5,652	925
84 Transylvania.	5,368	513
85 Tyrrell	3,000	1,225
86 Union	15,712	5,547
87 Vance	6,438	11,147
88 Wake	26,093	23,114
89 Warren	5,880	13,480
90 Washington	4,961	5,239
91 Watauga	10,180	431
92 Wayne	15,115	10,985
93 Wilkes	20,633	2,042
94 Wilson	10,884	7,760
95 Yadkin	12,421	1,369
96 Yancy	9,197	293

SOUTH CAROLINA.

	White.	Colored.
1 Abbeville	15,142	31,705
2 Aiken	13,761	18,059
3 Anderson	25,268	18,428
4 Barnwell	14,194	30,416
5 Beaufort	2,695	21,421

Counties.	White.	Colored.
6 Berkeley	7,686	47,739
7 Charleston	24,764	35,073
8 Chester	8,482	18,178
9 Chesterfield	10,988	7,479
10 Clarendon	6,987	16,246
11 Colletton	14,032	26,245
12 Darlington	11,749	17,384
13 Edgefield	17,340	31,916
14 Fairfield	7,139	21,460
15 Florence	10,471	14,554
16 Georgetown	4,053	16,840
17 Greenville	27,516	16,789
18 Hampton	6,827	13,717
19 Horry	13,706	5,550
20 Kershaw	8,550	13,810
21 Lancaster	10,411	10,349
22 Laurens	13,169	18,444
23 Lexington	13,766	8,411
24 Marion	14,519	15,436
25 Marlboro	9,062	14,435
26 Newberry	8,966	17,468
27 Oconee	13,678	5,008
28 Orangeburg	15,654	32,738
29 Pickens	12,253	4,136
30 Richland	11,993	24,885
31 Spartanburg	36,857	18,527
32 Sumter	11,813	31,792
33 Union	10,973	14,390
34 Williamsburg	9,355	18,420
35 York	18,245	20,525

TENNESSEE.

	White.	Colored.
1 Anderson	13,920	1,204
2 Bedford	18,411	6,327
3 Benton	10,609	621
4 Bledsoe	5,643	491
5 Blount	15,954	1,632
6 Bradley	11,816	1,788
7 Campbell	12,905	581
8 Cannon	11,250	947
9 Carroll	17,926	5,701

Counties.	White.	Colored.
10 Carter	12,688	701
11 Cheatham	7,297	1,548
12 Chester	7,228	1,841
13 Claiborne	14,577	526
14 Clay	6,880	380
15 Cocke	15,178	1,339
16 Coffee	12,127	1,699
17 Crockette	10,908	4,238
18 Cumberland	5,322	53
19 Davidson	66,612	41,549
20 Decatur	7,662	1,333
21 De Kalb	14.462	1,188
22 Dickson	14,493	2,152
23 Dyer	15,193	4,762
24 Fayette	8,264	20,614
25 Fentress	5,180	46
26 Franklin	15,313	3,610
27 Gibson	26,386	9,473
28 Giles	22,427	12,530
29 Grainger	12,470	716
30 Greene	25,047	1,566
31 Grundy	5,909	436
32 Hamblen	9,867	1,546
33 Hamilton	35,760	17,704
34 Hancock	9,598	744
35 Hardeman	12,082	8,947
36 Hardin	15,269	2,429
37 Hawkins	19,826	2,390
38 Haywood	7,835	15,723
39 Henderson	13,894	2,442
40 Henry	15,202	5,868
41 Hickman	11,729	2,770
42 Houston	4,553	837
43 Humphreys	10,178	1,542
44 Jackson	12,835	480
45 James	4,362	534
46 Jefferson	14,269	2,206
47 Johnson	8,478	377
48 Knox	48,422	11,127
49 Lake	4,226	1,070

Counties.	White.	Colored.
50 Lauderdale	10,810	7,946
51 Lawrence	11,492	794
52 Lewis	2,336	219
53 Lincoln	21,074	6,307
54 Loudon	7,805	1,459
55 McMinn	15,722	2,168
56 McNairy	13,602	1,908
57 Macon	10,095	782
58 Madison	15,809	14,684
59 Marion	12,977	2,434
60 Marshall	14,365	4,538
61 Maury	22,090	16,022
62 Meigs	6,208	721
63 Monroe	14,046	1,272
64 Montgomery	15,793	13,903
65 Moore	5,434	541
66 Morgan	7,303	336
67 Obion	22,936	4,335
68 Overton	11,767	272
69 Perry	7,114	671
70 Pickett	4,725	11
71 Polk	7,771	579
72 Putnam	13,045	638
73 Rhea	10,871	1,771
74 Roane	15,460	1,957
75 Robertson	14,524	5,548
76 Rutherford	20,595	14,502
77 Scott	9,423	371
78 Sequatchie	2,948	76
79 Sevier	18,134	627
80 Shelby	51,021	61,674
81 Smith	15,406	2,997
82 Stewart	10,015	2,177
83 Sullivan	19,457	1,422
84 Sumner	17,257	6,409
85 Tipton	12,436	11,835
86 Trousdale	4,018	1,832
87 Unicoi	4,388	231
88 Union	11,351	107
89 Van Buren	2,794	67

Counties.	White.	Colored.
90 Warren	12,391	2,022
91 Washington	18,389	1,964
92 Wayne	10,600	871
93 Weakley	24,330	4,625
94 White	11,513	835
95 Williamson	16,162	10,159
96 Wilson	19,798	7,350

TEXAS.

Counties.	White.	Colored.
1 Anderson	11,420	9,502
2 Andrews	24	
3 Angelina	5,705	607
4 Aransas	1,684	131
5 Archer	2,089	12
6 Armstrong	943	1
7 Atascosa	6,157	285
8 Austin	12,673	5,85
9 Bandera	3,669	126
10 Bastrop	11,836	8,898
11 Baylor	2,589	6
12 Bee	3,401	317
13 Bell	30,716	2,650
14 Bexar	43,662	5,504
15 Blanco	4,439	210
16 Borden	217	5
17 Bosque	13,583	641
18 Bowie	12,659	7,591
19 Brazoria	2,983	8,523
20 Brazos	8,213	3,433
21 Brewster	694	13
22 Brown	11,348	73
23 Buchel	287	11
24 Burleson	7,274	5,727
25 Burnet	10,440	307
26 Caldwell	10,890	4,878
27 Calhoun	647	168
28 Callahan	5,426	31
29 Cameron	14,307	108
30 Camp	3,328	3,296
31 Carson	355	1
32 Cass	14,041	8,512

Counties.	White.	Colored.
33 Castro	9	
34 Chambers	1,479	757
35 Cherokee	15,265	7,705
36 Childress	1,171	2
37 Clay	7,400	102
38 Coke	2,058	
39 Coleman	6,042	69
40 Collin	34,208	2,525
41 Collingworth	357	
42 Colorado	10,666	8,845
43 Comal	6,218	180
44 Comanche	15,600	8
45 Concho	1,051	14
46 Cooke	23,323	1,351
47 Coryell	16,413	459
48 Cottle	240	
49 Crane	15	
50 Crockett	194	
51 Crosby	345	1
52 Dallern	112	
53 Dallas	55,795	11,177
54 Dawson	28	1
55 Deaf Smith	179	
56 Delta	8,389	728
57 Denton	19,580	1,707
58 De Witt	10,311	3,995
59 Dickens	295	
60 Dimmit	1,012	37
61 Donley	1,012	40
62 Duval	7,591	7
63 Eastland	10,347	25
64 Ector	223	1
65 Edwards	1,964	6
66 Ellis	28,397	3,376
67 El Paso	14,996	377
68 Encinal	2,738	6
69 Ereth	20,869	723
70 Falls	12,745	7,961
71 Fannen	34,459	4,241
72 Fayette	23,031	8,446

Counties.	White.	Colored.	Counties.	White.	Colored.
73 Fisher	2,981	15	113 Iron	868	2
74 Floyd	529		114 Jack	9,643	97
75 Foley	8	17	115 Jackson	1,459	1,822
76 Ft. Bend	1,605	8,981	116 Jasper	3,214	2,378
77 Franklin	5,661	819	117 Jeff Davis	1,352	37
78 Freestone	9,311	6,675	118 Jefferson	3,638	2,218
79 Frio	3,010	102	119 Johnson	21,459	852
80 Gaines	68		120 Jones	3,790	7
81 Galveston	24,422	7,009	121 Karnes	3,093	544
82 Garza	14		122 Kaufman	18,418	3,176
83 Gillespie	6,947	108	123 Kendall	3,610	216
84 Glasscock	208		124 Kent	324	
85 Goliad	4,266	1,644	125 Kerr	4,355	106
86 Gonzalas	12,146	5,869	126 Kimple	2,238	5
87 Gray	202	1	127 King	171	2
88 Grayson	46,453	6,712	128 Kinney	3,527	253
89 Gregg	4,052	5,349	129 Knox	1,134	
90 Grimes	9,648	11,664	130 Lamar	27,883	9,378
91 Guadalupe	10,799	4,415	131 Lamb	4	
92 Hale	718	3	132 Lampasas	7,320	262
93 Hall	702	1	133 La Salle	2,072	67
94 Hamilton	9,300	13	134 Lavaca	17,631	4,253
95 Hansford	133		135 Lee	8,850	3,102
96 Hardeman	3,880	21	136 Leon	8,464	5,377
97 Hardin	2,989	967	137 Liberty	2,512	1,715
98 Harris	23,718	13,522	138 Limestone	17,217	4,459
99 Harrison	8,528	18,191	139 Lipscombe	632	
100 Hartley	251	1	140 Live Oak	2,006	49
101 Haskell	1,659	6	141 Llano	6,719	52
102 Hays	9,152	2,171	142 Loving	3	
103 Hemphill	508	9	143 Lubbock	31	2
104 Henderson	9,293	2,988	144 Lynn	24	
105 Hidalgo	6,457	76	145 McCulloch	3,205	12
106 Hill	25,485	2,096	146 McLennan	2,811	10,381
107 Hood	7,339	274	147 McMullen	994	44
108 Hopkins	17,726	2,838	148 Madison	6,439	2,070
109 Houston	10,892	8,467	149 Marion	3,861	6,989
110 Howard	1,165	34	150 Martin	264	
111 Hunt	28,917	2,953	151 Mason	5,149	31
112 Hutchinson	56	2	152 Matagorda	1,364	2,621

Counties.	White.	Colored.	Counties.	White.	Colored.
153 Maverick ...	3,547	142	193 San Jacinto .	3,027	4,328
154 Medina	5,445	283	194 San Patricio.	1,287	25
155 Menard	1,192	23	195 San Saba ...	6,588	53
156 Midland	1,028	3	196 Schlicher ...	134	4
157 Milam	18,548	6,220	197 Scurry.......	1,413	2
158 Mills........	5,436	57	198 Shackelford .	1,845	167
159 Mitchell	1,950	99	199 Shelby......	11,411	2,954
160 Montegue...	18,774	87	200 Sherman....	33	1
161 Montgomery	6,275	5,488	201 Smith	15,633	12,690
162 Moore	15		202 Somerville ..	3,413	6
163 Morris	3,968	2,610	203 Starr	10,739	10
164 Motley	136	3	204 Stephens....	4,921	5
165 Nacogdoches	11,713	4,257	205 Stonewall ...	1,021	2
166 Navarro	20,105	6,266	206 Sutton	659	1
167 Newton.....	3,092	1,558	207 Swisher.....	100	
168 Nolan	1,540	32	208 Tarrant.....	36,777	4,316
169 Nueces	7,384	707	209 Taylor......	6,768	174
170 Ochiltree ...	198		210 Terry.......	21	
171 Oldham.....	267	3	211 Trockmorten	891	11
172 Orange	3,937	829	212 Titus	6,430	1,760
173 Palo Pinto ..	8,253	67	213 Tom Greene	4,944	202
174 Panola......	7,978	6,350	214 Travis	26,222	10,090
175 Parker......	21,009	671	215 Trinity	5,740	1,903
176 Parmer	7		216 Tyler	8,484	2,392
177 Pecos	1,307	8	217 Upshur......	8,766	3,929
178 Polk	6,272	3,834	218 Upton	51	1
179 Potter	830	14	219 Uvalde	3,720	84
180 Presidio	1,669	26	220 Valverde ...	2,758	108
181 Rains........	3,494	415	221 Van Zandt..	15,127	1,098
182 Randall.....	187		222 Victoria.....	5,217	3,519
183 Red River ..	14,832	6,628	223 Walker	5,642	7,382
184 Reeves	1,224	7	224 Waller	4,184	6,703
185 Refugio	915	324	225 Ward	74	3
186 Roberts.....	324	2	226 Washington.	13,957	15,200
187 Robertson ..	12,326	14,142	227 Webb.......	14,625	214
188 Rockwall ...	5,756	216	228 Wharton ...	1,461	6,119
189 Runnels	3,162	31	229 Wheeler	761	16
190 Rusk	10,026	7,624	230 Whithita....	4,700	128
191 Sabine......	3,885	1,004	231 Wilbarger ..	7,057	26
192 S. Augustine	4,557	2,131	232 Williamson .	23,146	2,755

Counties.	White.	Colored.
233 Wilson	9,602	1,053
234 Winkler	18	
235 Wise	23,971	161
236 Wood	10,680	3,249
237 Yoakum	4	
238 Young	3,034	15
239 Zapata	3,561	
240 Zavalla	1,094	8

VIRGINIA.

Counties.	White.	Colored.
1 Accomac	17,547	9,730
2 Albemarle	18,252	14,127
3 Alexandria	11,361	7,236
4 Alleghany	6,955	2,328
5 Amelia	3,023	6,045
6 Amherst	9,923	7,628
7 Appomattox	5,254	7,336
8 Augusta	28,596	8,409
9 Bath	3,827	761
10 Bedford	20,064	11,149
11 Bland	4,888	241
12 Botetourt	11,122	3,782
13 Brunswick	6,651	10,584
14 Buchanan	5,843	24
15 Buckingham	6,786	7,587
16 Campbell	21,283	19,804
17 Carolina	7,359	9,322
18 Carroll	15,135	362
19 Charles City	1,348	3,718
20 Charlotte	5,716	9,361
21 Chesterfield	15,399	10,812
22 Clark	5,617	2,454
23 Craig	3,686	149
24 Culpepper	7,147	6,086
25 Cumberland	2,860	6,622
26 Dickenson	5,051	26
27 Dinwiddie	15,570	20,619
28 Elizabeth City	8,278	7,890
29 Essex	3,584	6,463
30 Fairfax	11,586	5,069
31 Fauquier	14,686	7,904
32 Floyde	13,230	1,175

Counties.	White.	Colored.
33 Fluvanna	5,051	4,457
34 Franklin	18,737	6,248
35 Frederick	15,652	2,228
36 Giles	8,253	837
37 Gloucester	5,437	6,216
38 Goochland	7,083	5,875
39 Grayson	13,473	921
40 Greene	4,114	1,508
41 Greensville	2,919	5,311
42 Halifax	15,008	19,416
43 Hanover	9,188	8,214
44 Henrico	59,775	43,619
45 Henry	9,928	8,283
46 Highland	4,930	422
47 Isle of Wight	6,169	5,144
48 James City	2,317	3,326
49 King George	3,433	3,208
50 King & Queen	4,235	5,434
51 King William	3,783	5,822
52 Lancaster	3,171	4,020
53 Lee	17,002	1,214
54 Loudoun	16,696	6,578
55 Louisa	7,192	9,805
56 Lunenburg	4,636	6,736
57 Madison	6,260	3,965
58 Mathews	5,447	2,136
59 Mecklenburg	9,329	16,030
60 Middlesex	3,141	4,317
61 Montgomery	14,227	3,515
62 Nansemond	8,925	10,767
63 Nelson	9,033	6,303
64 New Kent	1,956	3,555
65 Norfolk	37,497	39,571
66 Northampton	4,833	5,480
67 N'th'berland	4,795	3,090
68 Nottoway	3,959	7,623
69 Orange	6,573	6,241
70 Page	11,320	1,772
71 Patrick	12,079	2,068
72 Pittsylvania	30,847	29,094
73 Powhatan	2,358	4,433

Counties.	White.	Colored.
74 Pr. Edward.	7,770	9,924
75 Pr. George..	2,732	5,140
76 Pr. William..	7,210	2,595
77 Prin'ss Anne	4,131	5,379
78 Pulaski	9,669	3,121
79 Rappah'nock	5,863	2,818
80 Richmond...	3,998	3,148
81 Roanoke.....	21,082	9,019
82 Rockbridge .	17,931	5,131
83 Rockingham	28,485	2,814
84 Russell......	14,923	1,203
85 Scott	20,726	968
86 Smyth	12,136	1,224
87 Shenandoah.	18,829	842
88 Southampton	8,293	11,785
89 Spottsylvania	8,156	6,077
90 Stafford.....	5,893	1,469
91 Surry........	3,238	5,018
92 Sussex......	3,524	7,776
93 Tazewell....	16,395	3,504
94 Warren	7,016	1,264
95 Warwick....	2,884	3,866
96 Washington.	25,215	2,805
97 Westmorel'd	3,662	4,737
98 Wise........	8,763	582
99 Wythe......	14,849	3,170
100 York........	3,201	4,395
WEST VIRGINIA.		
1 Barbour	12,204	498
2 Berkeley.....	17,005	1,664
3 Boone	6,715	170
4 Braxton......	13,794	134
5 Brooke	6,545	114
6 Cabell	22,101	1,493
7 Calhoun	8,074	81
8 Clay	4,659	
9 Dodridge	12,052	131
10 Fayette	17,488	3,054
11 Gilmer.......	9,696	50
12 Grant........	6,423	379
13 Greenbier....	16,041	1,993

Counties.	White.	Colored.
14 Hampshire...	10,852	567
15 Hancock	6,392	21
16 Hardy	6,977	590
17 Harrison	21,158	760
18 Jackson......	18,934	87
19 Jefferson.....	11,437	4,116
20 Kanawka	39,554	3,402
21 Lewis	15,627	261
22 Lincoln	11,035	211
23 Logan	10,416	685
24 McDowell....	5,909	1,591
25 Marion	20,617	104
26 Marshall	20,499	236
27 Mason	22,104	759
28 Mercer.......	13,979	2,022
29 Mineral	11,604	481
30 Monongalia ..	15,477	227
31 Monroe	11,450	979
32 Morgan	6,469	275
33 Nicholas	9,287	21
34 Ohio.........	40,452	1,098
35 Pendleton....	8,585	126
36 Pleasants	7,530	9
37 Pocahontas ..	6,461	353
38 Preston	20,221	134
39 Putnam......	14,105	237
40 Raleigh......	9,518	79
41 Randolph ...	11,371	262
42 Ritchie	16,585	36
43 Roane	15,274	29
44 Summers	11,990	1,127
45 Taylor	11,785	362
46 Tucker	6,276	183
47 Tyler	11,960	2
48 Upshur	12,458	256
49 Wayne	18,491	160
50 Webster	4,772	11
51 Wetzel.......	16,805	36
52 Wirt	9,387	24
53 Wood........	27,700	910
54 Wyoming....	6,177	70

COLORED MEMBERS OF CONGRESS.

SENATORS.

Name.	Elected.	Length of Service.	State.
Bruce, B. K............	1875–81	6 years	Mississippi
Revells, Hiram.........	Feb. 23, 1870, to Mch. 3, 1871		Mississippi

REPRESENTATIVES.

Name.	Elected.		Length of Service.	State.
Cain, Rich. H.....	43d and 45th	Cong.	4 years	S. Carolina
Cheatham, H. P...	52d and 53d	"	4 "	N. Carolina
De Large, Robt. C.	42d	"	2 "	S. Carolina
Elliott, Robt. B...	42d	"	2 "	S. Carolina
Haalson, Jerry....	44th	"	2 "	Alabama
Hyman, John.....	44th	"	2 "	N. Carolina
Langston, John M..	51st	"	2 "	Virginia
Long, Jeff.........	41st	"	2 "	Georgia
Lynch, John R....	43d, 44th and 47th	"	6 "	Mississippi
Miller, Thos. H...	51st	"	2 "	S. Carolina
Murray, Geo. W..	53d and 54th	"	4 "	S. Carolina
Nash, Chas. E....	44th	"	2 "	Louisiana
O'Hara, Jas. E....	48th and 49th	"	4 "	N. Carolina
Rainey, Jos. H....	44th et seq	"	10 "	S. Carolina
Ransier, A J......	43d	"	2 "	S. Carolina
Rapier, Jas. T.....	43d	"	2 "	Alabama
Smalls, Robt......	44th, 45th and 47th	"	6 "	S. Carolina
Turner, Benj. S...	42d	"	2 "	Alabama
Wall, Josiah T....	42d, 43d and 44th	"	6 "	Florida
White, Geo. H....	55th	"	Present member	N. Carolina

DEPARTMENT OF STATE.—There are nine colored employes in the Department of State at Washington (all men).

DEPARTMENT OF JUSTICE.—There are ten colored employes in the Department of Justice at Washington—seven males and three females.